FUSSBALL
FOOTBALL

Ein Spiel – Viele Welten   One Game – Many Worlds

Herausgegeben von
Karin Guggeis im Auftrag des Münchner Stadtmuseums
und des Kulturreferats der Landeshauptstadt München

Edited by
Karin Guggeis commissioned by the Munich City Museum
and the Department of Culture, City of Munich

Unter konzeptioneller Mitarbeit von
Concept Team
Stefan Eisenhofer
Wolfgang Habermeyer
Christiane Lembert
Patricia Müller
Barbara Rusch

ARNOLDSCHE

Inhaltsverzeichnis

Vorwort *Lydia Hartl*	6
Fußball: Ein Spiel – Viele Welten	
Ein ethnologischer Blick auf eine weltweite Leidenschaft *Karin Guggeis*	10

WELTFUSSBALL – FUSSBALLWELTEN

Der Fußball eroberte die Welt – und die Welt den Fußball *Karin Guggeis*	16
Lokale Bälle – globale Bälle *Karin Guggeis*	28
Ein Derwisch, der Fußbälle näht Arif Sain aus Pakistan *Jürgen Wasim Frembgen*	32
Im Fußballschuh in eine andere Welt *Karin Guggeis*	34
Get Up – Stand Up!	
Ein Gespräch mit Anthony Baffoe über Rassismus auf dem Spielfeld *Anthony Baffoe / Patricia Müller*	38
Paradise Lost? Brasilien als Arkadien des Fußballs *Stefan Eisenhofer*	44
Fußball in politischen Karikaturen Ostafrikas *Jigal Beez*	52
Ist der Deutsche doch ein Brasilianer? Identität und nationale Spielstile im Fußball *Stefan Eisenhofer*	56
Langeweile, Kurzeweile *Zé do Rock*	62
Was Fußballer alles mit der Hand machen *Wolfgang Till*	70

IT'S A MAN'S WORLD?

It's a Man's Game? Der Kampf der Frauen um den Ball *Kathrin Steinbichler*	78
Dribbelkünstler und Dorfschönheiten	
Das Peladão-Fußballturnier in Amazonien *Wolfgang Kapfhammer*	88

IST GOTT RUND?

Fußball als »Clash« der Weltbilder *Stefan Eisenhofer*	94
Fußball in Japan Zwischen »Gehorsam« und Subkultur *Patricia Müller*	108
Die Jungfrau von Guadalupe Religiöse Bekenntnisse rund um den Fußball *Sinahí Venegas*	114
Unvermeidbare Siege *Stefan Eisenhofer*	116
San Pancracio – Der Heilige im Kühlschrank	
Fußballkultur und Heiligenkult in Südspanien *Natalie Göltenboth*	118
Fußball-Schrein-Fieber in Japan *Patricia Müller*	120

LOCAL HEROES – GLOBAL PLAYERS

Gemachte Männer Die Helden des Fußballs *Stefan Eisenhofer*	124
Diego Santissimo Maradona für immer im Herzen Neapels *Natalie Göltenboth*	132
D10S Maradonakult in Argentinien *Natalie Göltenboth*	138
Beckham meets Buddha *Patricia Müller*	142

FAN-TRÄUME – FAN-WIRKLICHKEITEN

In Treue ergeben Die Welt der Fans *Christiane Lembert / Barbara Rusch*	146
Die Welt der Fanartikel *Christiane Lembert / Barbara Rusch*	158
Passagen Ein Lebensweg mit dem Verein *Christiane Lembert / Barbara Rusch*	162
Memento mori Das Stadion als heiliger Ort *Christiane Lembert / Barbara Rusch*	166
Fankultur und Jugendkultur Die »Kutten« *Christiane Lembert / Barbara Rusch*	168
Karneval und Fußball in Brasilien *Alex Bellos*	170
Nippon Socca-Girlie Zwischen Kimono, Barbie und Nakata *Patricia Müller*	180
Kampf der Hütten gegen die Paläste?	
Reale und imaginierte Identitäten im Fußball *Kathrin Steinbichler*	182
Mehr als ein Spiel, mehr als ein Club!	
Fußball als Spielfeld regionaler Identitäten in Spanien *Christiane Hirsch*	188
Metropole versus Provinz im türkischen Fußball *Tanıl Bora*	194

BROT UND SPIELE

Fußball als Fortsetzung der Politik mit anderen Mitteln? *Stefan Eisenhofer*	202
Fußball und Demokratie in Südafrika	
Vom Honeymoon nach der Wahl zur Weltmeisterschaft *Fiona Rankin-Smith*	214
Bern 1954 Ein Finale und seine Folgen *Anikó Szalay*	222
Zuhause und in der Fremde Der Migrantensport Fußball *Christiane Lembert / Barbara Rusch*	228
Zinédine Zidane Kind von Migranten, Heros der Nation *Wolfgang Wohlwend*	232
KSK Beveren Belgiens »neue Diamanten« *Ben Kerste*	234
Anhang	236

Table of Contents

Foreword *Lydia Hartl* — 7

Football: One Game – Many Worlds
    Ethnological Perspectives on a World-wide Passion *Karin Guggeis* — 11

WORLD OF FOOTBALL – FOOTBALL WORLDS
Football Conquered the World – and the World has Conquered Football *Karin Guggeis* — 17
Local Balls – Global Balls *Karin Guggeis* — 29
A Dervish who sews Footballs Arif Sain of Pakistan *Jürgen Wasim Frembgen* — 32
To the Other World in a Football Boot *Karin Guggeis* — 34
Get Up – Stand Up!
    A Conversation with Anthony Baffoe about Racism on the Pitch *Anthony Baffoe / Patricia Müller* — 39
Paradise Lost? Brazil as Football Arcadia *Stefan Eisenhofer* — 45
Football in East African Political Caricature *Jigal Beez* — 53
Might the German be a Brazilian after all?
    Identity and National Styles of Playing Football *Stefan Eisenhofer* — 57
Contra Monotonie *Zé do Rock* — 63
What Footballers can do with their Hands *Wolfgang Till* — 71

IT'S A MAN'S WORLD?
It's a Man's Game? The Women's Battle for the Ball *Kathrin Steinbichler* — 79
Kings of Dribble and Village Beauty Queens
    The Peladão Football Championship in the Amazon Basin *Wolfgang Kapfhammer* — 89

IS GOD ROUND?
Football as the «Clash» of World-Views *Stefan Eisenhofer* — 95
Football in Japan Between «Obedience» and Subculture *Patricia Müller* — 109
The Virgin of Guadalupe Professing Religion in Football *Sinahí Venegas* — 114
Inevitable Victories *Stefan Eisenhofer* — 117
San Pancracio – A Saint in the Fridge
    Football Culture and a Devotional Cult in Southern Spain *Natalie Göltenboth* — 118
Football Shrine Mania in Japan *Patricia Müller* — 120

LOCAL HEROES – GLOBAL PLAYERS
Football-Made Men The Heroes of a Global Game *Stefan Eisenhofer* — 125
Santissimo Diego Maradona for Ever in Neapolitan Hearts *Natalie Göltenboth* — 133
D10S The Maradona Cult in Argentina *Natalie Göltenboth* — 139
Beckham meets Buddha *Patricia Müller* — 142

FAN DREAMS – FAN REALITIES
Devoted to the Last The World of Fans *Christiane Lembert / Barbara Rusch* — 147
The World of Fan Memorabilia *Christiane Lembert / Barbara Rusch* — 159
Passages Lifelong with the Club *Christiane Lembert / Barbara Rusch* — 163
Memento mori The Stadium as a Holy Place *Christiane Lembert / Barbara Rusch* — 166
Fan Culture and Youth Culture «Kutten» *Christiane Lembert / Barbara Rusch* — 168
Carnival and Football in Brazil *Alex Bellos* — 171
Nippon Socca Girlie Between Kimono, Barbie and Nakata *Patricia Müller* — 180
A Contest of Huts vs Palaces? Real and Imagined Identities in Football *Kathrin Steinbichler* — 183
More than a Game, More than a Team!
    Football as the Pitch for Regional Identity in Spain *Christiane Hirsch* — 189
Metropolis vs the Provinces in Turkish Football *Tanıl Bora* — 195

BREAD AND GAMES
Football as Politics with Different Means? *Stefan Eisenhofer* — 203
Soccer and Democracy in South Africa
    From Post-Election Honeymoon to World Cup *Fiona Rankin-Smith* — 215
Bern 1954 A Finals Game and its Repercussions *Anikó Szalay* — 223
At Home and Abroad Football as an Immigrant Sport *Christiane Lembert / Barbara Rusch* — 229
Zinédine Zidane Child of Immigrants, National Hero *Wolfgang Wohlwend* — 232
KSK Beveren Belgium's «New Diamonds» *Ben Kerste* — 234

Appendix — 236

Vorwort

Liebe Leserinnen und Leser,
es ist Fußball-Kultur-Zeit: Während der FIFA WM 2006™ rollt der Ball nicht nur im FIFA-WM-Stadion München, sondern über verschiedene Spielwiesen: Installation und Performance, Film und Fotografie, Videokunst, Theater, Literatur und Musik. Das Kulturreferat der Landeshauptstadt München und das Münchner Stadtmuseum nehmen dieses große Sportereignis zum Anlass, in einer Ausstellung und einem Kulturprogramm zu zeigen, dass das weltumspannende Phänomen Fußball sehr viel mehr zu bieten hat als jubelnde Sieger und geschlagene Helden: *Fußball: Ein Spiel – Viele Welten*.

Das Motto der FIFA WM 2006™, »Die Welt zu Gast bei Freunden«, lädt dazu ein, dem allgegenwärtigen Eurozentrismus der Fußballberichterstattung entgegenzutreten und einen tieferen Blick in die Fußball- und Alltags-Welten der Gäste zu werfen: Vom Stadion als »beliebtestem Versammlungsort« bis zu den Akteuren als Global Players und Local Heroes zwischen Pop, Heiligenverehrung und Polit-Ikonen, von der Fußball-Kunst bis zum Geschäft mit dem runden Leder – stets geht es um das Wechselspiel von Lokalem und Globalem, von Sportlichem und Sportfernem.

Der vorliegende Katalog *Fußball: Ein Spiel – Viele Welten* versammelt Autorinnen und Autoren aus Wissenschaft, Sport, Literatur und Journalismus, die sich der Thematik aus unterschiedlichen Perspektiven annähern. Die Beiträge reflektieren ebenso wie Ausstellung und Kulturprogramm, dass Fußball mehr ist als eine Sportart. Noch bis in die 1980er Jahre hing ihm das schmuddelige Image des Vulgären an. Doch wie kaum ein anderer Sport wurde er schließlich von der Maschinerie des globalen Kapitalismus vereinnahmt. Er ist ein inszeniertes Medienereignis, Inspiration für Künstlerinnen und Künstler und Bühne für Selbstdarstellungen und Projektionen nationaler Errungenschaften.

Ich wünsche Ihnen eine spannende Lektüre und möchte an dieser Stelle der Nationalen DFB Kulturstiftung in Berlin sowie allen kooperierenden Personen, Institutionen und Museen für ihre Unterstützung danken. Ohne sie hätte das Projekt nicht realisiert werden können.

Prof. Dr. Dr. Lydia Hartl
Kulturreferentin der Landeshauptstadt München

Foreword

Dear Readers,

It's football and culture time: during the 2006 FIFA World Cup™ the ball will not just roll in the Munich FIFA World Cup stadium but also across all sorts of pitches: installation and performance, film and photography, video art, theatre, literature and music. The Department of Culture, City of Munich, and the Munich Stadtmuseum are taking the opportunity afforded by this great sporting event to demonstrate in an exhibition and a programme of cultural events that the world-embracing phenomenon of football has a great deal more to offer than yelling victors and dejected losers: *Football: One Game – Many Worlds*

The 2006 FIFA World Cup™ motto «A time to make friends» invites us all to counter the Eurocentrism currently prevailing in football reporting and delve deeper into our guests' football and everyday worlds: from the stadium as «the most popular place to be» to the protagonists as global players and local heroes between pop, hagiography and political icons, from football art to the commercial side of the round leather ball – what is always at stake is the interplay of local and global, sports and fields unrelated to sports.

The present catalogue *Football: One Game – Many Worlds* assembles writers from the fields of science, sport, literature and journalism who approach the subject matter from different angles. Like the exhibition and the cultural events programme, their essays reflect the fact that football is more than just a sport. Until well into the 1980s the taint of vulgarity still clung to it. However, more than any other sport it has been caught up in the machinery of global capitalism. It is a staged media event, inspiration for artists and a stage for showcasing the self-image and projections of national achievements.

I hope you will enjoy this exciting book and should like to take this opportunity to thank the National DFB Kulturstiftung in Berlin and all persons, institutions and museums involved for their unstinting support. Without them this project could not have been realised.

Professor Dr. Dr. Lydia Hartl
Director of the Department of Culture, City of Munich

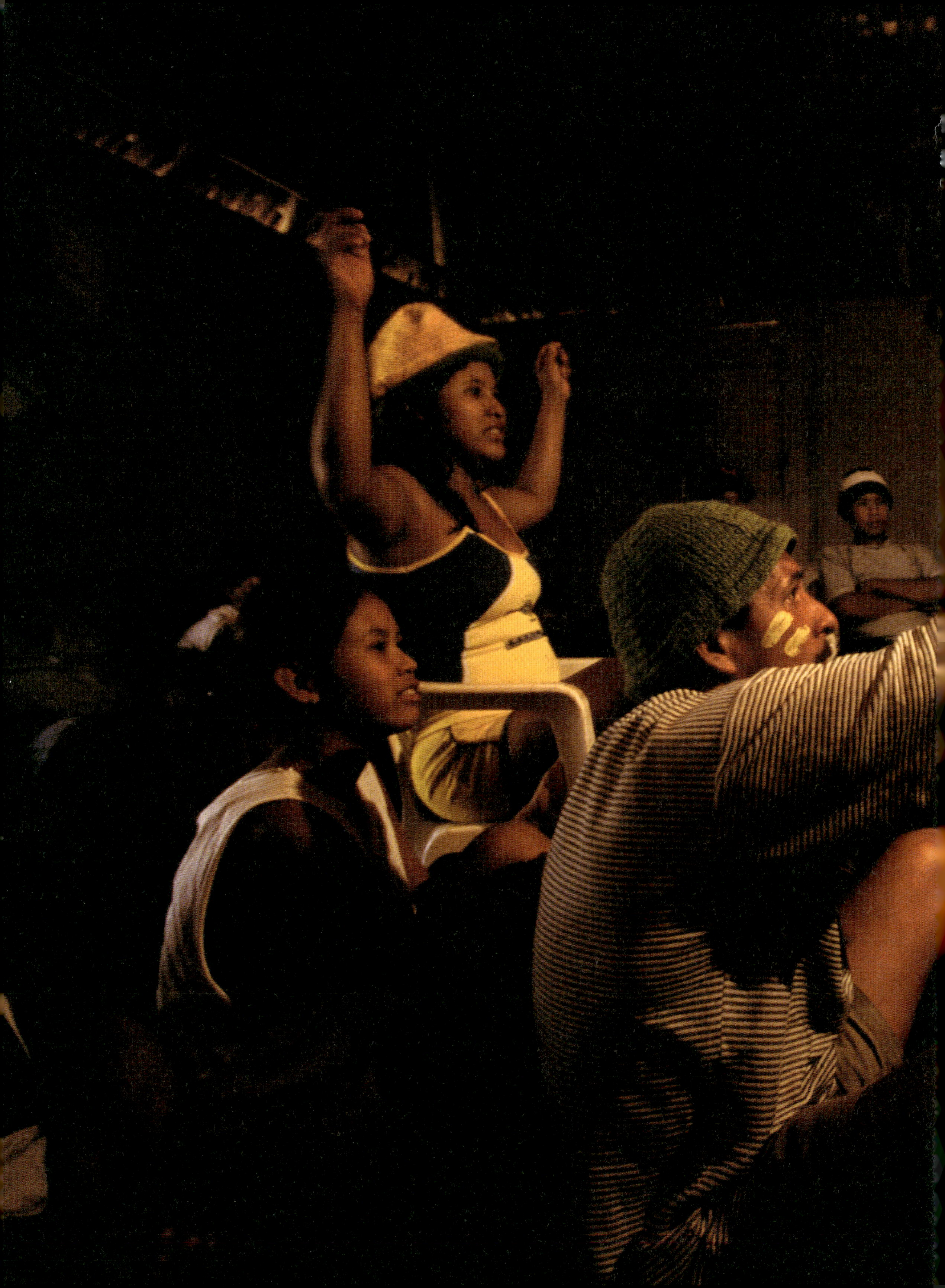

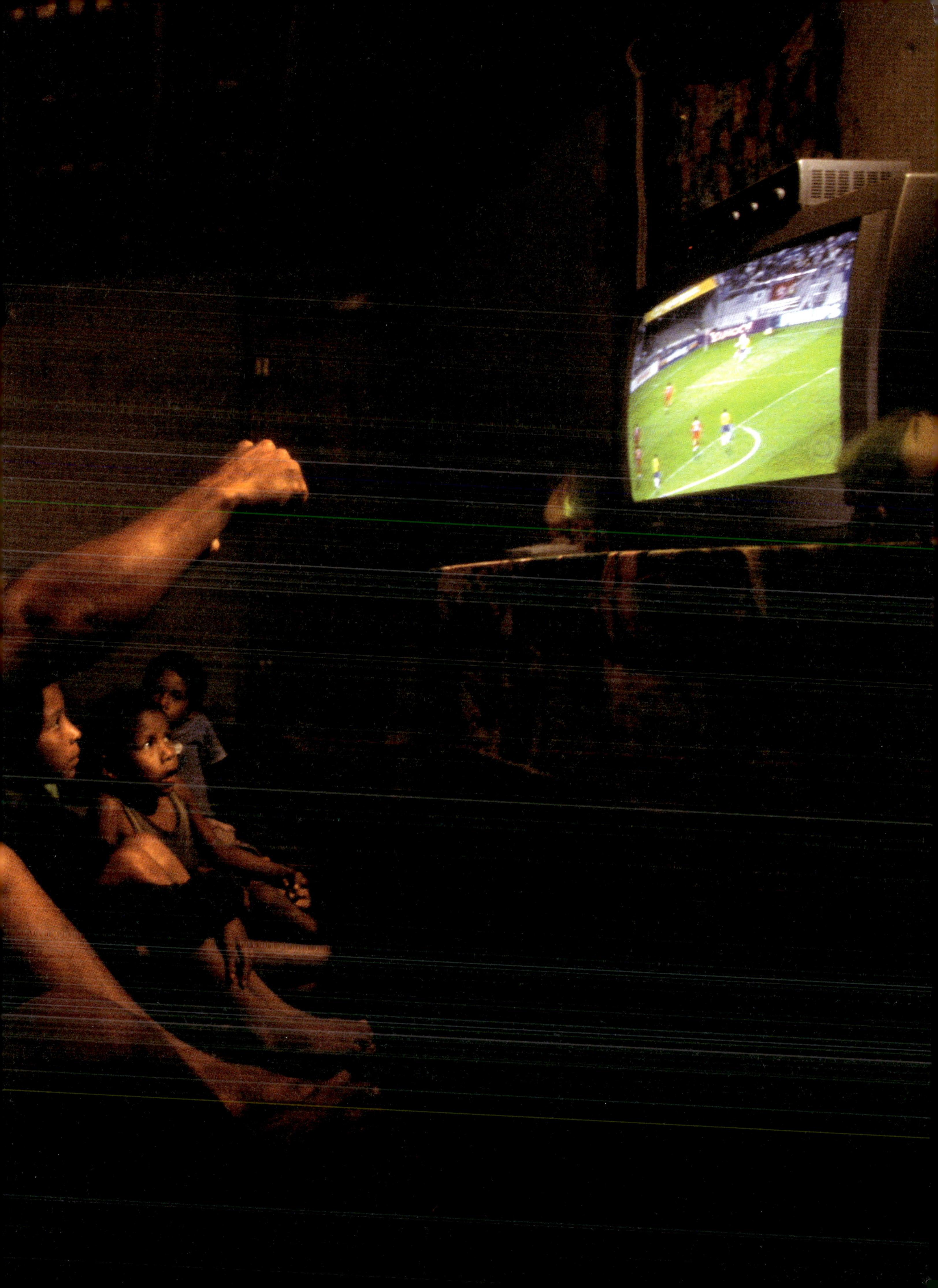

Fußball: Ein Spiel – Viele Welten
Ein ethnologischer Blick auf eine weltweite Leidenschaft

Karin Guggeis

Fußball besitzt für unzählige Menschen über den ganzen Globus hinweg eine einzigartige Faszination und Bedeutung. Ob auf Dorfplätzen oder in Vereinen, überall auf der Welt begegnet man Menschen, die voller Leidenschaft um den Ball kämpfen. Bei Weltmeisterschaften vereint Fußball mehr Erdenbewohner vor dem Bildschirm als irgendeine andere Sportart. Doch Fußball ist mehr als ein Sport: Er ist ein Spiegel der Gesellschaften, in denen er gespielt wird. Weltanschauungen, Religionen und Werte verschiedenster Kulturen finden in ihm Bühne und Arena. Kurz: In diesem einen Spiel entfalten sich viele Welten.

Mit ethnologischem Blick wird in Ausstellung und Publikation das weltumspannende Phänomen Fußball betrachtet. Kulturelle Ausprägungen und gesellschaftliche Einbettungen des Spiels auf und neben dem Platz stehen dabei im Mittelpunkt. Nicht das Exotische wird

Hervorragender Blick aufs Spielfeld jenseits der Business-Lounges: Fußball-Fans in einem Vorort von Accra, Ghana, 2004. A splendid view of the pitch beyond the business lounges: football fans in a suburb of Accra, Ghana, 2004.

← Globaler Zuschauersport Nummer eins: Auch Indianer im Amazonas-Gebiet sind vom Fußballfieber gepackt. The number one global spectator sport: even Indians in the Amazon Basin are in the grip of football mania. © Photo: Gerd Ludwig, Visum

Fußbälle aus verschiedensten Gegenden dieser Erde. Footballs from across the world.

Football: One Game – Many Worlds
Ethnological Perspectives on a World-wide Passion

Karin Guggeis

For countless people all around the globe, football holds a unique fascination and is of a unique importance. Everywhere in the world, whether on village squares or in clubs, people fight passionately for the ball. During world championships, football brings more people together in front of the television than any other sport. Yet football is more than a sport – it is a reflection of the societies in which it is played. It is a stage and an arena for the world views, religions and values of very diverse cultures. In short: this one game reveals many worlds.

In the exhibition and the accompanying publication, the world-wide phenomenon of football is looked at from the point of view of cultural anthropology. The focus is on the game's many cultural forms, both on the field and beyond it, and the way it is embedded in different

jedoch gesucht. Angestrebt ist vielmehr ein Blick auf das Fremde sowie auf das Eigene und vermeintlich so Selbstverständliche – auf gleicher Augenhöhe.

Den populären Phänomenen rund um den Fußball auf globaler Ebene nachzuspüren war weitgehend ethnologisches Neuland. Enzyklopädische Vollständigkeit ist deshalb nicht angestrebt, sondern eine Konzentration auf Schlaglichter, die aus unserer Sicht wichtig und aufschlussreich erscheinen. Diese kaleidoskopartige Annäherung soll möglichst treffende Einblicke in die Kulturen geben, die sich rund um den Fußball auf vielfältigste Weise entwickelt haben.

Was heute eine weltweite Faszination darstellt, begann in seiner modernen Ausprägung vor etwa 130 Jahren von England aus die Welt zu erobern. Doch die Welt eroberte auch den Fußball. Die einzelnen Gesellschaften der Erde eigneten sich das zunächst fremde Spiel auf jeweils sehr spezifische Weisen an und verschmolzen es mit einheimischen Elementen. Dies zeigen beispielsweise die Fan-Kulturen, die sich rund um den Globus unterschiedlich ausprägen. Globalisierung bedeutet eben auch bei einem Phänomen wie Fußball keineswegs kulturelle Gleichmacherei. Vielmehr sind gerade auch bei diesem Spiel Abhebung, Abgrenzung, Betonung von Eigenem und Suche nach spezifischen Identitäten ein wesentlicher Aspekt. Ebenso spiegeln sich grundlegende Strukturen und Werte der jeweiligen Gesellschaften im Fußball, etwa bei der Frage, für welches Geschlecht der Sport besser geeignet ist. Oder darin, welche Spieler wo und warum zu Helden werden. Unterschiedlichste Weltbilder offenbaren sich in der Wahl der Mittel, mit denen Siege herbeigeführt werden sollen. Und auch Politik und Wirtschaft versuchen den Fußball seit Beginn seines Siegeszuges rund um den Globus für sich zu vereinnahmen.

Aufgrund der Vielschichtigkeit des Themas sind die einzelnen Texte im Buch bewusst heterogen gehalten. Neben ethnologischen und anderen kulturwissenschaftlichen Annäherungen finden sich auch Beiträge von kundiger literarischer, journalistischer oder fußballerischer Seite.

Zahlreichen Institutionen und Privatpersonen, die uns bei unseren umfangreichen Recherchen oder bei der Beschaffung der Exponate aus vielen Ecken der Welt überaus kooperativ unterstützt haben, sind wir zu großem Dank verpflichtet.

Eiffelturm-Flasche, Weißbierglas und Mallorca-Eisbecher: Die Grenze zwischen lokaler Identitätssuche und kommerzialisierter Kitschproduktion ist im Umfeld des Fußballs oft fließend. An Eiffel Tower bottle, a wheat-beer glass and a Mallorca ice-cream dish: the boundaries between the search for local identity and the production of commercialised kitsch are often blurred when it comes to football.

societies. But the exhibition is not devoted to the exotic. Rather, it strives to show both other cultures and things we take for granted in our own culture – in the same light.

Investigating the popular phenomenon of football on a global level meant entering largely unknown territory within cultural anthropology. We therefore make no claim to encyclopaedic completeness but concentrate on highlights which are important and revealing from our point of view. This kaleidoscopic approach is intended to give a broad insight into the most diverse cultures that have grown up through and around football.

What is today a world-wide fascination began its conquest of the world in its modern form about 130 years ago, with England as the starting point. But the world has also conquered football. Different societies around the globe have appropriated in very specific ways a game which initially was foreign, and fused it with indigenous elements. This is seen for instance in the great variety of fan cultures. For globalisation, even in the case of a phenomenon such as football, does not mean cultural levelling. And especially in the case of this game, individuality, distinction from others, emphasis on what is one's own, and the creation of a specific identity are essential aspects. The fundamental structures and values of the different societies also play a role in football, for instance in the question as to which sex the sport is more suited to. Or in determining which players, where, and why become heroes. The most diverse worldviews are reflected in the means used to assure victories. And politics and business have tried to monopolise the game right from the beginning of its triumphant advance round the globe.

Due to the complexity of the topic, the texts in the book are deliberately heterogeneous. Besides anthropology and other areas of cultural studies, there are also contributions from the spheres of literature, journalism or football itself.

We would like to express our deep gratitude to the many institutions and private individuals who have helped us for their friendly co-operation during our extensive researches and their assistance in procuring exhibits from many corners of the world.

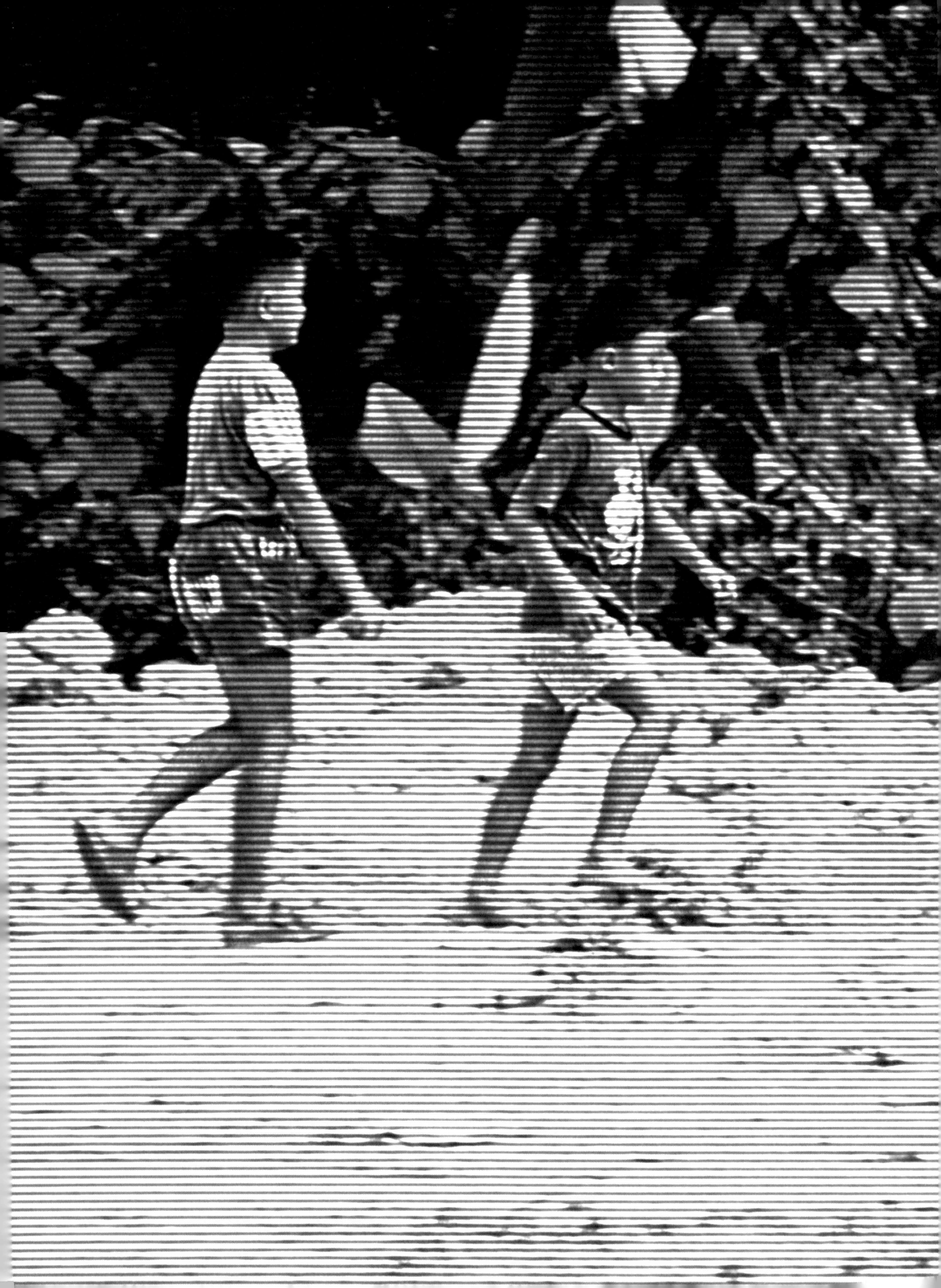

Weltfußball – Fußballwelten

World of Football – Football Worlds

Der Fußball eroberte die Welt – und die Welt den Fußball

Karin Guggeis

Klinssman lebt in Kolumbien, in einem Flüchtlingscamp. Sein Onkel, ein begeisterter Fußball-Fan, war bei der WM 1990 ein glühender Bewunderer der deutschen Nationalmannschaft und vor allem von Jürgen Klinsmann. Nach ihm sollte sein Sohn benannt werden. Seine Frau gebar eine Tochter, doch stellvertretend erhielt sein kurz darauf zur Welt gekommener Neffe den Namen seines Helden – allerdings mit Rechtschreibfehler, denn Schwierigkeiten mit den deutschen Doppelkonsonanten haben auch die Kolumbianer.

Kinder werden in Kolumbien gerne nach globalen Gütern oder Berühmtheiten benannt. Vielleicht erhoffte man sich von Klinssman Alexander Delgado Molina einen sozialen Aufstieg, ein Entfliehen aus den eigenen ökonomischen Verhältnissen. Klinssmans Stärken liegen allerdings mehr jenseits des Fußballfeldes. Mit dem Fußball werden viele Träume geträumt, doch nur wenige gehen in Erfüllung.

Ob bei Wartenden an einem Busbahnhof im nigerianischen Lagos, bei einem Ladenbesitzer in einem kleinen Ort in Myanmar oder beim Strandstuhl-Nachbarn in Italien: Die Antwort auf die Frage nach meiner Heimatstadt zaubert häufig ein Lächeln auf das Gesicht des bis dahin fremden Gegenübers. München ist weltberühmt, München kennt jeder – wenn auch nicht die Stadt, so doch den FC Bayern München. Jenseits nationaler, sozialer oder kultureller Unterschiede offenbart sich eine gemeinsame Gesprächsbasis, ein geteiltes und somit verbindendes Interesse. Fußball ist Türöffner in den verschiedensten Winkeln dieser Erde.

Fernsehübertragungen von Fußballspielen aus fernen Weltregionen haben mittlerweile ihren festen Platz in der Unterhaltungskultur zahlloser Länder. Die Spiele der englischen Premier League, der spanischen Primera División oder der deutschen Bundesliga erzielen in vielen Regionen der Erde hohe Einschaltquoten. Nicht zu vergessen die Weltmeisterschaft, die wie kein anderes Ereignis Milliarden von Menschen vor die Bildschirme dieser Welt zieht. Und gleich nach den Fernseh-Übertragungen versuchen Millionen kleiner Ronaldinhos, Ronaldos oder Ballacks nahezu überall auf den Bolzplätzen, Straßen, Stränden oder Dorfplätzen dieser Erde, den neuesten Spielzügen und Tricks ihrer Idole nachzueifern. Als Zuschauer- wie Aktivensport ist Fußball heute unangefochten der globale Sport Nummer eins.

Der moderne Fußball entstand – lässt man die vielfältiger Vorformen rund um den Globus einmal außer Acht – im England des 19. Jahrhunderts. Berühmte *public schools* wie Rugby oder Eton hatten die erzieherischen Werte dieser Mannschaftssportart – hart, aber fair – als neues Männlichkeitsideal ihrer Schüler erkannt und »zähmten« den einst in den Straßen gespielten Massenfußball mit jeweils eigenen Regeln. Diese für den Spielverkehr untereinander zu vereinheitlichen war im Jahre 1863 das Ziel von elf Londoner Clubs. Die Football Association – von der sich die in einigen Ländern gebräuchliche Bezeichnung *soccer* ableitet – wurde gegründet, allerdings ohne die Verfechter der Rugby-Variante, die auf

Der Fußball eroberte von England aus die Welt. Toraufsatz am Eingang eines Fußballvereins, England, 1880er Jahre. From England football conquered the world. The top of a gate to a football club, England, 1880s.

Wie nahezu überall auf der Welt war Fußball auch in Deutschland anfangs ein Sport für die »besseren Kreise«. As almost everywhere at first, football was initially a «posh» sport in Germany.

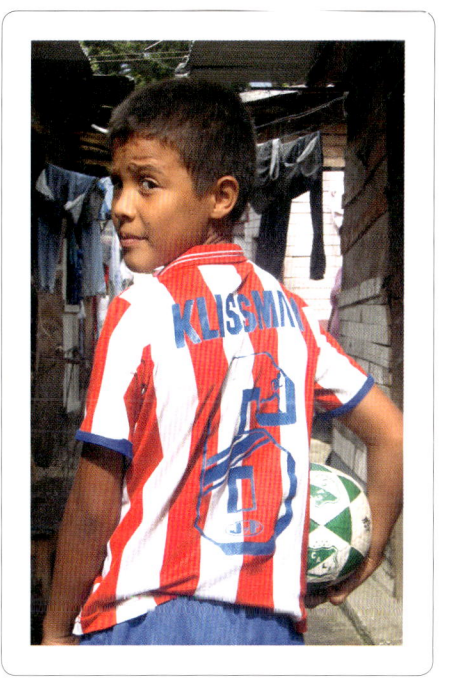

Klinssman Alexander Delgado Molina aus Kolumbien – auf Wunsch seines Onkels benannt nach dem damaligen deutschen Stürmer Jürgen Klinsmann. Klinssman Alexander Delgado Molina of Colombia – his uncle wanted him to be named after the former German forward Jürgen Klinsmann. © Photo: catlinafilm, 2005

Football Conquered the World – and the World has Conquered Football

Karin Guggeis

Klinssman lives in Colombia, in a refugee camp. His uncle, an enthusiastic football fan, was such an ardent admirer of the German national team, and especially of Jürgen Klinsmann, at the 1990 World Cup, that his son was to be named after the footballer. His wife bore a daughter but in her stead a nephew born not long afterwards was given the name of his hero – spelt incorrectly because Colombians are not the only people in the world to have difficulties with the German double consonants.

In Colombia children are often named after global commodities or celebrities. Perhaps his parents hoped that Klinssman Alexander Delgado Molina's name would be the key to improving his social status, to fleeing the economic conditions he was born into. Klinssman's strengths, however, tend to be demonstrated off the pitch more than on. Many dreams have been dreamt with football but only a few ever come true.

Be it people waiting at a bus station in Lagos, Nigeria, be it the proprietor of a shop in a small town in Myanmar or the occupant of the neighbouring deck chair on an Italian beach: my answer to the question of where I come from often brings a fleeting smile to the face of a person who has been till then a complete stranger. Munich is world-famous. Every-

Charakteristisch für Südafrika: Kreativ verzierte Fan-Helme aus Plastik, die an die Grubenhelme der Goldminen-Arbeiter erinnern. Typically South African: creatively decorated plastic fan helmet reminiscent of the helmets worn by goldminers in the pit.

Mit seiner Torjubel-Tanzeinlage an der Eckfahne eroberte Roger Milla aus Kamerun bei der WM 1990 die Herzen der Zuschauer. Roger Milla of Cameroon won spectators' hearts at the 1990 World Cup by celebrating goals with a special dance around the corner posts.

Schienbeintritte oder Beinstellen nicht verzichten wollten. Bald begann dieses sich in seinen Regeln stets entwickelnde Spiel auch die Arbeiterschaft zu erobern, und durch Werte wie den individuellen Einsatz für ein gemeinsames Ziel bewegte es vielfach auch Fabrikbesitzer zur Gründung und Unterstützung von Werkvereinen. Es blieb jedoch nicht ausschließlich ein Sport für Männer: Frauen begeisterten sich ebenfalls in großer Zahl für den Fußball und stellten dadurch auch die Vorherrschaft der männlichen Gesellschaft in Frage.

Ferne Ufer erreichte der Fußball zunächst vor allem im Handgepäck von Geschäfts- und Seeleuten der damaligen wirtschaftlichen Großmacht Großbritannien. Erst allmählich konnten sich auch die jeweiligen einheimischen Oberschichten Zugang zu dem Spiel verschaffen, das für sie den bewunderten *English Way of Life* und »Modernität« repräsentierte. Auch in einigen europäischen Ländern wie Deutschland verhalf die Anglophilie gewisser Bildungsschichten dem »englischen Spiel« zu seiner Verbreitung. Die weltweite Fußballgemeinde wuchs ständig, doch nicht ohne Widerstände und Rückschläge. Die Argumente gegen das Spiel waren vielfältig: So verletzten die nackten Knie der Spieler den herrschenden Sittenkodex in Deutschland, während in Übersee gerne das tropische Klima als Hemmnis für eine Verbreitung angeführt wurde. Trotz aller Widerstände: Fußball hat die Welt erobert.

Und die Welt den Fußball. Roger Milla brachte bei der WM 1990 Kamerun durch seine Tore bis ins Viertelfinale – so weit wie zuvor keine andere afrikanische Mannschaft. Doch wurde er nicht nur aufgrund seiner sportlichen Leistung zu einer Legende der Fußballgeschichte, sondern weil er eine bisher unbekannte Variante des Torjubels zelebrierte: Jeden Treffer feierte er mit einer Tanzeinlage an der nächstgelegenen Eckfahne. Und rund um den Globus wurde versucht, diese Bewegungen nachzuahmen, die zu Makossa, einem in Kamerun beliebten, schweißtreibenden Afro-Pop-Rhythmus getanzt werden. Roger Milla wurde mit diesem Freudentanz weltweit zur Symbolfigur des afrikanischen Fußballs und verschaffte seinem Land, das auf anderen Feldern international nur wenig Beachtung genoss, eine globale Welle der Sympathie. Kamerun – und mit ihm der ganze Kontinent Afrika – hatten

Fußballspielende Kinder, Pangkor Island, Malaysia. Boys playing football, Pangkor Island, Malaysia.
© Photo: Earl & Nazima Kowall, Corbis

one knows Munich – if not the city, at least FC Bayern München. At a far remove from national, social or cultural differences, a basis is thus revealed for a conversation on a shared and, therefore, linking interest. Football opens many doors all over the world.

Television broadcasts of football matches from far distant lands are by now an integral part of the entertainment culture of innumerable countries. English Premier League, Spanish Primera División or German Bundesliga matches notch up high viewer quotas in many places round the world, not to mention the World Cup, which keeps billions of spectators glued to their screens like no other event. And no sooner has the broadcast finished than millions of little Ronaldinhos, Ronaldos or Ballacks are trying out their heroes' newest plays and feints across the world in backyards and streets, on beaches and village squares. Football is undeniably the Number One global sport, both as a spectator sport and as a game actively played.

Modern football originated – leaving aside the many early forms engaged in round the world – in 19th-century England. Celebrated public schools such as Rugby and Eton had recognised the educational value of this – hard but fair – team game as a new ideal of masculinity for their pupils and »tamed« the mass game of football once played in the street by applying new rules that differed from school to school. In 1863 eleven London clubs concurred in the aim of standardising the rules. The Football Association – the term »soccer« used in some countries derives from the name – was founded. It did not include the advocates of Rugby football, who did not want to abolish practices such as kicking opponents in the shins or tripping them up. The game kept on developing rules and soon swept through the working class. Moreover, values such as the commitment of the individual to a common goal inculcated by football induced industrialists to found and support works clubs in many places. Football did not, however, remain a sport that was exclusively a male prerogative: a great many women were enthusiastic about it, contesting male domination in society.

Football reached distant shores mainly in the luggage of travelling merchants and seamen from Great Britain, then the economic world power. Gradually the upper classes of

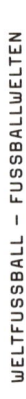

Armband eines Fans von Real Madrid in Mexiko, hergestellt aus Glasperlen, 2005. Bracelet of glass beads, made in Mexico for a Real Madrid fan, 2005.

Ein globales Phänomen lokal angeeignet: Schal aus Frottee für Fans aus dem westafrikanischen Kamerun. A global phenomenon adapted to local use: a fan scarf made of towelling from Cameroon, West Africa.

»Kölsch«-Glas mit dem Emblem des 1.FC Köln. «Kölsch» glass for the typical Cologne beer with the emblem of 1.FC Köln.

die Bühne des Weltfußballs betreten und bereichert. Freude, so war die Botschaft, kann unterschiedlich ausgedrückt werden.

Doch nicht nur einzelne Spieler spiegeln prägende Verhaltensmuster der eigenen Gesellschaft. Fußball ist vor allem auch ein wichtiger Ausdruck der Identität von Gemeinschaften. Er bietet den Mannschaften wie auch den Fans eine breitenwirksame Arena für die Zurschaustellung ihrer Einzigartigkeit, Eigenständigkeit und Besonderheit. Zudem offenbart sich gerade im Fußball als populärster Sportart rund um den Globus der Doppelpass zwischen Globalität und Lokalität. Globalisierung führt keineswegs nur zur Vereinheitlichung und Standardisierung der Welt, wie ein oberflächlicher Blick vielleicht vermuten lässt. Globales und Lokales treffen aufeinander und treten somit gegeneinander an, vermischen sich und führen zu neuen kulturellen Elementen und Formen. Gerade das Eigene wird durch die globale Herausforderung oft gestärkt. Auch aus fast vergessenen Quellen werden Reserven mobilisiert, die dem Lokalen neuen Auftrieb geben, und einheimische Traditionen werden an neue Bedürfnisse angepasst. Diese Neuinterpretation lokaler Elemente im Wechselspiel mit globalen Phänomenen ist gerade im Fußball mit seiner immensen Breitenwirkung und seinem hohen Unterhaltungsfaktor wichtig. Sie macht den Sport in zahllosen Weltregionen zu einer der lebendigsten Populärkulturen.

So werden Fan-Utensilien und andere materielle Güter im Umfeld des Fußballs nicht einfach überall gleichförmig übernommen. Vielmehr werden sie mit örtlichen Bedeutungen und Versatzstücken versehen und aufgeladen und dadurch zu etwas Neuem und Eigenem umgewandelt. Das eigene Beckham-Trikot beispielsweise ist für einen nigerianischen Jungen auch Ausdruck seiner Teilhabe am Welt-(Fußball-)Geschehen, für einen weiblichen japanischen Teenager hingegen steht es für Individualität und Abkehr von den Traditionen und Werten der Elterngeneration.

Und selbst bei einem globalem Gut wie den Fan-Schals lassen sich bei genauerer Betrachtung entscheidende Unterschiede erkennen. Denn meist sind solche Schals aus Baumwolle oder billigen Kunstfasern gefertigt. Die Variante aus dem westafrikanischen Kamerun hingegen ist aus Frottee hergestellt, einem weitaus saugfähigeren Material – und dient damit nicht nur als Bekenntnis zur Nationalmannschaft, sondern auch als Schweißtuch.

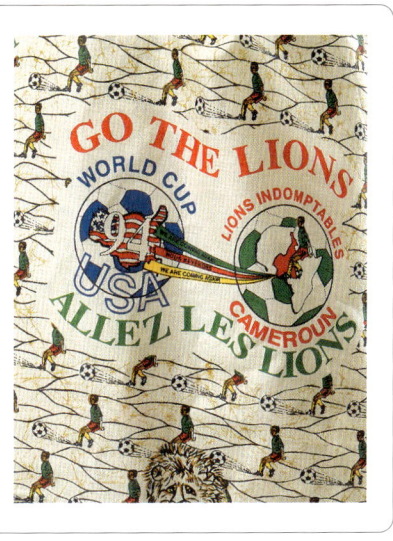

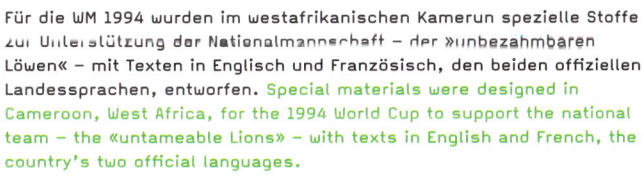

Für die WM 1994 wurden im westafrikanischen Kamerun spezielle Stoffe zur Unterstützung der Nationalmannschaft – der »unbezähmbaren Löwen« – mit Texten in Englisch und Französisch, den beiden offiziellen Landessprachen, entworfen. Special materials were designed in Cameroon, West Africa, for the 1994 World Cup to support the national team – the «untameable Lions» – with texts in English and French, the country's two official languages.

Auch in Ostasien erobert der Fußball zunehmend öffentliche und private Räume: Ein WC im chinesischen Jining, 2005. Football is invading both public and private spaces in East Asia, too: a toilet in Jining, China, 2005.

other countries gained access to the game, which to them represented the »English way of life« and »modernity« which they admired. Anglophilia in some European countries, including Germany, promoted the spread of the »English game« among the educated classes. The football community grew apace world-wide yet not without encountering resistance and setbacks. The arguments against the game were legion: players' bare knees infringed the prevailing moral code in Germany whereas overseas the tropical climate was used as a reason for preventing the spread of football. Yet despite all the resistance it has met, football has conquered the world.

And the world has conquered football. In the 1990 World Cup Roger Milla brought Cameroon to the quarter finals with his goals – further than any other African team had gone before. However, he did not only become a football legend because of his sporting achievements but also made history because he introduced a previously unknown variant of goal celebration: he marked each goal by dancing at the nearest corner post. And all around the world his movements were imitated, which were danced to Makossa, an African pop rhythm popular in Cameroon. With this way of celebrating goals, Roger Milla came to symbolise African football world-wide and brought his country, which in other respects had previously attracted little attention, a global tide of sympathy. Cameroon – and with it the entire African continent – had entered the stage of global football and enriched it with its presence. Rejoicing, that was the message, can be expressed in all sorts of different ways.

But individual players are not the only ones to reflect the formative behaviour patterns of the societies they come from. Football is also an important expression of communal identity. It provides both teams and fans with a global arena for showcasing their uniqueness, independence and distinctiveness. Moreover, football, as the most popular sport throughout the world, reveals a give-and-take of global and local aspects. Globalisation does not lead just to world-wide uniformity and standardisation as it might seem when viewed superficially. The global and the local meet and, in so doing, clash, blend and lead to new cultural elements and forms. The individual aspect is often strengthened by dint of being a global challenge. Reserves from almost forgotten sources are mobilised to give fresh impetus to the local aspect and indigenous traditions are adapted to new needs. The re-interpretation of local elements

Fan-Gesänge offenbaren ebenfalls lebendige Populärkulturen im Wechselspiel zwischen Globalität und Lokalität. In den 1960er Jahren in Großbritannien erfunden, verdanken sie auch der in diesem Land 1966 ausgetragenen Weltmeisterschaft ihre schnelle und globale Verbreitung. In Europa werden für Gesänge innerhalb und außerhalb des Stadions meist aktuelle oder altbekannte Lieder aus dem Schlager- und Popmusik- sowie dem Volksliedbereich umgedichtet. Manche überdauern Jahrzehnte, andere entstehen aus einer Situation heraus und sind schon nach einem Spiel wieder vergessen. Schmähgesänge auf gegnerische Vereine erfreuen sich weltweit größter Beliebtheit. So auch in Deutschland, wo die eingängige Refrain-Zeile aus *Yellow Submarine* umgetextet wurde in das jedem Fußball-Fan bekannte »Zieht den Bayern die Lederhosen aus!« Die Melodie wird aber durchaus auch auf andere Gegner umgemünzt, wie etwa auf den 1. FC Köln als »Ihr seid nur ein Karnevalsverein!« Dennoch überdauern in Europa – auch wegen der gesanglich meist ungeübten Fans – nur Lieder, die auf einfache Melodiebestandteile reduziert sind. In afrikanischen Ländern wie Uganda sind die Gesänge hingegen melodischer, harmonischer und weniger kämpferisch. Auch versetzen konzertreife Percussionisten mit lokal verwurzelten, mitreißenden Rhythmen den ganzen Platz in Schwingung. Ein mittlerweile weltweit verbreiteter Rhythmus, der keineswegs nur brasilianische Stimmbänder und Hüften in Bewegung versetzt, ist der Samba. Denn dieser ertönt selbst in japanischen Stadien, um zusammen mit »Olé, Olé, Olé«-Liedern ihre brasilianischen Stars anzufeuern. Auch katalanische Lieder, US-amerikanische Hits oder Auszüge

Den Stars auch jenseits des Platzes nacheifern: Die Haarschnitte populärer Fußballer sind nicht nur bei Fans beliebt. Reklameschild eines Frisörs in Südafrika, gemalt von dem Kongolesen Bruno Ngumbare Bihiza. Emulating the stars even off the pitch: the haircuts worn by popular footballers are not just a hit with fans. Advertisement for a barber in South Africa, painted by Bruno Ngumbare Bihiza of the Republic of Congo.

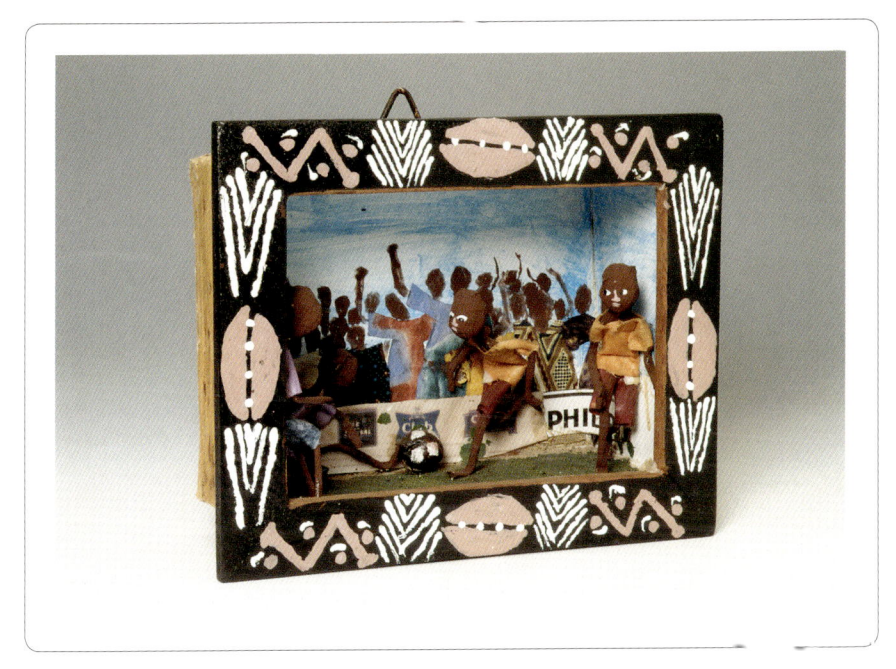

Fußballbegeisterung macht sich nicht an Weltranglistenplätzen fest: Bambus-Schaukästchen mit Fußball-Szene aus dem ostafrikanischen Uganda. Enthusiasm for football is not just demonstrated by where one stands on the world-ranking list: bamboo display case with football scene from Uganda in East Africa.

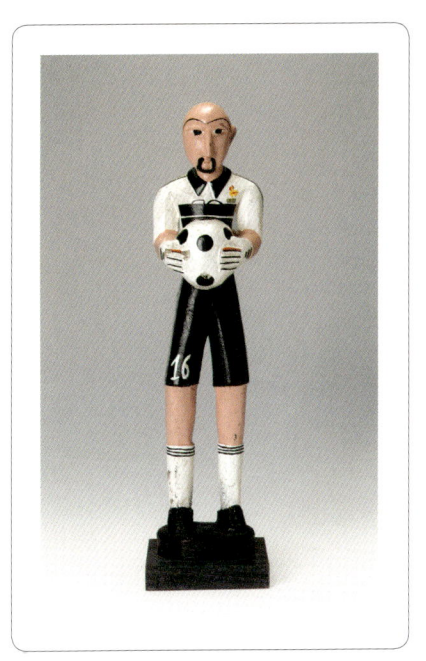

Der französische Nationalturhüter Barthez als Colon-Figur. Siegreiche Europäer werden immer wieder in westafrikanische Kulte eingebunden. The French national goalkeeper Barthez as a colon figure. Victorious Europeans have often been linked with West African cults. Anonymus, Republik Elfenbeinküste / Anonymous, Rep. Ivory Coast, 2002.

in interplay with global phenomena is particularly important in football with its mass appeal and its high entertainment value. This is what makes the sport one of the most lively popular cultures in so many regions across the world.

Fan articles and other football-related material goods are not just simply taken over. On the contrary, they are embellished with local significance and ready-made elements and in this way transformed into something new and distinctive to a particular region. Owning his own Beckham jersey is, for a Nigerian boy, an expression of his participation in world (football) events. For a Japanese teenage girl, on the other hand, it stands for individuality and a rejection of the traditions and values espoused by her parents' generation.

And even global commodities such as fan scarves reveal crucial differences on closer scrutiny. After all, most scarves of this type are made either of cotton or cheap synthetic fibres. The Cameroon variant in West Africa, on the other hand, is made of towelling, a much more absorbent material – it does not just serve as a profession of allegiance to the national team but is also used to wipe the fan's sweating brow.

Fan songs also reveal lively popular cultures at the interface of globalism and localism. Invented in 1960s Britain, they also owe their rapid spread around the world to the World Cup hosted in England in 1966. In continental Europe songs sung inside and outside the stadium are usually remakes of current hits or golden oldies and are drawn from both pop music and folk music. Some survive for decades, others arise spontaneously, only to be forgotten once a game is over. Songs sung to insult opposing clubs are enormously popular all over the world. In Germany, too, where the catchy refrain from *Yellow Submarine* was re-texted to mean »Strip the Lederhosen off the Bavarians!« The melody is also re-coined to insult other rivals, such as 1. FC Köln, to mean: »You are nothing but a Carnival club!« Nevertheless, the only fan songs to survive in Europe – partly because most fans are unpractised singers outside the stadium – are those that can be reduced to simple melodic elements. In African countries such as Uganda, by contrast, songs are more melodic and harmonic but less belli-

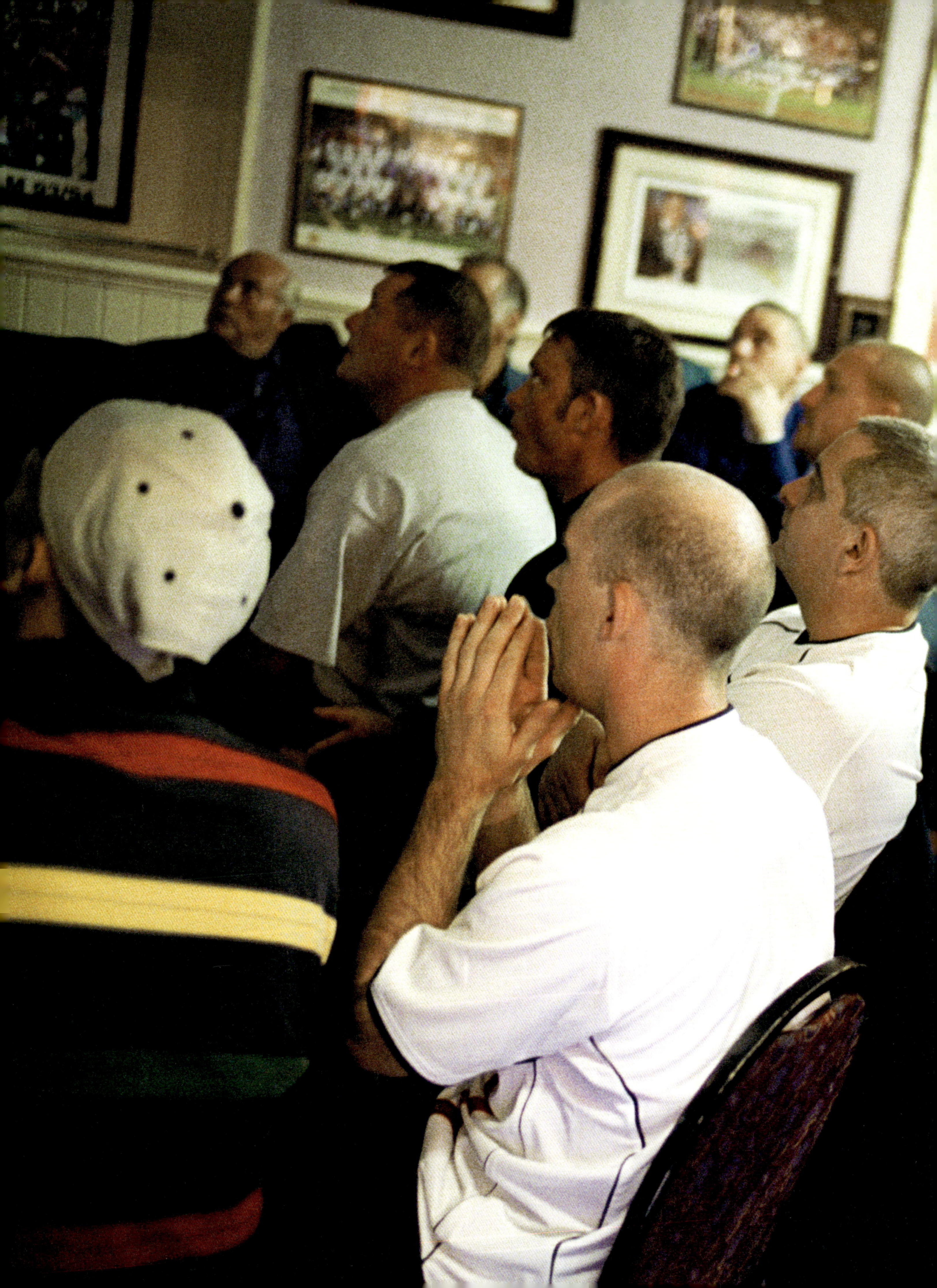

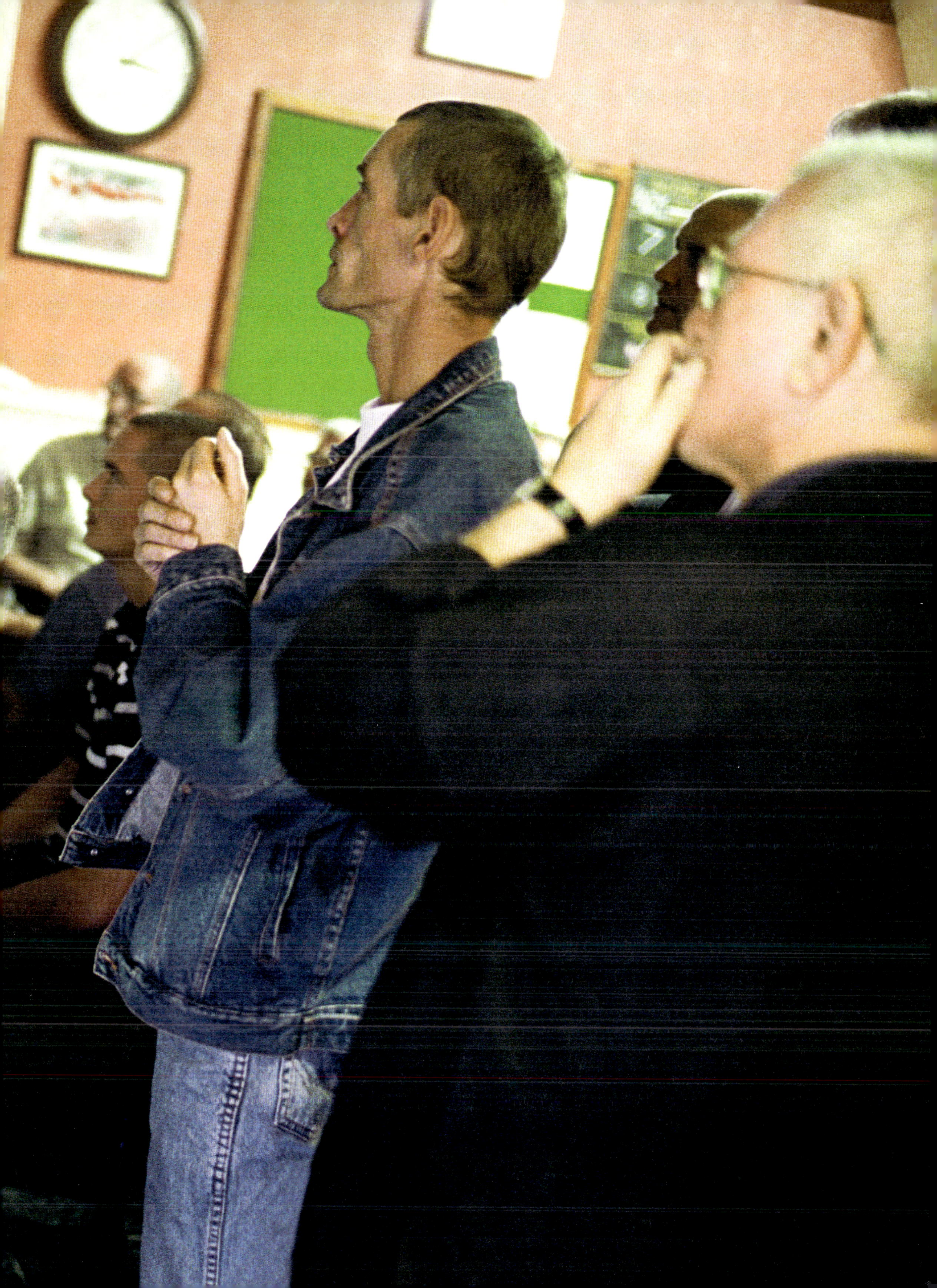

Auch in Europas Städten – hier in St. Etienne, Frankreich – bietet Fußball gerade Migrantenkindern eine geschätzte Freizeitbeschäftigung: Kaum ein anderer Sport ist materiell so bedürfnislos. In European cities, too – here at St. Étienne, France – football gives immigrant children especially a highly appreciated leisure activity: no other sport is so inexpensive. ©Photo: Oliver Heisch

← Kollektives Hoffen und Bangen: Englische Fans verfolgen 2001 in Manchester ein Fußballspiel in einem Pub. Collective hopes and fears: English fans following a football match in a Manchester pub, 2001.
©Photo: Helen King, Corbis

aus klassischen Opern tragen zur einzigartigen kosmopolitischen Atmosphäre in der J-League bei, die die grundsätzliche Offenheit Japans gegenüber fremden Phänomenen spiegelt. Bei der Abwandlung von Text und teilweise auch der Melodie gibt es allerdings ein Tabu: Die »Urhymne« aller Fangesänge, das Lied *You'll Never Walk Alone,* das erstmals in den 1960er Jahren im Liverpooler Anfield-Stadion erklang.

Seine außergewöhnliche Faszination bezieht Fußball für die Zuschauer auch aus seinen Unwägbarkeiten und Unsicherheiten. Denn keineswegs gewinnt immer der Beste. Wie im »richtigen Leben« spielen der Faktor »Glück« oder auch der Ausgang anderer Spiele eine große Rolle. Sieg und Niederlage wechseln sich ab, der eigene Status ist ungewiss. Diese Unkontrollierbarkeiten begünstigen das Streben nach zusätzlicher Unterstützung des Teams. Und auch hier vermischen sich im Fußball unterschiedlichste lokale und globale Religionen, Vorstellungen, Welterklärungsmuster und rituelle Praktiken. Darüber hinaus werden globale Fußballstars in einheimische Kulte, Rituale oder Religionen rund um den Globus eingebaut. So verschmolz Diego Maradona im italienischen Neapel mit der lokalen Tradition der Heiligenverehrung. Fabien Barthez, französischer Nationaltorwart, sollte in der Republik Elfenbeinküste als Colon-Figur einem einheimischen Kult zu mehr Kraft und Macht verhelfen. Und von David Beckham steht heute eine Statue in einem buddhistischen Tempel in Thailand. Dabei ist weltweit zu beobachten: Was den einen selbstverständlich erscheint, ist für andere oft unverständlich.

Auch Fußballkleidung ist kulturell geprägt: Iranische Mädchen spielen im Rahmen eines Programms der Swiss Academy for Development, das sich um traumatisierte Kinder in der 2003 von einem Erdbeben verwüsteten Stadt Bam kümmert. Football apparel is also culturally tinged: Iranian girls play under the auspices of a Swiss Academy for Development programme helping children traumatised by the earthquake that ravaged the city of Bam in 2003.
© Photo: Frank Baumann

cose. Concert-standard percussionists make the whole stadium throb to locally rooted, catchy rhythms. A familiar rhythm world-wide that does not just set Brazilian vocal chords and hips in motion is the samba. Along with the chorus of »Olé, Olé, Olé«, it reverberates even in Japanese stadiums to spur on their Brazilian stars. Catalan songs, US hits or passages from classical operas contribute to the uniquely cosmopolitan atmosphere prevailing in the J-League, which reflects Japan's fundamental receptivity to foreign cultural phenomena. There is, however, one taboo. The text and even much of the melody of that »primal hymn«, the mother of all fan songs, *You'll Never Walk Alone,* which was first sung in Anfield Stadium, Liverpool, in the 1960s, are sacrosanct and may not be changed.

Its incalculability and uncertainty are part of the extraordinary fascination football exerts on spectators. The best team does not always win. As in »real life«, »luck« and the outcome of other games are factors to be reckoned with. Victories alternate with defeats, one's own status is uncertain. Such imponderables tend to make fans, players and coaches strive all the harder to give more support to their team. And here all sorts of local and global religions, ideas, world-views and ritual observances fuse in football. Moreover, global football stars are built into local indigenous cults, rituals and religions world-wide. Diego Maradona, for instance, has been fused in Naples, Italy, with the local tradition of venerating a patron saint. Fabien Barthez, the French national goalkeeper, was alleged in the republic of Côte d'Ivoire to enhance the strength and power of an indigenous cult as a *colon* figure. And a statue of David Beckham now stands in a Buddhist temple in Thailand. As can be seen anywhere in the world: what is taken for granted in one culture is utterly incomprehensible in another.

Lokale Bälle – globale Bälle

Karin Guggeis

Seine weltweite Popularität verdankt der Fußball vor allem auch einer Besonderheit: Man braucht nur einen Ball oder ein anderes irgendwie mit dem Fuß tretbares Ding, um diesem Spiel zu frönen.

Und so wird jenseits des Vereins- oder gar Star-Fußballs rund um den Globus mit den unterschiedlichsten Gegenständen gekickt. Es reizen bereits alltägliche Dinge, die am Weg liegen – etwa eine Orange, eine Mango oder eine Dose. Auch wird oft rasch ein kurzlebiger Ballersatz aus gerade vorhandenen Materialien hergestellt. Eine zusammengeknotete Plastiktüte, in die weitere zusammengeknüllte Tüten gesteckt sind, benutzten z.B. Kinder in Kamerun (Abb. 1). Papier und Klebeband wiederum fanden in Mexiko neben dem Schulunterricht in der Pause eine neue Verwendung (Abb. 2).

Strapazierfähigere selbstgefertigte Bälle, mit denen gerade jüngere Kinder aus ärmeren Verhältnissen mancher Weltregionen Fußball spielen, sind ebenfalls aus jeweils leicht und ohne große Unkosten verfügbaren Materialien hergestellt. So der Ball aus Maniok-Blättern, den nigerianische Kinder anfertigten, oder jener aus Kochbananenblättern ihrer kamerunischen Nachbarn (Abb. 3). Beide Pflanzen gehören in Westafrika zu den Grundnahrungsmitteln, und so legen die Bälle auch beredtes Zeugnis von den dortigen Alltagswelten ab. Zwei weitere Bälle aus Kamerun sind aus Gummifäden hergestellt (Abb. 4) und künden damit von kolonialen weltwirtschaftlichen Weichenstellungen: Bereits in der deutschen Kolonialzeit wurden in diesem Gebiet großflächige Kautschukplantagen angelegt, und der billige Export dieses Rohstoffs verhalf der deutschen Automobil- und Elektro-Industrie zu einem starken Aufschwung. Auf eine ideale Recycling-Methode industrieller Wegwerfprodukte verweist der kompakt aus dünnen Plastiktüten gewickelte Ball aus Sambia (Abb. 6). Wie der kamerunische »Ersatzball« zeigt dieser eine für Länder ohne flächendeckende Müllabfuhr beispielhafte Art kreativer Wiederverwertung. Bemerkenswert sind auch die beiden Bälle aus Rotang (Abb. 7), die weit voneinander entfernten Weltregionen entstammen – dem indonesischen Java und dem westafrikanischen Kamerun. Die Bälle unterscheiden sich nur in Flechttechnik und Gewicht, nicht jedoch hinsichtlich Material und Größe. Generell fällt bei den aufwändigeren, in Eigenproduktion hergestellten Bällen auf, dass fast alle annähernd den selben Durchmesser besitzen wie die industriell gefertigten Norm-Bälle der Größe »Mini«.

Neben diesem Spektrum an lokal gefertigten Bällen sind in allen Weltgegenden auch industriell gefertigte Standard-Bälle verbreitet. So z. B. der hier gezeigte »Norm-Fußball«, mit dem die Kindergruppe eines javanischen Dorfes etwa zwei Jahre lang jeden Tag spielte (Abb. 9). Ebenfalls in täglichem Gebrauch war der hier gezeigte Ball, den die Projektmitarbeiterin Sinahí Venegas von einem Nachbarsjungen aus ihrem mexikanischen Heimatort geschenkt bekam (Abb. 10).

Ob man seine Spieltechnik und -stärken täglich mit einem winzigen Kautschukball, einem andauernd Luft verlierenden Gummiball oder einem industriellen Norm-Fußball entwickelt, prägt – neben Faktoren wie Größe und Beschaffenheit des Platzes, Mannschaftsstärke oder Vorhandensein eines Trainers mit seinen Vorgaben – die Spielweise entscheidend.

Local Balls – Global balls

Karin Guggeis

Football owes its world-wide popularity mainly to one peculiarity: only one ball or something else that can be kicked around is needed for playing the game.
So all sorts of objects are being kicked around the world far from club and Premiership football. Things lying in the street are enough to invite a kick – an orange, a mango or a tin can. A short-lived substitute for a ball may also be made of whatever materials happen to be available. Children in Cameroon might use a crumpled-up plastic bag with other bags in it (fig. 1). Paper and adhesive tape have been put to use in Mexican schoolyards in breaks from class (fig. 2).
More durable home-made balls with which younger children, especially those from disadvantaged homes, play in many parts of the world are also made of light materials available at little expense, for instance a ball of manioc leaves made by Nigerian children or one made of plantain (green bananas used in cooking) leaves by their neighbours in Cameroon (fig. 3). These two plants are basic food staples in West Africa, so balls made of their leaves attest eloquently to everyday living there. Two other balls from Cameroon are made of strings of latex (fig. 4) and, therefore, bear witness to the economic conditions established by colonialism. Large rubber plantations were laid out in these regions during the German colonial era and the export of this cheap raw material contributed substantially to a strong upturn in the fledgling German automobile and electrical industries. A compact ball from Zambia made of tightly wound thin plastic bags (fig. 6) demonstrates an ideal method for recycling throwaway industrial products. Like the «ball substitute» from Cameroon, this one exemplifies creative recycling in a country that does not have large-scale rubbish disposal systems. Two balls made of rattan (fig. 7) are also remarkable. They come from regions that are very far apart indeed – Java in Indonesia and Cameroon in West Africa. The balls differ only in the technique of weaving used and in weight, but they are both made of the same material and are the same size. On the whole, more elaborate home-made balls tend, remarkably, to match closely the standard diameter of industrially manufactured «mini»-sized balls.
Industrially manufactured standardised balls are also widespread throughout the world wherever the range of locally handmade balls exists. The «standard ball» with which a group of children played every day for two years in a Javanese village (fig. 9) attests that this is so. Another standard ball used daily is the one shown here, which project assistant Sinahí Venegas was given by a neighbourhood boy from her Mexican hometown (fig. 10). Whether you practise your technique and strengths on a tiny latex ball, a rubber ball that deflates continually or a standard industrially made football makes a huge difference – along with such factors as the size and properties of the place where you play, the number of players in a team or the availability of a coach who can give precise instruction – in the way you play.

1 Fußballersatz aus Plastiktüten. Bamenda, Kamerun, 2006. A substitute football made of plastic bags. Bamenda, Cameroon, 2006. B 18 cm, H 10 cm, 45 g, Sprunghöhe / bounce 9 cm.

2 Ballersatz aus Papier. Mexiko, 2006. Substitute football made of paper. Mexiko, 2006. Ø 10 cm, 80 g, Sprunghöhe / bounce 9 cm.

3 Links: Ball aus Streifen von Maniok-Blättern, gefertigt von Kindern im nigerianischen Akuma, 2006. Rechts: Ball aus Bananenblättern. Kamerun, 2005. Left: Ball fashioned of strips of manioc leaves, made by children in Akuma, Nigeria, 2006. Right: ball made of banana leaves. Cameroon, 2005. Links / left: Ø 12 cm, 210 g. Rechts / right: Ø 12 cm, 160 g.

4 Zwei Bälle aus Gummifäden, Kamerun. Links: Sehr kompakt, wird ziemlich schnell, für schuhgewohnte Füße schmerzhaft und schwer zu kontrollieren. Rechts: 2006 in Tiko erworben. Er hebt leicht ab und schlägt durch seine Ei-Form so manch überraschenden Haken. Two balls made of latex strings, Cameroon. Left: very compact, is quite fast but painful for feet accustomed to shoes and difficult to control. Right: acquired in Tiko in 2006. This ball bounces lightly and spins unexpectedly because it is egg-shaped. Links / Left: Ø 5 cm, 100 g, Sprunghöhe / bounce 110 cm. Rechts / right: Ø 13 cm, 135 g, Sprunghöhe / bounce 55 cm.

Bei den abgebildeten Bällen angegeben sind Größe und Gewicht sowie Sprunghöhe bei einem Aufprall aus zwei Metern Höhe (laut der Norm »FIFA approved« soll ein Ball dabei mindestens 1,35 m, auf keinen Fall aber mehr als 1,55 m hoch springen). Fragilere Bälle wurden diesem Test nicht ausgesetzt. The size and weight as well as bounce height when thrown from a height of two metres (according to the «FIFA approved» standard a ball must bounce at least 1.35 m but not more than 1.55 m) of the footballs shown are given below. More fragile balls were not subjected to this test. Tests der Spiel- und Sprungeigenschaften der Bälle / Testing play and bounce qualities: Peter Niedersteiner, Sinahí Venegas.

Abkürzungen / abbreviations
B   Breite / breadth
H   Höhe / height
Ø   Durchmesser / diametre

5 »Meereswellenball«, Küstenregion Kameruns. Nur die Wellen des Meeres formten diese kurzlebige Fußball-Variante aus kleinen Pflanzenteilen. «Waves of the Sea» ball, coastal region of Cameroon. This short-lived football variant made of small bits of vegetable matter was formed solely by the waves of the sea. Ø 10 cm, 125 g.

6 Ball aus gefundenen und gewaschenen Plastiktüten – mit Schnüren umwickelt. Lusaka, Sambia, 2003. Ball made of found and washed plastic bags – wrapped with twine. Lusaka, Zambia, 2003. Ø 15 cm, 320 g.

7 Zwei Bälle aus Rotangstreifen. Leicht zu kontrollieren, erlauben sie auch hohe Pässe. Links: Kamerun, 2005. Rechts: Java, 2005. Ganz rechts: Ein Norm-Ball der Größe »Mini«. Two balls made of strips of rattan. Easy to control, they make high passes possible. Left: Cameroon, 2005. Right: Java, 2005. Far right: a standard «Mini»-size ball. Links / left: Ø 12 cm, 160 g. Rechts / right: Ø 12 cm, 80 g.

8 Seine zahlreichen Flicken offenbaren die Wertschätzung, die dieser Gummiball bei seinen Vorbesitzern erfuhr. Bamenda, Kamerun, 2006. Its many patches show how highly appreciated this rubber ball was by its previous owners. Bamenda, Cameroon, 2006. Ø 10 cm, 70 g.

9 Mit diesem Ball aus Java spielten zwei Jahre lang jeden Tag Kinder und Jugendliche des Dorfes Pekayon-Bekasi bei Jakarta. Children and teenagers played with this Javanese ball for two years in the village of Pekayon-Bekasi near Jakarta. Ø 20,5 cm, 210 g, Sprunghöhe / bounce 120 cm.

10 Norm-Ball aus Mexiko. A standard ball from Mexico. Ø 22 cm, 370 g, Sprunghöhe / bounce 80 cm.

11 Norm-Fußball aus den 1940er Jahren. A 1940s standard football. Ø 20 cm, 210 g, Sprunghöhe / bounce 120 cm.

Ein Derwisch, der Fußbälle näht
Arif Sain aus Pakistan

Jürgen Wasim Frembgen

An einem schwül heißen Augusttag im Sommer 2004 unweit der pakistanisch-indischen Grenze: Der Wanderderwisch Arif Sain hat gemeinsam mit seinen Begleitern ein Zelt in der Stadt Kasur aufgeschlagen. Tausende Pilger treffen sich hier jedes Jahr am Schrein des Sufi-Heiligen Baba Bullhe Shah und verbringen die Nacht mit ekstatischen Hymnen der Gottesliebe, berauschender Musik und Trancetanz. Am Morgen nach dem Fest kramt Arif in seinen Beuteln und Jutesäcken und zieht schließlich zu unserem Erstaunen mehrere Fußbälle hervor. »Komm Nadim«, meint er beim Abschied zu meinem Sohn, »du bist von soweit hergekommen, ich möchte dir etwas schenken. Suche dir einen Ball aus, vielleicht hier den schwarzen, ich habe ihn selbst gemacht!«
Ein islamischer Mystiker, noch dazu ein in der Bruderschaft der Qalandariyya weithin geachteter »großer Derwisch«, halbnackt und mit Flickenkappe, der Fußbälle herstellt – wie ist das möglich, wie passt das zu einem religiösen Wanderleben am Rande der Gesellschaft? Arif beginnt zu erzählen: Er wuchs im Pandschab, dem »Fünfstromland«, in der Stadt Sialkot auf, bekannt für die Produktion von Sportartikeln, aber auch für die damit verbundene Kinderarbeit. Seit seinem sechsten Lebensjahr half er im Kreis seiner Familie beim Zusammennähen der Lederstücke für Fußbälle, die bis heute in alle Welt verkauft werden. Mit 16 Jahren begann er dann ein ungebundenes Leben als Wanderderwisch. Zunächst zog er zu Fuß und später mit einem Eselskarren von einem Heiligenschrein zum anderen, heute benutzt er manchmal die Eisenbahn. Wenn er Geld benötigt, um seine Anhänger und Gäste zu bewirten, dann repariert er ein paar Fahrräder oder näht eben einige Fußbälle, die er weiterverkauft.

A Dervish who sews Footballs
Arif Sain of Pakistan

Jürgen Wasim Frembgen

On a muggy August day in 2004 near the border between India and Pakistan: together with his followers, Arif Sain, an itinerant dervish, has pitched his tent in the town of Kasur. Thousands of pilgrims assemble here every year at the shrine of the Sufi saint Baba Bullhe Shah and spend the night singing ecstatic hymns showing their love for God, playing intoxicating music and dancing in a trance. The morning after the celebration, Arif Sain rummages in his bags and to our astonishment comes up with several footballs. «Come, Nadim,» he says to my son in farewell, «You've come such a long way to get here, I want to give you something. Pick out a ball for yourself, maybe this black one here, I made it myself!»
An Islamic mystic, and a widely acclaimed «Great Dervish» in the Qalandariyya Brotherhood, at the moment half-naked and wearing a patchwork cap, who makes footballs – how is this possible, indeed compatible, with an itinerant life as a holy man? Arif starts to tell us about it. He grew up in the Punjab, the «Land of Five Rivers», in the city of Sialkot, which is known for producing sports articles, which children also help to make. Since he was six years old he has helped his family to sew together the pieces of leather that make the footballs that are sold throughout the world to this day. At sixteen he began his life as an itinerant dervish. At first he went everywhere on foot but later he had a donkey cart to take him from one holy shrine to the next. Now he sometimes goes by train. When he needs money to be hospitable to followers and guests, he repairs a bicycle or two or sews footballs, which he then sells.

Der pakistanische Wanderderwisch Arif Sain sichert seinen Lebensunterhalt unter anderem durch das Nähen von Fußbällen. One of the ways the Pakistani itinerant dervish Arif Sain earns his livelihood is by sewing footballs.

← Ein von Arif Sain zusammengenähter Lederfußball. A leather football sewn by Arif Sain.

Im Fußballschuh in eine andere Welt

Karin Guggeis

In einem Sarg in Form eines Fußballschuhs in die jenseitige Welt befördert zu werden ist auch im westafrikanischen Ghana etwas Außergewöhnliches. Es bedeutet, dass man es im Leben zu etwas gebracht hat – und zwar als Fußballer.

Man muss »Großes« im Leben geleistet haben, damit die Hinterbliebenen einen so extravaganten Sarg in Auftrag geben. Dessen jeweilige Gestalt soll an die besonderen Leistungen des Verstorbenen erinnern: etwa ein als Kakaoschote gestalteter Sarg an einen erfolgreichen Pflanzer oder ein als Thunfisch gestaltetes Modell an einen herausragenden Fischer. Am Tag der Beerdigung wird der Sarg dann inmitten einer großen Trauergemeinde durch den Ort eskortiert. Durch aufwändige Bestattungsriten soll der Verstorbene von der Welt der Lebenden getrennt und in seine neue Welt im Jenseits eingegliedert werden. In dieser, so glaubt man, führt der Tote eine dem irdischen Dasein ähnliche Existenz.

Fußball ist in Ghana – wie auch in vielen anderen, wirtschaftlich schlechter gestellten Regionen der Welt – nicht nur ein Sport. Er öffnet das Tor zu Welten, die sonst oft verschlossen bleiben – zu Berühmtheit, Reichtum und vielleicht auch zu anderen Ländern der Erde.

Die Tradition, figürliche Särge zu gestalten, hat ihren Ursprung in den 1950er Jahren in der Nähe der ghanaischen Hauptstadt Accra. Als Erfinder gilt der mittlerweile verstorbene Sargtischler Kane Kwei. Bei dessen Neffen und Schüler Paa Joe lernte wiederum Dr. Joe, der den hier gezeigten Fußballschuh-Sarg fertigte. Einst beschränkte sich der Kundenkreis für diese ausgefallenen letzten Ruhestätten auf die lokale Bevölkerung, die Ga. Seit den 1970er Jahren sind die Motiv-Särge aber bei wohlhabenden Bewohnern in ganz Ghana in Mode. Und auch der westliche Kunstmarkt zeigt immer mehr Interesse an ihnen.

To the Other World in a Football Boot

Karin Guggeis

Even in Ghana, West Africa, it's something special indeed to be carried to the next world in a coffin made in the form of a football boot. It means you have made something of your life – and specifically as a footballer.

You have to have achieved «great things» in life for those you leave behind to commission such an extravagant coffin. The form given to a coffin is supposed to commemorate the dead person's particular personal achievements: a coffin shaped like a cocoa pod would recall an excellent farmer or a model designed to look like a tuna fish would commemorate an exceptional fisherman. The day of the funeral the coffin is carried through town escorted by a large crowd of mourners. Through elaborate funerary rites, the dead is supposed to be separated from the world of the living and integrated in a new world beyond. In this world, the dead are believed to lead lives similar to their earthly existence.

In Ghana – as in so many of the world's economically disadvantaged regions – football is not just a sport. It opens doors to worlds – fame, wealth and perhaps also to other countries – that might otherwise often remain closed.

The tradition of designing figurative coffins originated near Accra, the capital of Ghana, in the 1950s. The man now generally credited with inventing the figurative coffin was the late Kane Kwei, a coffin maker. Dr. Joe, who made the football boot coffin shown here, learned his trade under Paa Joe, nephew and pupil of Kane Kwei. The clientele for such unusual last resting places used to be limited to the local population, the Ga. Since the 1970s, however, motif coffins have also been fashionable among the affluent throughout Ghana. And the western art market is also revealing a growing interest in them as collectibles.

Sarg in Form eines Fußballschuhs. A coffin in the form of a football boot.
Dr. Joe, Labadi, Ghana, 2005. 195 × 95 cm.

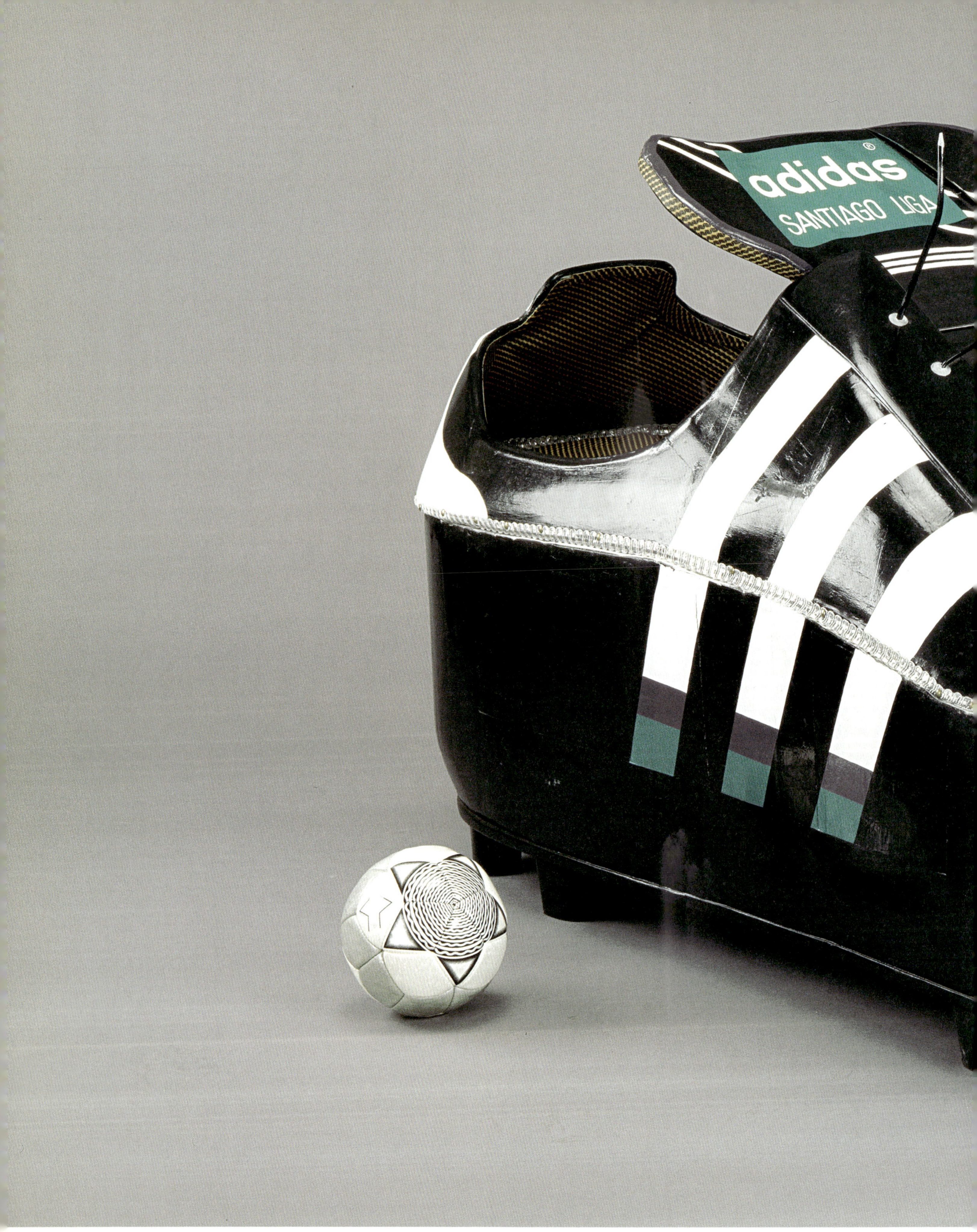
adidas
SANTIAGO LIGA

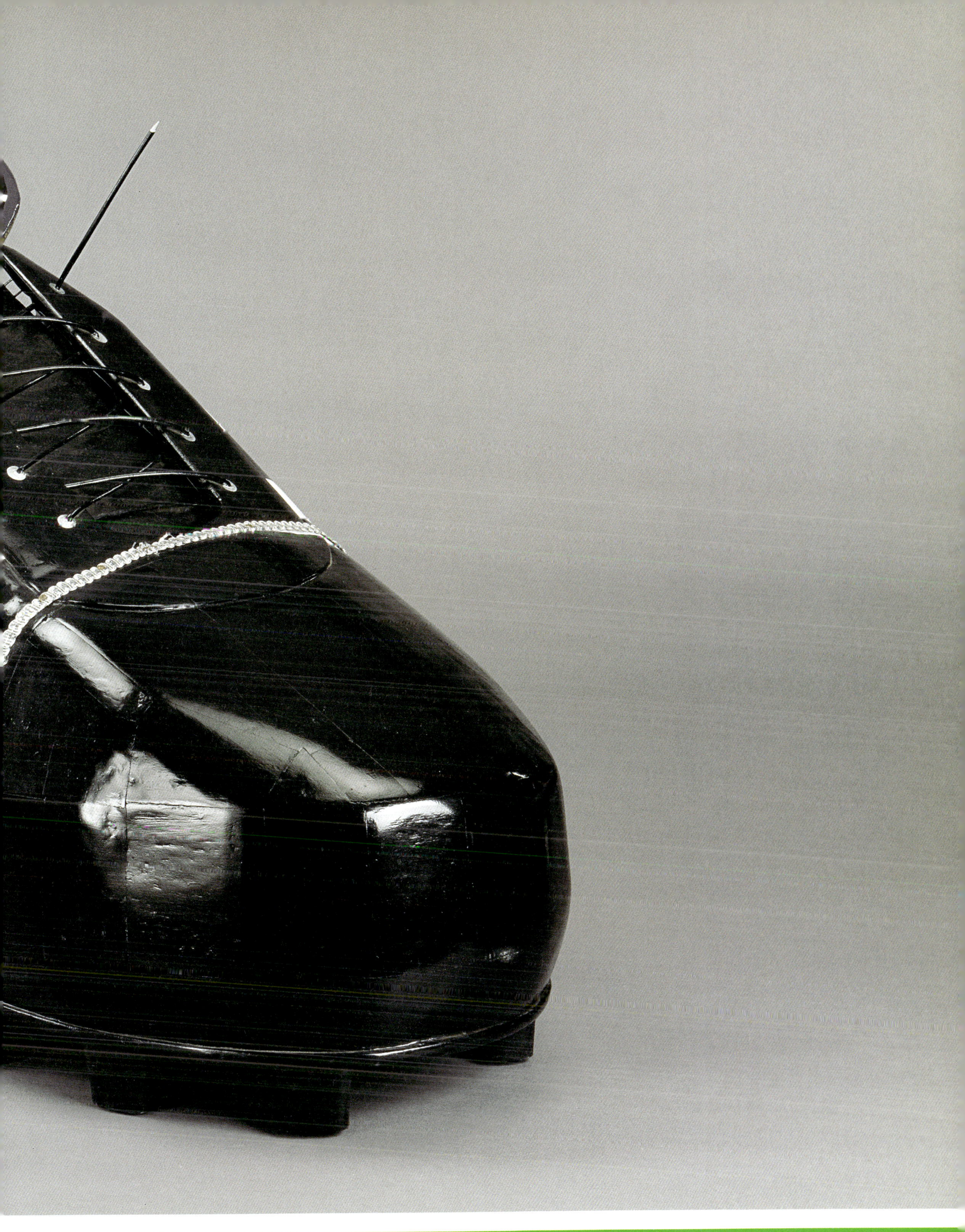

Anthony Baffoe nimmt den Jean-Kahn-Preis der Europäischen Stelle zur Beobachtung von Rassismus und Fremdenfeindlichkeit (EUMC) im Namen des Netzwerks Fußball gegen Rassismus in Europa (FARE) entgegen. Anthony Baffoe accepting the Jean Kahn Prize from the European Monitoring Centre on Racism and Xenophobia (EUMC) in the name of the Football Network Against Racism in Europe (FARE). ©Photo: EUMC, W. Vogelhuber, www.eumc.eu.int

Get Up – Stand Up!
Ein Gespräch mit Anthony Baffoe über Rassismus auf dem Spielfeld

Anthony Baffoe, Ex-Bundesliga-Profi und ehemaliger Nationalspieler Ghanas, war einer der ersten »schwarzen« Spieler in der Bundesliga und der erste afrikanische Sportmoderator im deutschen Fernsehen. In einem Telefon-Interview mit Patricia Müller spricht er über seine Erfahrungen mit und sein Engagement gegen Rassismus im Fußball.

Patricia Müller: Herr Baffoe, in letzter Zeit gab es europaweit wieder verbale Übergriffe nicht nur von Fans, sondern auch von Trainern und Spieler-Kollegen auf »schwarze« Fußballer: Von einem bekannten deutschen Coach stammt der Spruch »Die Neger nehmen uns die Arbeitsplätze weg«. In Italien hagelte es rassistische Schmäh-Rufe aus den Rängen gegen Messina-Verteidiger Marco André Zoro aus der Elfenbeinküste, Thierry Henry wurde vom spanischen Nationaltrainer beleidigt, Patrick Vieira musste sich von einem Gegenspieler als »Negerbastard« beschimpfen lassen und Barcelonas Star Samuel Eto'o hat in Spanien eine Debatte über Rassismus ausgelöst, als er drohte, wegen übler Affenlaut-Schmähungen seitens der ZuschauerInnen den Platz zu verlassen. Dies spiegelt eine traurige Realität wider: Wie kann man verhindern, dass die »faschistischen Gesichter Europas« überhand nehmen? Hat

Get Up – Stand Up!
A Conversation with Anthony Baffoe about Racism on the Pitch

Anthony Baffoe, formerly Bundesliga professional and once a national player for Ghana, was one of the first «black» players in the Bundesliga and the first African sports-caster on German television. In a telephone interview he talks to Patricia Müller about his experiences with racism in football and his commitment to countering it.

Patricia Müller: Mr Baffoe, recently verbal assaults have once again been made on «black players» throughout Europe, not just by fans but also by coaches and fellow players: a well-known German coach came up with «The Niggers are taking our jobs.» In Italy racist insults have been raining down from the blocks on Messina defender Marco André Zoro from the Ivory Coast. Thierry Henry was insulted by the Spanish national coach, Patrick Vieira had to put up with being called a «Nigger bastard» by a player from the opposing team and Barcelona star Samuel Eto'o triggered off a debate on racism in Spain when he threatened to leave the pitch when accosted by spectators with nasty monkey grunts. All this mirrors a sad reality: how can we prevent the «Fascist faces of Europe» from getting the upper hand? Has something changed in the Germany of an Asamoah and an Owomoyela, which seemed to have become, at least symbolically, more diverse?

  Anthony Baffoe: What Zoro, Henry, Vieira, Eto'o and many other players are experiencing today is what I myself used to experience. It really is true: as an African you have to be twice as good. When we played well, we were super, but when we played badly, we were at the bottom of the league. That was when there were monkey noises and bananas were thrown at us. I think that Zoro and Eto'o were right to defend themselves against those insults by threatening to leave the pitch. Not just those concerned, but their fellow players, too, must join forces in making a stand against intolerance in football. I'm actively committed against racism. As the ambassador of the Football Against Racism Network in Europe (FARE), I recently took part in an anti-racism conference in Barcelona. The subject was also raised of how players, coaches and referees can contribute to the fight against discrimination. By the way, fining highly paid professional footballers and coaches who make racist remarks and then letting them back on the pitch isn't much of a punishment. I wonder where the punishment is in that? Here much, much harsher measures have to be taken.

  P. M.: The round leather also took you to France, where the burning *banlieue* in which mainly immigrants live recently made headlines. What is going on with racism in France, a country that is fond of leaning on its multicultural *équipe tricolore* and the *black blanc beurre* philosophy as a sign of its open-mindedness and tolerance? What experiences have you brought back from there?

Afrika bringt zahllose vielversprechende Fußballer hervor – hier ein junges Talent im liberianischen Monrovia. Africa produces a great many promising football players – here is a talented young player in Monrovia, Liberia.
© Photo: Pieter van der Houwen, Amsterdam

sich im Deutschland der Asamoahs und Owomoyelas, das zumindest symbolisch vielfältiger geworden zu sein scheint, etwas verändert?

Anthony Baffoe: Das, was Zoro, Henry, Vieira, Eto'o und viele weitere Spieler heute erleben, habe ich alles früher selbst erfahren. Es ist in der Tat so: Als Afrikaner muss man zweimal so gut sein. Wenn wir gut gespielt haben, waren wir super, doch wenn wir schlecht gespielt haben, waren wir ganz unten. Da gab es Affengeräusche und es wurden Bananen nach uns geworfen. Ich finde es richtig, dass sich Zoro und Eto'o selbst gegen die Beleidigungen zur Wehr setzten, indem sie vom Platz gehen wollten. Doch nicht nur die Betroffenen selbst, auch ihre Mitspieler müssen gemeinsam ein Zeichen gegen Intoleranz im Fußball setzen. Ich engagiere mich selbst aktiv gegen Rassismus. Als Botschafter des Netzwerks Fußball gegen Rassismus in Europa (FARE) habe ich erst kürzlich an einer Anti-Rassismus-Konferenz in Barcelona teilgenommen. Dabei ging es auch um das Thema, wie Spieler, Trainer und Schiedsrichter ihren Beitrag zum Kampf gegen Diskriminierung leisten können. Übrigens: Hochdotierten Profi-Fußballern und Trainern, die rassistische Äußerungen von sich geben, eine Geldstrafe aufzubrummen, um sie dann wieder aufs Feld zu lassen, ist keine große Sanktion. Ich frage mich: Wo ist da die Strafe? Hier müsste man viel, viel härter durchgreifen.

P.M.: Das runde Leder führte Sie auch nach Frankreich, das vor kurzem durch die vorwiegend von MigrantInnen bewohnten, brennenden *Cités* in die Schlagzeilen geriet. Wie verhält es sich mit dem Rassismus in Frankreich, einem Land, das sich gerne auf seine multikulturelle *Equipe tricolore* und die Philosophie *black blanc beurre* als Zeichen seiner Offenheit und Toleranz stützt? Welche Erfahrungen bringen Sie von dort mit?

A.B.: Aus Frankreich bringe ich sehr positive Erfahrungen mit. Von Unruhen war damals nichts zu spüren. Ich bin Anfang der 1990er Jahre nach Frankreich zum FC Metz gewechselt, wurde schon nach drei Monaten zum Kapitän gewählt und habe mit und gegen so große Spieler wie den algerischstämmigen Zidane, den aus dem Senegal stammenden Vieira oder den Basken Lizarazu gespielt. Der Umgang zwischen und mit Spielern verschiedener Herkunft ist dort anders, einfach »normal«. Das hängt natürlich damit zusammen, dass Frankreich viel mehr Kolonien besaß, aus denen zahlreiche Menschen im Laufe der Zeit nach Frankreich emigrierten. Dies spiegelt sich auch in den einzelnen Vereinen wider. Die französische Gesellschaft und der französische Fußball sind somit seit jener Zeit »schwarz-weiß-arabisch« geprägt. Heute hast du in jeder Mannschaft »Schwarze«, die allein dadurch schneller integriert sind, dass sie die Staatsbürgerschaft leichter kriegen. Das Ergebnis sieht man im Nationalteam. Die afrikanischen Spieler werden trotzdem als Franzosen gesehen.

P.M.: Sie selbst sind ja mit dem Thema Rassismus immer sehr offensiv umgegangen. Bereits 1990 haben Sie zusammen mit Ihren Spieler-Kollegen Souleymane Sané und Anthony Yeboah in einen offenen Brief an die Presse auf den Rassismus in deutschen Stadien hingewiesen. Und einmal sagten Sie nach einem rassistischen Übergriff: »Du kannst auf meiner Plantage arbeiten«. Was waren die Auslöser hierfür? Hatten bzw. haben Sie eine wichtige Vorbild-Funktion für Afrikaner in der Bundesliga inne?

A.B.: Im ersten Fall waren diese so genannten »Dschungelgeräusche« der Auslöser und im zweiten Fall war es eine verbale Attacke eines Spielers gegen mich … Ich drehe den Spieß gerne um und agiere stets nach dem Motto, die Rassisten mit ihren eigenen Waffen zu schlagen. Es ist wichtig, den Spielern zu zeigen, dass ich nicht alles mit mir machen lasse.

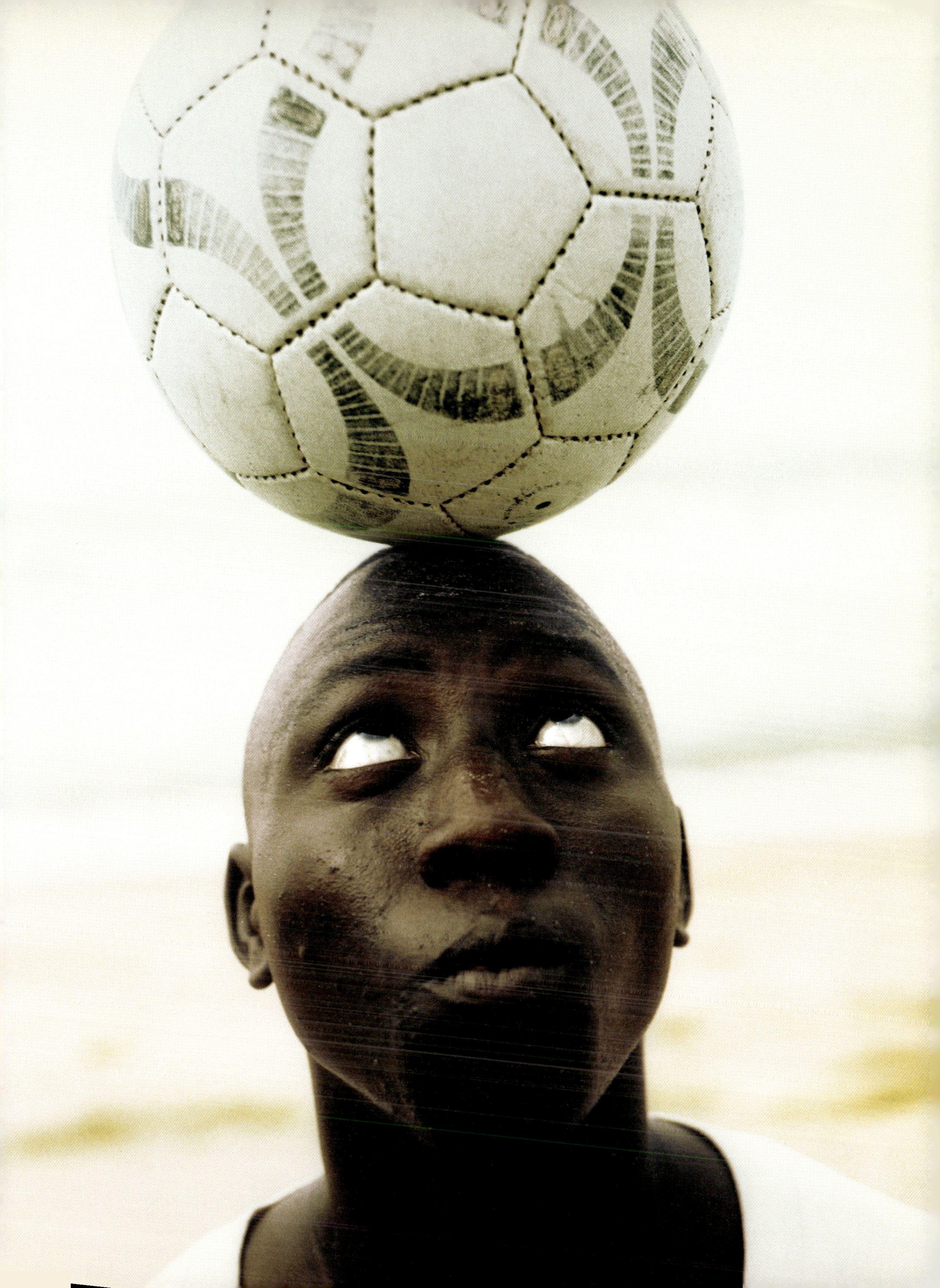

Der Bundesligaprofi Otto Addo engagiert sich für die Antirassismus-Kampagne »Stand up, speak up«. Bundesliga professional Otto Addo is committed to the anti-racism campaign «Stand up, speak up».
© Photo: firo, 2006

Am Anfang, als ich noch sehr jung war, war es mir nicht so bewusst, welche wichtige Vorbild-Funktion ich für meine »schwarzen« Brüder in der Bundesliga innehatte. Doch mit steigender Popularität wurde es mir immer klarer: Ich war der Fußballprofi, der es einfacher hatte. Schließlich hatte ich den Vorteil, sehr gut Deutsch zu sprechen und ein größeres Selbstbewusstsein zu besitzen als so mancher Deutsche. Doch wie ergeht es unbekannten Studenten, Asylbewerbern oder Spielern, die der Sprache noch nicht mächtig sind und sich nicht so gut artikulieren können? Da sich für mich in meiner Position immer alles positiver auswirkt, muss ich sehr genau auf das, was ich sage, achten. Ich möchte Vorbild in dem Sinne sein, dass andere es auch schaffen.

P.M.: Wie sehen Sie Ihre Rolle heute als Sport-Entertainer? Inwieweit können Sie in Ihren Sendungen zu einem offenen interkulturellen Dialog beitragen?

A.B.: Ich habe viele Spieler afrikanischer Herkunft in meine Sportsendungen eingeladen ... nicht, weil sie »schwarz« sind, sondern um zu zeigen, dass sie genauso gut sind wie alle anderen. Und ich möchte vor allem eine Botschaft für junge Leute rüberbringen, sie für das Thema Rassismus sensibilisieren. So habe ich z.B. eine Sendung über Thierry Henrys Kampagne *Stand Up Speak Up* gemacht, eine Initiative gegen Alltagsrassismus im Fußball, die Henry als Reaktion auf diskriminierende Beschimpfungen durch seinen Trainer ins Leben gerufen hat. Es ist sehr wichtig, dass Fußballstars als Idole vieler Millionen Kinder und Jugendlicher ihren Einfluss zur Geltung bringen. Ich mag auch keine Klischees. Viele meinen: «Typisch Afrikaner, barfuß, Fußball...», doch es gibt auch die andere Seite. Warum zeigt man die nicht? Das sind Dinge, wo ich mir mehr Aufklärung wünsche.

A.B.: I brought back very positive experiences from France. There wasn't a sign of unrest when I was there. I transferred to FC Metz in France in the early 1990s, was made captain after only three months and have played alongside and against great players like Zidane, who is of Algerian origin, Vieira, who comes from Senegal, or Lizarazu, a Basque. Players of different origins deal with each other and are dealt with differently there, simply «normally». That, naturally, has something to do with the fact that France had many more colonies, from which a great many people emigrated to France over the years. This is also reflected in the individual clubs. French society and French football have been «black-white-Arab» since then. Nowadays you've got «blacks» in every team, who are more quickly integrated for the simple reason they can be naturalised more quickly. You see the results in the national team. The African players are nevertheless viewed as French.

P.M.: You have always dealt with the subject of racism by going very much on the offensive. Back in 1990 you wrote an open letter together with your fellow players Souleymane Sané and Anthony Yeboah in which you drew attention to the racism in German stadiums. And you once said after a racist attack: «You can work on my plantation.» What triggered that off? Did you have or do you have an important role-model function for Africans in the Bundesliga?

A.B.: In the first instance it was those so-called «jungle noises» that triggered it off and in the second it was a player's verbal attack on me ... I like to turn it against them and always act on the motto you can only beat racists with their own weapons. It's important to show players that I won't let them do whatever they want with me. In the beginning, when I was still very young, I wasn't so aware of what an important role-model function I had for my «black» brothers in the Bundesliga. But as my popularity grew, it became clearer and clearer to me: I was the professional footballer who had it better. After all, I had the advantage of speaking German very well and of being more self-assured than many Germans. But what happens with unknown students, asylum-seekers or players who don't master the language yet and can't express themselves so well? Since everything works out more positively for me all the time in my position, I have to be very careful about what I say. I want to be a role-model in the sense that others can make it too.

P.M.: How do you view your role today as a sport entertainer? To what extent can you contribute to an open intercultural dialogue on your television shows?

A.B.: I have invited many players of African origin to my sports shows ... not because they're «black» but to show that they are just as good as everyone else. And I'd particularly like to get the message across to young people, sensitise them to the subject of racism. So I did a show on Thierry Henry's *Stand Up Speak Up* campaign, for instance, a campaign against everyday racism in football which Henry started as a reaction against discriminating insults from his coach. It's very important for football stars to make their influence felt as the idols of millions of kids and young people. I can't stand clichés, either. So many people think: «Typically African, barefoot, football ...» but there is another side. Why isn't it shown? Those are things where I'd like to see more enlightenment

Paradise Lost?
Brasilien als Arkadien des Fußballs

Stefan Eisenhofer

Der amtierende Fußball-Weltmeister ist seit Jahrzehnten auch Fußballer-Export-Weltmeister. Kein anderes Land der Erde versorgt die Welt derart reichlich mit Fußballern und Fußballerinnen wie Brasilien. Auf allen Kontinenten und in über 70 Ländern kicken brasilianische Spieler als mehr oder weniger gut bezahlte Profis: Von Island über den Senegal bis nach Südafrika, von Australien über Japan, Vietnam und Armenien bis hin zum Libanon sind weit mehr als 5000 Brasilianer außerhalb der eigenen Landesgrenzen in Vereinen verpflichtet. Alex Bellos bemerkt treffend, dass der Begriff »brasilianischer Fußballer« mittlerweile einen ebenso branchen-dominierenden Klang besitzt wie »französischer Chefkoch« oder »tibetanischer Mönch«.

Tatsächlich sind talentierte Kicker nicht nur ein wichtiges »Exportgut«, sie bestimmen als »kulturelle Botschafter« und als »Markenzeichen« neben Karneval und Samba das Fremd- und Selbstbild Brasiliens ganz erheblich. »Fußball-Land« nennt der brasilianische Schriftsteller Zé do Rock denn auch seine Heimat – zwar nicht ohne Ironie, aber durchaus ernst gemeint. Denn nahezu weltweit werden brasilianische Fußballer überhöht als Verkörperungen des »idealen Fußballs« und als leibhaftige Vertreter eines »verlorenen Fußball-Arkadiens«. Und je eintöniger dieser Sport andernorts empfunden wird, desto häufiger verpflichtet man die Abkömmlinge dieses »Fußball-Paradieses«, um das Verlangen nach dem Ideal des »reinen Spiels« mit dem Ball zu befriedigen. Glücklicherweise. Denn die unerfüllten Fußball-Träume in anderen Ländern und Vereinen der Welt machen so manchen Traum in Brasilien selbst erst wahr. Tatsächlich ermöglicht der Fußball dort zahllosen Menschen ein besseres Leben, vermittelt Aufstiegschancen und gesellschaftliche Anerkennung. Heute ist Brasilien das Land mit den meisten Fußballspielern und den größten Stadien der Welt, als Aktiven- und Zuschauersport durchdringt er nahezu alle gesellschaftlichen Bereiche.

Diese gesellschaftliche Vormachtstellung und der internationale Rang des brasilianischen Fußballs sind jedoch zugleich auch ein Lehrstück für die außerordentlich erfolgreiche Aneignung eines an sich fremden Phänomens vor gut einhundert Jahren – auf dem Höhepunkt der kolonialen Expansion Europas: Denn erst in den Jahren 1894 und 1895 kamen die ersten beiden Fußbälle nach Brasilien, und diejenigen, die der »britischen Fußlümmelei« dort frönten, waren zunächst europäische Seeleute.

Die darauf folgende Etablierung des Fußballs in Brasilien war allerdings keineswegs frei von Widerständen. Lange stand der Fußball im Schatten des englischen Kricket. Und mehr noch: Es gab Stimmen, die behaupteten, es mache keinen Sinn, Fußball in Brasilien etablieren zu wollen, da er als »europäischer Sport« für die Tropen nicht geeignet sei. Den Fußballbegeisterten und den Förderern dieses Sports in Brasilien kamen daher die Berichte über indianische Ballspiele, die mehr oder weniger große Ähnlichkeiten mit dem europäi-

Brasilianische Sandstrande wie hier in Salvador da Bahia dienen nahezu weltweit als Symbol für einen kreativen und »unverdorbenen« Fußball. Sandy beaches in Brazil, as here in Salvador da Bahia, symbolise creative, «unspoilt» football almost world-wide. © Photo: Silke Eberspächer, 2003

Paradise Lost?
Brazil as Football Arcadia

Stefan Eisenhofer

The current world champion team has for decades also been world champion at exporting football players. No other country on earth has given the world as many football players, both men and women, as Brazil has. Brazilian players, all of them more or less well paid professionals, are kicking balls in over seventy countries: from Iceland through Senegal to South Africa, from Australia, through Japan, Vietnam and Armenia to Lebanon more than five thousand Brazilians are committed to clubs far beyond the borders of their own country. Alex Bellos has made the apposite observation that the term «Brazilian footballer» has come to mean cornering the market the way «French chef» or «Tibetan monk» does.

Talented kickers are not just an important «export ware». As «cultural ambassadors» and as «trade names» alongside Carnival and the Samba they have considerably enhanced the Brazilian self-image. It is only logical, therefore, that the Brazilian writer Zé do Rock calls

schen Fußball aufwiesen, sehr gelegen – konnte man damit doch beweisen, dass Fußball irgendwie schon immer brasilianisch gewesen sei und auf diese Weise eine alte lokale Fußball-Tradition konstruieren. Einen kuriosen Höhepunkt erreichte diese brasilianische Wurzelsuche im Jahr 1922, als 16 Angehörige der indianischen Pareci-Bevölkerungsgruppe über 2000 Kilometer durch den Regenwald reisen durften (oder mussten), um im größten Stadion von Rio de Janeiro vor einer beachtlichen Zuschauermenge ihr *Zicunati*-Spiel vorzuführen – eine Mischung aus Volleyball und Fußballtennis im weitesten Sinne, bei dem der Ball mit dem Kopf in der Luft gehalten werden musste. In einer breiteren brasilianischen Gesellschaft setzten sich die einheimischen Spiele freilich nicht durch – ganz im Gegensatz zum »britischen Fußball«. Dieser war aber anfangs kein Sport der einfachen Leute, sondern eine Freizeitbeschäftigung für Wohlhabende: ein Amateursport, bei dem englische Sitten gepflegt und die angebliche Überlegenheit eines europäischen Lebensstils demonstriert wurden. Menschen, deren Haut etwas stärker pigmentiert war, ließ man hier nicht zu. Erst nach und nach erreichte der Fußball die Massen der brasilianischen Gesellschaft und wurde bei den armen und einfachen Leuten populär. Von den Vorstädten von Rio de Janeiro und São Paulo aus setzte die »Tropikalisierung« des britischen Oberschichten-Spiels ein. Dort wurde schnell erfasst, dass Fußball ein Sport war, für den man lediglich die Lust am Spiel und weder Geld noch teure Ausstattung benötigte. Man brauchte auch keine unerschwinglichen Sportanlagen oder kostspielige Gerätschaften. Gespielt werden konnte fast überall – auf Wiesen, in Hinterhöfen, auf Straßen, an den Stränden. Und Bälle ließen sich aus billigsten Materialien wie Lumpen oder Fetzen herstellen. Auch genügten Steine, Bäume oder Türen als Tore. So entwickelte sich aus der Nachahmung des europäischen elitären Fußballs eine dynamische und schöpferische Aneignung dieses Spiels, befruchtet vom *Capoeira* der afrikanisch-stämmigen Sklaven und den Tänzen aus den Armenvierteln. Darüber hinaus wurde Fußball zur Arena, in der sich die europäisch-stämmigen Tagelöhner mit den einheimischen Landflüchtigen friedlich treffen, sich annähern und Gemeinsames finden konnten.

Die neu entfachte Liebe und Leidenschaft der Massen zum einstigen Elitesport Fußball wurde freilich keineswegs von allen mit Wohlwollen betrachtet. Dies belegt ein Auszug aus der brasilianischen Zeitschrift *Sports* aus dem Jahr 1915, in dem es heißt: »Die, die wir eine Stellung in der Gesellschaft innehaben, sind gezwungen, mit einem Arbeiter zu spielen, mit einem Chauffeur … Diesen Sport zu betreiben, wird langsam zur Qual, zum Opfer, und hört auf, ein Vergnügen zu sein.«

Vasco da Gama ging wie viele andere brasilianische Fußballvereine aus einem Ruderklub hervor und gilt als erster Club in Brasilien, der Farbige und sozial Benachteiligte als Mitglieder aufnahm. Vasco da Gama, like so many other Brazilian football clubs, grew out of a rowing club and is believed to be the first club in Brazil to have accepted non-whites and socially disadvantaged as members.

his country the «country of football» – with a bit of tongue in cheek, to be sure, but also seriously. Brazilian footballers enjoy virtually world-wide the lofty status of embodying «ideal football» and being incarnations of a «lost football Arcadia». And the more uniformly the sport is viewed elsewhere, the more frequently the children of this «football paradise» are bought in to still the universal longing for the ideal of the «pure game» with the ball. And a good thing, too. After all, the unfulfilled football dreams in other countries and clubs are what make many a dream in Brazil come true. The fact of the matter is football allows innumerable people there to live better lives. Football makes it possible to rise up the social ladder and achieve social status and recognition. Brazil is today the country with the most football players and the biggest stadiums in the world. As both an actively played game and a spectator sport, football pervades almost all areas of society there.

The social supremacy of football in Brazil and its international ranking, however, exemplify the extraordinarily successful naturalisation of a phenomenon that was foreign about a century ago – when European colonial expansion was at its height: not until 1894 and 1895 were the first footballs sent to Brazil and the first people to indulge in this new British sport there were European seamen.

Football did not become established in Brazil without resistance. It was overshadowed for a long time by the English game of cricket. And what is more, voices were heard asserting that there was no sense in trying to establish football in Brazil because it was a «European sport» and as such not suitable for tropical countries. Aficionados of the game and its promot-

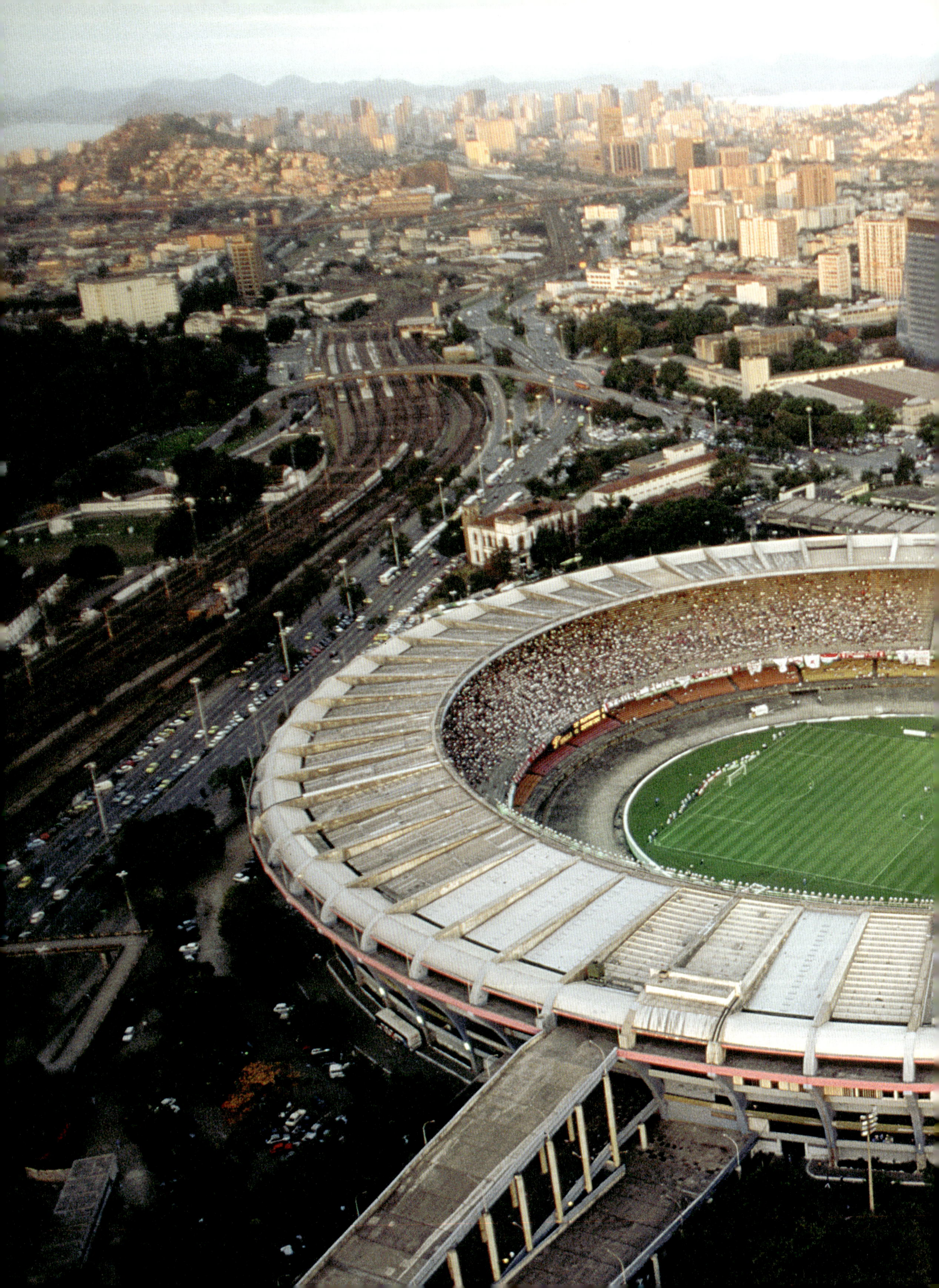

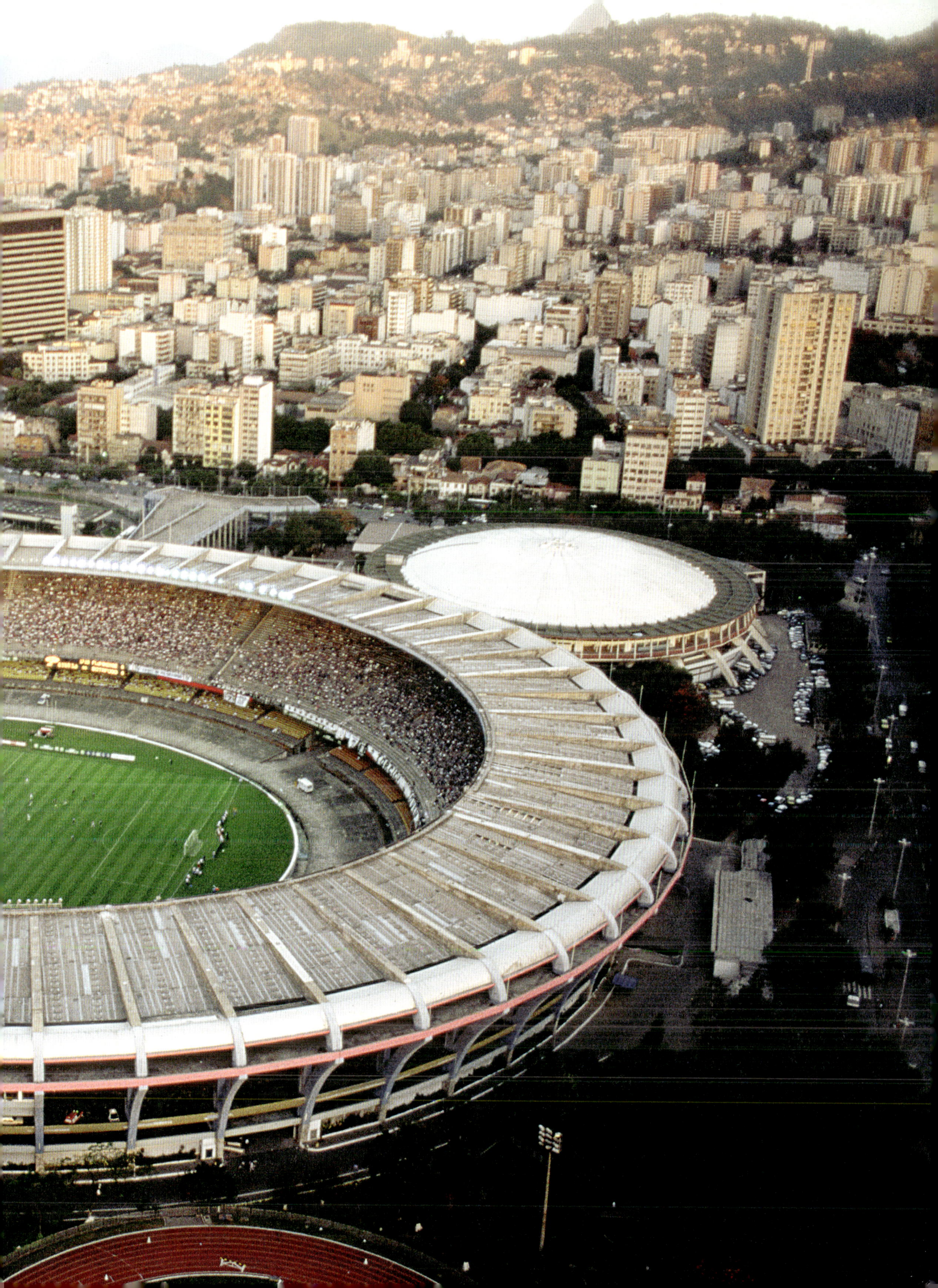

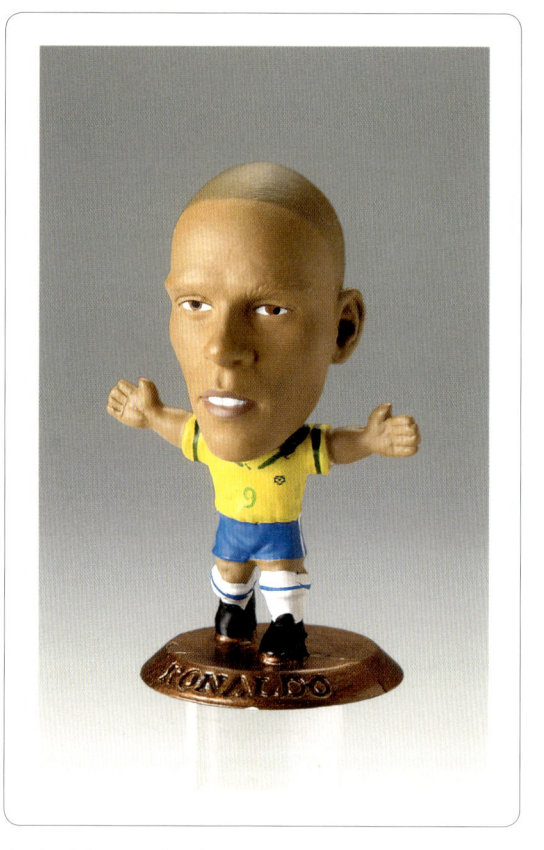

Herausragende brasilianische Export-Fußballer funktionieren sowohl als lokale wie auch als globale Werbe-Ikonen: Taschentücher-Tasche mit Ronaldinho-Portrait und Ronaldo als Corinthian-Figur. Outstanding Brazilian export footballers are both local and global advertising icons: Handkerchief bag with portrait of Ronaldinho and Ronaldo as a Corinthian figurine.

← Trotz des Exports zahlloser überragender Spieler: In Brasilien selbst füllt der Fußball noch immer riesige Arenen wie das Maracanã-Stadion in Rio de Janeiro. Despite the export of so many outstanding players: in Brazil football still packs enormous arenas like Maracanã Stadium in Rio de Janeiro. © Photo: Yann Arthus-Bertrant, Corbis

ers in Brazil were more than pleased to hear reports of Indian games that somewhat resembled European football – this was incontrovertible evidence that football had somehow always been Brazilian so a venerable local football tradition could be constructed. This Brazilian digging for roots reached bizarre heights in 1922, when sixteen members of the Pareci Indian tribe were permitted (or were forced) to travel more than two thousand kilometres through the rain forest to demonstrate their game of *Zicunati* in the biggest stadium in Rio de Janeiro, which was packed with spectators – in the broadest sense a blend of volleyball and football tennis, in which the players had to keep the ball in the air by butting it with their heads. The native games did not cut much of a swathe through Brazilian society at large – unlike «British football». It was initially not a sport for the common man but rather a leisure activity engaged in by the affluent: a sport for amateurs entailing the cultivation of English manners and demonstrating the alleged superiority of the European lifestyle. People whose skin was more strongly pigmented were not admitted to the sport. It took quite some time for football to trickle down to the masses in Brazilian society and become popular with the poor and underprivileged. The «tropicalisation» of what had been an upper-class British game began in the suburbs of Rio de Janeiro and São Paulo. There it soon became apparent that football was a sport for which all that was needed was enjoying the game. No unaffordable sports facilities and expensive gear were needed. It could be played almost anywhere – in meadows, on streets and beaches. And balls could be made of rags or scraps of the cheapest materials. Similarly, stones, trees or doors could be used as goalposts. Thus a dynamic and creative adaptation of this game developed out of an imitation of the elitist European football, fertilised, as it were, by the *Capoeira* played by slaves of African descent and the dances performed in the favelas of the poor. Moreover, football became the arena in which working-class men of European descent could meet peacefully with the indigenous population that had fled to the cities, get closer to them and find they had points in common.

The love, the passion for football, once an elite sport, that had so recently flared up among the masses was certainly not always regarded with a benevolent eye. That this was so is shown by an excerpt from a 1915 issue of the Brazilian magazine *Sports:* «Those of us who occupy a position in society are forced to play with a working man, a chauffeur ... Engaging in this sport has gradually become torture, a sacrifice, and is ceasing to be pleasurable.»

Fußball in politischen Karikaturen Ostafrikas

Jigal Beez

Fußball ist Volkssport Nummer eins, auch in Ostafrika. Insofern ist es kein Wunder, dass sich Comics dieses Themas annehmen. Swahili-Comics gibt es seit über 60 Jahren. Und schon in Reklamecomics aus den 1950er Jahren sind es Kicker-Cartoons, die Schmerztabletten oder Zigaretten anpreisen – neuerdings auch den Gebrauch von Kondomen. Auch gibt es unzählige Fußballwitze, die als Comicstrips erzählt werden, oder Abenteuercomics, in denen etwa tansanische Fußballer für Real Madrid spielen. Besonders gerne greifen ostafrikanische Karikaturisten auf Bilder aus dem populären Spiel zurück, um politische Vorgänge aufs Korn zu nehmen.

Im Jahr 1998 zum Beispiel interpretierte der tansanische Karikaturist Ali Masoud Kipanya das Verhältnis zwischen der Regierungspartei CCM (Chama cha Mapinduzi, der Partei der Revolution) zu den Oppositionsparteien folgendermaßen: Jede Partei wird von einer Fußballmannschaft repräsentiert, die gerade ins Stadion einläuft, angeführt von den Spielführern, den Parteivorsitzenden. Es fällt auf, dass die Mannschaften der Opposition relativ »schmächtig« aussehen und das Spielfeld barfuß betreten. Der Spielführer der Regierungspartei hingegen, der damalige tansanische Präsident Benjamin Mkapa, ist ein gut genährter »Hüne«. Nicht nur, dass er mit Fußballschuhen aufläuft, es wird auch mit seinem Ball gespielt. Zudem hat er die Schiedsrichterpfeife im Mund und hält die Fahnen der Linienrichter in der Hand. Es ist ganz offensichtlich, wer hier das Spiel gewinnen wird: Die Regierungspartei ist materiell besser ausgerüstet als die Opposition und bestimmt als Schiedsrichter auch noch die Spielregeln. Die tansanische Politik wird hier als abgekartetes Spiel dargestellt, dessen Ergebnis schon vor dem Anpfiff fest steht.

Vielsagend ist eine Maus in Schiedsrichterkleidung am rechten Bildrand, die die Szene ärgerlich betrachtet. Hier setzt sich der Karikaturist Masoud *Kipanya* selbst ins Bild. Als »Mäuschen« – so die Übersetzung seines Spitznamens Kipanya – taucht er in seinen Zeichnungen häufig auf und kommentiert das Geschehen. In diesem Fall mit dem missmutigen Blick eines neutralen Schiedsrichters, dem das unfaire Schauspiel bitter aufstößt.

Eine derartige Bildsprache voller beißender Ironie wird von den tansanischen Lesern sehr geschätzt – weniger jedoch von den Politikern, und bis in die frühen 1990er Jahre hinein waren prominente Politiker in Ostafrika für die Karikaturisten auch noch tabu.

Fußball dient aber nicht nur zur Analyse des politischen Tagesgeschehens, auch auf andere sozio-politische Kontexte wird von ostafrikanischen Comic-Künstlern mit Hilfe von Fußballmetaphern hingewiesen. In der kenianischen Tageszeitung *Daily Nation* etwa kommentiert der bekannte Cartoonist Gado die Probleme der HIV-Forschung wie folgt (Abb. S. 54): Die »Menschheit« *(mankind)* wird von einem Fußballspieler repräsentiert, der verzweifelt einem Ball hinterher rennt, auf dem der Begriff »Forschung« *(research)* steht. Der Fußballer ist gerade dabei, ein entscheidendes Tor im Kampf gegen die Pandemie zu erzielen. Doch

Tansanische Politik als Fußballspiel. Tanzanian politics as a football game. Cartoon von / by Ali Masoud Kipanya, 1998. Aus / From Friedrich-Ebert-Stiftung 2001: 116

Football in East African Political Caricature

Jigal Beez

Football is the number one popular sport and it is in East Africa, too. No wonder then that comics have taken up the theme. There have been comics in Swahili for over sixty years. And in 1950s advertising comics, kicker cartoons praise the efficacy of painkillers or the taste of cigarettes – recently they also advocate the use of condoms. And football jokes are legion, which are told in the form of strip cartoons or adventure comics, for instance, about a Tanzanian player signed on to Real Madrid. East African cartoonists often revert to images from the popular game to make fun of what is going on in the political arena.

Just to take one example, in 1998 the Tanzanian cartoonist Ali Masoud Kipanya interpreted relations between the governing CCM party (Chama cha Mapinduzi, the Party of Revolution) and the opposition parties as follows. Each party is represented by a football team shown running into the stadium, led by their captains, who are the heads of the parties. The opposition teams are noticeably quite «scrawny» by comparison and are depicted walking

leider spielt »Aids« – dargestellt als Skelett mit Fußballstiefeln und schwarzer Robe – sein eigenes, heimtückisches Spiel. »Aids« ergreift die Pfosten des Tores und trägt es – höhnisch lachend – an einen anderen Ort. Der Künstler Gado führt seinem Publikum damit die Tödlichkeit und Hinterhältigkeit von HIV/Aids vor Augen: Die Krankheit hält sich an keine Regeln. Sobald die Menschheit nach langen und aufwändigen Forschungen glaubt, einen Weg zur Kontrolle der Seuche gefunden zu haben, verändert sich das Virus und macht alle Hoffnungen zunichte. Gado erweist sich hier als ein Meister seiner Kunst. Mit nur wenigen Pinselstrichen und durch die Übertragung auf das populäre Sujet »Fußball« gelingt es ihm, ein an sich komplexes Thema eingängig und leicht verständlich zu machen.

Fußball als Metapher für den Kampf gegen AIDS. Football as a metaphor for the fight against AIDS. Cartoon von / by Gado, 1998. Aus / From »The Daily Nation«, 2.12.1998

barefoot on to the pitch. The captain of the governing party, on the other hand, Benjamin Mkapa, who was then president of Tanzania, is shown as a well-fed «hunk». Not only is he running in shod in football boots but it is his ball that is being used for the game. Moreover, the referee's whistle is sticking in his mouth and he is holding the linesmen's flags in his hand. It's only too obvious who is going to win the game: the governing party is, from the material standpoint, better kitted out than the opposition and, *qua* referee, also makes the rules. Tanzanian politics is represented here as a playing with loaded dice, the outcome determined before the whistle blows.

On the right-hand margin, a mouse dressed as a referee and watching the scene with annoyance says a lot about what is going on. Cartoonist Masoud Kipanya has put himself into the picture. He often surfaces in his drawings as a «mouse» – thus the translation of *Kipanya,* his nickname and *nom d'artiste* – to comment on what is happening. In the present instance, with the despondent air of a neutral referee who finds the taste of the unfair spectacle before his eyes bitter indeed.

A pictorial idiom so full of biting sarcasm is highly appreciated by Tanzanian readers – less so by politicians. Until the early 1990s high-ranking politicians were still a taboo for cartoonists in East Africa.

Football, however, is not only used to analyse everyday politics. East African comics artists also allude to other social and political contexts via metaphors drawn from football. In the Kenyan daily the *Daily Nation,* for instance, the acclaimed cartoonist Gado has commented as follows on the problems bedevilling HIV research. «Mankind» is represented by a football player who is running desperately after a ball with the word «research» written on it. The football player is about to make a crucial goal in the battle against the pandemic. Unfortunately, however, «AIDS» – represented as a skeleton wearing football boots and a black robe – is playing an insidious game of his own. «Aids» grabs the goal posts and – sporting a malicious grin – moves them to a different place. Thus Gado as an artist confronts his public in visual terms with the deadly insidiousness of HIV/AIDS: this is a disease that does not abide by any rules. No sooner does mankind begin to believe, after time-consuming, costly and labour-intensive research, that a way of bringing the disease under control has been found than the virus mutates and destroys all hopes that have been raised. Gado thus proves his consummate mastery of his art. With just a few strokes of his brush and by transferring his imagery to «football» as a universally popular theme, he succeeds in making complex subject matter accessible and easy to grasp.

Ist der Deutsche doch ein Brasilianer?
Identität und nationale Spielstile im Fußball

Stefan Eisenhofer

Für manche Briten gibt es auf der Welt nur zwei wirklich unterschiedliche Arten, Fußball zu spielen. Die eine ist die alte britische Schule des *kick and rush* mit den Hauptelementen: »Auf dem Spielfeld rauf und runter rennen, den Ball in die gegnerische Hälfte schlagen, den schnellen Schuss aufs Tor riskieren«. Die andere ist der »kontinentale Stil«, der alle übrigen Spielweisen umfasst. Losgelöst von Längen- und Breitengraden wird so beispielsweise auch den Brasilianern nachgesagt, sie würden einen »kontinentalen Fußball« pflegen.

Solche Zuschreibungen haben selbstredend nur sehr wenig mit Fußball-Wirklichkeiten, mit den realen Stärken und Schwächen von Mannschaften zu tun. Es geht vor allem um das »Wir« und »die Anderen«, um Selbst- und Fremdbilder.

Zwar ist unbestritten, dass Spielbedingungen und fußballerische Sozialisation den Stil, die Fähigkeiten und die Vorlieben eines Fußballspielers und auch ganzer Teams beeinflussen und prägen. Es ist ja durchaus ein Unterschied, ob man barfuß, ohne Trikots und mit einem Lumpenball das Kicken gelernt hat – auf einem kleinen Spielfeld, drei gegen drei und ohne Torwart –, oder als Fünfjähriger in einem Fußballverein, mit Fußballschuhen, auf einem regulären Spielfeld und unter Trainer-Anleitung. Bei den Eigenschaften, die den einzelnen Nationalmannschaften zugeschrieben werden, stehen aber nicht wirklich deren Spielweisen zur Debatte. Es geht dabei um nichts weniger als um die fundamentalen Werte der jeweiligen Gesellschaften, die – gerade bei Spielen der Nationalmannschaft – zugespitzt und konstruiert, verfestigt und weitergetragen werden. Vor allem in den Medien und in Berichten über Fußballspiele werden die Mannschaften zu Repräsentanten, ja zu Symbolen bestimmter Werte, Lebensstile, Tugenden und Untugenden.

Wenn also die französische Mannschaft gut spielt und gewinnt, wird der Begriff vom »Champagnerfußball« bemüht. Wenn sie aber verliert, wird dies sowohl in Frankreich wie auch anderswo als Beweis dafür genommen, dass Franzosen bekanntlich gerne in entscheidenden Momenten versagen und zu wenig Vertrauen in die eigenen Fähigkeiten besitzen. Der Spielstil der Mannschaft wird so zum Ausdruck der französischen Kultur und Gesellschaft und dient – von innen wie auch von außen gesehen – als Bestätigung einer imaginierten Identität.

Dabei sind solche Zuschreibungen keineswegs unwandelbar. Durch die Erfolge im Laufe der WM 1998 zum Beispiel wurden in Frankreich nationale Sport-Stereotypen neu erfunden. Es wurde ein neues Bild von *frenchness* konstruiert – sowohl fähig, mit Kreativität und Eleganz Siege einzubringen, als auch in der Lage, heroisch und würdevoll Niederlagen

Might the German be a Brazilian after all?
Identity and National Styles of Playing Football

Stefan Eisenhofer

To some British people there are only two really different ways of playing football. One is represented by the old British «kick and rush» school, whose main features are: «Keep running up and down the field, slam the ball over the half-way line and risk a quick rush to the goal.» The other is the «Continental style», which means all the other ways of playing can be subsumed in it. Disregarding longitude and latitude, the Brazilians are also said to play «Continental football».

It goes without saying that such stylistic attributions have very little to do with the realities of football, with a team's real strengths and weaknesses. What matters most is «us» and «them», self-image and how others are viewed.

It may be undisputed that playing conditions and the primary socialisation of players affect, indeed shape, the skills and preferences of a particular player and even of an entire team. There is certainly a difference between barefoot boys without jerseys learning to kick around a battered ball – on a tiny pitch, three on three and without a goalkeeper – or, on the other hand, boys joining a club as five-year-olds, kitted out with football boots, playing on a regular pitch under a trainer's supervision. Whatever qualities may be ascribed to individual national teams, however, the way they play is not really what we are talking here. Instead, what is at stake are the fundamental values upheld by each society concerned, values which – particularly when national teams are playing – are exaggerated and construed, consolidated and disseminated. In the media especially and in reports on games, teams become representatives, indeed symbols of particular values, lifestyles, virtues and vices.

So when the French national team, to take one example, is in superb form and winning, the term «champagne football» is bandied about. When they have a losing streak, however, this is taken in France and elsewhere as proof that Frenchmen are known for not being up to scratch just when it counts and for having too little confidence in their own abilities. The team playing style thus becomes an expression of French culture and society, going to confirm – viewed from within as well as without – an imagined national identity.

Of course such attributions of national character are not immutable. National sport stereotypes had to be reinvented in France during the 1998 World Cup. A new image of «Frenchness» was constructed – implying both capable of winning elegantly, through deployment of hidden reserves of creativity, and able to accept defeat heroically and with unimpeachable dignity. The media abounded in parallels with French military history. As attributions of qualities are in fact continually oscillating back and forth in football – from the pitch to

hinzunehmen. Parallelen zur französischen Militärgeschichte wurden dabei gerade in den Medien gerne bemüht. Wie überhaupt beim Fußball ein ständiges Hin und Her von Zuschreibungen stattfindet – vom Spielfeld auf andere Bereiche der Gesellschaft und umgekehrt. So wird etwa für Brasilien gerne betont, dass gängige Verhaltensmuster auf den Straßen Brasiliens, wo man durch Eleganz und Vortäuschung Angelegenheiten erledige, auf das Spielfeld übertragen werden. Daraus sei der »Fußball aus der Hüfte« entstanden, bei dem der Gegner nicht direkt angegriffen wird, sondern seitwärts und indirekt. Dass man damit weder der brasilianischen Gesellschaft noch dem Spiel der brasilianischen Nationalteams so ganz gerecht wird, ist offensichtlich. Entsprechendes gilt für Italien, für dessen Spielweise es zwischen 1930 und 1980 gerne heißt, es hätte sich um eine Demonstration des *Italian way of life* gehandelt – ohne viel Methode und Organisation zwar, aber geprägt von kreativer Genialität und Vielfältigkeit.

Und auch wenn in Massenmedien und an Stammtischen kolportiert wird, schottischer Fußball sei »Englische Härte plus x«, »Eine deutsche Mannschaft gibt nie auf« oder »Afrikanische Mannschaften zelebrierten das Credo der totalen Offensive«, wird deutlich, dass Mannschaften selten so spielen, wie ihre entsprechenden Gesellschaften tatsächlich sind, sondern eher so, wie diese gerne sein wollen – oder aber sich fürchten zu sein. Dass diese nationalen Spielweisen dann als tatsächlich existierend wahrgenommen werden, hängt von mehreren Faktoren ab: Zum einen steuern die genannten Stereotypen die Wahrnehmung, so dass Unpassendes ausgeblendet wird. Zudem wirken sie als sich selbst erfüllende Prophezeiungen. Und drittens erfolgt auch eine Anpassung der Mannschaften an diese Stereotypen.

Nationale Fußballmannschaften tragen so in vielen Ländern der Welt nicht unerheblich zur Konstruktion nationaler Identitäten bei und sorgen dafür, dass Fußball mittlerweile ein wichtiger Bestandteil dessen ist, was es heißt, in einer modernen globalisierten Welt Deutscher, Kroate, Brasilianer oder Nigerianer zu sein.

Gottfried Müller: »Kick-and-Rush«, 2006, Papier, Tusche, Aquarell / paper, India ink, watercolour.

Gottfried Müller: »Samba-Fußball vs. Tango-Fußball«, 2006, Papier, Tusche, Aquarell / paper, India ink, watercolour.

Gottfried Müller: »Rumpelfüßler«, 2006, Papier, Tusche, Aquarell / paper, India ink, watercolour.

Gottfried Müller: »Shaolin Soccer«, 2006, Papier, Tusche, Aquarell / paper, India ink, watercolour.

other areas of society and *vice versa*. It is often emphasised about Brazil, for instance, that common behaviour patterns learnt in the street, where affairs are handled with deftness and deception, are transferred to the pitch. This is said to explain the Brazilian «football from the hip» which does not directly attack an adversary but goes about it deviously and indirectly. It should be obvious that this does justice neither to Brazilian society nor the Brazilian national team. The same holds for Italy, of whose playing style it was often said between 1930 and 1980 that it was a demonstration of the «Italian way of life» – perhaps rather short on method and organisation but nonetheless long on creative genius and versatility.

And even though the buzzword in the mass media and on pub nights may be that Scottish football is «English toughness and then some», that «a German team never gives up» or «African teams celebrate the creed of the all-out offensive», it becomes clear that teams rarely play the way the societies that produce them really are but rather the way these societies want to be – or are afraid of being. That these national ways of playing are actually perceived as existing depends on several factors: first of all, the stereotypes touched on above steer perception so that anything that doesn't match them is filtered out. Moreover, they turn out to be self-fulfilling prophesies. And third, teams do end up conforming to these stereotypes.

National football teams thus contribute to creating constructs of national identity in many parts of the world and, in so doing, ensure that football has become an important constituent of what it means to be a German, Croatian, Brazilian or Nigerian in the modern globalised world.

Langeweile, Kurzeweile

Zé do Rock

Hallo Leute, normal schreib ich fast nur noch auf wunschdeutsch, aber zur abwechslung werd ich jeden satz in einer anderen sprachvariazion schreiben, die ich kreiert hab. Und zwar Siegfriedisch (dem rrreingermanischen Deutsch), ultradoitsh-S (seriös, mit der ferainfachten rechtschreibung), ultradoitsh-U (unseriös, mit de ferainfachte gramatik), wunschdeutsch (wie die meisten deutschen schreiben würden, wenn sie wüssten, das sie das dürfen) und schließlich kauderdeutsch (super multiculti). Natürlich alles im progressiven modus, das heißt, schwerdeutsch beginnend und dann immer weiter weg davon.

Als ich durch Afrika trampte, kam ich immer wieder an fußballfeldern vorbei und sah, wie gut und schön man fußball spielen kann. Oft haben mich die Leute gefragt, wo ich herkomme, und als ich ihnen sagte, ich komm aus Brasilien, waren sie begeistert und baten mich, mitzuspielen und ihnen ein Bisschen Fußball beizubringen. Ich sagte dann, ich hab gerade ein problem mit meinem rycken und kann mich kaum bewegen. Die hätten mich ausgelacht, wenn sie mich beim fußballspielen gesehen hätten. Nicht, dass ich ein saumäßig schlechter spieler wäre, aber ich bin eher durchschnittlich. Momentan spiel ich überhaupt nicht, weil ich nach einem kreuzbandriss operiert wurde und immer noch probleme hab, entweder weil ich zu wenig Knieübungen mache oder weil der Heilmann beim Eingriff pfuschte. Aber ich leg mich momentan wieder ins zeug und hoff, dass ich im näxten sommer mit meinen freunden wieder spielen kann. Wenigstens noch ein paar jährchen, bis ich definitiv ein greis geworden bin und das aufstehen von der baduwanne als größte sportliche leistung des tages betrachten muss.

Ich frag mich manchmal, wieso fussball in der ganzen welt zur beliebtesten sportart geworden is – ausser naturlich in den USA, aber bei denen muss sowieso alles immer anders sein – frauenfussball is dort populär, schon wider alles anders. Ich nehm mal an, dass er mehr dem Leben entspricht, weil in ihm das unwahrscheinliche so möglich, so präsent is. In den meisten sportarten gibt es viele tore oder punkte, und da wird es unwahrscheinlicher, dass schwächere Mannschaften oder schwächere Spieler gewinnen. Im baskettball oder im volleyball kann man nich als schwächeres team versuchen, auf 0:0 zu spielen und dann in lezte sekunde ein ding bei den andren rein zu plazieren. Sein glück beim elfmeterschiessen zu versuchen, wird wahrscheinlich auch nicht klappen. Ausserdem ist Fussball eine Mannschaftsleibesertüchtigung, hat dann auch ein psychosoziales element, hat drama, theater, intrige. Keine Frage, das haben manche andere sportarten auch, aber dann haben sie viele tore, viele punkte, und der schwächere ha kaum eine chanse ...

Ich sehe äusserst selten Fussball im Fernsehen, weil die Deutsche Bundesliga stinklangweilig is. Normaleweise gewinne die Bayern, und manchmal schafft es eine andere mannschaft, mit einem halbe punkt vorsprung vor den Bayern antukomme. Das bereitet kein Vergnügen. Einmal hab ich einen marketing-manager der Bayern darauf angesprochen, und

fischerartwork: »Auf dem Weg ins Netz« («On the Way into the Net»), 2005, Buchenholz, bemalt / beech, painted.

Contra Monotonie

Zé do Rock

Hi fokes, usualy i rite in an english spelling sistem calld «house stile», eesy to reed, but for a change i'l rite in all english spelling variations i hav: House Stile, RITE (Redusing Iregularitys in Tradissional English), diacritical english, fonetic english (i dont hav a proper naim for them) and IPI (Internasionale Pijin Inglish, pronunset «ippy»). But i'l start from traditional spelling, so u can get used to them graddualy ...

When i hitchhiked thru Africa, i saw people playing football and was amazed to see how beautiful this sport can be. Of course i'm talking about the sport americans call «soccer», the japanese «sakka» and the rest of the world football – i dont know much about american football. Often the players asked me where i come from, and when i told them that i come from Brazil, they were very excited, they asked me to play with them and give them some lessons. Normally i told them i was having a funny problem with my back and was hardly able to move. They would have laughed at me if they saw me playing. Not that i'm such a bad player, but i'm rather average. At the moment i'm not playing at all, i had surgery on my knee after i tore a cruciate ligament and still have problems with it, either becauze i dont train enough or becauze the doctor botched it. But i'm making an extra effort at the moment and hope i can play with my friends again next summer. At least for a few years to come, until i'm definitely too old for it and getting out of the bathtub has to be seen as my greatest athletic performance of the day.

er saget, dafür, dat die andere teams schwächer sind, können die Bayern doch nichts. Natyrlich hat er recht, langweilig is es aber trozdem.

Der brasilianische fussball würde mich eher interesieren, no, weil ich ihn so toll finde, sondern weil alles offener is. Es gib ungefähr 15 klubs, bei denen man sich kein bisschen wundern würde, wenn dei meister werde. Und manchmal gewinnt doch noch ein Anderer, von dem ma nie was gehört hat. Leider wird sehr wenig yber de sydamericanische fussball in den europäische medie berichtet. Viele europäer glauben, die sudamerikaner mögen gute national teams aufstelle, aber vereinsmäßig können sie mit dem europäischen Fussball nicht mithalten: wir ham doch ihre besten spieler aufgekauft. Das kann schon sein, aber diese besten brasilianischen spieler müssen in einem tim spielen, ki not aus brasilis bestee, während in der brasilianischen Mannschaft (meistens) 11 brasilis spiele. Fakt is, dat osso so ein milionäre club wie Real Madrid den suxessu no kaufe konet. Man kann mit Geld die Erfolgswahrscheinlichkeit erhöhen, aber kaufen kann man ihn nich, genauso weni wie de liebu. Das is ja das schöne am fussball. Und wen ma die resultus der Wold Cup der Clubs observ (in der der weissenerdteilische Meister auf den südneuweltlichen trifft), siet man auch, das de sydamerikis ofter gewinnet denn de europis.

Joe Big-Big: »Dribblings«, 2004, Draht / wire.

Sometimes i ask myself why football has become the most popular sport of the world – except of course in the USA, but in that country everything has to be different. They like womens football there, though – they always have to be different. I suppose football is so popular becauze it is more like life itself, it is so unpredictable! In most sports you have many goals, scores, points, so it is less likely that a weaker team or a weaker player defeats a stronger one. In basketball or in volleyball you cant try tu play 0:0 and then score in the last second, or try to win the mach in the penaltys. Besides, futball is a team sport, so you also have the psycho-social element, you have drama, theater, intrigue. Sure, not only football is a team sport, but then again the uther sports usually have many goals, scores, and the weaker player/team hardly stands a chanse …

I rarely wach futball on TV, because the German Championship is terribly boring. Usually Bayern wins, and sometimes anuther team manages to become a champion with half a point lead over Bayern. That is no fun. Once i spoke with a Bayern secretar about it, and he said that it's not their falt that the uther teams are so much weaker. Of corse he was right, but it is boring all the same.

I think the brazilian championship would interest me more. No becauze i consider brazilian futball that great, it is just that it is mor open somehow. Anything can happen. There are around 15 clubs that can win, and nobody wuud be surprized. And sometempos still un othre club win, a club we had nevver heard about. Unfortunately there isnt much tauk about south american football in the european media. Many europeans believe that the south americans can hav güd national teams, but in terms of clubs they cant keep up with us europeans: we have bought their best players! That can be true, but in the european football clubs u see one brazilian number 1 playing tugether with 10 europeans number 10, while in Brazil 11 brazilians number 2 play together, if u allow me this litle exaggeration. Telepathy does no work when brazilians play with foreigners. The fact is that not even a millionaire club like Real Madrid was able to by success – it is the same with love, u cant by it. That is the nise thing about fuutball. And when we look at the rezultus of the Wold Cup of Clubs (in which the european champion meets the south american champion), we see that the south americans win more often than the europeans.

What remains is the enthuzlasm for the World Cup, with all its dramas and its fatalitys. It takes plass solo every 4 years and nobody can be sure his country wil partisipate next time and he'l be invitet again tu the nasional team, so every movement can decide if u'l be a hero or a villain in your country – for the rest of your life. A singel second or a singel sentimeter can mean the fruntier between paradise and hel.

If Brazil wins, i wil be hapy, of corse. But i wood prefur if a «weak team» like Costa Rica or Angola wins. This monopolization of the brazilians is geting boring, like the monopolization of Bayern in the German Championship or Schumachers monopolization in the formula 1 sircus (til a mini while agou, at least …). And it is a fact that many people think like that tu. In the 80s Brazil had a wunderful team, that never manajed to win the titel. And the tot wold was pro Brazil. Now u see a lot of people who seem to be fed up with Brazil winning. Worse than that, brazilians ar geting arogant, and thats not wat we wanted, no?

By the way, the player hoo shot the greatest number of goals in history was the brazilian Arthur Friedenreich. He played til 1935 and was the sun of a german-brazilian man with

Sind brasilianische Fußballmannschaften per se unbesiegbar? Are Brazilian football teams per se unbeatable?
Anonymus, Brasilien: Keramik / Anonymous, Brazil: pottery, 2005.

→ Wann kommt der Fußball-Weltmeister endlich aus Afrika? Colon-Figur von Roger Milla – der Ikone des afrikanischen Fußballs. When will the football world champions come from Africa? A colon figurine of Roger Milla – the icon of African football. Bemaltes Holz, / Wood, painted, 2005.

Bleibt die begeisterung für die WM, mit al its dramen und its fatalität. Dadurch, das si nur einmal alle fir iare stattfindet und keiner sich sicher sein kann, das sein tim es de nexte mal schaffen und er dabei sein werd, kann eine einzige bewegung darüber entscheiden, if man in his land ein hero or ein bädy sein verd – für die übriggebliebene Zeit seines Lebens. Eine einzige sekunde oder ein zentimeter kann di grenze zwischen paradis und hölle bedoiten.

Wenn Brasil gewinnt, froi ich mich naturlich. Aber mir wär's liber, if ein otre tim win. Diese Monopolisierung der Brasilianer geht mir auf den Wecker, genauso wi di Monopolisierung der Bayern in der Bundesliga oder fon Schumacher in der Formel 1 (bis vor kurzem, zumindest..). Un es is ein fakt, das es vilen menschen in der welt auch so get. In den 80er anos had Brazil ein wunderfole tim, das es nie geschafft hat, meister zu werden, un de ganze welt war fyr Brasil. Heutzutage sit ma schon vile leute, ki die sigus der brasilis sat ha. Ausserdem werden die Fussballländler allmählich überheblich, und das is doch nich der sinn der sache.

Ybrigens, der spiler, ki la moste goules da historie shot ha, war der Fussballländler Arthur Friedenreich. Er spielte bis 1935 und war der sohn aines deutschbrasilianas mit aina afrobrasilianerin, a heller mulatte mit grünen augen und krausen haren. Der verein, in dem er spielen wollte, nahm keine nichtweissen Spieler auf, und so musste er sich täglich in mühsama arbait das har mit gel glätten, um als waisser durchzukommen.

Bei der nächsten WM haben die deutschen den heimvorteil, die spielen nicht shlecht und haben eha rar shlecht gespielt, sonst wären sie nicht Rang 2 in der ewigen WW-Liste – unta 190 ländan is das doch nicht übel. Und die shießen soviele tore, wie sie nur shießen können. Aba »german-bashing« is nicht nur in England or in den Niederlanden popular, sondern vor allem in Deutschland. Spilen di deutshen 8:0 gegen ain asiatishes team, sagt man »naja, gegen so a team cann doh jeder gewinnen«. Spielen sie 1:0 gegen eine starke Mannschaft wie Nudelland, sagt man »naja, 1:0 is nicht grade berauschend, aussadem spilten die

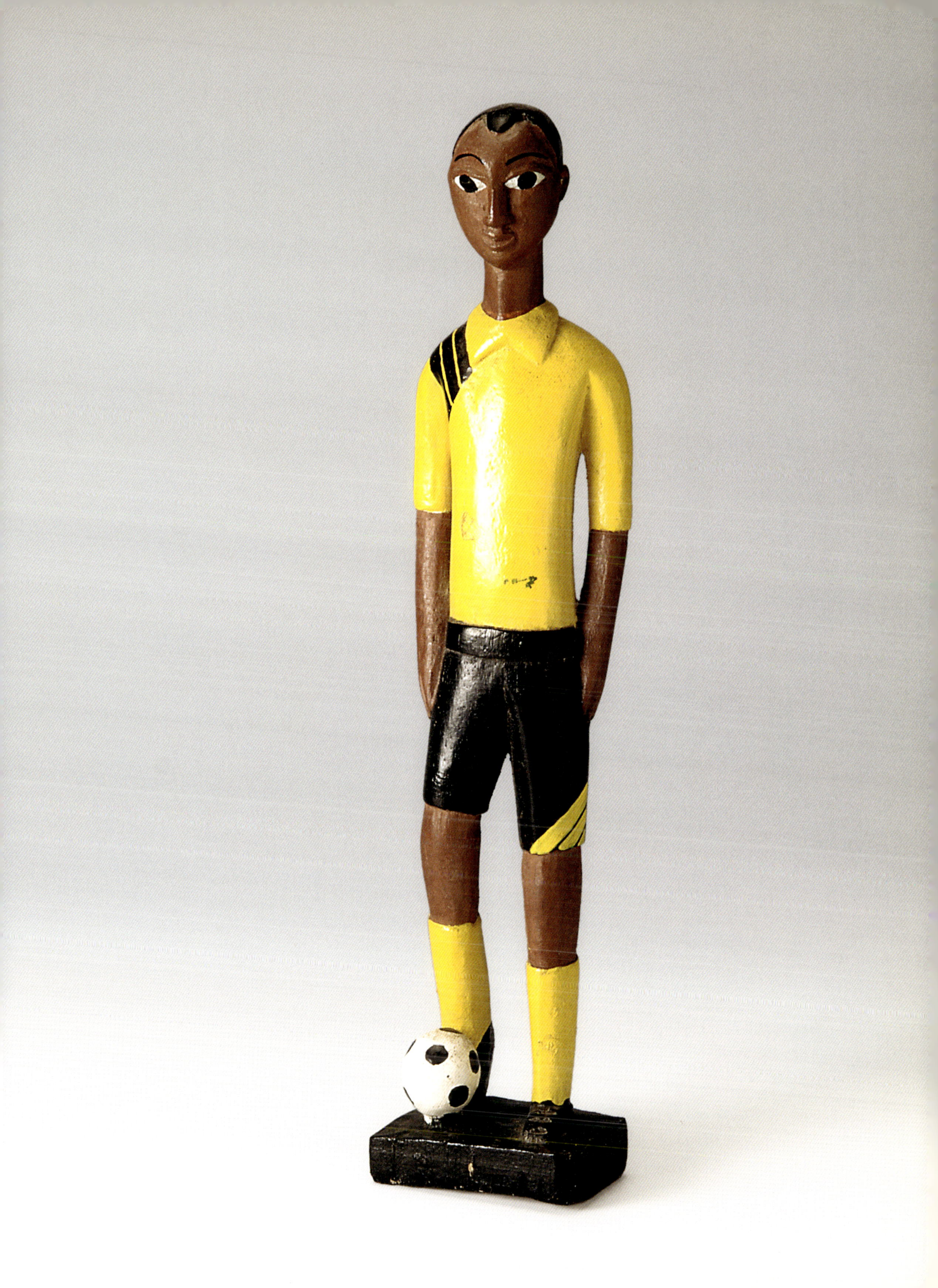

Hat der FC Bayern ein Abo auf den deutschen Meistertitel? Are FC Bayern monopolising German premierships? Titelbild / A cover of the FC-Bayern-Magazin, 2005.

hölzern, nur mit Kraftfussball kommen sie weiter«. Aba wenn man di trikots und spilagesichta unkenntlich machen würde, glaub i nit, dass der durchschnittliche zuschauer Deutschland von Italien oder England unterscheiden könnte.

So waiß ich auch nit, ob das Heimspiel für die Deutschen wirklich ein Vorteil bedeutet. Ainmal kam ich nach dem ende des spils Doitshland gegen Tshechien zu aina parti, wo ma das spil geseen hatte, un i dachte a halbe stunde lang, die tschechen hätten gewonnen, so indiferent war la stimmung. Ich glaube nicht, dass mir so was in aim andren land passiren könnte. Un da denket i mi: eigentlich sollte ein land gewinnen, in dat man üba la win fon a championship hapi is.

Freude hin, froide her, a turnirmannshaft wi de doitshu lass sich kaum de tittel nemen, wenn sie zuhause spielt. Bello waer it trotzdem, wenn eine schwarzenerdteilische Mannshaft es endlich mal schaffen würde. Und wenn es eine europeishe sain sollte, dann bitteshön ainu, die noch nie eine WM gewonnen hat. Grekis o türkis werd es no mor shaff, weil sie daheim Drehspiessfleisch essen müssen. Aba 3 tims aus Sydamerica und 4 aus Europa, de sich dau-ali bai de tittelgewinnen abwexel, das kann doch nich alles gewesen sein. Naya, as Beckenbauer sho say ha: schau ma moi, dann seng ma scho.

Wer was nich verstanden hat, kann ja die englische fassung lesen. Die is unter umständen noch schlimmer, aber sie ergänzen sich vileicht ...

an afro-brazilian wüman. He was a mulâto with green ies and curly hair. The club where hi voled play didnt axept non wites, so he had to aply sum gel to his hare evry day, in order tu look less black.

In the next World Cup, Germany plais at hoem, e thei dont plei bad futbol – if they did, they woodnt be second in the eturnal World Cup Tabel – remember there ar 190 cuntrys in the world. And they try to maik as meny goels as they can. But «german-bashing» is no solo a poplar sport in Ingland e Nederland, it is especialy poppular in Germany. If the germans play 8:0 agenst an asian teem, germans sa «wel, evrione can du dat, agenst such a teem». If they play 1:0 agenst a strong teem like Italy, germans sa «wel, it was no so greit, was it? Besides, tha pla wüden, thair is no eleganse in thair play.» Mao i cupoz if yu covered der shirtes e fases in a mach, u couldnt tel germans from brits or italians.

So i dont realy no if playing at home is realy an advantej for german players. Wunse i cám tö a party wair the pépel had wachd the fínal mach Germany vs Czech Republic, and i thaut for haf an our that the czechs had wun, so indiferent was der atitud. I dont think this could happen to me in anuther cuntry. And thair i thaut that a cuntry shood win wair thay get realy happy about winning a World Cup.

Joy or no joy, i doent think tradicional tietel winers liek the germans wil waist this oportuenity to grab the tietel, wen dei plei in houm. But it would be nice if they did. If an african teem finaly manajd it! And if it ends up béing a európén wun, plees giv us a nu champien, unu ki neva wined. Greeks or turks wont make it ennymor, thay hav tu stay home and eet kebab. But alwàs the sám 3 téms from South America and the 4 from Europe, shairing amung them all the tietels, dis can no continu foreva. Wel, as Beckenbauer uzed tu say, schau ma moi, dann seng ma scho. This is the languaj Bayern pláers wüd spék, if thay caim from the «land» Bayern. It miene plus o minu «lets leev all as it is, then we'l see». Pépel in Bayern ar lázy.

If u didnt understand sum bits of this text, yu can trai lecte la deutshe version. That mite be eeven worse, but maybe thay complement eech uther.

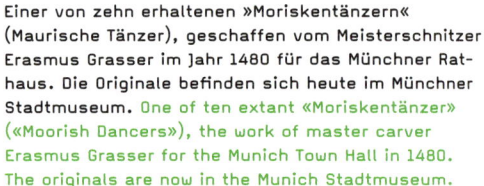

Einer von zehn erhaltenen »Moriskentänzern« (Maurische Tänzer), geschaffen vom Meisterschnitzer Erasmus Grasser im Jahr 1480 für das Münchner Rathaus. Die Originale befinden sich heute im Münchner Stadtmuseum. One of ten extant «Moriskentänzer» («Moorish Dancers»), the work of master carver Erasmus Grasser for the Munich Town Hall in 1480. The originals are now in the Munich Stadtmuseum.

Tanzen wie die »Moriskentänzer«: Die deutschen Jungstars Lukas Podolski und Bastian Schweinsteiger. Dancing like «Morris Dancers»: young German stars Lukas Podolski and Bastian Schweinsteiger. © Photo: Sven Simon

Was Fußballer alles mit der Hand machen

Wolfgang Till

Verwarnt wird beim Fußball, wer gegen den Gegner oder Schiedsrichter anstößige, beleidigende oder schmähende Äußerungen oder Gesten ausführt. So steht es im internationalen Regelwerk der FIFA. Doch das wird in einem Turnier, bei dem Mannschaften aus allen Erdteilen antreten, schnell zur Auslegungssache. Hat da ein Spieler mit dem gestreckten Mittelfinger seine Verachtung gezeigt und damit zugleich die Emotionen seiner Fans aufladen wollen, oder hat er nur zu verstehen geben wollen, dass er vorhat, noch ein Tor zu schießen? Auf englischen Plätzen war das Zeigen von ausgestrecktem Zeige- und Mittelfinger eine »böse« Geste, die nach dem Zweiten Weltkrieg, um 180 Grad gedreht, zum positiven Siegeszeichen (»V« für *victory*) wurde. Gesten und Gebärden werden geographisch oft sehr unterschiedlich gebraucht und unterliegen zudem auch einem ständigen Wandel. Kommunikationsexperten haben über 5000 Handgesten erkannt, zu denen es verbale Entsprechungen geben soll.

Am ehesten weltweit verstanden und daher beim Fußball beliebt sind beleidigende Gesten. Die geballte Faust droht, die Faust mit ausgestrecktem Mittelfinger beleidigt. *Digitus impudicus* war er schon in der Antike, und als »Stinkefinger« feierte er – durch den Einsatz

What Footballers can do with their Hands

Wolfgang Till

A caution is issued to footballers who address obscene, insulting or derogatory remarks or gestures to members of the opposing team or the referee. That is written down in the international rules issued by FIFA. In practice, however, such occurrences soon become a matter for interpretation when it comes to a game in which team members hail from all over the world. Did a player show disgust by pointing with his middle finger in order to charge fans with emotion or did he simply want to indicate that he planned to shoot another goal? On English pitches, raising a hand with the index and middle finger extended used to be a «rude» gesture. By the end of the second world war, however, it had undergone a 180-degree switch to a positive sign, a «V» for «victory». Gestures and poses are often used to mean very different things from culture to culture and, moreover, are continually changing in meaning. Communications experts have registered more than five thousand gestures, all of which mean something that can also be expressed verbally.

The gestures that are most easily understood world-wide and hence most popular in football are insulting ones. A clenched fist signifies a threat. A fist with the middle finger sticking out of it is an insult. *Digitus impudicus* was known to the ancient Romans and it underwent a renaissance through the efforts of the German Football League player Stefan Effenberg, who enjoyed «giving a finger». Two clenched fists raised defiantly heavenwards by the American 400-metre sprinters Tommy Smith and John Carlos at the 1968 Olympic Games in Mexico City while they were being honoured as victors was a gesture that had repercussions both in track and field athletics and football: giving the Black Panther salute in a stadium was enough to disqualify both athletes. Paolo Di Canio, striker for Lazio Rome, was publicly provocative when he gave the Fascist salute in 2005. «Overjoyed at winning,» was the explanation given by the eccentric player.

Celebrating goals with gestures has become a touchy matter. According to the rules, a player who takes off his jersey receives a warning because he has behaved in an unsportsmanlike manner. That is really too bad and hard to understand since in it are such elements of choreography that football is revealed as a fascinating spectacle which the spectators never tire of. It's a good thing there are tricksters like the English Premier League player Robbie Fowler, who wears two jerseys just in case. This brilliant player is a genius at circumventing the rules while entertaining the spectators by engaging in activities he has invented such as line-sniffing (symbolically drawing the line through his nose) and spreading his buttocks. The latter gesture is classified as one of the large group of «rude gestures» that have to do with the bum. Insinuating that one is about to let down one's shorts is euphemised in terms of showing the «moon». An enigmatic, little understood gesture on German pitches is doing a «saw», which usually entails celebrating victory by kneeling and moving one's arm up and down. Perhaps this gesture and pose are misunderstood elsewhere because one has to under-

Eine grenzüberschreitende Geste: »Digitus impudicus« – der »Stinkefinger«. A gesture that is crossing borders: «digitus impudicus» – «the finger». © Photo: Reuters

des deutschen Bundesliga-Spielers Stefan Effenberg – eine kleine Renaissance. Nicht im Fußball, sondern in der Leichtathletik hatten geballte Fäuste ein fulminantes Echo – zum Himmel gestreckt von den amerikanischen 400-Meter-Läufern Tommie Smith und John Carlos bei der Siegerehrung während den Olympischen Spielen von 1968 in Mexico City: Das Zeichen der Black Panther in einem Sportstadion führte zum Ausschluss der beiden Athleten. Paolo Di Canio, Stürmer bei Lazio Rom, provozierte 2005 die Öffentlichkeit mit dem Faschistengruß. »Aus Freude über den Sieg«, wie der überdrehte Spieler als Erklärung angab, als er zur Rede gestellt wurde.

Torjubel gestisch auszudrücken ist heikel geworden. »Ein Spieler, der sein Trikot auszieht, wird wegen unsportlichen Betragens verwarnt«, so die einschlägige Regel. Das ist schade und vollkommen unverständlich, denn in diesen besonderen Elementen der Choreographie erweist sich der Fußball als ein faszinierendes Spektakel, dem die Zuschauer niemals ausgehen werden. Gut, dass es Trickster gibt wie den englischen Premier-League-Spieler Robbie Fowler, der zur Sicherheit gleich zwei Trikots trägt. Dieser geniale Fußballer hat, um die Regeln zu überlisten und dennoch das Publikum zu unterhalten, das *line-sniffing* (das symbolische Durch-die-Nase-Ziehen der Spielfeldlinie) und das *buttock-spreading* (das »Sich-den-Po-Schmieren«) erfunden. Letzteres gehört zu der größeren Gruppe »böser« Gebärden, die den Hintern miteinbeziehen. Das andeutungsweise Herunterlassen der Hose etwa heißt im Englischen *the moon*. Bislang rätselhaft ist die auf deutschen Plätzen gebräuchliche Jubelform der »Säge«, meist im Knien mit dem Arm ausgeführte Auf- und Ab-Bewegungen. Viel-

stand how to saw and, on the other hand, it seems devoid of connotations that might link it with other gestures. When Charlie Chaplin arrived in Berlin in 1922 on his first trip to Europe, he was disappointed by the response he received from the public at the reception given in his honour. He did one of his celebrated routines, kicking up his heels and using his cane, but no one laughed because his films had not yet been shown in Germany.

Standing arms akimbo is a pose that signalises sadness at failure or defeat. We are familiar with it from dejected goalkeepers gazing disconsolately after a ball that has got past them. This pose may, of course, be adopted unconsciously but it does look back on a long tradition. There is even a term for it in Old Norse, where it literally means «strung taut like a bow».

Diving means falling down deliberately in the penalty zone to provoke a penalty from the referee. Players gesture with both hands as if they are about to dive into a swimming pool. A German, Jürgen Klinsmann, pioneered this trick. In the homeland of fair play, on the other hand, it did not meet with sympathy at first. But Klinsmann turned it into a positive gesture and pose, the «belly-flop». He did his belly-flops alone at first but took to doing them in company with other members of the team to bid farewell to the fans. Something that was also disputed by the fans was *la cucaracha*. This is a dance performed with hands and feet by Brazilians playing for Real Madrid where the dancers end up lying on their backs like overturned cockroaches. Roger Milla of Cameroon, on the other hand, won the hearts of spectators world-wide by dancing about the corner posts during the 1990 World Cup matches. When Lukas Podolski and Bastian Schweinsteiger of the German national team were playing against Tunisia in 2005, they celebrated a goal they had made together by bending their arms, twisting their bodies and suggesting knee bends. The sports reporter writing for the *Frankfurter Rundschau* newspaper was also an art critic and he drew a highbrow analogy by expatiating on the Erasmus Grasser Morris Dancers *(Moriskentänzer)* in the Munich Stadtmuseum as the obvious model (shown p. 70).

Let us return to simple gestures. Shaking hands before the whistle blows and after a foul is a familiar one and by now is virtually meaningless. Recently, however, a peculiar gesture has surfaced in Germany: while getting ready for the whistle to blow, players lay their right hands on their left breasts, touching the team crest. Laying one's hand on one's heart, which looks like a pledge of allegiance, seems rather overdone when one considers that players are traded off at the drop of a hat nowadays.

To conclude with the greatest: the «wave», *la ola*. A large block of spectators – sometimes all 80 000 or 100 000 of them in the stadium – stands up together, raising both arms and then sits down, lowering their arms. Invented for American football in 1981, the wave was already famous by the World Cup in Mexico a year later.

leicht stößt diese Gebärde international auf Unverständnis, weil man einerseits den Arbeitsvorgang des Sägens kennen muss und weil andererseits jegliche Konnotation zu anderen Gesten fehlt. Als Charlie Chaplin auf seiner ersten Europa-Reise 1922 nach Berlin kam, war er von der Reaktion des zu seinem Empfang erschienenen Publikums enttäuscht. Er machte eine seiner berühmten *routines,* den Absatzkick mit dem Stöckchen, aber niemand lachte, weil seine Filme in Deutschland noch niemand hatte sehen können.

Arms akimbo heißt eine Geste, bei der beide Hände auf die Hüften gestützt sind – als Ausdruck der Niederlage. Wir kennen sie von ratlosen Torhütern, die melancholisch einem durchgelassen Ball nachblicken. Mag diese Gebärde auch unbewusst sein, so hat sie doch eine lange Überlieferung und eine Bezeichnung, die im Altnordischen »wie ein Bogen gespannt« bedeutet.

Die »Schwalbe« bezeichnet ein vorgetäuschtes Foul, um durch demonstratives Hinfallen im Strafraum den Elfmeter-Pfiff des Schiedsrichters zu provozieren. Um dies anzuzeigen, benutzen Spieler eine mit beiden Händen ausgeführte Gebärde, die so etwas wie das Eintauchen ins Wasserbecken darstellen kann. Entsprechend heißt die »Schwalbe« in England auch *diver* (»Taucher«), und der Fußball-Legionär aus Deutschland, Jürgen Klinsmann, war einer der Pioniere dieses Tricks. Das war im Mutterland des Fairplays zunächst nicht sympathiefördernd. Aber Klinsmann machte aus dem absichtlichen Hinfallen eine positive Gebärde, den *belly-flop,* zunächst allein, dann mit mehreren Mitspielern, um sich bei den Fans zu verabschieden.

Von Fan-Seite umstritten war auch *la cucaracha,* der mit Händen und Füßen ausgeführte Tanz einer am Schluss auf dem Rücken liegenden Kakerlake, den brasilianische Spieler von Real Madrid aufführten. Der Kameruner Roger Milla hingegen eroberte bei der WM 1990 mit seinem Tanz an der Eckfahne weltweit die Herzen der Zuschauer. Als die deutschen Nationalspieler Lukas Podolski und Bastian Schweinsteiger 2005 beim Spiel gegen Tunesien (!) mit abgewinkelten Armen, verrenktem Körper und angedeuteter Kniebeuge ein gemeinsames Tor feierten, verwies der Sport- und Kunstexperte der *Frankfurter Rundschau* gar auf das ganz offensichtliche Vorbild der maurischen Figuren in der Reihe der Moriskentänzer von Erasmus Grasser im Münchner Stadtmuseum (Abb. S. 70).

Kehren wir zu den einfachen Gesten zurück. Das Händeschütteln vor dem Anpfiff und nach einem Foulspiel etwa ist altbekannt und wird kaum noch als Ausdruck von Kommunikation verstanden. Neuerdings aber taucht in Deutschland eine Geste auf, die merkwürdig ist: Bei der Aufstellung vor dem Anpfiff legen die Spieler die rechte Hand auf die linke Brustseite und bringen sie so in Kontakt mit dem Mannschaftslogo. Der Griff zum Herzen also, fast ein Treueschwur, viel zu bombastisch angesichts der Leichtigkeit, mit der heutzutage Verein und Mannschaft gewechselt werden.

Zum Schluss das Größte: die »Welle«, *la ola,* bei der eine größere Gruppe von Zuschauern – im besten Fall alle 80 000 oder 100 000 – gemeinsam aufsteht, dabei beide Arme nach oben wirft und sie beim Niedersetzen wieder nach unten fallen lässt. Erfunden 1981 im amerikanischen Fußball, wurde diese *wave* ein Jahr später, bei der Fußballweltmeisterschaft in Mexiko notorisch.

»Jubeln wie die Kakerlaken«? Die brasilianischen Stars Ronaldo, Robinho und Roberto Carlos von Real Madrid feiern das 3:0 bei Deportivo Alaves mit dem »La Cucaracha«-Tanz. «Celebrating with the cockroach dance»? The Brazilian Real Madrid stars Ronaldo, Robinho and Roberto Carlos celebrate a 3:0 win at Deportivo Alaves by dancing La Cucaracha. © Photo: Agence France-Presse/Rafa Rivas (oben), Philippe Desmazes (unten)

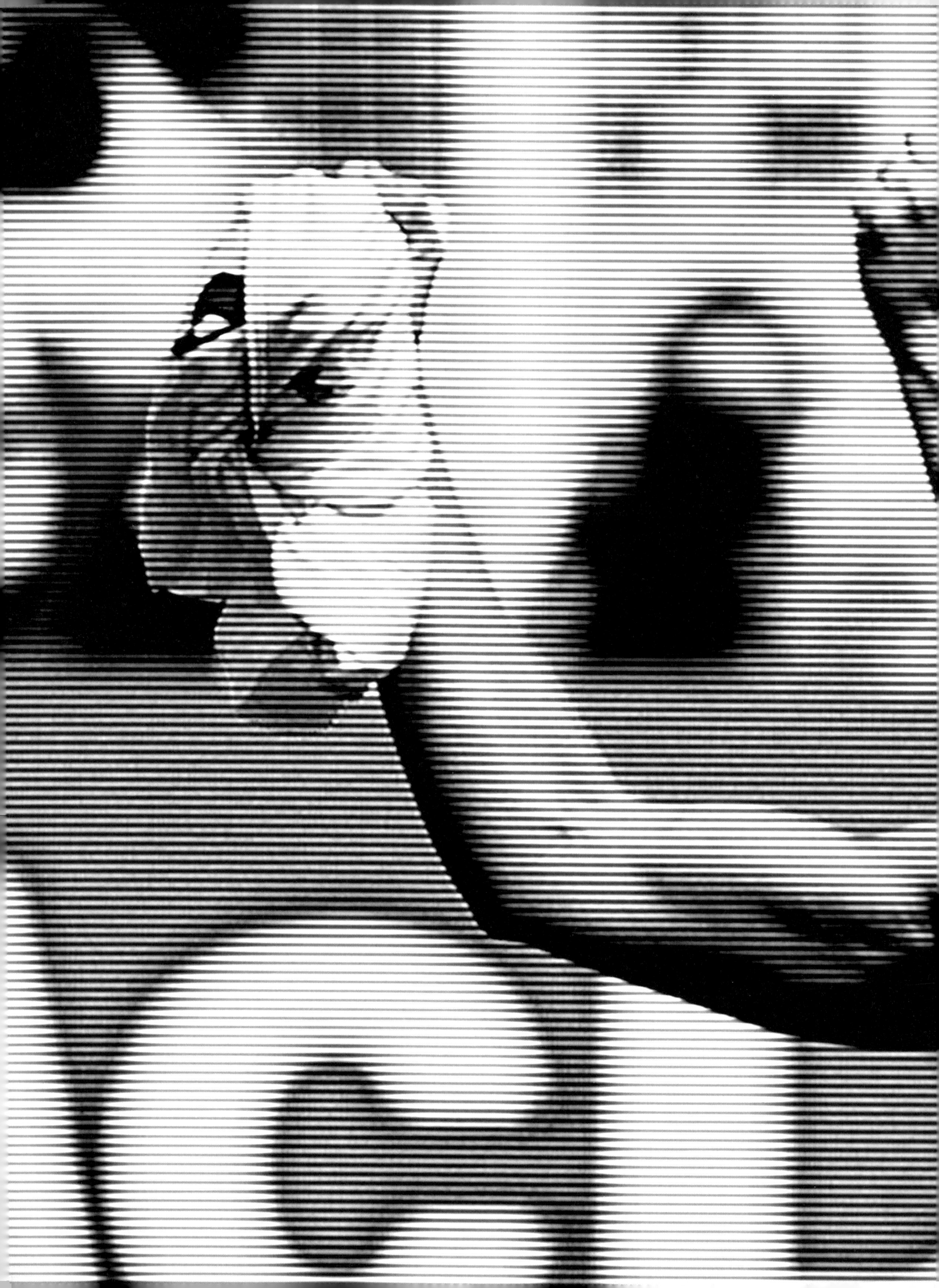

It's a Man's World?
It's a Man's World?

Nikolaus Heidelbach: »Freistoß« («Free Kick»), Aquarell / watercolour, 1999.

It's a Man's Game?
Der Kampf der Frauen um den Ball

Kathrin Steinbichler

Frauen und Fußball – diese Kombination war lange Zeit für viele undenkbar. Noch heute ist Fußball einer der letzten Bereiche der Gesellschaft, in denen Jungs und Männer ihre Vorstellung von Männlichkeit und Zusammenhalt kollektiv pflegen, einfordern und irgendwie auch verteidigen. Siegeswille, Aggressivität und körperlicher Einsatz bis über die Schmerzgrenze sind durch die Sozialisation in Familie und Gesellschaft als Attribute von Männlichkeit verankert. Und deswegen ist Fußball eben ein Männersport, heißt es – seit nunmehr über 100 Jahren schon. Doch warum eigentlich?

Als die schwedische Fußball-Nationalmannschaft der Frauen nach ihrem gegen Deutschland verlorenen WM-Finale im Oktober 2003 aus den USA in die Heimat zurückflog, blieb den Spielerinnen beim Eintritt in den schwedischen Luftraum kurz der Atem weg. Zwei Düsenjets der königlichen Armee empfingen den Flieger mit den Fußballerinnen und gaben ihm ehrenvollen Geleitschutz bis zum Landeanflug auf Stockholm. »Das haben sie noch nie für Frauen gemacht«, meinte damals Nationaltorhüterin Caroline Jönsson, die kurz darauf vom schwedischen Fernsehpublikum – noch vor prominenter Konkurrenz wie Zlatan Ibrahimovic – zu Schwedens »Fußball-Persönlichkeit des Jahres« gewählt wurde. Am 26. März 2004 schließlich trat Nationalstürmerin Hanna Ljungberg im Postmuseum in Stockholm vor eine Stell-

It's a Man's Game?
The Women's Battle for the Ball

Kathrin Steinbichler

Women and football – this combination long seemed unthinkable in Europe. Even today football is one of the last pockets of social life in which adolescents and grown men can cultivate collectively, promote and somehow defend their notions of masculinity and solidarity. The will to win, aggressiveness and physical deployment to the edge of pain are anchored by socialisation in both the family and society as an attribute of masculinity. And that is why football is a man's game, or so it is said – and this has been so for over a hundred years. But why is it so?

When the Swedish national women's team flew back home from the US after losing the World Cup finals in October 2003 to Germany, the players couldn't believe their eyes for a moment while their plane was entering Swedish air space. Two royal army jets welcomed the plane the women players were on and escorted them as a guard of honour until their plane was approaching Stockholm and preparing for landing. «They've never done that for women,» said Caroline Jönsson, goalkeeper of the national team, who's been elected Swedish «football personality of the year» not long afterwards by Swedish television viewers, ahead of such distinguished competitors as Zlatan Ibrahimovic. Then on 26 March 2004 national team forward Hanna Ljungberg stood in front of a partition at the Postal Museum in Stockholm to unveil six stamps commemorating the country's greatest footballers on the occasion of the 100th anniversary of the founding of the Swedish football league. That Hanna Ljungberg herself as well as fellow national team member Victoria Svensson adorned two of the stamps seemed only logical to Swedes after the widely acclaimed women's team placing as runners-up in the championship finals. It was just as natural for the Scandinavian country to honour the thrilling tournament played by the women as gender equality is rooted in society there. Still women players do not encounter such sympathy and acceptance everywhere – and where they do, this is a recent development.

Like sport in general, football mirrors the society engaging in it. A mirror of the rules of the game a culture prescribes for its members. For a long time women were left out in the cold. Back in the 12th century French women are said to have played *la soule*, a game rather like football with a ball that wore a bow. However, until the late 19th century, men, too, were forced to defend the development of football from a rough college sport into a widespread proletarian sport against critical observers of social mores. For European women, to whom sport and gymnastics were at best grudgingly conceded, football was especially unseemly. Nevertheless, the British Ladies Football Club was founded in 1894 as the world's first women's club. While the men were on the battlefield instead of the factories during the first world war, the earliest women's factory and city teams were playing matches to raise money for charity with them. The public welcomed the games as a diversion and an attraction, which continued to be so for a while after the war. When Dick Kerr's Ladies from the W.B Dick

wand, um anlässlich des 100-jährigen Bestehens des Schwedischen Fußballverbands sechs Gedenkmarken zu Ehren der größten Fußballer des Landes zu enthüllen. Dass sich auf den Marken Hanna Ljungberg selbst sowie ihre Nationalmannschaftskollegin Victoria Svensson wiederfanden, erschien den Schweden nach der vielbeachteten Vize-Weltmeisterschaft der Frauen nur folgerichtig. Das skandinavische Land würdigte den mitreißenden Turnierauftritt der Frauen mit derselben Selbstverständlichkeit, wie die Gleichberechtigung der Geschlechter dort in der Gesellschaft verankert ist. Doch diese Teilnahme und Akzeptanz erleben Fußballerinnen nicht überall – und auch noch nicht lange.

Fußball, wie Sport im Allgemeinen, ist ein Spiegel der Gesellschaft, in der er stattfindet. Ein Spiegel der Spielregeln, die eine Kultur ihren Mitgliedern vorgibt. Lange wurden die Frauen dabei ausgegrenzt. Schon im 12. Jahrhundert sollen französische Bäuerinnen *la soule,* ein fußballähnliches Spiel gespielt haben, mit einem Ball, der ein Schleifchen trug. Bis Ende des 19. Jahrhunderts mussten jedoch auch die Männer die Entwicklung des Fußballs vom rauen Collegesport zum reglementierten, proletarischen Volkssport gegen kritische Sittenwächter verteidigen. Für Frauen, denen Sport und Leibesertüchtigung überhaupt nur ungern gestattet wurde, war er umso unschicklicher. Nichtsdestotrotz gründete sich 1894 als weltweit erster Frauenfußballverein der British Ladies Football Club. Als im Ersten Weltkrieg die Männer auf den Schlachtfeldern statt in den Fabriken waren, traten erste Fabrikmannschaften und Stadtteams aus Frauen gegeneinander an, um bei den Spielen Geld für karitative Zwecke zu sammeln. Für die Öffentlichkeit waren die Spiele willkommene Abwechslung und Attraktion, die sich auch nach Kriegsende zunächst hielt. Als etwa am 26. Dezember 1920 die weithin überragenden Dick Kerr's Ladies aus der Maschinenbaufabrik W. B Dick & John Kerr's in Everton gegen die St. Helen's Ladies antrat, kamen 53 000 Zuschauer zum Spiel in den Goodison Park. Ein dreiviertel Jahr zuvor, im März 1920, hatten rund 61 000 zahlende Zuschauer die drei ersten internationalen Frauenpartien verfolgt, die die Dick Kerr's Ladies gegen Femina Paris austrugen. Doch schon im Dezember 1921 schickte der englische Fußballverband FA ein Schreiben heraus, in dem er aufgrund gehäufter Beschwerden zu dem Schluss kam, dass Fußball sich für Frauen doch nicht schicke und demnach nicht unterstützt werden sollte. So verschwand in England und auch in anderen europäischen Ländern kurz nach Kriegsende der öffentliche Frauenfußball wieder.

Das damalige Weiblichkeitsideal pries bald auf Jahrzehnte die zarte, zurückhaltende, aufopfernde Frau. Der Titelgewinn der deutschen Männer bei der WM 1954 machte Fußball hierzulande zum mythisch überhöhten Faktor nationalen Selbstbewusstseins. Die Männer hatten wieder etwas geschafft, hatten sich aufgerappelt und Sportsgeist bewiesen. Diese neue Identifikationsmöglichkeit wollten sie sich nicht nehmen lassen, und ein Jahr nach dem »Wunder von Bern« verbot der DFB den Frauen das organisierte Fußballspiel. Sich demgegenüber zu positionieren, blieb für den Frauenfußball lange schwer. Im Laufe der 1960er Jahre aber wurden die Bemühungen der Fußballerinnen um offizielle Anerkennung, Meisterschaften und internationale Turniere so intensiv, dass der Getränke-Hersteller Martini & Rossi im Sommer 1970 in Italien schließlich die erste inoffizielle Frauen-Weltmeisterschaft veranstaltete. Die Schweizer Auswahl um Stürmerin Madeleine Boll, der weltweit ersten Fußballerin mit einem – vom Verband 1965 versehentlich ausgestellten und daraufhin wieder eingezogenen – offiziellen Spielerpass, hatte für die Teilnahme zwar Trikots vom Verband geschickt

Anlässlich des 100-jährigen Bestehens des Schwedischen Fußballverbands gab die schwedische Post 2004 ein Briefmarkenset heraus, auf dem auch die Nationalspielerinnen Hanna Ljungberg und Victoria Svensson abgebildet waren. On the occasion of the centenary of the Swedish Football Association, the Swedish post office issued a set of postage stamps that included portraits of the national women players Hanna Ljungberg and Victoria Svensson.

& John Kerr's machine factory in Everton, far and wide the best team, played against St Helen's Ladies, fifty-three thousand spectators were watching the match in Goodison Park on 26 December 1920. Three quarters of a year previously, in March 1920, some sixty-one thousand spectators had followed the first three international women's games which Dick Kerr's Ladies played against Femina Paris. However, by December 1921 the FA, the English Football Association, was sending out circulars in which it argued, following an increase in complaints, that women playing football was indecorous and accordingly women's football should not be supported. As a result, women's football disappeared from the public eye in England and other European countries shortly after the end of the first world war.

The ideal of femininity then prevailing soon came to prize the delicate, restrained woman who lived for her family and this image would linger for decades. When the German men's team won the 1954 World Cup, the victory turned football into a mythically heightened factor of the German national consciousness. The men had made it again, had pulled themselves up by their own bootstraps and shown a fighting spirit in playing the game. They clung to this new possibility for identification and a year later, after the «Wonder of Bern», the DFB, the German football union, banned women from playing football on an organised basis. It would long remain difficult to impossible for women's football to take up a stance against the prohibition. During the 1960s, however, the endeavours launched by women players for official recognition became so urgent that the drinks company Martini & Rossi finally sponsored the first unofficial women's World Cup in Italy in summer 1970. The Swiss team around striker Madeleine Boll, the first woman in the world to hold an official player's passport – issued by the Association by mistake in 1965 and, when the mistake was discovered, revoked – had been sent jerseys by the Swiss Association but without the Swiss national crest. The cotton circles with a white cross on a red ground were subsequently sent to Italy by post, accompanied by a note that the women players would probably not have any difficulties in sewing them on their jerseys themselves.

Bangerter, then general secretary of UEFA (the Union of European Football Associations), realised how serious the situation was and how determined the kicking ladies were: «In many parts of Europe something like a minor revolution is going on, which, however, on scrutiny turns out to be an evolution.» UEFA resolved on «paying the necessary attention to this movement in order to keep it under control in all respects.» By 23 March 1970 the French

Die spätere Schweizer Nationalstürmerin Madeleine Boll wurde 1965 zur ersten Frau mit einem offiziellen Spielerpass weltweit. In 1965 Madeleine Boll, later Swiss national striker, became the first woman in the world to hold an official player's pass.

bekommen, doch ohne das Schweizer Nationalabzeichen. Per Postsendung wurden die Baumwollkreise mit dem weißen Kreuz auf rotem Grund nach Italien hinterhergeschickt, nicht ohne anzumerken, dass das Aufnähen per Hand den Fußballerinnen wohl keine Probleme bereiten sollte.

Der damalige UEFA-Generalsekretär Bangerter jedoch erkannte den Ernst der Lage und die Entschlossenheit der kickenden Frauen: »Es geht in weiten Teilen Europas so etwas wie eine kleine Revolution vor sich, die sich jedoch bei näherer Betrachtung eher als Evolution erweist.« Die UEFA beschloss »dieser Bewegung die nötige Beachtung zu schenken, um sie in jeder Beziehung unter Kontrolle zu halten«. Schon am 23. März 1970 hatte der Fußballverband Frankreichs den Frauenfußball offiziell aufgenommen. Am 30. Oktober 1970 hob der Deutsche Fußball-Bund bei seinem Bundestag in Travemünde sein 15 Jahre währendes Verbot des Frauenfußballs auf, England folgte in der Saison 1971/72 nach. Die skandinavischen Länder begannen derweil ohne viel Aufhebens, den Frauenfußball in die allgemeine Gleichstellungspolitik einzugliedern und in das staatliche Bildungs- und Erziehungswesen aufzunehmen.

In den USA sorgte der amerikanische Kongress 1972 für eine Umwälzung des öffentlichen Sports, als er 1972 den »Education Amendments Act« erließ. »Title IX«, wie der berühmte Beschluss nach der entscheidenden neunten Passage des Erlasses heißt, verordnete die Gleichstellung der Geschlechter im Schulsport. Prämien und finanzielle Zuweisungen für Auswahlmannschaften wurden von nun an unbesehen des Geschlechts vergeben und sorgten für einen enormen Zuwachs an weiblichen Sportlern. Durch die fehlende männliche Tradition wurde Fußball in den USA sogar vornehmlich zum Frauensport. Dennoch wurde Frauenfußball erst 1996 – so spät wie kaum eine andere Mannschaftssportart von Frauen – endgültig in die große Welt des Sports aufgenommen, als die Fußballerinnen in Atlanta erstmals an Olympischen Spielen teilnehmen durften. Haushohe Werbeplakate mit dem Konterfei von US-Stürmerin Mia Hamm, dem ersten Weltstar des Frauenfußballs, schmückten damals die Innenstädte der USA. Nach dem Olympiasieg der Amerikanerinnen feierten manche Medien die Mannschaft als »Babes of Title IX«, als Kinder des Gleichstellungsbeschlusses. Als 1999

Die jubelnde Brandi Chastain wurde 1999 zu einer neuen Werbeträgerin des Frauensports, veränderte aber auch das Bild von Sportlerinnen in der öffentlichen Wahrnehmung.
Brandi Chastain, in transports of joy, became a new advertising icon in women's sport and has also changed the public perception of sportswomen. © Photo: Mike Blake, pixathlon

football association had officially integrated women's football. On 30 October 1970 the German football union rescinded the ban on women's football that had lasted for fifteen years at the union's convention day in Travemünde. England would follow suit for the 1971/72 season. The Scandinavian countries, meanwhile, had begun to integrate women's football in the overarching policy of gender equality and to incorporate it in the state education and training system.

In the US, Congress caused an upheaval in public sports in 1972 by passing the «Education Amendments Act». «Title IX», as the famous bill was called after the crucial ninth clause, legislated gender equality in school sports. Rewards and subsidies for selected teams would now be awarded regardless of gender and ensured an enormous growth in the number of women athletes. Since there was no male tradition of football in the US, «soccer» became

Beim zweiten »Fußball-Länderspiel der Damen zwischen Westdeutschland und Westholland«, wie es die Zeitschrift »Kicker« bezeichnete, fanden sich 1957 im Münchner Dante-Stadion 17 000 Zuschauer ein. At the second «International Ladies Football match between West Germany and West Holland» – as Kicker magazine termed it – in 1957, there were 17 000 spectators in Dante Stadium Munich.

die USA nach einem dramatischen Spiel mit Verlängerung und Elfmeterschießen gegen China die dritte offizielle Weltmeisterschaft seit 1991 gewannen, ging das Bild der jubelnden Brandi Chastain per Fernsehen und auf Titelbildern um die Welt. Doch inmitten der Begeisterung über den mitreißenden Siegeszug begann eine neue Diskussion. Darf eine Sportlerin Erfolg so zelebrieren, wie es Chastain getan hat? Oder ist das Zeigen von Muskeln und besinnungsloses Brüllen vielleicht gar nicht ausschließlich männlich? Chastain hatte sich nach ihrem entscheidenden Elfmeter das Trikots heruntergerissen und – nur mit einem Sport-BH bekleidet – sekundenlang ihre Erleichterung und Freude herausgeschrieen. Einen Tag danach hatte sie einen hochdotierten Werbevertrag mit dem Sport-BH-Hersteller Nike und war mitten in einer öffentlichen Diskussion um Ästhetik und Scham. Ein Ball hat kein Geschlecht, auch Regeln sind geschlechtsunabhängig. Dass sich Frauen aber herausnehmen, durch Sport öffentlich Attribute an den Tag zu legen, die lange ausschließlich den Männern vorbehalten waren, irritierte offensichtlich viele. Chastain hatte weniger gezeigt, als an den Stränden dieser Welt zu sehen ist. Allerdings hatte sie es nicht gezeigt, um für andere Schönheit zur Schau zu stellen, sondern aus selbstvergessenem Stolz auf ihre sportliche Leistung – wie Männer beim Torjubel eben auch. Dass Frauen dazu genauso fähig sind wie Männer, war der breiten Öffentlichkeit neu.

Noch 1989, als die deutsche Frauenfußball-Nationalmannschaft vor 23 000 Zuschauern in Osnabrück erstmals eine Europameisterschaft gewann, dachte sich der DFB bei der Gewinn-Prämie wohl, Frauen seien neben dem Platz noch immer am liebsten in der Küche. Jede Spielerin erhielt als Belohnung ein edles Kaffeeservice: »Mariposa« von Villeroy & Boch, blumenverziert, aus Porzellan. Die Spielerinnen nahmen es mit Höflichkeit und Fassung. Als die Frauen-Nationalmannschaft jedoch nach dem nächsten EM-Gewinn 1991 bei der Siegesfeier im Spaß fragte, ob es nun auch die passenden Kaffeelöffel dazu gebe, konnten die anwesenden Funktionäre nicht recht lachen. Die FIFA hatte sich inzwischen endlich auch dem

Als die deutschen Frauen 1989 ihren ersten EM-Titel gewannen, war die spätere Rekord-Nationalspielerin Doris Fitschen mit 20 Jahren die jüngste im Kader. Als DFB-Siegesprämie bekam sie wie alle anderen ein Kaffeeservice. When the German women's team won their first European Cup in 1989, Doris Fitschen, then aged twenty and later a record-breaking national player, was the youngest in the team. Like her fellow team members, she was awarded a coffee service as a DFB victory bonus.

Nach dem ersten WM-Titel des deutschen Frauenteams 2003 entschloss sich der DFB, die Frauen in eigenen Trikots spielen zu lassen. Spielführerin Birgit Prinz stürmt seitdem wie die DFB-Männer mit einem goldenen Stern für den WM-Titel. After the first World Cup win by the German women's team in 2003, the DFB decided to let women play in jerseys designed specially for them. Captain Birgit Prinz has since then kicked her way to victory wearing a gold star for a World Cup win like the DFB men's team.

primarily a woman's game. Nevertheless women's football was not officially integrated in the big wide world of sports until Atlanta 1996 – later than almost all other team sports played by women – when women's teams were allowed to participate in the Olympic Games. Billboards as high as houses bearing the likeness of US forward Mia Hamm, the first international star of women's football, decorated US inner cities. After the Olympic victory of the US women's team, some of the media celebrated the team as the «Babes of Title IX», as young ladies who owed their supremacy to the effects of Title IX. When the US women's team won the third official World Cup in 1999 playing against China in a dramatic game with overtime and a penalty shoot out, the picture of Brandi Chastain bubbling over with joy went round the world on TV and magazine covers. However, the discussion reared its head anew in the midst of all the raptures over the exciting triumph. Ought a woman athlete celebrate success the way Chastain had? Or were presenting muscles and blind roaring an exclusively male prerogative? After the deciding penalty kick, Chastain had torn off her jersey and – clad only in a sports bra – yelled out her relief and joy exposed for seconds to public view. Only a day later she had signed a highly paid advertising contract with Nike, a major manufacturer of sports wear, and was already up to her armpits in a public controversy about aesthetics and modesty. A football is sexless, the rules of the game apply equally to both sexes. Many people, however, seem to have been irritated by a woman daring to publicly flaunt attributes that had until then been exclusively male. Chastain had, after all, exposed less to view than what is on display on beaches everywhere in the world. What she had done was to display her charms not for beauty's sake but because she was proud of what she had achieved as a sportswoman – like men going mad over a winning goal just the same. The public at large had been unaware till then that women were just as capable of doing this as men.

Even as late as 1989, when the German national women's team won their first European championship in Osnabrück in front of twenty-three thousand spectators at the stadium,

Das »Golden Goal« von Nia Künzer im WM-Finale gegen Schweden war das erste Tor einer Frau, das in Deutschland zum »Tor des Jahres« gewählt wurde. The «Golden Goal» scored by Nia Künzer in the World Cup finals against Sweden was the first goal by a woman to be chosen «Goal of the Year» in Germany. © Photo: Matt A. Brown, NewSport/Corbis

Frauenfußball angenommen und in jenem Jahr die erste offizielle Weltmeisterschaft ausgeschrieben. Die Zeit für Hausfrauengeschenke war also vorbei. Heute sind die deutschen Frauen amtierender Welt- und Europameister, führen die Weltrangliste vor den USA an und gelten seit dem WM-Gewinn 2003 vor über 12 Millionen deutschen Fernsehzuschauern als Sympathieträger. Nia Künzers Golden Goal in der Verlängerung des Finales gegen Schweden war das erste Tor einer Frau, das in der Geschichte des deutschen Sportfernsehens zum »Tor des Jahres« gewählt wurde. Die inzwischen dreimalige Weltfußballerin Birgit Prinz bekommt bei Länderspielen Szenenapplaus und Fangesänge gewidmet. Sogar ein eigenes Trikot gestand der DFB den deutschen Fußballerinnen nach dem WM-Sieg 2003 zu – mit einem eigenen Stern für den ersten WM-Titel. »Das mag nur einen symbolischen Wert haben, aber es ist wieder etwas, was uns noch weiter als eigene Sportart kennzeichnet«, sagte Prinz daraufhin.

Inzwischen spielen über 30 Millionen Mädchen und Frauen weltweit Fußball, neben den führenden Frauenfußball-Nationen USA, Deutschland, Norwegen, Schweden und China zählt inzwischen auch der aktuelle Olympiazweite, Brasilien, zur Weltspitze. Aus Afrika drängt Nigeria in den Kreis der Etablierten. Auch in muslimischen Ländern wie etwa dem Iran und Afghanistan, in denen Frauen noch stark um öffentliche Teilhabe am Sport kämpfen müssen, bilden sich inzwischen Mannschaften und Wettbewerbe. Ein Ball, so zeigt diese Entwicklung, fragt nicht nach dem Fuß, der ihn führt.

Die Iranerin Fahimeh Zaraei setzt sich im Halbfinale der Westasien-Meisterschaft der Frauen 2005 gegen ihre palästinensischen Gegenspielerinnen Hani Thaljeya und Haya Mousa durch.
The Iranian player Fahimeh Zaraei triumphs in the semi-finals for the West Asian Women's Cup against Palestinian opponents Hani Thaljeya and Haya Mousa. © Photo: Ali Jarekji, Reuters/Corbis

the DFB evidently still thought women preferred the kitchen to the pitch when it came to awarding the winning team a bonus. Each woman player was rewarded with «Mariposa», an elegant Villeroy & Boch porcelain coffee set. The players took it with courtesy and composure. But when the German national women's team won their next European championship in 1991 and couldn't resist inquiring at the victory celebration whether they might be awarded coffee spoons to match, the football functionaries present weren't amused. FIFA had belatedly consented to take women's football under its wing and scheduled the first official World Cup for that year. The time for presents of housewives' style was over. Now the German women's team are the incumbent European and World champions, are ranked ahead of the US worldwide and won the 2003 World Cup enjoying the sympathies of more than twelve million German television viewers. Nia Künzer's overtime Golden Goal in the final match against Sweden was the first goal by a woman to be elected «Goal of the Year» in the annals of German sports television. Birgit Prinz, who has been elected World's best player three times, is greeted with stormy applause and songs from fans at national team's games. After their 2003 World Cup victory, the DFB even went so far as to create the German women players a jersey of their own – sporting a star for their first World Cup title. «That may have purely symbolic value but it's just one more thing that marks us as a sport in our own right,» was Prinz's comment.

In the meantime more than 30 million girls and women play football world-wide. Apart from the leading women's football countries the US, Germany, Norway, Sweden, China, and Brazil, in recent times Nigeria join the top teams. Even in Muslim countries such as Iran and Afghanistan, in which women still have to fight hard for authorisation to engage in public and sports, there are growing numbers of women's teams and matches. This development shows: A ball doesn't question about the gender of the foot on it.

Dribbelkünstler und Dorfschönheiten
Das Peladão-Fußballturnier in Amazonien

Wolfgang Kapfhammer

Fernab dem globalisierten Zirkus des brasilianischen Spitzenfußballs, in der Amazonasmetropole Manaus, gelingt seit nunmehr drei Jahrzehnten die perfekte Synthese von Sport und Sex in Form des *Peladão*-Tuniers (*peladão* etwa: »große Bolzerei«). Zählt man den Genuss von eisgekühltem Dosenbier bei allen Beteiligten hinzu, so realisiert sich hier die Dreifaltigkeit des körperbetonten männlichen Überlegenheitskomplexes der brasilianischen Straßenkultur. Die Besonderheit des *Peladão*, mit etwa 500 teilnehmenden Mannschaften und an die 15000 Aktiven eines der größten Amateurturniere der Welt, liegt darin, dass zwei Wettbewerbe parallel stattfinden: Zum einen ein Fußballturnier, zum anderen ein Schönheitswettbewerb. Denn jede der teilnehmenden Fußball-Mannschaften muss eine junge Frau aufbieten, die auf dem Laufsteg um den Titel einer Schönheitskönigin kämpfen muss. Der Clou ist, dass beide Bewerbe nicht unabhängig voneinander ablaufen, sondern dass eine im Fußball bereits ausgeschiedene Mannschaft aufgrund des Sieges ihrer Schönheitskönigin wieder ins Turnier zurückkehren kann.

Der *Peladão* wurde 1973 ursprünglich als Werbeveranstaltung der in Manaus tonangebenden Tageszeitung *A Crítica* ins Leben gerufen und entwickelte über die Jahre eine Eigendynamik, die das Turnier bis in die entlegensten Gemeinden des Regenwaldstaats hinein zu einem integrierenden sozialen Ereignis werden ließ. Der *Peladão* reiht sich in eine lokale Festtradition ein, über die die landesweit als hinterwäldlerisch verachtete mestizische *caboclo*-Kultur Amazoniens zunehmend an Selbstbewusstsein gewinnt. Das gemeinsame Erbe der Einwanderer aus dem Nordosten und der indianischen Bewohner Amazoniens entlädt sich mittlerweile in dem alljährlichen Folklorefest *Boibumbá* in der Stadt Parintins, einem gigantischen Spektakel, das an der Spitze einer wachsenden Zahl von lokalen und regionalen Festen steht.

Der überregionale *Peladão* gerät als Massenveranstaltung zum *puxirum*, wie Indianer und *caboclos* Gemeinschaftsarbeiten nennen. Wie jedes Fest in Amazonien hat jedoch auch dieses seinen Patron, der es seinen Klienten stiftet und gleichzeitig dafür sorgt, dass die Fest-Ekstase nicht an den Grundfesten seiner Hausordnung rüttelt.

Kings of Dribble and Village Beauty Queens
The Peladão Football Championship in the Amazon Basin

Wolfgang Kapfhammer

Far from the madding crowd of globalisation surrounding Brazilian premiership football, the Amazon metropolis of Manaus has been celebrating the perfect synthesis of sport and sex in the guise of the *Peladão* Championship (*peladão* means roughly «a lot of kicking around») for more than three decades. Factor in the enjoyment of ice-cold cans of beer by all and sundry and the Holy Trinity of the muscle-bound macho male superiority complex that is Brazilian street culture materialises here. What is so special about the *Peladão*, which comprises some five hundred teams and fifteen thousand active fans in one of the world's biggest amateur championships, is that two contests take place in parallel: on the one hand, a football championship and on the other, a beauty contest. Each participating football team must propose a young lady, who for her part must compete on the catwalk for the title of Beauty Queen. The point is that the two contests do not take place independently of each other. On the contrary, a team that has already been eliminated on the pitch is readmitted to competition if their particular beauty queen happens to win the beauty contest.

The *Peladão* was originally started in 1973 as advertising for the posh daily in Manaus, A *Crítica*, but over the years it has developed a dynamic of its own which has seen the championship become a socially integrative event pervading even the most remote communities in the rain-forest state. The *Peladão* has become part of local festival tradition and through it the Mestizo *caboclo* culture of the Amazon basin, which is decried throughout the country as backwoods in the extreme, has grown increasingly self-confident. Meanwhile the heritage shared by immigrants from the north-east and the Indian inhabitants of the Amazon basin erupts annually in the *Boibumbá*, a folklore festival in the city of Parintins and a spectacle on a truly grand scale, which heads the ever-lengthening roll of local and regional festivals.

The *Peladão* is supra-regional and, as a mass event, has become a *puxirum*, as Indians and caboclos dub a collective or joint undertaking. Like all the other festivals in the Amazon Basin, this one, too, has a patron who throws it for his clientele while ensuring that festival ecstasy does not shake the pillars of his own particular establishment.

→ Die Schönheitskönigin der Männer-Fußballmannschaft kann für den Turniererfolg entscheidend sein. Manaus, 2005. The beauty queen of the men's football team can decide the outcome in the tournament. Manaus, 2005. © Photo: Sophie Brandström, Focus

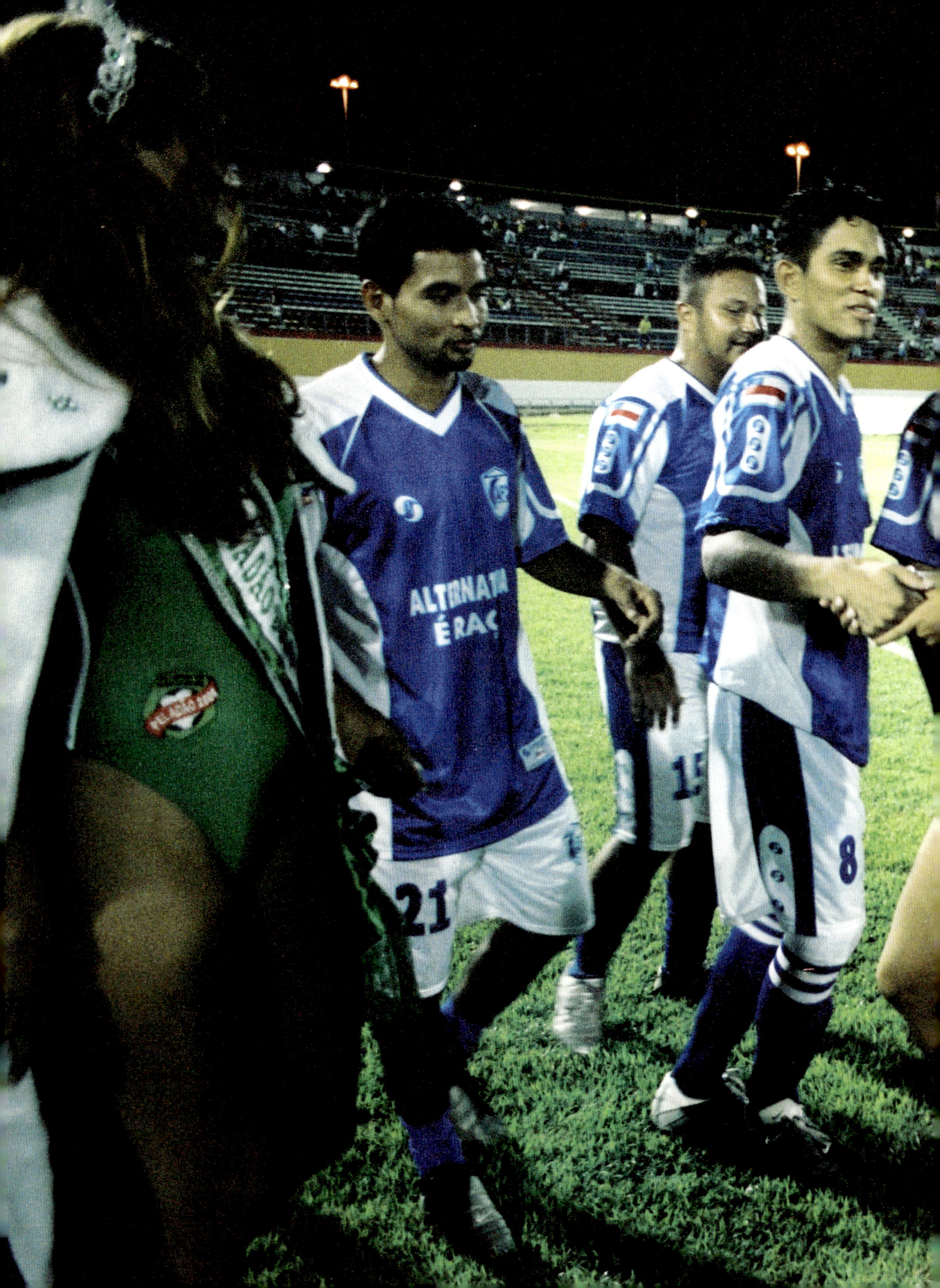

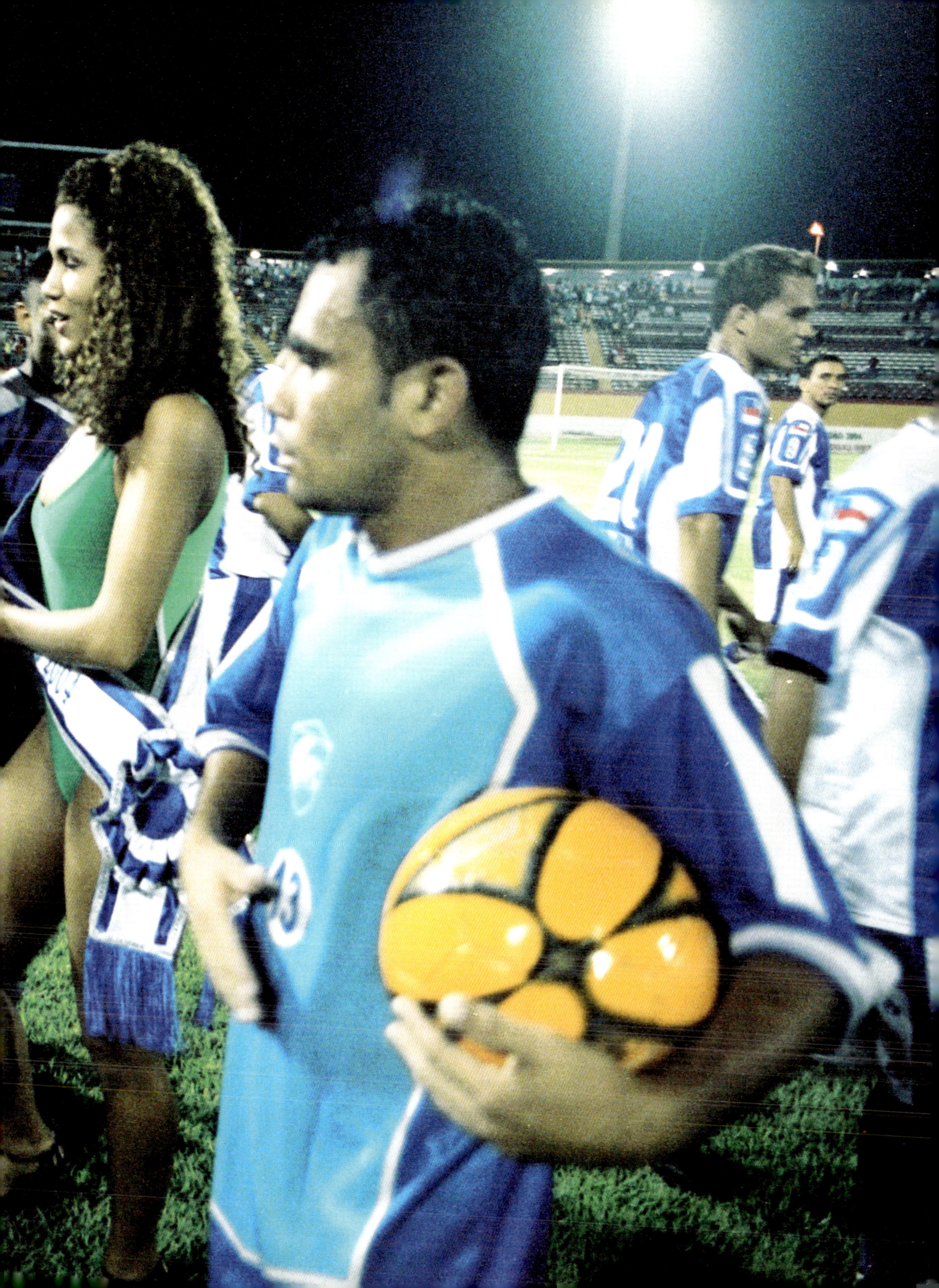

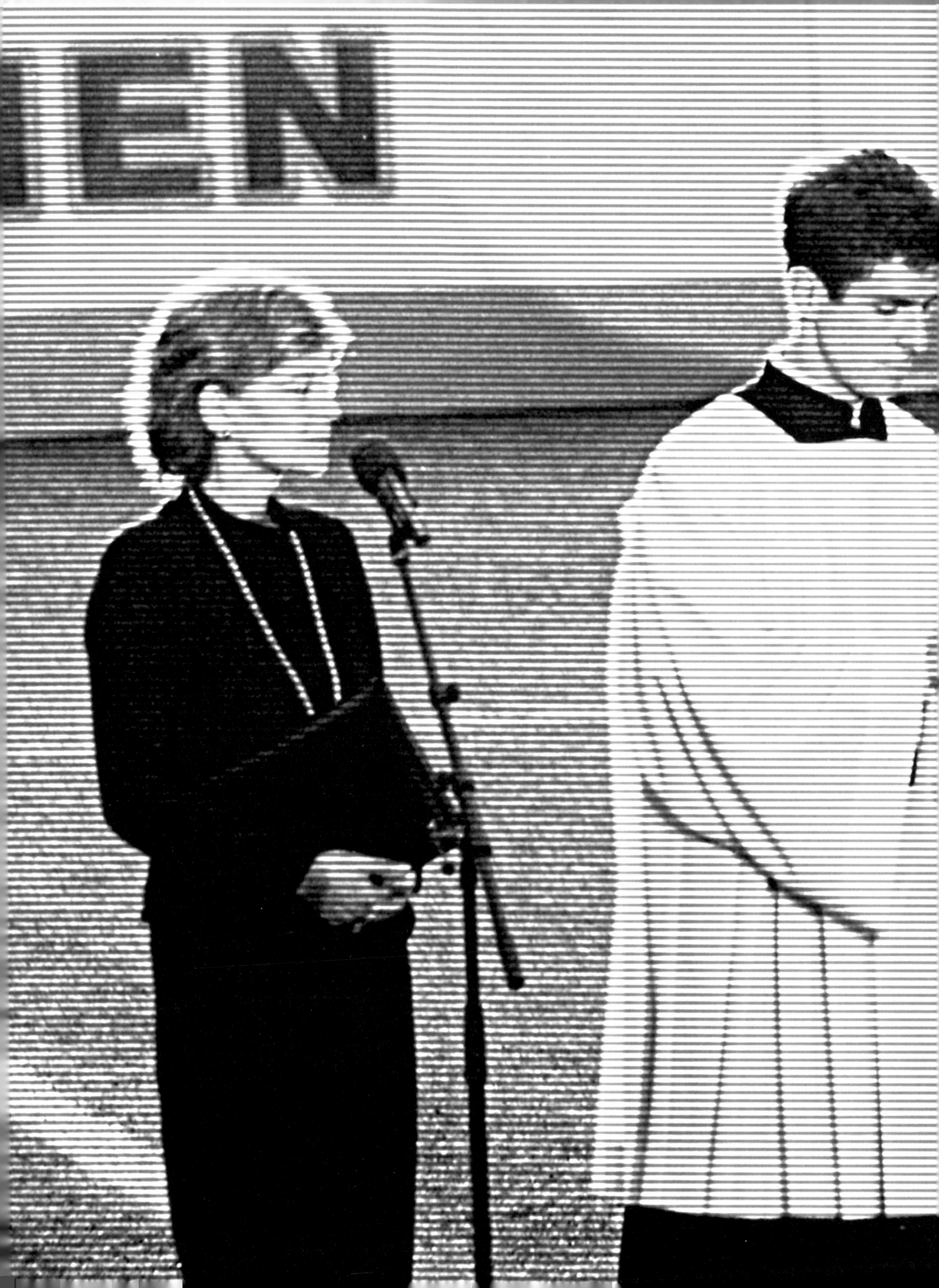
IEN

Ist Gott rund?

Is God Round?

Fußball als »Clash« der Weltbilder

Stefan Eisenhofer

Nicht nur die Welt an sich, sondern auch der Fußball wird an verschiedenen Orten, in verschiedenen Kulturen und durch verschiedene Herzen und Hirne unterschiedlich definiert, erfahren und erlebt. Überall auf der Welt besitzen Menschen andere Gewohnheiten und Selbstverständlichkeiten – und was dem einen unfraglich und gewiss ist, bleibt dem anderen unverständlich oder entlockt diesem sogar Kopfschütteln. Überall glaubt man an andere Götter, hegt für das Leben vor oder nach dem Tode unterschiedliche Erwartungen und Hoffnungen. Die Weltbilder besitzen andere Gesetzmäßigkeiten, ein unterschiedliches Aussehen und eine andere Logik. Von der westlichen Welt oft völlig unterschiedliche Wirklichkeiten durchdringen auch den Fußball.

Im Fußball spiegeln sich unterschiedliche Weltsichten vor allem darin, wie Siege herbeigeführt oder Niederlagen verhindert werden sollen. Denn in diesem Spiel, das wegen seiner zahllosen Unwägbarkeiten und Unsicherheiten nur schwer planbar und zu kontrollieren ist, reflektieren die Rituale und Handlungen vor, während und nach dem Spiel, unterschiedliche Auffassungen von den Fähigkeiten und Möglichkeiten des Menschen. Jeder versucht, Kontrolle über das Unkontrollierbare zu bekommen. Dies gilt insbesondere da, wo Fußball nicht nur Zeitvertreib, sondern Beruf und Broterwerb ist, wo sich an dieses Spiel existentielle Fragen knüpfen.

In technologieorientierten Gesellschaften stützt man sich bei der Lösung dieser Herausforderung auf wissenschaftliche und pseudowissenschaftliche Methoden, entwickelt exakte Trainingslehren und Ernährungspläne, sucht nach messbaren Kriterien zur Sicherstellung des Erfolgs, wechselt Trainer und Spieler. Ein kurioser Höhepunkt an Technologiegläubigkeit wurde in der alten Sowjetunion erreicht, wo mehr oder weniger fußballrelevante Daten in Computer eingespeist wurden und danach die Auswahl der Spieler erfolgte. Der Versuch, ein derart komplexes Spiel wie Fußball auf bestimmte festgelegte Faktoren zu reduzieren, erscheint nur bedingt rationaler als andere Riten, die sich um den Fußball ranken.

Was den einen ihre exakten Trainingspläne und Ernährungsvorschriften sind, sind den anderen die Kontaktaufnahmeversuche zu höheren Mächten und die Sicherung übermenschlichen Beistands. Es ist daher kein Zufall, dass in so ziemlich allen Religionen dieser Welt – von den großen Weltreligionen bis hin zu anderen religiösen Systemen – eine Verbindung mit dem Fußball existiert.

In vielen Teilen der Welt ähneln die Rituale, die sich um den Fußball ranken, jenen, die in Jäger- und Fischergesellschaften vor Jagdzügen durchgeführt werden, um den Lebensunterhalt zu sichern. Diese Riten sind ein menschlicher Versuch, Ordnung und Sicherheit in eine unsichere, beängstigende und chaotische Situation zu bringen. Und je unsicherer und wichtiger der Erfolg bei solchen Unternehmungen ist, desto größer sind die Anstrengungen, diesen Erfolg kalkulierbarer zu machen. Oftmals sind diese Riten irrational in dem Sinne, dass sie in keinem offensichtlichen kausalen Zusammenhang zu den erwünschten Ergebnissen

Football as the «Clash» of World-Views

Stefan Eisenhofer

Not just the world as such but football as well is variously defined, experienced and lived, depending on place, culture, hearts and minds. Throughout the world people have different customs and different things they take for granted – and what is to one person unquestionable and a certainty remains a mystery to others, even eliciting marked disapproval. People everywhere believe in different gods, entertain different expectations and hopes of life before and after death. World-views possess differing systems of rules, appearances and internal logic. Realities that often differ entirely from those prevailing in the West often pervade football as well.

In football, differing world-views are primarily reflected in the ways in which victories are won or defeat is to be prevented. After all, this is a game which is difficult to plan and control because it is so full of imponderables and uncertainties. As a result, its pre- and postgame rituals and acts reflect differing ideas of human capabilities and potential. Everyone tries to keep something uncontrollable under control. This is especially true when football is a profession and a livelihood and not just a leisure activity, where existential issues are linked with this game.

In technology-oriented societies, solutions to this challenge are based on scientific and pseudo-scientific methods, training becomes rigid dogma and nutrition plans are developed, quantifiable criteria for ensuring success are sought, trainers and players are traded off. A peculiar high point of faith in technology was attained in the former Soviet Union, where data that are more or less relevant to football were stored in databases, according to which players were selected. The attempt to reduce a game as complex as football to certain predetermined factors seems only slightly more rational, if at all, than other rituals entwined with football.

What precise training schedules and prescribed diets are for one society, attempts to curry favour with higher powers and ensuring divine benevolence are to another. Consequently, it is no coincidence that a link with football exists in virtually all the world's religions – from the major world religions to other religious systems.

In many places throughout the world, the rituals associated with football resemble those observed in hunter-gatherer societies before men set out to hunt or fish in order to secure their livelihoods. Rites of this kind are a human attempt to bring order and security into an insecure, frightening and chaotic situation. And the more insecure and important success in such undertakings is, the greater are the efforts made to ensure that the outcome is calculable. Such rites are irrational in the sense that they are not overtly causally linked with the desired outcome. They are, however, often rational in so far as they instil assurance and self-confidence in those observing them.

The standard kit of many players includes amulets and other unusually efficacious objects that are supposed to reinforce positive trends or ward off harm. Their range is a broad

Der Fußballplatz als »ritueller Grund«? – Vertreter der katholischen und der evangelischen Kirche bei der Einweihung der »Allianz-Arena« 2005 in München. The football pitch as «ritual ground»? – Representatives of the Catholic and Lutheran Protestant Churches at the 2005 inauguration of the «Allianz Arena» in Munich. ©Photo: Fred Joch

stehen. Sie sind aber sehr wohl oft rational darin, dass sie den Praktizierenden Zuversicht und Selbstbewusstsein verleihen.

Zum Standardrepertoire vieler Spieler gehören Amulette und andere außergewöhnlich wirksame Gegenstände, die Positives unterstützen oder vor Schädlichem schützen sollen. Sie umfassen eine große Bandbreite – von speziellen Unterhemden über Anhänger in Kreuzform bis hin zu Koransprüchen. Gemeinsam ist allen, dass durch sie übermenschliche Energien auf einzelne Spieler oder die gesamte Mannschaft übertragen werden sollen.

Viele mit dem Fußball verknüpfte Rituale entstammen der Vorstellungswelt der sympathetischen Magie. Wenn etwa Dinge eines Gegenspielers verbrannt und dann als Asche während des Spiels im Fußballschuh mitgetragen werden oder wenn symbolische Bestattungen des zukünftigen Gegners das erwünschte Ergebnis herbeiführen sollen, werden auf einer übermenschlichen Ebene Dinge vor-vollzogen, die sich dann im realen Leben erfüllen sollen.

In vielen Teilen der Welt werden die im Spiel verwendeten Gegenstände wie Bälle, Trikots, Fußballschuhe und Torwarthandschuhe keineswegs als neutrale Spielgeräte betrachtet, sondern als Dinge, die mit erfolgsbringender wie mit schädlicher Energie aufgeladen werden können. Auch das Spielfeld ist nicht einfach nur ein Stück Rasen, sondern ein Ort, der positiv wie negativ aufgeladen sein kann, der Sieg und Niederlage entscheidend beeinflussen kann. Entsprechendes gilt für Torpfosten und Spiellinien. Nicht nur in Brasilien werden Mannschaften daher oftmals außer von Trainern und Masseuren auch von rituellen Spezialisten betreut, die man als »spirituelle Platzwarte« bezeichnen könnte. Diese sollen von der Mannschaft Schädliches abwehren, Positives bewirken und gegebenenfalls auch den Gegner schädigen. Der Sieg einer Mannschaft über eine andere wird daher nicht selten als Erfolg der eigenen Ritualspezialisten über die der anderen verstanden. Entsprechendes gilt

Unterstützung von ganz oben? Eine 84-jährige Nonne trifft als Vorsitzende des Fanclubs des Vittoria Fußball-Clubs Vorbereitungen für ein bevorstehendes Spiel. Support from above? An eighty-four-year-old nun, head of the Vittoria Football Fan Club, preparing for a game. **Salvador da Bahia, Brasilien /** Brazil, 1998. ©Photo: Américo Mariano, Paris

↑ Hilfreicher als eine Trainerschelte? – In der Halbzeitpause platziert ein Fußballer seine Schuhe auf einem Altar, um die zweite Hälfte für sein Team erfolgreich werden zu lassen. More effective than a coach blasting off? – A player placing boots on an alter during half-time to guarantee a win. Salvador da Bahia, Brasilien / Brazil 1998. ©Photo: Américo Mariano, Paris

↓ Nicht nur das Ergebnis des Spiels im Stadion ist wichtig. Fans beim Africa Cup 2002. It isn't just the outcome in the stadium that matters: Fans at the 2002 Africa Cup. ©Photo: Américo Mariano, Paris

↳ Eine Fußballmannschaft genießt ihren Sieg unter dem »Letzten Abendmahl« und bedankt sich für die himmlische Unterstützung.
Last moments below the «Last Supper»: after the game the winning team relaxes and gives thanks for divine guidance. Juazeiro do Norte,
Ceara, Nordost-Brasilien / north-eastern Brazil 1998. © Photo: Américo Mariano, Paris

↳ Ballspielende Jungs in einem Vorort von Salvador da Bahia, der »Hauptstadt des afrikanischen Brasilien« und des Candomblé, einer
Kombination aus afrikanischen Religionen und Christentum. Boys playing ball in a suburb of Salvador da Bahia, the «capital of African Brazil»

Viele Fußballmannschaften dieser Welt versuchen, sich übermenschliche Kräfte nutzbar zu machen – wie hier durch einen Marabout in einem Vorort von Bamako, Mali. Many football teams recruit the support of supernatural powers – here through the intercession of a Marabout in a suburb of Bamako, Mali.

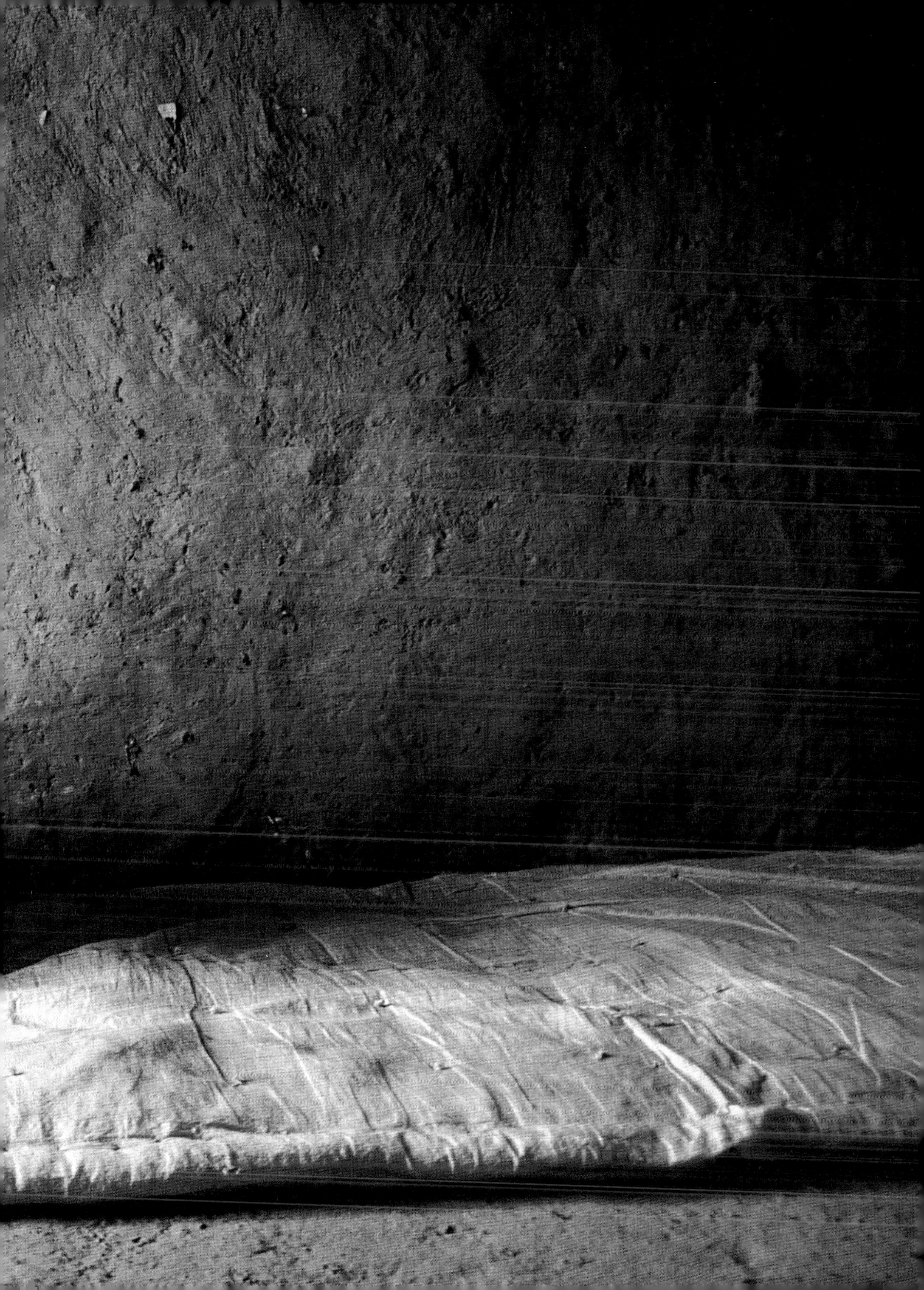

Trotz seiner schadenabwehrenden Amulette erlebt ein brasilianischer Fan fassungslos die Niederlage seines Teams gegen Frankreich bei der WM 1998. A stunned Brazilian supporter watches Brazil lose to France in the 1998 World

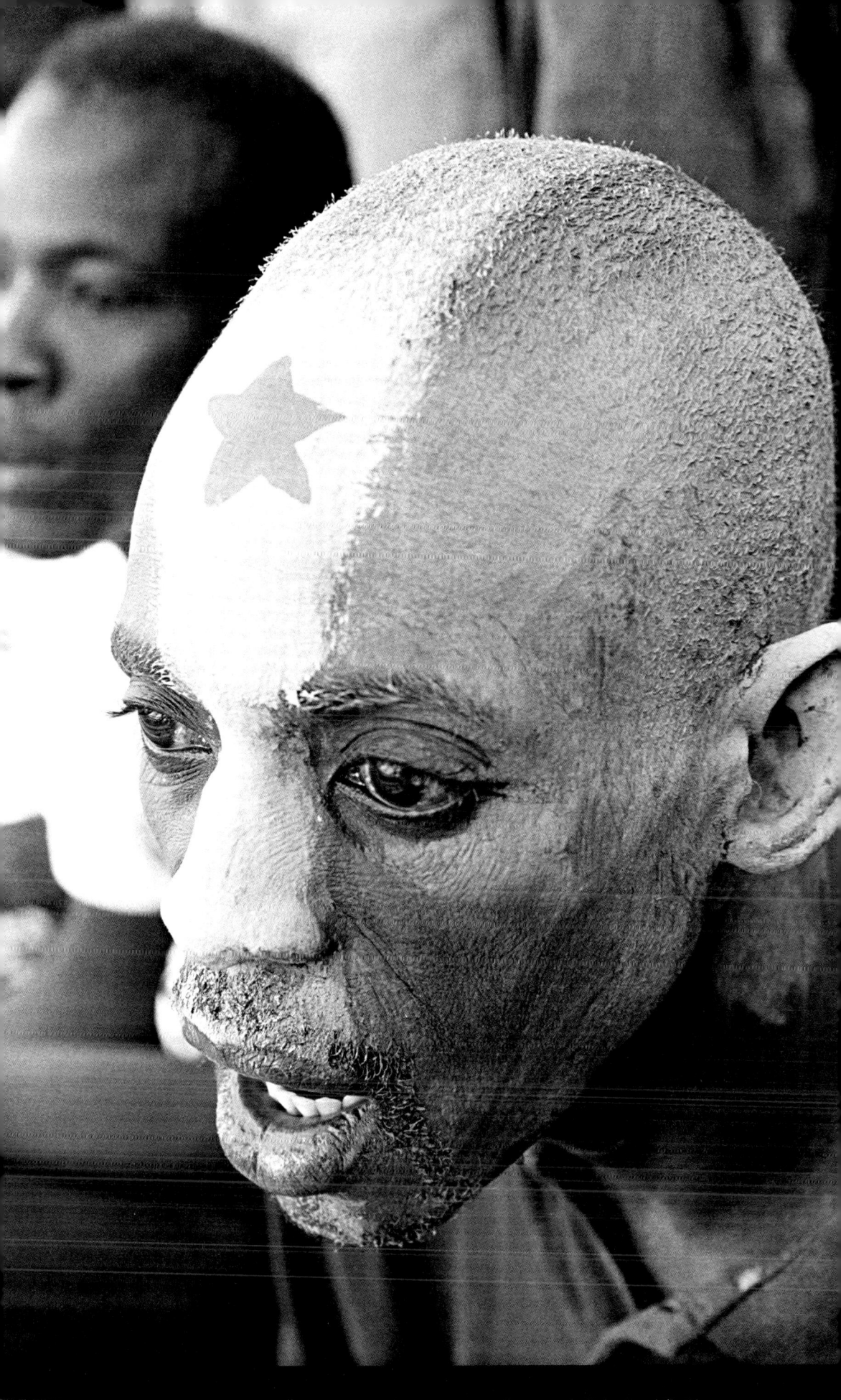

Ein besorgter Fan des senegalesischen Teams kurz vor der Niederlage gegen die Mannschaft der Republik Elfenbeinküste beim Africa-Cup 2002. An anxious Senegal supporter just before his team loses to Côte d'Ivoire in the 2002 Africa Cup, Bamako, Mali.

oyalität, sichtbar auf der Haut getragen: Ein senegalesischer Fan beim Africa-Cup 2002. Loyalty shows:

Fans von Sambia bei einer symbolischen Bestattung des Gegners Senegal vor dem Qualifikationsspiel für die FIFA WM 2006™. Senegal gewann das Spiel anschließend 1:0.
Zambian fans symbolically burying their opponent, Senegal, before the 2006 FIFA World Cup™ qualifying match, which Senegal won 1:0. Chililabombwe, Sambia / Zambia 2005.
© Photo: Mike Hutchings, Reuters/Corbis

one – from the special vest through crosses to be worn round the neck to sayings from the Koran. What they all have in common is that through them superhuman energies are supposed to be transferred to individual players or an entire team.

Many of the rituals associated with football derive from the imaginative realm of sympathetic magic. Whenever things belonging to a player from an opposing team are burnt and then carried during a game in a player's football boot or if symbolic burials of a future adversary are supposed to bring about the desired outcome, things are being predetermined on a superhuman plane which are then expected to come true in real life.

In many parts of the world objects used during a game such as balls, jerseys, boots and goalkeeper's gloves are not regarded as neutral football gear but instead as things that can be charged with energies that can bring about either success or harm. Nor is the pitch merely a field of turf. Instead it is a place that can be charged positively or negatively, which can have a crucial bearing on victory or defeat. The same holds for the goalposts and the halfway, touch and goal lines. It is not just in Brazil, therefore, that teams are often accompanied by specialists in rituals, who might be termed «spiritual groundsmen» as well as trainers and massage experts. These supernumeraries are supposed to ward off harm from the team, to have a positive effect and, in some cases, even to harm the team's adversaries. The victory of one team over another is, therefore, quite frequently viewed as the success of one specialist in rituals against another. The same goes for unsuccessful saves by goalkeepers or the defence or particularly spectacular goals made by forwards.

The rites associated with football are often highly complex, quite often take fairly long to perform and exact strictest observance of what is prescribed from those performing them. It is not just articles of clothing which are linked with success or failure but even the

Rituelle Erhöhung des Spielfeldes oder einfach nur kurioses Erinnerungsstück? Ein Stück des Rasens – in Kunstharz eingegossen –, auf dem Deutschland in Rom im Jahr 1990 Fußball-Weltmeister wurde. Ritual enhancement of a pitch or just a peculiar memento? A piece of the turf – set in hardened acrylic resin – on which Germany won the 1990 World Cup in Rome.

Schlüsselanhänger-Amulett eines Fußballfans aus Marokko mit Koranversen. A keyring amulet with verses from the Koran owned by a Moroccan football fan.

bei gravierenden Fehlern von Torhütern oder Verteidigern oder besonders herausragenden Toren von Stürmern.

Die Riten, die sich um das Fußballspiel ranken, sind oft sehr komplex, ziehen sich nicht selten über längere Zeiträume hin und erfordern das genaueste Einhalten von Vorschriften. Dabei sind es nicht nur die Kleidungsstücke selbst, die mit Erfolg und Misserfolg verknüpft werden, sondern auch die Reihenfolge des Ankleidens. Zudem trifft man immer wieder auf regelrechte Kleidungs-Tabus: Niederlagen-Trikots werden nicht mehr angezogen, bestimmte Rückennummern werden vermieden, Sieger-Trikots dürfen nicht gewaschen werden. Auch bestehen zahlreiche Regeln bezüglich Ernährung und Geschlechtsverkehr vor dem Spiel sowie dem Betreten von Umkleidekabine und Spielfeld.

Im Fußball zeigt sich auch, wie unterschiedlich der Zugang zu Heiligen und übermenschlichen Mächten sein kann. Das Spektrum reicht vom demütigen Bitten über das genaue Befolgen von Riten bis hin zu drohenden Forderungen. Tatsächlich trifft man nicht nur auf Dankesrituale nach Siegen, sondern auch auf Strafrituale nach Niederlagen, wenn etwa San Pancracio nach unerwünschten Ergebnissen als Heiligenfigur für einige Zeit in den Kühlschrank gesperrt wird.

Freilich geht es bei den Riten rund um den Fußball keineswegs immer ausschließlich um Sieg und Niederlage. Ebenso häufig wird Verletzungsfreiheit erbeten oder auch, dass man anderen keinen körperlichen Schaden zufügt. Und viele bringen einfach nur ihren Dank zum Ausdruck, dass sie mit Hilfe der entsprechenden überirdischen Macht durch den Fußball der Armut entfliehen konnten.

order in which they are donned. In addition, regular kit taboos are frequently encountered: jerseys worn at a lost game are never worn again, certain numbers on the back are eschewed as unlucky, jerseys worn by members of a victorious team must not be washed. Further, there are numerous rules governing diet and sex before games as well as stepping into the changing-room and on to the pitch.

How much invoking saints and superhuman powers can differ is also revealed in football. The gamut ranges from humble supplication through precise performance of rituals to demands uttered as threats. In fact, both punitive rituals after defeats and thanksgiving rituals after victories are encountered, for example when a figurine of San Pancracio (St Pancras) is consigned to cold storage in the fridge for a while after a lousy performance at a game.

Of course rituals are connected with all aspects of football and not just victory and defeat. Freedom from injury is often prayed for or even that one may not do physical harm to others. And many a player simply expresses his gratitude for having been able to flee poverty through football with the aid of the superhuman power invoked.

Nach dem Sieg des Außenseiters Nordkorea über den haushohen Favoriten Italien während der Weltmeisterschaft 1966 stand Ginseng als »mysteriöse Wurzeldroge« einige Zeit wie ein Dopingmittel auf der Liste verbotener Substanzen. After the victory won by outsider North Korea over Italy, the hands-on favourite, during the 1966 World Cup, ginseng featured for a while as a «mysterious root drug» on the list of prohibited substances.

Valery Lobanowsky hat als Trainer des ukrainischen Topclubs Dynamo Kiew und als herausragender Vertreter eines »wissenschaftlich-systematischen Fußballs« über Jahrzehnte den europäischen Fußball mitgeprägt. Valery Lobanovsky, the coach of the Ukrainian premiership club Dynamo Kiev and a distinguished representative of «scientific-systematic football», exerted a strong influence on European football for decades.

Fußball in Japan
Zwischen »Gehorsam« und Subkultur

Patricia Müller

In einem Interview mit der *Zeit* behauptete der Pekinger Amateurfußballer Cheng Fanglin: »Stars wie Ronaldinho und Zidane wird es in Ostasien nicht geben. Unsere Profis lernen früh, sich in der Mannschaft einzufügen. Ihr Individualismus wird nicht gefördert.« Realität oder Klischee? Ein Blick nach Japan soll Aufschluss geben:

Noch bis Ende der 1970er Jahre wurde Sport in Japan als Erziehungsinstrument und Bühne zur Präsentation nationaler Erfolge betrachtet. Spätestens seit dem aufkeimenden Olympiagedanken um 1920 diente auch der damals noch eng an die Bildungsstätten geknüpfte Fußball verstärkt als Medium zur Disziplinierung und Erzeugung von Loyalität gegenüber Schule, Universität, Staat und Firma. Diese Werte harmonierten gut mit der konfuzianischen Lehre, eine die Gesellschaft strukturierende Moralphilosophie, die bis heute den sozialen Umgang in ostasiatischen Staaten prägt. In den 1960ern gesellten sich im Namen des wirtschaftlichen Aufschwungs und Innovationsstrebens noch drei weitere Aspekte hinzu: technische Perfektionierung, Flexibilität und Stärkung des Kampfgeists. Vor allem das im Fußball geforderte blitzschnelle Umschalten von Abwehr auf Angriff oder rasante Sprints sollten entsprechend geschult werden, da man glaubte, durch diese Fähigkeiten den Anschluss an »moderne« Nationen leichter und schneller bewältigen zu können. Sowohl in Bildungseinrichtungen als auch in der 1921 eingeführten Nationalliga lautete das Motto *ganbaru* – »nicht aufgeben«.

Als sich in den 1970ern zeitweise eine wirtschaftliche Rezession anbahnte und klar war, dass das Konzept des »zur Hochleistung getrimmten Körpers im Dienste des Fortschritts« nicht zu den erhofften Erfolgen führen würde, kam es unter Japans Studentenschaft zu Protesten: Nicht länger gewillt, sich dem Diktat des strikten Gehorsams zu unterwerfen, forderten die Studierenden Reformen in der Sporterziehung, die zwischen 1978 und 1988 teilweise umgesetzt wurden: Zum ersten Mal sprach man in Japan von »Spaß an der körperlichen Ertüchtigung«. Die Wende bedeutete eine abrupte Freisetzung der lange unter Verschluss gehaltenen Emotionen. Insbesondere der Fußball, den man fortan als autonomen Lifestyle betrachtete, fand nun immer mehr AnhängerInnen unter der Jugend.

Zwar sucht man in Japan auch heute noch vergebens nach bolzenden Straßenfußballern, aber spätestens seit 1998, als sich die »Blue Samurai« erstmals für eine Weltmeisterschaft qualifiziert hatten, grassiert unter Nippons Jugend das »Blaufieber«. Der steigende Zuspruch hängt auch damit zusammen, dass Fußball in Japan für Internationalität und Individualität steht: Seit Anbeginn prägten Sportler und Trainer aus verschiedenen Ländern – von Dettmar Cramer über Littbarski bis Zico – die einheimische Szene. Exzentrische Fußballhelden wie die britische Pop- und Stilikone David Beckham avancierten im Lande des »gehorsamen Körpers« schnell zu Symbolen für Freiheit und Selbstbestimmung. Immer

Hidetoshi Nakata – Die Verkörperung des Traums vieler junger Japaner von einer internationalen Karriere. Hidetoshi Nakata embodies the dreams many young Japanese have of an international career. Japanische Fußball-Zeitung / *Japanese Football Magazine*, 2005.

Der japanische Fußballstar Mioto – verewigt als goldbemalte Mini-Plastikfigur. Mioto, the Japanese football star – immortalised as a gilded plastic miniature figurine.

Football in Japan
Between «Obedience» and Subculture

Patricia Müller

In an interview with the German weekly *Die Zeit*, Cheng Fanglin, an amateur football player from Beijing, maintained: «There'll never be stars like Ronaldinho and Zidane in East Asia. Our pro footballers learn early on to fit into the team. Individualism is not encouraged.» Reality or cliché? A look at Japan is informative.

Until the late 1970s sport in Japan was regarded as an instrument of education and a stage for showcasing national successes. At the latest since the Olympic ideal had burgeoned in 1920, football, which was then still closely tied to educational institutions, began to grow into a medium for discipline and inculcating loyalty to school, university, state and company. These values were easy to reconcile with Confucian doctrine, a moral philosophy

mehr japanische Spieler wie Hidetoshi Nakata, Shinji Ono oder Jun'ichi Inamoto fanden ihren Weg in westliche Vereine.

Einige der Kicker mit internationaler Erfahrung, allen voran Nakata, der »japanische Beckham«, wurden sogar zu Identifikationsfiguren des Anti-Establishments. Der Mittelfeldspieler ist einer von nur zwei Asiaten in Pelés »Top 100« der größten noch lebenden Fußballer. Der Profi des italienischen Erstligisten AC Florenz wird in seiner Heimat wie ein Popstar verehrt. In seiner Fernsehserie Nakata.net-TV empfängt er ebenso berühmte wie »eigenwillige« Gäste, in Tokios Innenstadt betreibt er sein chices Nakata.net.Café und mit seinen extravaganten, im Monats-Rhythmus *à la* Beckham wechselnden Frisuren irritiert der Individualist Trainer und Teamkollegen.

Scharfe Zungen der japanischen Gesellschaft betrachten Fußball deshalb als Sport der Unangepassten und Außenseiter. Ein Sprecher des Tokioter Finanzministeriums formulierte es dagegen etwas vorsichtiger: »Das Land wäre nicht reif für einen Regierungschef vom Typ Nakata. Nakata trifft seine Entscheidungen auf dem Spielfeld selbstständig und verantwortet sowohl Sieg als auch Niederlage. Unsere PolitikerInnen handeln dagegen auf Anweisung von Interessensgruppen.« Doch ein Typ wie Nakata mit vielen jugendlichen AnhängerInnen scheint einer der größten Wirtschaftsnationen der Welt, die seit etlichen Jahren in der Wachstumsflaute dümpelt, gut zu tun: Sie braucht, um Reformen auch von unten durchzusetzen, das lose Miteinander einer freien Bürgerschaft, wie sie sich im Fußball ansatzweise konstituiert.

Und für viele JapanerInnen unter 30 definiert sich Fußball, die letzte Nische außerhalb des Einflussbereichs der Firma, tatsächlich als sportlicher Weg, dem von ihnen als bedrückend empfundenen Konformismus in Schule, Universität und Beruf zu entfliehen. So begibt sich mancher Junge oder manches »Girlie« zumindest in seinen Träumen auf die Spuren kickender Comicfiguren à la Captain Tsubasa, die in bunten Manga-Heftchen ihrer Heimat den Rücken kehren, um im »freien« Europa ein unabhängiges Leben als Fußballstar zu beginnen.

Auch die alternative (Sub-)Kulturszene lässt sich vom Fußball mitreißen: Jugend-Bands aus den japanischen Grunge- und Punk-Reihen mixen Underground mit Soccer-Manie: So erschien vor einigen Jahren eine schräge Single mit dem Titel *Come on United,* auf der die vier jungen Untergrund-Punker Ki-Chan, Pooly, Kazu und Mu alias The Hat Trickers ausgerechnet einem der Global Players des Fußballkapitalismus – nämlich ManU – huldigten.

Fazit: Es gibt sie doch, die Individualisten und Popikonen rund um den japanischen Fußball. Nippons Soccer ist auf dem besten Weg, das zu schaffen, was zuvor kaum eine politische Bewegung in Japan vermochte: ein Solidaritätsgefühl jenseits des sozialen Mehrheitsempfindens ohne weitergehende Pflichten.

that purported to structure society and down to the present day informs social conduct in East Asian countries. In the 1960s three further aspects were added to promote the economic upswing and striving for innovation: technical perfection, flexibility and strengthening morale. The lightning switch from defence to offence and fast running required in football were to be schooled since the belief prevailed that these capabilities would make it easier to catch up with «modern» countries more quickly. At educational institutions as well as the National League introduced in 1921 the motto was *ganbaru* – «Don't give up».

When a recession dawned during the 1970s and it became clear that the concept of the «body drilled to body achievement in the service of progress» would not lead to the desired success, Japanese students began to voice protests. No longer willing to subject themselves to the dictates of reflexive obedience, students demanded reforms in physical education, some of which were actually implemented between 1978 and 1988. For the first time in Japan, there was talk of «physical training being fun». The turnaround entailed the abrupt release of emotions long throttled. Football in particular, which from then on was regarded as a lifestyle in its own right, attracted a growing throng of youthful aficionados of both sexes.

Die Raumknappheit in Japan spiegelt sich auch in den Bolzplätzen: Fußballfeld auf einem Hausdach in Tokio. The lack of space in Japan is also reflected in the places people find to kick a ball around: pitch on the roof of a Tokyo house. © Photo: Stefan Seifert, Chemnitz

Zwei der populärsten Phänomene im aktuellen Japan – Fußball und Manga – verbinden sich in der Serie »Captain Tsubasa« zum illustrierten Traum von einem unabhängigen Leben im »freien Europa« als Fußballstar. Two of the most popular cultural phenomena in Japan today – football and Manga – are linked in the «Captain Tsubasa» series illustrating the dream of an independent life as a football star in «free Europe».

Of course even today you would look in vain in Japan for kids kicking balls in the streets. However, at the latest since 1998, when the «Blue Samurai» qualified for the first time for the World Cup, «blue fever» has been rampant among young Japanese. The growing prospects of the game there are also related to the circumstance that football stands for internationalism and individuality in Japan. From the outset Japanese players and trainers – from Dettmar Cramer through Littbarski to Zico – from many different countries have shaped the Japanese football scene. Eccentric football heroes such as the British pop and style icon David Beckham were quick to advance to the status of symbols of freedom and self-determination in the «land of the obedient body». A growing number of Japanese players such as Hidetoshi Nakata, Shinji Ono and Jun'ichi Inamoto found their way to Western teams.

Some of these kickers with international experience, headed by Nakata, the «Japanese Beckham», even became counterculture identity figures. A midfield player, Nakata is one of only two Asians in Pelé's «Top 100», the roll of living football greats. Now with first league AC Florence, Nakata is venerated in his home country like a pop star. He welcomes guests who are as «eccentric» as they are celebrated to his TV series Nakata.net-TV. In downtown Tokyo he runs the chic Nakata.net.Café. An individualist to the core, he irritates both his trainer and fellow team members with extravagant hair styles that change monthly *à la* Beckham.

That all goes to explain why sharp-tongued members of Japanese high society regard football as the sport of misfits and outsiders. A speaker for the Tokyo Ministry of Finance, on the other hand, was more cautious in the way he put it: «The country is not ready for a premier like Nakata. Nakata takes all his decisions on the pitch independently and holds himself accountable for both victories and defeats. Our politicians, both men and women, however, act according to the instructions issued to them by the lobbies.» Yet a type like Nakata, with his hordes of youthful male and female fans, seems to be doing good to one of the world's great economies, which for some years has been caught up in the doldrums of stagnation and deflation. To effect reforms from the bottom up and not just from top down, it needs the casual ad hoc arrangements made by a free citizenry which are beginning to show up in football.

And for many Japanese men and women under thirty football is defined as the last niche outside the company's sphere of influence, in fact an athletic way of fleeing the conformity so many of them found so oppressive at school, university and on the job. So many a boy or «girlie» is beginning, at least in their dreams, to follow kicking comic figures such as Captain Tsubasa, in turning their backs on their country in lively Mangas to embark on an independent life in «free» Europe.

The counter-(sub)culture scene is also enthralled with football. Youth gangs from the ranks of Japanese grunge and punk blend underground music with soccer mania. Some years ago a bizarre single entitled *Come on United* was launched, in which the four young underground Punkers Ki-Chan, Pooly, Kazu and Mu alias The Hat Trickers pay tribute to, of all things, a team of Global Players – ManU.

In brief, they do exist: Japanese football has plenty of individualists and pop icons. Japanese soccer is well on the way to creating what no political movement in Japan has hitherto managed to produce: a feeling of solidarity transcending majority thinking without further obligations.

Die Jungfrau von Guadalupe
Religiöse Bekenntnisse rund um den Fußball

Sinahí Venegas

Ein bis heute unvergessenes Ereignis in Mexiko ist das Eröffnungsspiel der dortigen Fußballsaison 1994/95: Die Sportler trugen vor dem Spiel ein großes Abbild der heiligen Jungfrau von Guadalupe – *La Virgen de Guadalupe* – in das Azteken-Stadion von Mexiko-Stadt. Das, was in weiten Teilen Europas gegenwärtig zu Debatten und sogar Verboten führt, ist in Gesellschaften, in denen der Alltag stark von Religiösem durchdrungen ist, eine Selbstverständlichkeit: Religiöse Bekenntnisse in den öffentlichen Raum Fußballstadion zu tragen.

So ist im mexikanischen Fußball die Jungfrau von Guadalupe eine der wichtigsten Figuren. Viele Spieler tragen während des Spiels Unterhemden mit ihrem Abbild und zeigen dies nach einem Tor, wodurch sie der *Virgen* nicht nur ihre Verehrung erweisen, sondern sich auch für sportlichen Erfolg und Verletzungsfreiheit bedanken. Einige Fans erbitten bei der »Brünetten« – wie sie auch liebevoll genannt wird – zudem Erfolg für ihren Verein oder ihren Lieblingsspieler. So werden etwa Bilder oder Figuren wichtiger Fußballspieler auf die zahlreichen Altäre der Jungfrau gelegt, die sich nicht nur in Kirchen, sondern auch an einigen Trainingsplätzen und Stadien befinden.

The Virgin of Guadalupe
Professing Religion in Football

Sinahí Venegas

An event that has never been forgotten in Mexico is the first game of the 1994/95 football season: before the match the players carried a large image of the Virgin of Guadalupe – *La Virgen de Guadalupe* – into Aztec Stadium in Mexico City.
What has led to controversy and even bans in large parts of Europe is a matter of course in societies in which everyday living is still imbued with religiosity: professing religion overtly in public spaces like football stadiums.
Not surprisingly, the Virgin of Guadalupe figures prominently in Mexican football. During games many players wear vests with a picture of her on them and show them after a goal to demonstrate their veneration for the *Virgen* and to give thanks to her for granting them success in the game and safeguarding them from injury. Fans, too, supplicate the «brunette» – a nickname for her – for success for their club and favourite players. Pictures or figurines of important players are placed on the many Lady altars in churches and the altars consecrated to the Virgin at training grounds and stadiums.

Eine der wichtigsten Figuren im mexikanischen Fußball: Die Jungfrau von Guadalupe. A leading light in Mexican football: the Virgin of Guadalupe. Altarnachbau / Altar reconstruction: Sinahí Venegas und / and Münchner Stadtmuseum.

Videostills aus dem dokumentarischen Kurzfilm »Coupe des Lebbé – Fußball in Togo« von Boris Tomschiczek, Togo 2000. Video stills from the short documentary film «Coupe des Lebbé» – Fußball in Togo by Boris Tomschiczek, Togo, 2000.

Unvermeidbare Siege

Stefan Eisenhofer

Nicht alle Rituale vor Fußballspielen dienen dem unbedingten Herbeizwingen von Siegen und dem Vermeiden von Niederlagen. Bisweilen wird der Ritualspezialist – wie hier im westafrikanischen Togo – von den Spielern vor dem Spiel befragt, wie das Spiel ausgehen wird. Der Ritualexperte nimmt mittels einer kleinen Holzfigur Kontakt zur übermenschlichen Welt auf und offenbart die in unsichtbaren Sphären bereits feststehenden Wirklichkeiten. Dahinter steckt die Vorstellung, dass die Abläufe und Ordnungen in der außermenschlichen Welt bereits existieren und sich in der Folge lediglich in der sichtbaren Welt – hier auf dem Spielfeld – manifestieren. Bereits vor dem Spiel ist also festgeschrieben, welches Ergebnis zustande kommen wird. Aus einer westlichen Sicht betrachtet wirken solche Rituale insofern in die Zukunft, als sie in der Wahrnehmung und im Glauben und somit in der Psyche und im Selbstbewusstsein der Spieler bestimmte Grundbedingungen und Möglichkeiten schaffen. Die Spieler beider Mannschaften verhalten sich gemäß der vom Ritualspezialisten vorformulierten Rolle und passen sich den Erwartungen des Systems an. Sie fügen sich in die vorgesehenen Strukturen und Positionen ein. Das Spielergebnis bewahrheitet sich schließlich als *self-fulfilling prophecy* – als »sich selbst erfüllende Prophezeiung«: Das Spiel endet wie vorhergesagt und vorherbestimmt.

Inevitable Victories

Stefan Eisenhofer

Not every ritual that takes place before a football match is intended to ensure victories and prevent defeat. Occasionally, a specialist in rituals – as here in Togo in West Africa – is asked before a game what the outcome will be. Using a small wooden figure, the expert contacts the other world and reveals realities predetermined in spheres invisible to us. The idea behind this is that events and arrangements pre-exist in the extraterrestrial sphere and simply become manifest in the visible world – in the present instance on the football pitch. Even before the game is played the outcome has, therefore, been pre-determined. Viewed from the European standpoint, such rituals seem to have a bearing on the future in so far as they create particular conditions and possibilities in the perception and beliefs, that is, in the psyche and consciousness, of the players concerned. The players of both teams behave according to the role formulated in advance by the specialist in rituals and conform to the expectations of the system. In so doing, they fit into prescribed structures and positions. Finally, the outcome of the game reveals itself as a self-fulfilling prophecy: the game ends as predicted and predetermined.

San Pancracio – der Heilige im Kühlschrank
Fußballkultur und Heiligenkult in Südspanien

Natalie Göltenboth

Auf einer Kommode zwischen angezündeten Kerzen und frischen Petersilienbüscheln steht der Heilige San Pancracio, auf dem erhobenen Finger das obligatorische 25-Pesetenstück. Der erklärter Zuständigkeitsbereich des Heiligen ist die Lotterie und im weitesten Sinne all jene Ereignisse, die mit den Freuden des Gewinnens und den Enttäuschungen des Verlierens einhergehen, also auch die Siege und Niederlagen der Fußballmannschaften.
So beschwören die Fans ihren übernatürlichen Helfer in Sachen Sieg indem sie Kerzen und andere Opfergaben für ihn bereitstellen.
Der Legende nach stammt San Pancracio aus der heutigen Türkei. Im Jahre 287 n. Chr. wurde er als christlicher Märtyrer unter Kaiser Diokletian in Rom geköpft. Heute floriert der Kult um den wundertätigen Heiligen vor allem in den Städten Andalusiens, wo er in kürzester Zeit die Grenze des kirchlichen Bereichs überschritten, und Einzug in Haushalte, Läden und Bars gehalten hat. Man braucht San Pancracio weil man nicht ohne ihn leben kann – so die Gläubigen –, denn der Heilige bringt nicht nur Glück und Fußballsiege, sondern auch Gesundheit und Wohlstand ins Haus. Doch um seine wundertätigen Kräfte voll zur Entfaltung zu bringen bedarf es zuweilen auch härterer Maßnahmen. Hilft kein Bitten und kein Beten, muss San Pancracio in den Kühlschrank oder gar ins Gefrierfach bis er willig wird.

San Pancracio – A Saint in the Fridge
Football Culture and a Devotional Cult in Southern Spain

Natalie Göltenboth

San Pancracio, or St Pancras, stands on a chest of drawers between lit candles and bunches of fresh parsley, the compulsory twenty-five peseta piece balanced on a raised finger. He is, as everyone knows, the patron saint of the lottery and, in the broadest sense, watches over all events accompanied by delight in winning and disappointment in losing, which includes the victories won and the defeats suffered by football teams. Unsurprisingly, fans invoke the intercession of the saint to ensure victory by lighting candles to him and propitiating him with votive offerings.
As the legend goes, St Pancras came from what is now Turkey. He was beheaded as a Christian martyr in Rome during the reign of Diocletian in 287 AD. Nowadays the cult of this miracle-performing saint flourishes particularly in the cities of Andalucia, where he soon transcended the ecclesiastical sphere to enter households, shops and bars. St Pancras is needed because you cannot live without him – thus the devout – since the saint not only brings good luck and football victories but also health and wealth to households. However, more stringent measures are occasionally called for to exploit his miraculous powers to the full. If supplication and prayers have been to no avail, San Pancracio must remain shut in the fridge or even the freezer until he unbends.

Strafritus wegen abgewiesener Fürbitten: Eine Figur von San Pancracio in einem spanischen Kühlschrank.
Punitive rite because supplication fell on deaf ears: a San Pancracio figure consigned to a Spanish fridge.
Nachbau / Reconstruction: Münchner Stadtmuseum, Anikó Szalay, Natalie Göltenboth.

Fußball-Schrein-Fieber in Japan

Patricia Müller

Seit Jahren schleppen FußballerInnen und Fans Opfergaben zum legendären Shiramine Shinto-Schrein in Kyoto, um Seidaimyojin, den Gott der Ballspiele, um sportlichen Erfolg zu bitten. Ursprünglich wurde Seidaimyojin als Gottheit des aus China importierten traditionellen Kemari-Ballspiels verehrt, das von Hofadligen während der Heian-Zeit (794–1185) praktiziert wurde. Doch infolge der steigenden Popularität moderner Sportarten entwickelte sich Seidaimyojin zum *Kami* aller Ballspiele und – seit Japans erster WM-Teilnahme 1998 – vor allem auch zum Soccer-Gott. Laternen, Holztafeln oder Sake-Flaschen mit Gebeten und Wünschen vermischen sich mit Wimpeln und Logos von Kawasaki Verdy und Yokohama FC. Täglich lockt der Schrein kickende Schulkinder und Fußball-Profis aus ganz Japan an, die auf diese Weise den Sieg auf dem Sportfeld sichern oder sich dafür bedanken wollen. So berichtet einer der Shinto-Priester von Shiramine, dass sich die japanische Nationalmannschaft bei Seidaimyojin aus Dank für ihre erste WM-Teilnahme mit einem Beutel voller Fußbälle und France 98-Logos erkenntlich gezeigt hat. Und im Zuge der WM 2002 wurden sogar weitere kleine Soccer-Schreine, in denen Seidaimyojin durch einen Fußball repräsentiert wird, in Sportmuseen und Privathäusern installiert.

Soccer und Kult im HighTech-Land – ein Widerspruch? Nicht für die Japaner, zeigt sich hier doch einmal mehr ihre spezifische Fähigkeit, »Fremdes« mit »Eigenem« bzw. Modernes mit Traditionellem zu verschmelzen und auf diese Weise Neues entstehen zu lassen.

Football Shrine Mania in Japan

Patricia Müller

For years men and women football players and fans have been bearing votive offerings to the legendary Shiramine Shinto shrine in Kyoto to propitiate Seidaimyojin, Goddess of ball games, so that she will make them win. Seidaimyojin was originally venerated as the deity of Kemari, a ball game imported from China and played at court during the Heian period (794–1185). However, along with the growing popularity of modern sports, Seidaimyojin has evolved into the *Kami* of all ball games and – since Japan first reached the World Cup finals in 1998 – in particular the goddess of «soccer». Lanterns, wooden plaques and bottles of sake inscribed with prayers and wishes rub shoulders with the banners and crests of Kawasaki Verdy and Yokohama FC. Every day the shrine attracts hordes of football-playing school children as well as professional footballers from all over Japan, who are hoping in this way to ensure victory on the pitch or want to express their gratitude for winning. A Shinto priest at Shiramine recalls that the Japanese national team showed their gratitude to Seidaimyojin for reaching the World Cup finals the first time by taking a sack full of footballs and France 98 logos to the shrine. And during the 2002 World Cup matches little soccer shrines featuring Seidaimyojin represented as a football were even set up in sport museums and homes.

Soccer and a full-blown cult in the land of high-tech – a contradiction in terms? Not as the Japanese see it. This is just one more example of their distinctive ability to fuse «foreign» and «domestic» or modern and traditional to create something entirely new.

Ein dem Gott der Ballspiele gewidmeter Fußball-Shinto-Schrein, Japan, 2006. A Shinto football shrine dedicated to the god of ball games, Japan, 2006.

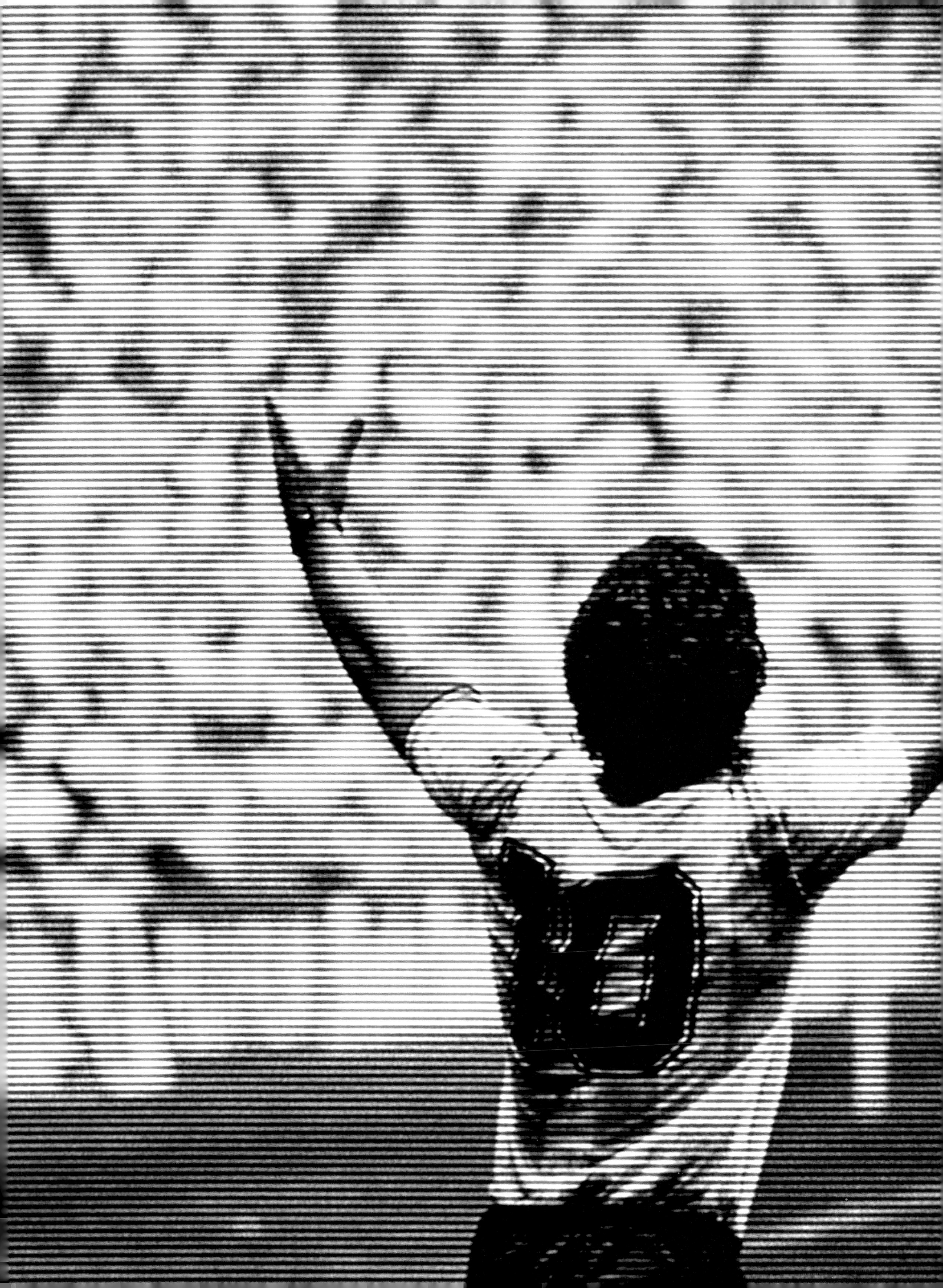

Local Heroes – Global Players
Local Heroes – Global Players

Ein früher Held des Münchner Fußballs: »Haxentoni« Anton Hübel. Von seinem fußballerischen Glanz blieb nur eine Postkarte erhalten, die ihn auf einem Bärenfell stehend vor Blumengirlanden und antiken Säulen zeigt. Um 1900. An early Munich football hero: «Haxentoni» Anton Hübel. All that remains of his vanished football glory is a postcard showing him standing on a bear rug with garlands of flowers and ancient Greek columns. Ca 1900.

Gemachte Männer
Die Helden des Fußballs

Stefan Eisenhofer

Jede Gesellschaft hat die Helden, die sie braucht und verdient. Helden werden nicht geboren – Helden werden erschaffen. Helden verkörpern populäre Einstellungen, stehen für Hoffnungen, Ideale und Gegen-Ideale von Einzelnen und Gemeinschaften. Sie personifizieren Wünsche und Träume, aber auch Ängste und Vorbehalte. Gerade die Helden des Massenphänomens Fußball lassen Werte erkennen, die in den jeweiligen Gemeinschaften einen besonderen Stellenwert einnehmen. Tatsächlich lässt sich viel über eine Gesellschaft erfahren, wenn man untersucht, welche »Fußball-Helden« wo und warum eine Rolle spielen. Denn nicht jeder außergewöhnliche Fußballer wird überall zum Helden. Ein und dieselbe Figur kann in unter-

Football-Made Men
The Heroes of a Global Game

Stefan Eisenhofer

Every society has the heroes it needs and deserves. Heroes are made – not born. Heroes embody popular attitudes, stand for the hopes, ideals and counter-ideals of individuals and communities. However, they personify fears and reservations as well as desires and dreams. The heroes of the mass phenomenon that is football especially reveal values which have particular status in the communities with which they are associated. One can learn a great deal about a society by studying its «football heroes» and where and why they play the roles they do. It must be borne in mind that not every exceptional footballer becomes a hero everywhere. A figure can be evaluated differently from society to society and environment to environment – as is the case with the goalkeeper Oliver Kahn, whose will to win is viewed by many as symbolic of the overly ambitious German. In East Asia, on the other hand, this quality is what has made him one of the most popular sportsmen. Moreover, Kahn has become an icon in Japan because he has accepted bitter defeats with composure and dignity – an achievement which has gone virtually unnoticed in Germany.

In football especially the creation of heroes is closely linked with the modern mass media and has been given a fresh dynamic in recent decades since the world has become globalised. In the early 20th century, the well-known Munich footballer nicknamed «Haxentoni» was primarily a local hero. And even the first international football idol, José Andrade of Uruguay in the 1920s could not match the popularity of such present-day football heroes as Ronaldinho and Ronaldo, who are known to tens of millions of people virtually throughout the world. Reporting on football had not yet reached anything like the scale on which it operates today.

In the latter half of the 20th century, numerous footballers attained local and national fame beyond the bounds of the pitch without becoming global stars. The Bengali player Bhutia and Azikiwe of Nigeria played important roles on a national level in their countries as symbols of resistance against all-powerful colonial overlords.

Diego Armando Maradona did meet with world-wide acclaim as a player. However, he was primarily important on the national and regional levels, where he enjoyed cult status, venerated as the saviour and avenger of the honour of Argentina and Naples.

Maradona also embodied a certain type of masculinity – the «lad», footloose and fancy-free, who stood for the playfulness and freedom that are usually lost with adulthood. In this Maradona matches certain patterns that made Franz Beckenbauer an idol in Germany. Beckenbauer, too, had something of a «Peter Pan» about him, the boy who never grows up and would really rather keep on playing outside and not have to worry about the more serious things in life. In a certain sense Beckenbauer was the «Peter Pan of Blue and White-Collar Germany».

Fußballer und Popsängerin – hochstilisiert zu religiösen Ikonen: David Beckham und seine Frau Victoria als Heiliger Josef und Jungfrau Maria in Madame Tussauds Wachsfiguren-Kabinett. Footballer and pop singer – stylised to the hilt as religious icons: David Beckham and his wife Victoria as St Joseph and the Virgin Mary in Madame Tussaud's Waxworks.
© Photo: Rune Hellestad, Corbis

schiedlichen Gesellschaften und Milieus verschieden betrachtet und deren Eigenschaften unterschiedlich bewertet werden – so etwa beim Torhüter Oliver Kahn, dessen Siegeswille von vielen als Sinnbild des überehrgeizigen Deutschen betrachtet wird, während ihn gerade dies in Ostasien zu einem der populärsten Sportler überhaupt macht. Darüber hinaus wurde Kahn in Japan auch deshalb zur Ikone, weil er schwere Niederlagen gefasst und würdevoll hingenommen hat – eine Leistung, die etwa in Deutschland kaum thematisiert wurde.

Gerade auch im Fußball ist das Erschaffen von Helden eng mit den modernen Massenmedien verknüpft und hat in den letzten Jahrzehnten in einer globalisierten Welt eine neue Dynamik erfahren. So war zu Beginn des 20. Jahrhunderts etwa der bekannte Münchner Fußballer mit dem Spitznamen »Haxentoni« (»Fuß-Anton«), vor allem eine lokale Berühmtheit. Und selbst das erste internationale Idol des Fußballs, José Andrade aus Uruguay in den 1920er Jahren, ist in seinem Bekanntheitsgrad nicht mit heutigen Fußball-Heroen wie Ronaldinho oder Ronaldo zu vergleichen, die Milliarden von Menschen in nahezu allen Winkeln der Welt ein Begriff sind. Damals hatte die Berichterstattung über Fußball eben bei weitem noch nicht die heutigen Ausmaße angenommen.

In der zweiten Hälfte des 20. Jahrhunderts erlangten zahlreiche Fußballer überragende regionale und nationale Bedeutung jenseits des Fußballfeldes, ohne zu globalen Stars zu werden. So spielten etwa der Algerier Mekhloufi oder der Nigerianer Azikiwe als Symbolfiguren des Widerstands gegen übermächtige Kolonialherren oder Besatzer herausragende Rollen.

Zwar erntete Diego Armando Maradona auch als Fußballer globale Anerkennung. Seine wichtigste Bedeutung entfaltete er jedoch ebenfalls auf nationaler und regionaler Ebene, wo er als Retter und Rächer der Ehre Argentiniens bzw. Neapels geradezu kultische Verehrung genoss.

Gleichzeitig war Maradona die Verkörperung einer bestimmten Art von Männlichkeit – des verantwortungsbefreiten »Burschen«, der für das Spielerische und die Freiheit stand, die

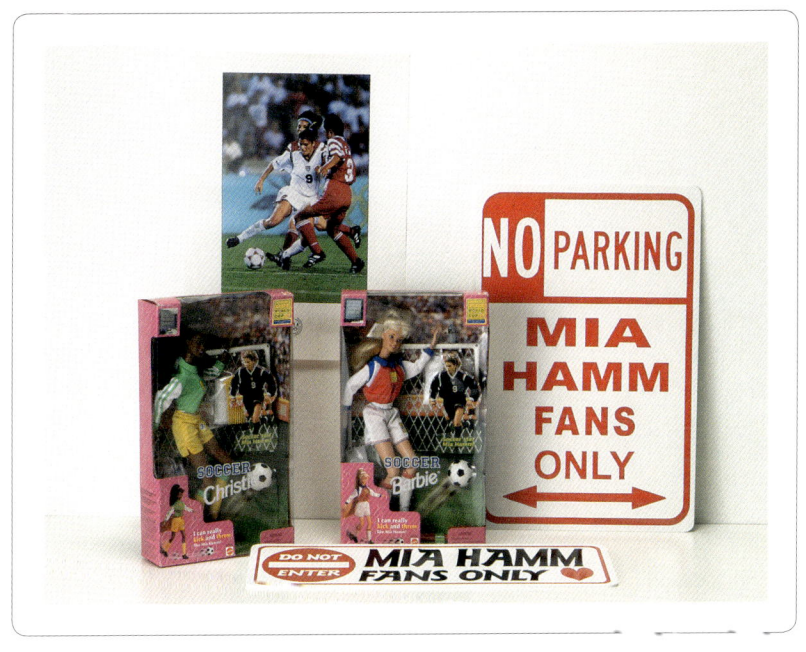

Mia Hamm wurde für eine ganze Generation junger Fußballerinnen zum Vorbild und verhalf dem Frauenfußball in den USA zu einem unverhofften Höhenflug. A role model for a whole generation of young women football hopefuls, Mia Hamm raised women's football to unexpected heights in the US. Installation: Münchner Stadtmuseum.

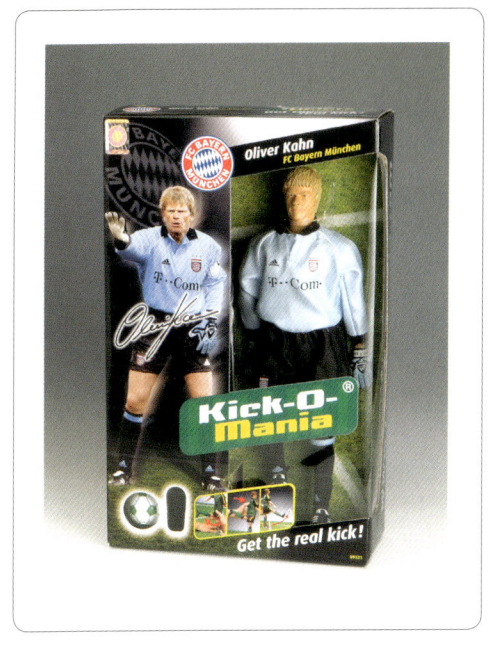

Idol für die nachwachsende männliche Generation: Oliver Kahn als Spielfigur. The idol of the next generation of men players: an Oliver Kahn doll.

There are more aspects of Beckenbauer, however, that are relevant in the present context. They are his rise from a relatively modest background to stardom world-wide: a «gentleman player», the «emperor» who pulled himself up by his own bootstraps. This leads into another characteristic common to numerous football heroes – ranging from George Weah of Liberia through Maradona of Argentina to Zidane, a French national of Algerian origin: they all owe their success to their athletic achievements and not to «coming from good families». In many countries a rise to success of this kind is closely linked with bare survival. Consequently, the hopes of social and economic advancement cherished by impoverished demographic groups converge on many a football hero. The story of the guttersnipe without a chance who flees poverty through his prowess as a sportsman is encountered in the biographies of many football luminaries.

Garrincha, as Brazil's most famous footballer a «hero of the Brazilian people», is unequivocally rooted in a culture of poverty. He made the most of his physical appearance, his dark skin and dramatic, alcohol-soaked life he led as confirming all stereotypes of the «poor black». In his style of playing he epitomised the «backyard footballer». As the incarnation of a particular culture of the common people he was particularly suitable as an identification figure for the poor. That other world star of Brazilian football, Pelé, became a sign of how successful a person could be regardless of the colour of his skin or the class he belonged to. Regarded in their home countries as representing the hopes of the deprived, these players were reinterpreted in Europe as embodying the popular spirit in the romantic sense – exotic street players as «geniuses» who rose from the people.

Viewed in retrospect, football heroes tend to be stylised in Europe into national representatives of entire eras. Johan Cruyff, for instance, developed into a symbol of cosmopolitan and tolerant 1970s Holland because of his discreetly intelligent manner both on the pitch and away from it. In contrast, twenty years later in England the ruddy-faced, beefy and anti-intel-

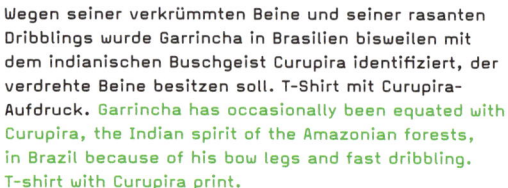

Wegen seiner verkrümmten Beine und seiner rasanten Dribblings wurde Garrincha in Brasilien bisweilen mit dem indianischen Buschgeist Curupira identifiziert, der verdrehte Beine besitzen soll. T-Shirt mit Curupira-Aufdruck. Garrincha has occasionally been equated with Curupira, the Indian spirit of the Amazonian forests, in Brazil because of his bow legs and fast dribbling. T-shirt with Curupira print.

Diego Maradona ist trotz oder gerade wegen seiner Ambivalenzen eine verehrte Identifikationsfigur – sowohl in Argentinien als auch im italienischen Neapel, wo er jahrelang spielte. Feuerzeug für Maradona-Fans. For all his flaws, Diego Maradona is a venerated identification figure – both in his native Argentina and in Naples, Italy, where he played for years. A lighter for Maradona fans.

man gewöhnlich beim Eintritt ins Erwachsenenalter verliert. Hier trifft sich Maradona mit bestimmten Mustern, die Franz Beckenbauer in Deutschland zum Idol werden ließen. Denn auch dieser besaß Züge eines »ewigen Jungen«, der eigentlich lieber draußen spielt als sich daheim um die ernsteren Dinge des Lebens zu kümmern. In gewisser Weise wurde Beckenbauer so zum »Peter Pan der deutschen Angestelltengesellschaft«.

In Beckenbauer kommen aber auch noch andere Aspekte zum Tragen. Und zwar sein Aufstieg aus vergleichsweise bescheidenen Verhältnissen zum Weltstar, »Gentleman« und »Kaiser« aus eigener Kraft. Damit ist ein weiteres Merkmal vieler Fußball-Helden genannt – vom Liberianer George Weah über den Argentinier Maradona bis zum algerisch-stämmigen Franzosen Zidane: Sie alle haben ihre Erfolge durch sportliche Leistung selbst errungen, und nicht aufgrund ihres »guten Elternhauses«. In vielen Ländern der Welt ist ein solcher Weg eng mit elementaren Überlebensfragen verknüpft. So bündeln sich in so manchem Fußball-Helden die Hoffnungen verarmter Bevölkerungsgruppen auf gesellschaftlichen Aufstieg und ein wirtschaftliches Auskommen. Die Geschichte vom chancenlosen Gassenjungen, der durch seine sportlichen Fähigkeiten der Armut entkommt, findet sich daher in vielen Biographien von Fußball-Stars.

Auch der berühmteste Fußballer Brasiliens und »Held des brasilianischen Volkes«, Garrincha, ist eindeutig in einer Kultur der Armut verortet. Durch seine körperliche Erscheinung, seine Dunkelhäutigkeit und sein vom Alkohol bestimmtes, dramatisches Leben bediente er alle Stereotypen des »armen Farbigen«. In seinem Spielstil war er die Verkörperung des »Hinterhofspielers« schlechthin. Als Inkarnation einer bestimmten Kultur des einfachen Vol-

lectual Paul «Gazza» Gascoigne was the very incarnation of the British anti-Continental attitude at a time when British euroscepticism was at its height. And because pop elements have been pouring into football under the growing influence of the media since the 1960s, a brilliant Irish player who was also a beau and breaker of hearts, the late George Best, became the first football pop star and came to symbolise «the permissive sixties». Undisciplined and alcoholic he may have been but Best was unlike the current crop of stellar footballers in a globalised game. They are – and here Beckham inevitably comes to mind – also marketed with «sex appeal» and «pop culture». However, as global advertising icons, these footballers have to – as Christian Eichler has diagnosed – «get their rebellion at the hairdresser's».

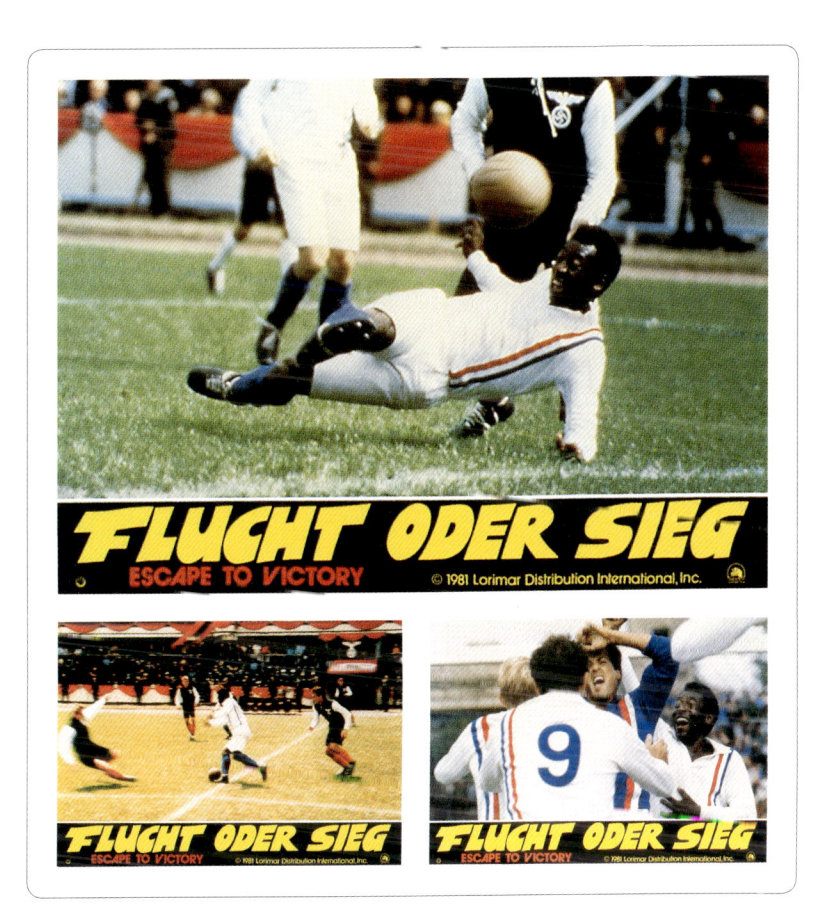

Auch außerhalb des Fußballplatzes ein Held: Pelé im Jahr 1981 als Schauspieler im Film »Victory« unter der Regie von Meisterregisseur John Huston an der Seite von Sylvester Stallone. Stills aus dem Film »Victory«. A hero off the pitch, too: Pelé acting in the film «Victory» in 1981, with master director John Huston and co-starring Sylvester Stallone. Stills from the film «Victory».

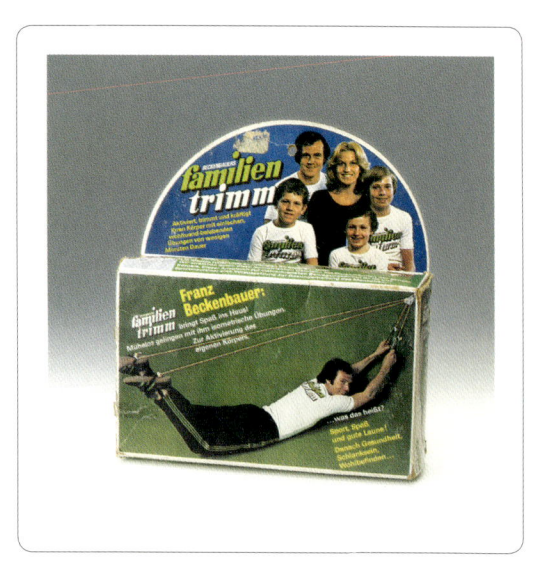

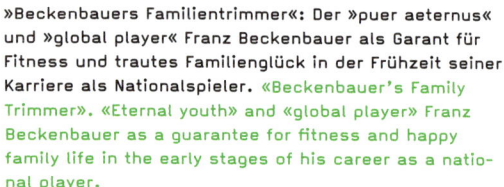

»Beckenbauers Familientrimmer«: Der »puer aeternus« und »global player« Franz Beckenbauer als Garant für Fitness und trautes Familienglück in der Frühzeit seiner Karriere als Nationalspieler. «Beckenbauer's Family Trimmer». «Eternal youth» and «global player» Franz Beckenbauer as a guarantee for fitness and happy family life in the early stages of his career as a national player.

»Kraft in den Teller, Knorr auf den Tisch« – Der »Kaiser Franz« wurde schon früh zur vielseitig einsetzbaren Werbe-Ikone. Knorr-Löffel mit eingraviertem Namenszug von Franz Beckenbauer. «Power on the plate, Knorr on the table» – «Emperor Franz» soon became a multi-purpose advertising icon. Knorr spoon with the name «Franz Beckenbauer» engraved on it.

kes eignete er sich daher besonders als Identifikationsfigur für die Armen. Auch der andere Weltstar des brasilianischen Fußballs, Pelé, wurde zum Zeichen dafür, dass man Erfolg haben kann, egal welcher Hautfarbe oder Klasse man angehört. In ihrer Heimat als Hoffnungsträger für die Benachteiligten betrachtet, interpretierte man diese Spieler in Europa zu Verkörperungen des Volksgeists im romantischen Sinne um – exotische Straßenfußballer als »Genies aus dem Volke«.

Im Nachhinein wurden Fußball-Helden in Europa gerne zu nationalen Vertretern ganzer Epochen stilisiert. Der Holländer Johan Cruyff etwa entwickelte sich wegen seines intelligenten Auftretens auf und neben dem Platz zum Sinnbild eines weltoffenen und toleranten Holland der 1970er Jahre. In England avancierte 20 Jahre später, in Zeiten großer britischer Europa-Skepsis also, der rotgesichtige, übergewichtige und anti-intellektuelle Paul »Gazza« Gascoigne zur fleischgewordenen Anti-Festland-Haltung. Und da seit den 1960er Jahren durch den wachsenden Einfluss der Massenmedien immer mehr Elemente des Pop in den Fußball Einzug hielten, wurde der fußballerisch begnadete irische Mädchenschwarm George Best zunächst zum ersten Popstar des Fußballs und später zum Spiegelbild der »zügellosen 68er Jahre«. Dennoch steht der undisziplinierte und alkoholsüchtige Best im Gegensatz zu den aktuellen Stars der globalisierten Fußballwelt. Diese werden zwar – wie etwa Beckham – ebenfalls gerne mit »Sex« und »Pop« vermarktet, als globale Werbe-Ikonen müssen sie sich aber – wie Christian Eichler diagnostiziert – »das Rebellische beim Friseur holen.«

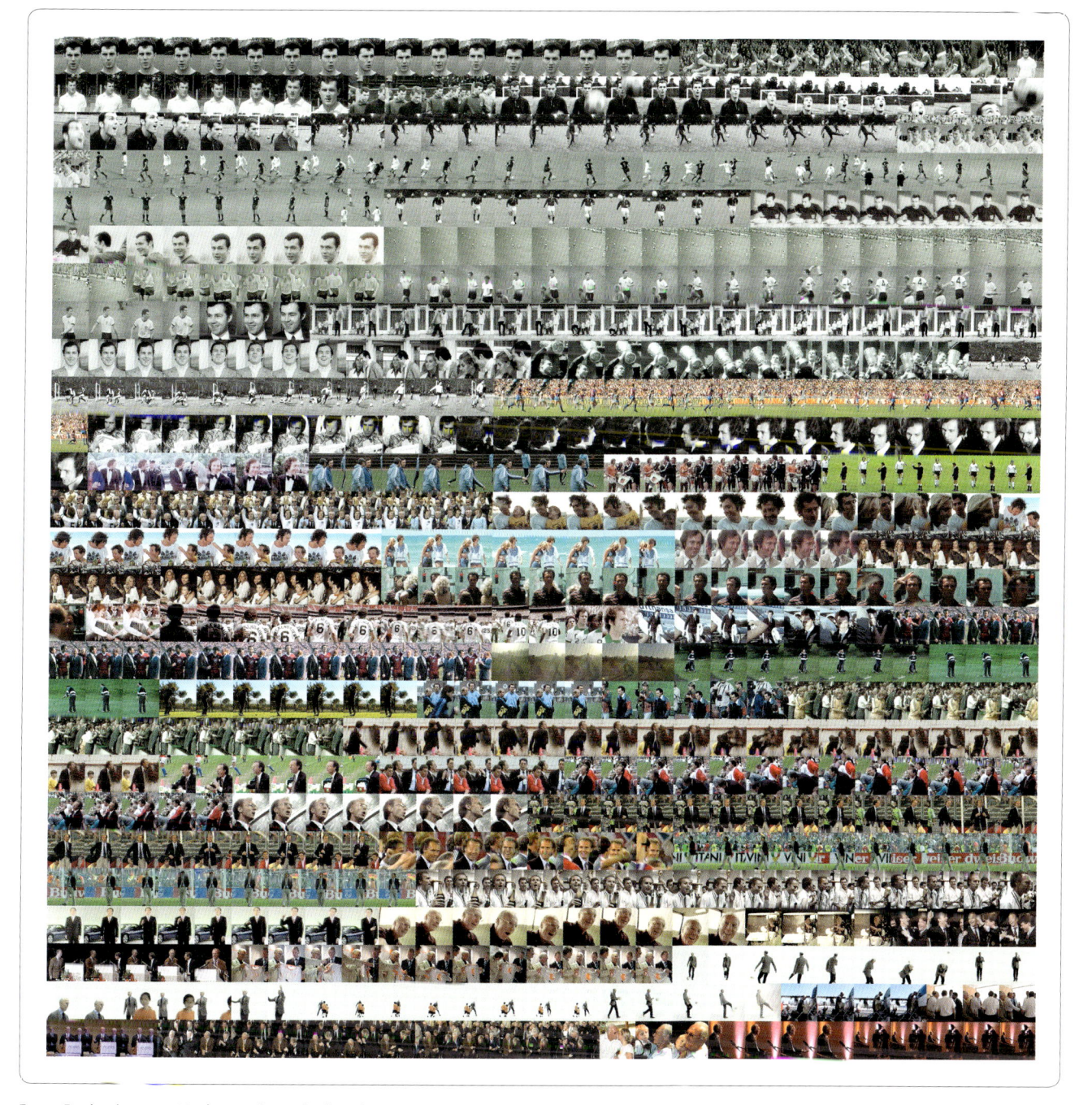

Franz Beckenbauer – Stationen eines einzigartigen Fußballer-Lebens. Franz Beckenbauer – stages in the unprecedented life of a footballer. Volker Hildebrandt: »Beckenbauers Leben« («Life of Beckenbauer»), 2005, Offsetlitho auf Papier / offset litho on paper, 80 x 80 cm. Courtesy Galerie Jörg Heitsch, München

Diego Santissimo
Maradona für immer im Herzen Neapels

Natalie Göltenboth

Der Lesart moderner kulturanthropologischer Studien zufolge lässt sich Fußball als das Ritual *par excellence* beschreiben, an dem moderne Gesellschaften derzeit ihr Vergnügen finden. Auf den sakralen Plätzen der Stadien werden in zyklischer Wiederkehr kämpferische Rituale vollzogen, in deren Verlauf die verinnerlichten Werte einer Gesellschaft dramatisch zur Darstellung kommen. Um vollständig in den Stand eines modernen und quasi religiösen Kultes zu avancieren, fehlt dem Fußball – so der französische Ethnologe Bromberger – nur noch eine Kleinigkeit: der Glaube an übernatürliche Wesen.

Auf der Suche danach stoßen wir auf ein kleines Figürchen im blau-weißen Trikot, das mit Engelsflügeln versehen einen Ball am Rande einer der zahlreichen, Maradona gewidmeten Internetseiten entlangdribbelt, und wir lesen:

Maradona unser	Maradona nostro
der du aufs Feld herabgestiegen bist	che scendi in campo
geheiligt sei dein Name	abbiamo santificato il tuo nome
Napoli ist dein Königreich …	Napoli é il tuo regno …
Wiege uns nicht in Illusionen	Non ci indurre in illusioni
sondern führe uns zum Siegertitel	ma conducici allo scudetto
Amen	Amen

Gebete, Lieder und Gedichte für Maradona finden sich zahlreich auf den Internet-Seiten der Fangemeinden in Neapel und Buenos Aires, den zentralen Stationen in Maradonas Karriere als Fußballgott und -heiliger – Orte, an denen seine Verehrung und »Kanonisierung« Höhepunkte in der Geschichte der Fußball-Liturgie erreichen.

Zwischen den neapolitanischen Straßenaltären zu Ehren der Stadtheiligen San Genaro und Madonna dell'Arco finden sich seit den spektakulären Fußball-Siegen Ende der 1980er Jahre auch Altäre für den Retter des »Napoli«. In Siegerpose sieht man da Maradona dem Vesuv entsteigen – Wahrzeichen der immer bedrohten Stadt – den Ball zum Himmel erhoben. Neapel, so erfahren wir, ist im Besitz dreier Dinge, die seine Schönheit repräsentieren: dem Golf, dem Vesuv und Maradonas!

Neapel – die Stadt mit dem Hang zum Kultischen, mit ihren Märtyrern und ihren Blutwundern, hat einen neuen Heiligen – Diego Maradona – der dort mit Inbrunst vereinnahmt, verehrt und rituell bewirtschaftet wird. Die Stadt ging sogar soweit, anlässlich des glücklich errungenen Titels von 1989 die Fusion von Heiligenkult und Fußball in Gestalt einer neuen Figur zu inszenieren. Auf einem Prozessionswagen wurde San Genarmando, bestehend aus der Büste San Genaros und dem Kopf Maradonas, durch die Stadt geführt.

Drei Wahrzeichen Neapels: Der Vesuv, der Golf und Diego Maradona. Naples landmarks: Mt Vesuvius, the Gulf of Naples and Diego Maradona. Loomit: Graffiti auf Wandkarte / graffiti on a wall map, 2006.

Santissimo Diego
Maradona for Ever in Neapolitan Hearts

Natalie Göltenboth

From the standpoint of cutting-edge studies in cultural anthropology, football can be described as the ritual *par excellence* currently enjoyed by contemporary societies. With the stadium as cult place, bellicose rituals are observed at regular cyclical intervals during which the values internalised by a society are dramatically displayed. All that football needs to advance entirely to the status of a modern, quasi religious cult – according to the French ethnologist Bromberger – is a mere trifle: belief in a higher power.

On our quest for it, we encounter a little figure clad in a blue-and-white jersey, winged like an angel and dribbling a ball on one of the myriads of homepages dedicated to Maradona and we read:

Our Maradona	Maradona nostro
Which art come down to us on the pitch	che scendi in campo
Hallowed be Thy name	abbiamo santificato il tuo nome
Thy kingdom come in Naples …	Napoli è tuo regno …
Let us not languish in disappointment	Non ci indurre in illusioni
But lead us to the Cup	ma conducici allo scudetto
Amen	Amen

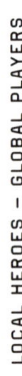

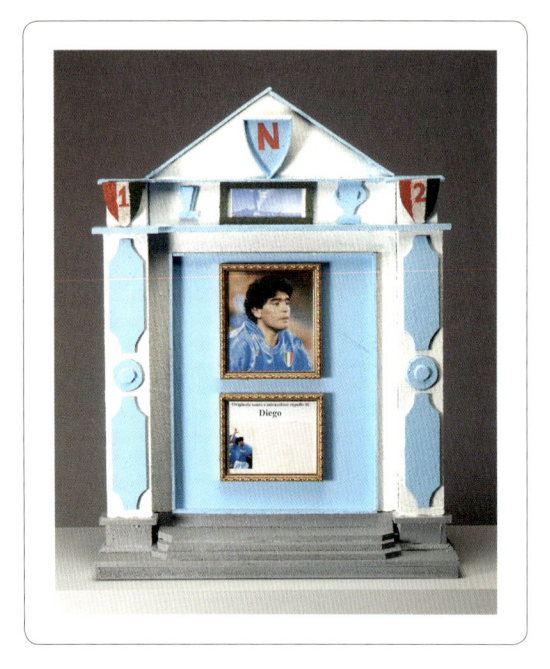

Maradona – noch heute in Neapel verehrt. Außen an seiner »Bar Nilo« hat Carmine Alcide seit fast einem Jahrzehnt einen Maradona-»Altar« angebracht. Maradona – still venerated in Naples. Carmina Alcide annexed a Maradona «altar» to his Bar Nilo nearly a decade ago. Nachbau, Neapel / Reconstruction, Naples, 2006.

Detail des Maradona-»Altars«: »Originale santo e miracoloso capello di Diego« – »Ein echtes heiliges und wundersames Haar von Diego«. Detail of the Maradona «altar»: «an original sacred and miraculous hair of Diego's».

Neapel besitzt ohne Zweifel eine alte Tradition dramatischer religiöser Inszenierungen, einen Fundus an Gesten und Ikonografien, der bei besonderen Anlässen wie dem *scudetto* von 1987 abgerufen werden kann. Fußballkultur verschmilzt dann mit lokaler Heiligenverehrung und dem Mythenvorrat der Stadt.

Doch ein Blick auf das Selbstverständnis Neapels macht weitere Gründe für die Adoption des argentinischen Helden offensichtlich. 1926 wurde der erste offizielle Fußballclub in Neapel – der »Napoli« gegründet. Während Rom und Turin edle Tiere wie Wölfin und Stier als Symbole ihrer Clubs wählten, entschieden sich die Neapolitaner für den *ciuccio* – den Esel. Wirtschaftlich abgestiegen, von Chaos und Verelendung bedroht gilt Neapel den Norditalienern als Inbegriff des verarmten, unkultivierten Südens, kurz – als Afrika inmitten von Europa. Vom Norden in dieser Weise verachtet, identifiziert sich Neapel mit der Rolle des Esels, dürstet dabei aber nach Anerkennung und Wiederherstellung seiner Ehre. Die Dynamik des Fußballs befeuert diesen latenten Konflikt, der im verbalen Schlagabtausch zwischen den Fanclubs offenkundig wird. So lautet ein norditalienischer Schlachtruf:

»Ihr habt euch noch nie mit Seife gewaschen
Napoli Scheiße, Napoli Cholera
Du bist die Schande von ganz Italien.«

Neapel kontert gegen die Norditaliener:
»Neapel – Champion des Fußballs, der Kultur und der Zivilisation.«

Hier wird deutlich, dass ein Spiel des »Napoli« gegen Juventus Turin weit über den Bedeutungsrahmen eines sportlich-spielerischen Ereignisses hinausgeht. Für Neapolitaner ist ein Sieg gegen eine Mannschaft aus dem Norden eine erträumte Gelegenheit der Revanche. Es ist

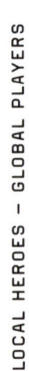

Prayers, songs and poems addressed to Maradona are legion on the fan homepages in Naples and Buenos Aires, the pivotal stations on Maradona's path to a career as the patron saint, if not the deity, of football – places where the veneration, nay the «canonisation», of a player have attained their zenith in the annals of football liturgy.

In the 1980s there were altars consecrated to the «Saviour of Napoli» amid the altars erected in the streets of Naples in veneration of the city's patron saints, San Genaro and the Madonna dell'Arco. There Maradona appeared in the pose of a victor arising from Mt Vesuvius – the landmark of a city that is always threatened by it – raising the ball to the heavens. Naples, we learn, possesses three things incarnating its beauties: the Gulf of Naples, Mt Vesuvius and Maradona!

Naples – that city with cultic leanings and miracles of the blood, had a new saint – Diego Maradona – who was taken to its heart, venerated and ritually consumed. On the felicitous occasion of capturing the title in 1989, the city even went to the lengths of staging a merger between the cult of a saint and football by creating a new cult figure. San Genarmando, consisting of a bust of San Genaro with the head of Diego Armando Maradona on its shoulders, was borne on a processional cart through the city.

There is no doubt about it, Naples looks back on a long tradition of religious dramatisation, possessing a treasure trove of gestures and iconographies which can be retrieved on special occasions such as the 1987 *scudetto*. When they are invoked, the culture of football fuses with the local hagiography and the city's repertory of myth.

However, a glance at the Neapolitan self-image reveals further reasons for adopting the Argentine hero. In 1926 the first official football club in Naples – «Napoli»– was founded. Whereas Rome and Turin chose such noble animals as a she-wolf and a bull as the symbols of their clubs, the Neapolitans opted for the *ciuccio* – the humble donkey. Down in the dumps economically, threatened with chaos and squalor, Naples is regarded by northern Italians as the epitome of the impoverished, uncultured south. In short – as Africa right in Europe. Thus despised by the North, Naples identifies with the role of the donkey but still yearns for recognition and the restitution of its honour. The dynamic peculiar to football has inflamed this latent conflict, which comes to a head in the exchange of verbal abuse between fan clubs. A northern Italian battlesong runs as follows:

«You've never washed with soap
Napoli shit, Napoli cholera
You're the disgrace of all Italy.»

Naples flung at the northern Italians:
«Naples – Champions in football, culture and civilisation.»

Here it becomes obvious that a match between «Napoli» and Juventus Turin goes far beyond the paradigm of a sporting or staged event. To Neapolitans, a victory against a team from the North means a long desired chance for revenge. This is the battle of the poor and downtrodden against the rich and recognised. Diego Armando Maradona, too, seems to have perceived this shift of planes. As he wrote in *El Diego,* his autobiography, he realised that the battle fought

der Kampf der Armen und Verachteten gegen die Reichen und Anerkannten. Auch Maradona scheint diese Verlagerung der Ebenen wahrgenommen zu haben, er schreibt in seiner Autobiografie *El Diego:* »… ich begriff, dass der Kampf Neapels nicht nur mit dem Fußball zu tun hatte … es spielte der Norden gegen den Süden, die Rassisten traten gegen die Armen an«.

Mitte der 1980er Jahre beginnt Maradona den »Napoli« zu strukturieren, einen Club, an dem vor ihm noch wenige jemals Interesse gezeigt hatten. Mit den nun folgenden Siegen feiert Neapel seine Auferstehung und Maradona wird zum Heiligen stilisiert, der der verachteten Stadt den verlorengegangenen Stolz zurückbringt.

Schon immer bedurfte Neapel der Hilfe übernatürlicher Retter – Heiliger, die die allgegenwärtigen Bedrohungen abwenden konnten und gegen Vulkanausbrüche, Erdbeben, Krankheiten und Armut halfen, und bezeichnenderweise entsprachen diese sakralen Retter stets der »katastrophischen Struktur« der Stadt. Die Blutverflüssigungen des San Genaro und die wundersamen Tötungen der Madonna dell'Arco sind bizarr, ihre jährlichen Vergegenwärtigungen bilden die ekstatischen Höhepunkte der neapolitanischen Gemeinschaft.

Maradona, selbst von der Kultur der Armut geprägt, genial, kapriziös, undiszipliniert, überschwänglich und stets in Skandale verwickelt, ist mit diesen Eigenschaften ein echter Sohn Neapels. Seine Tore hatten infolgedessen eine ähnliche Wirkung wie die Wunder der Heiligen – sie banden die Identität der Neapolitaner noch enger an ihre Stadt:

Oh du Gassenjunge aus Neapel	Oh tu scugnizzo
Wisse, dass diese Menschen,	ricorda que questa gente
dieses Land	questa terra
deine Heldentaten in sich aufnimmt	serberá le tue gesta nel punto
bis in die verborgensten Winkel seines Herzens.	piú reondito del cuore.

(Gedicht eines Fans aus Neapel)

Die Heldentaten Maradonas waren keineswegs immer edler Natur. Drogenprobleme, Betrügereien, Kontakte zur Mafia, schöne Frauen und schnelle Autos – Aufstieg und Fall – das liest sich wie das Einmaleins neapolitanischer Überlebensstrategie. Für die Bevölkerung Neapels und deren Ressentiments gegen alles »Offizielle« musste dieser allzu bekannte »Cocktail« Maradona geradezu unwiderstehlich gemacht haben. Und so hat sich die Stadt nach Maradonas großem Auftritt nicht von ihm abgewendet, sondern drückt ihn noch immer an ihr großes gefühlvolles Herz, als ihren *scugnizzo* – ihren Gassenjungen, ihren Heiligen – den Retter mit dem Ball.

Maradona-Büste und -Tamburin aus Neapel, 2005. A Maradona bust and tambourine from Naples, 2005.

by Naples had to do with more than football. It represented in fact North vs South, racists against the poor.

In the mid-1980s Maradona proceeded to restructure «Napoli», a club only a few people had shown any interest in before his time. Naples celebrated its resurrection in the victories that followed and Maradona was turned into a saint who had restored its lost pride to the city.

Naples had always invoked the aid of supernatural saviours – saints who might ward off the threats on all sides and protect against volcanic eruptions, earthquakes, diseases and poverty. Characteristically, these holy protectors always matched the city's «catastrophe structure». San Genaro's deliquescent blood and the miraculous killings performed by the Madonna dell'Arco are indeed bizarre. Invoking them annually represents the zenith of communal ecstasy in Naples.

Maradona himself, moulded as he was by the culture of poverty, brilliant, moody, undisciplined, exuberant and always involved in some scandal or other, was revealed in these qualities as a true son of Naples. His goals, therefore, made an impact similar to the miracles performed by the saints – they bound up Neapolitans' identity even more closely with their city:

Oh, you street urchin,	O tu scugnizzo
Know that this people,	ricorda que questa gente
this country	questa terra
will enshrine your deeds	serberá le tue gesta nel punto
in their inmost secret hearts.	più recondito del cuore.

(Poem by a fan from Naples)

Maradona's deeds were certainly not always heroic or noble. Drug problems, embezzlement, Mafia contacts, beautiful women and fast cars – his rise and fall – the roll reads like a Neapolitan brief for survival strategies. This all too notorious but heady «cocktail» must have been what made Maradona so utterly irresistible to Neapolitans. So the city did not spurn Maradona after his great days were over but instead continues to press him to its great, throbbing heart as its very own *scugnizzo* – its street urchin, its saint – its saviour with a football.

D10S
Maradonakult in Argentinien

Natalie Göltenboth

»Bei meinem Sprung aus dem Fenster hatte ich eigentlich gehofft, Gott zu sehen, aber du warst nicht da«, sagte der argentinische Star Charlie García zu Diego Maradona in dessen Fernsehshow »Die Nacht der 10« (*la noche del 10* – eine Anspielung auf Maradonas Nummer auf dem Spielfeld).

Diego Armando Maradona, in Neapel als Heiliger verehrt, ist in seinem Heimatland Argentinien gleich auf die nächste Stufe in der sakralen Hierarchie befördert worden. Als *D10S,* als Gott verehrt, ist ihm in Buenos Aires inzwischen eine eigene Kirche gewidmet worden. In der Iglesia Maradoniana wird Diegos Kult mit allen liturgischen Mitteln betrieben: Weihnachten feiert man am 30. Oktober, dem Geburtstag des neuen Gottes – mit Christbaumkugeln, in denen sich Maradonas Gesicht zu einem Lächeln verklärt. Die Rosenkränze bestehen aus vielen kleinen Fußbällchen, Gebete beginnen grundsätzlich mit »Unser Diego, der du bist ...«, es werden maradonianische Taufen zelebriert, die vom Täufling ein umfassendes Glaubensbekenntnis fordern, und die zehn maradonianischen Gebote weisen die Gläubigen an, ihre uneingeschränkte Liebe zu Diego unter Beweis zu stellen. Ein einzigartiger Kult, gestrickt aus religiösem Eifer und Starkult, Politik und einem guten Schuss des ganz besonderen argentinischen Sinns für Parodien – auch in ernsten Angelegenheiten.

Doch das argentinische Gefühl für Diego ist echt. Man verfolgt im Fernsehen jeden seiner Lebensabschnitte öffentlich – von der Fettabsaugung bis hin zur wiedererworbenen Wendigkeit in der Rolle des Showmasters. Rührende Geschichten machen die Runde, die Kirche Maradonas gewinnt an Mitgliedern.

Angesichts dieses Ausmaßes an Idolkult oder Idolatrie setzt bei den meisten Mitteleuropäern Kopfschütteln ein. Doch an eben dieser Stelle, an der das mitteleuropäische Kopfschütteln beginnt, wird in argentinischen Vorstellungswelten die Erinnerung wach. Maradona erscheint dann auf das engste verknüpft mit dem Krieg um die Falklandinseln, die Niederlage gegen die Engländer und das Blut der jungen Kämpfer. Mit dieser Niederlage aber werden alle Niederlagen lebendig – vergangene und gegenwärtige, politische und wirtschaftliche –, die Argentinien und mit ihm ganz Lateinamerika gegen die reichen Nordländer erlebt hat.

Ähnlich wie in Italien liegt auch hier der erlebten Intensität des Fußballs ein Konflikt zwischen Norden und Süden zugrunde. Hier allerdings handelt es sich um ein interkontinentales Nord-Süd-Gefälle, innerhalb dessen sich die südlichen Parteien meist mit der Rolle des Betrogenen identifizieren. Doch bei diesem schlechten Spiel gibt es eine Ausnahme, ein Kampffeld, auf dem der zu gewinnen scheint, der die größere Wut hat. »Was niemand je verstanden hat, war, dass unsere Kraft und Einigkeit aus der Wut kamen, der Wut darüber, dass wir gegen alles ankämpfen mussten« – so Maradona über das Spiel England gegen Argentinien in Mexiko 1986. Von argentinischer Seite aus wurde der Kampf von damals auf der Ebene

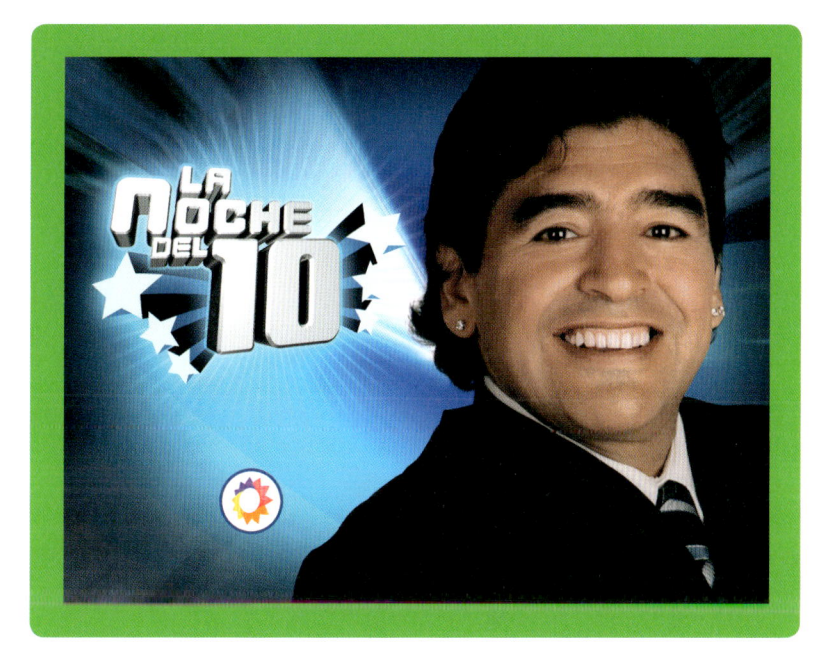

Auch nach dem Ende seiner Fußballerkarriere blieb Maradona in Argentinien eine höchst öffentliche Figur – hier als Showmaster einer eigenen Fernsehsendung.
Even after his football career ended, Maradona remained a conspicuous public figure in Argentina – here as the presenter of his own television show.
© Photo: Artear Canal Trece Argentina

D10S
The Maradona Cult in Argentina

Natalie Göltenboth

«When I jumped out the window, I had actually hoped to see God but You weren't there,» was how Argentine star Charlie García put it to Diego Maradona on his TV show «Night of 10» (*la noche del 10* – an allusion to the number Maradona wore on his jersey).

Venerated as a saint in Naples, Diego Armando Maradona was promoted upwards to the next echelon in the sacred hierarchy in his native Argentina. Worshipped as *D10S*, as deity, he has been honoured in Buenos Aires by having a church consecrated to him. The cult of San Diego is observed with all liturgical pomp in the Iglesia Maradoniana: Christmas is celebrated on 30 October, the new deity's birthday – with Christmas-tree baubles in which Maradona's face is transfigured by a smile. Rosaries are made up of minuscule footballs as beads. Prayers invariably begin with «Our Diego, which art…». Maradonian baptisms are celebrated. A person undergoing baptism is required to recite a comprehensive creed and the Maradonian Ten Commandments exhort believers to demonstrate boundless love for Diego. A unique cult, fabricated from religious fervour and the star cult with a good pinch of the distinctive Argentine sense of the ridiculous thrown in for good measure– parody is never very far away, even in serious matters.

For all that the Argentine feelings for Diego are genuine. Every phase of his life is followed publicly on television – from liposuction to the revival of his adroitness in the guise of TV presenter. Touching tales are told. The Maradonian congregation continues to grow.

des Fußballs wieder aufgenommen und so verstand man Maradonas Sieg als echte Revanche, die dem Land sein Selbstwertgefühl zurückgab. »Wer einen Dieb beklaut, dem wird tausendfach verziehen werden« kommentierte Maradona später sein berühmtes, durch »göttliches Handanlegen« errungene Tor und gibt damit zu verstehen, dass er sich in diesem Moment durchaus als Werkzeug göttlicher Gerechtigkeit verstanden hat.

Die Tatsache, dass Maradonas Wurzeln in Villa Fiorito, einem der armen Vorstadtviertel von Buenos Aires zu finden sind, lässt ihn um so mehr zu einem argentinischen Jedermann – einer Identifikationsfigur werden, die Argentinien in einem Wir-Gefühl zusammenschweißt. Die Figur eines der Armut entstiegenen Streiters und Retters der Betrogenen jedoch ist nichts neues, sie hat ihre Vorlagen in der Welt der Mythen und Märchen, von Robin Hood bis zu El Zorro. Mythologische Vorlagen aber sind mächtig – und Diego Maradona ist offensichtlich in der Lage, sich in dieser Form zu präsentieren. Und so ist der neue argentinische *D10S* auf der einen Seite siegreich und stark wie die Helden der Märchen, gleichzeitig mit seinen menschlichen Schwächen aber gerade auch jenseits aller Perfektion und damit liebenswert: Ein menschlicher *D10S,* dem Argentinien immer wieder verzeiht.

»In ihm manifestiert sich Göttliches!« – Maradona vor der kochenden Menge nach seinem »Tor des Jahrhunderts« gegen England bei der WM 1986 in Mexiko. «In him the divine is manifest!» – Maradona before the seething crowd after his «goal of the century» against England at the 1986 World Cup in Mexico. © Photo: John Vink, Magnum

In Buenos Aires grüßen im Stadtviertel Boca in der Flaniermeile El Caminito drei argentinische Helden von einem Balkon: Die populäre Politikerin Eva Perón, der Tango-Weltstar Carlos Gardel und Diego Maradona. Three Argentinian heroes greet their devoted followers from a balcony on El Caminito boulevard in the Boca section of Buenos Aires: popular politician Eva Perón, international tango star Carlos Gardel and Diego Maradona. © Photo: Arno van de Graat

Most central Europeans frown in disbelief at the scale on which this cult of an idol, which very simply more than borders on idolatry, is observed. Just at the point at which central Europeans start to frown, memories are triggered off in the Argentine consciousness. Maradona then appears in close association with the Falklands War, which was a defeat against England. The recollection of this defeat in turn brings all defeats to the surface – past and present, political and economic – which Argentina has suffered at the hands of rich northern countries.

As in Italy, the intensity with which football is experienced in Argentina is based on the conflict between North and South. Here, however, the difference between the rich North and the poor South is on an intercontinental scale, with the Southern countries usually identifying with the underdog role. However, in this bad hand of cards dealt to the South, there is one exception, a battlefield on which he who is angriest seems to win. As Maradona put it when discussing England vs Argentina in Mexico in 1986, no one realised that the Argentinian strength and unity was fed by anger at the fact that Argentina had to fight against everything. From the Argentinian side the battle that was fought then was taken up again on the level of football. Consequently Maradona's victory was viewed as genuine revenge, which restored the country's sense of self-worth – as in the case of Naples. Maradona would later comment on the goal he made then because «God laid His hand on him» by citing the proverb that «He who steals from a thief will be rewarded a thousandfold», thus implying that he viewed himself in that moment as the instrument of divine retribution.

That Maradona's roots lie in an impoverished suburb of Buenos Aires makes him an Everyman – a figure with whom Argentinians identify, who bonds them in a feeling of us vs them. The figure of the striver and saviour of the disadvantaged is nothing new. It goes back to myth and fairy tale, ranging from Robin Hood to El Zorro. Mythological models are, however, powerful ones – and Diego Maradona is evidently able to present himself convincingly in this guise. And so the new Argentinian *D10S* is, on the one hand, victorious and strong like a fairy-tale hero and, on the other, loveable just because he has so many human weaknesses despite his perfection: a very human *D10S,* who Argentina always forgives.

Beckham Meets Buddha

Patricia Müller

Der englische Fußballstar David Beckham wird künftig nicht nur im Stadion, sondern auch in einem thailändischen Tempel verehrt. Im kleinen Bangkoker Wat Pariwas hat der Mittelfeldspieler nun seinen Platz als »niedere Gottheit« in Gestalt einer vergoldeten Skulptur zu Füßen einer Buddha-Figur gefunden. Erschaffen wurde das Werk von dem jungen Thai-Bildhauer Jumnong Yantaphant, der seit vielen Jahren ein glühender Manchester United- und Real Madrid-Fan ist. Als die Pariwas-Mönche Jumnong baten, doch »etwas Modernes« für ihre buddhistische Stätte zu kreieren, erschuf er – eine 30 cm hohe Beckham-Skulptur. Obwohl die Statue zunächst auch Kontroversen unter einigen Älteren der thailändischen Bevölkerung, die zu 95 % aus Buddhisten besteht, hervorrief, wendete sich das Blatt im Beckham- und ManU-philen Thailand schnell zu Gunsten der Skulptur. Vor allem junge Thais begrüßten das Vorhaben; schließlich genießt Beckham im südostasiatischen Königreich Kultstatus. Bei seinen letzten Besuchen in Bangkok mussten Sicherheitskräfte im sonst als ruhig und diszipliniert geltenden Thailand an die 1000 kreischende Fans vor seinem Hotel zurückhalten. Nicht nur manch jugendlicher Beckham-Fan geriet beim Anblick der Skulptur im Tempel fast in Ekstase. Auch die buddhistischen Pariwas-Mönche zeigten sich mit dem Ergebnis vollauf zufrieden. Und Vorsteher Chan Theerapunyo erläuterte: »Fußball ist eine Religion geworden. Um mit der Zeit zu gehen, müssen wir uns öffnen.« Schließlich ist der Buddhismus ja auch mehr als nur Religion. Er ist eine Philosophie, ein Lebensweg, der alle Bereiche erfassen, durchdringen und transformieren will.

Beckham Meets Buddha

Patricia Müller

The English football star David Beckham is venerated not just in the stadium but also in a Thai temple. The midfield player now occupies a niche as a «lower deity» in the guise of a gilded sculpture at the foot of a Buddha in the small Bangkok temple of Wat Pariwas. The statue is the work of the young Thai sculptor Jumnong Yantaphant, who has been a fervent fan of both Manchester United and Real Madrid. When the Pariwas monks asked Jumnong to create «something modern» for their Buddhist place of worship, he came up with – a statuette of Beckham 30 cm high. Although the statue at first caused some controversy among older Thais, ninety-five per cent of whom are Buddhist, the tide soon turned in favour of the sculpture. Young Thais especially welcomed the project; after all, Beckham enjoys cult status in the south-east Asian kingdom. On his most recent visits to Bangkok, security cordons had to restrain some thousand screeching fans in front of his hotel although Thailand is otherwise known for being peaceful and disciplined. Not only are some youthful Beckham fans almost thrown into raptures on catching sight of the sculpture in the temple. The Buddhist Pariwas monks are also completely satisfied with the result. And head monk Chan Theerapunyo explained: «Football has become a religion. To go with the times, we have to be open to it.» After all Buddhism is also more than just a religion. It is a philosophy, a way of life that aims at embracing, pervading and transforming all aspects of life.

Vergoldete Beckham-Skulptur des Bildhauers Jumnong Yantaphant im buddhistischen Pariwas-Tempel, Bangkok, Thailand. A gilded statue of Beckham by the sculptor Jumnong Yantaphant in the Buddhist Pariwas Temple, Bangkok, Thailand.

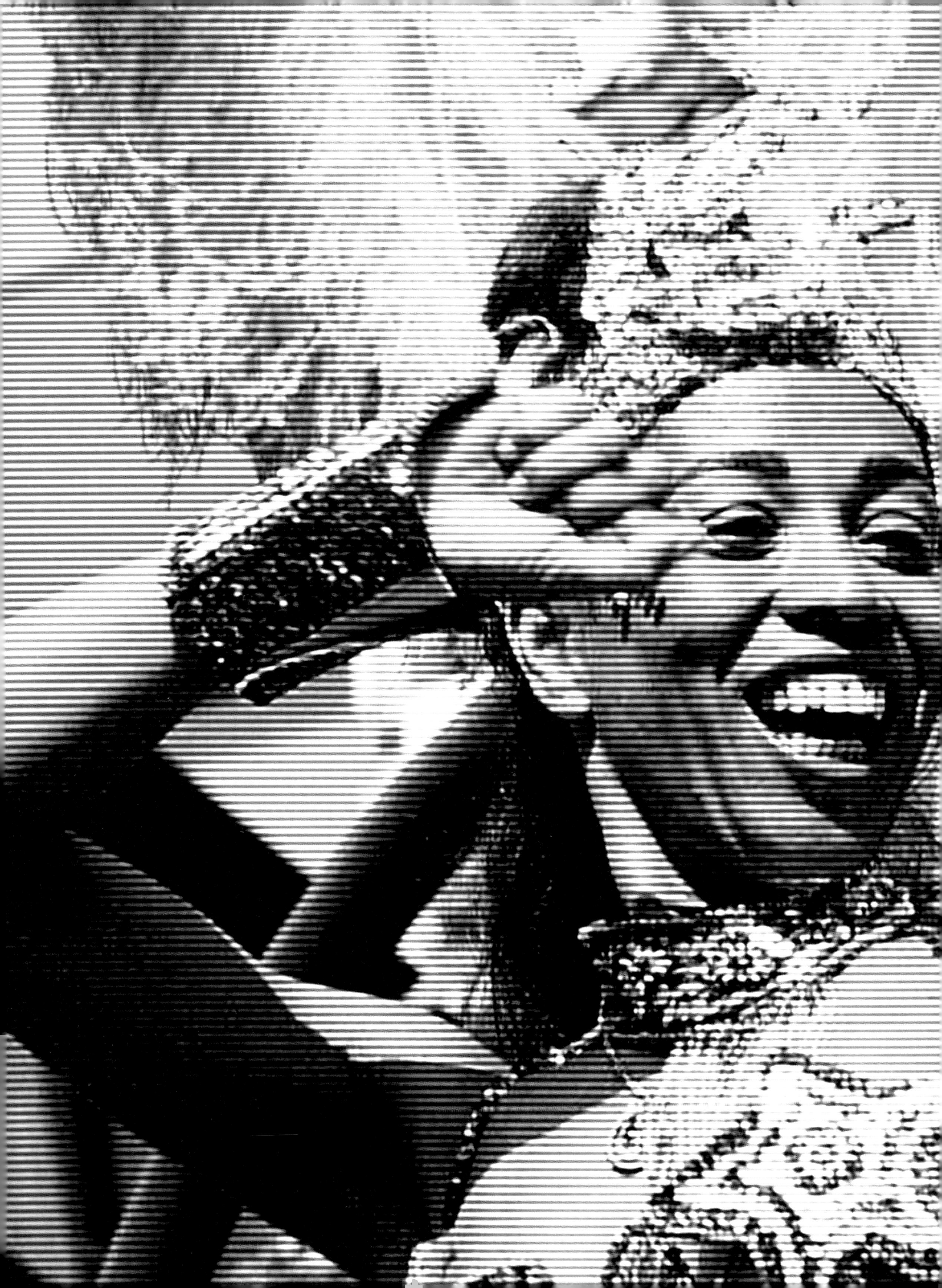

Fan-Träume – Fan-Wirklichkeiten
Fan Dreams – Fan Realities

In Treue ergeben
Die Welt der Fans

Christiane Lembert / Barbara Rusch

Vor dem Stadion des englischen Sunderland AFC steht ein Denkmal mit den Figuren eines Mannes, einer Frau und zweier Kinder. Der Verein hat das Monument den Generationen von Fans gewidmet, die dem Verein seit über 125 Jahren anhängen und auch in Zukunft unterstützen werden. Es verwundert nicht, dass gerade ein englischer Club seine Anhänger ehrt, schließlich ist England nicht nur die Wiege des Fußballs, sondern auch der Fankultur. Selbst die Bezeichnung *fan* stammt aus dem Englischen. Sie geht auf die lateinischen Begriffe *fanum,* »Tempel«, und *fanaticus* zurück. Letzterer beschreibt einen Menschen, der »von der Gottheit ergriffen und in rasende Begeisterung versetzt« wurde. Der Fußball-*Fan* frönt seinem Fanatismus für einen Verein, eine Mannschaft oder den Sport an sich und bringt diesen auf unterschiedliche Weisen zum Ausdruck. Im Portugiesischen heißen die enthusiastischen Anhänger *torcederos,* die »sich Windenden«, im Italienischen *tifosi,* »Typhuskranke«, die ihr Mit-Leiden am Spiel körperlich ausdrücken. Doch sind nicht alle Fußballzuschauer oder Anhänger einer Mannschaft als »Fans« zu bezeichnen. Auch bilden Fans keine homogene Gruppe, sondern eine vielschichtige Gemeinde mit den unterschiedlichsten sozialen und kulturellen Hintergründen, deren kleinster gemeinsamer Nenner die Leidenschaft für den Fußball ist. In seiner weitesten Definition ist ein Fußballfan ein Mensch, für den Fußball den Lebensmittelpunkt darstellt oder zumindest eine zentrale Rolle spielt. Und: Ein echter Fan ist bereit, für den Fußball einiges auf sich zu nehmen.

    Die Faszination am Fußball beruht sicher zu einem großen Teil auf seiner Fähigkeit, Emotionen und Leidenschaften zu entfachen. Eine wichtige Rolle spielt dabei die Unvorhersehbarkeit des Spiels und seine überraschenden Wendungen, die als eine Parabel auf das ungewisse Schicksal des menschlichen Daseins verstanden werden können. Zwischen Sieg und Niederlage reicht die Palette der erlebbaren Gefühle von tiefer Trauer über rasende Wut bis zu höchster Freude, umfasst Spannung, Aggression und Glück, Hass und Liebe. Fußball befriedigt ein Bedürfnis nach emotionaler Katharsis, die vor allem während und am Ort des direkten Geschehens durchlebt werden kann. Hierzu trägt die besondere Architektur des Stadions bei. Nach außen abgegrenzt, auf das Spielfeld konzentriert und als »Rund« konzipiert ermöglicht es ein kommunikatives Wechselspiel zwischen Spielern und Zuschauern sowie unter und zwischen den Anhängern der jeweiligen Mannschaften. Doch ist die fußballspezifische Gefühlswelt nicht nur auf die Arena beschränkt: Die Emotionen sind in allen fußballbezogenen Situationen möglich – während der Fahrt zum Stadion, vor dem Fernseher, beim »Nachtarocken« nach dem Spiel oder bei Gesprächen über Fußball.

    In der direkten Situation des Spiels sind Fans als Zuschauer zur Passivität bestimmt. Sie dürfen weder in den Spielverlauf eingreifen, noch bei der Mannschaftsaufstellung mitreden. Auch haben sie keinen Einfluss auf die Auswahl der Spieler, Trainer und Funktionäre.

Spezielle Fanbekleidung gab es schon seit den Anfängen des organisierten Fußballs. In Großbritannien etwa waren auffällige, in den Clubfarben gestaltete Schals, Mützen und Hüte verbreitet. There has always been special fan gear ever since organised football has existed. In Britain scarves, caps and hats in the club colours have always been widespread. ©Photo: Corbis 1923 »Hulton-Deutsch Collection«

Devoted to the Last
The World of Fans

Christiane Lembert / Barbara Rusch

In front of the Sunderland AFC stadium stands a monument consisting in the figure of a man, a woman and two children. The club dedicated the monument to the generations of fans who have been true to the team for more than one hundred and twenty five years and forthcoming generations who will continue to be supportive. It is not surprising that an English club would honour its fans. After all, England is the cradle of both football and fan culture. Even the term «fan» is English. It derives from the Latin noun *fanum*, meaning «temple», and from it in turn the adjective *fanaticus* is derived. In English «fanatic», this last concept describes a person who «is struck by the deity and is overcome by transports of rapturous enthusiasm». The football fan devotes his enthusiasm to a club, a team or the sport as such and finds various ways of expressing his feelings. In Portuguese enthusiastic aficionados are called *torcederos,* who «writhe» in their transports. In Italian, on the other hand, they are dubbed *tifosi,* «ill with typhus», people who physically express their passionate feelings about the game. Nonetheless, not all football spectators or even devotees of a team can be termed «fans».

Dennoch nehmen sie im Stadion mit ihrer Emotionalität aktiv und inbrünstig am Geschehen teil und schaffen so als »12. Mann« den Rahmen für das Spiel, der auch dessen Verlauf mitbestimmt.

Die emotionalisierende Kraft des Fußballs trägt dazu bei, dass er Loyalitäten mobilisieren und darstellen und auf diesem Weg auch Identität vermitteln kann. Von lokalen Nachbarschaftsspielen bis zu internationalen Turnieren bietet er ein Forum für den Ausdruck kollektiver Identitäten. Deren Ausbildung geht Hand in Hand mit einer deutlichen Abgrenzung zum »fußballerischen Gegenüber« – dem Verein aus dem anderen Stadtviertel, dem Konkurrenten um die nationale Meisterschaft oder die Nationalmannschaft eines anderen Landes. Identifikation und Emotion werden in positiver Unterstützung, aber auch in negativer Herabsetzung ausgelebt und verschiedenst geäußert – die Palette reicht von Anfeuerungen und Beschimpfungen, Lob- und Schmähgesängen, Banner und Graffiti mit Treueschwüren oder Beleidigungen bis hin zu freudiger Verbrüderung oder purer Gewalt.

Auch wenn die Berichterstattung über internationalen Fußball häufig die Unterstützer der Nationalmannschaften ins Bild rückt: Die Fanszene bestimmen in vielen Ländern

Fans von Manchester United gedenken der verstorbenen Fußball Ikone George Best im Spiel gegen West Bromwich Albion, November 2005.
Manchester United fans commemorating the late great football icon George Best at the match against West Bromwich Albion in November 2005.

Club-Loyalität wird auch an den Jüngsten mit Hilfe von Baby-Fanartikeln demonstriert. Auf diese Weise wird in einem ersten Schritt die nächste Generation in eine »Familien-Fantradition« aufgenommen. Club loyalty is demonstrated even by the youngest citizens sporting baby fan articles. Thus the first step is taken towards keeping up the «family fan tradition» in the next generation.

Fanshop des Middlesbrough Football Club: Die Fanartikelpalette der großen Clubs füllt heute ganze Läden. Jeder kann sich seine persönliche Umgebung – von der Handytasche bis zur Bettwäsche – mit den Farben und Emblemen »seines« Clubs gestalten. The Middlesbrough Football Club fan shop: the range of fan articles purveyed by the big clubs fills entire shops nowadays. Everyone styles his personal environment – from mobile phone pouch to bed linen – with the colours and crests of «his» club. © Photo: Roger Penn, Lancaster University

Nor do fans themselves form a homogeneous group. On the contrary, they are a multi-layered community from all sorts of social and cultural backgrounds whose smallest common denominator is their passion for football. The broadest definition of a football fan is a person for whom football represents the centre of his or her life or at least plays a pivotal role in it. And: a genuine fan is willing to put up with quite a lot for football.

The fascination of football certainly rests for the most part on its capacity for unleashing emotions and passion. An important role in this process is played by the unpredictability of the game and the surprising turns it can take, qualities which can be interpreted as a parable of the uncertain fate of human existence. Between victory and defeat, the gamut ranges from tense excitement, aggression and happiness, hatred and love. Football satisfies a need for emotional catharsis, which can best be experienced on site while a game is going on. The special stadium architecture also does its bit. Closed to the outside world, concentrated on the pitch and conceived «in the round», the stadium makes possible the interplay of communication between players and spectators as well as among and between the adherents of each team. Nonetheless the world of emotions specific to football is not limited to the arena; these are emotions that can be elicited in all situations related to football – during the trip to the stadium, in front of the television, while one is «reliving» the game afterwards or simply talking about football.

In the immediate situation of the game, fans are condemned to passivity as onlookers. They are not permitted to intervene in the game nor do they have a say in determining which members of a team are to play. Nor do fans exert any influence on the choice of players, trainers and functionaries. For all that they partake in what is happening in the stadium with their emotional approach and, therefore, as «twelfth man on the team», create the setting for a game, which also contributes to determining its outcome.

In Trinidad/Tobago erklärte Premier Manning den 17.11. anlässlich der Qualifikation des Nationalteams »Soca Warriors« zur FIFA WM 2006™ zum Feiertag. »Soca« ist keine Verballhornung von »soccer«, sondern ein landestypischer Musikstil. In Trinidad-Tobago, Prime Minister Manning declared 17 Nov. a holiday when the national team, the «Soca Warriors» qualified for the 2006 FIFA World Cup™. «Soca» isn't a dialectal form of the word «Soccer». It's a style of music typical of the islands. © Photo: AP

eher die Vereinsfans. Sie durchlaufen in der Beziehung zu ihrem Club einen komplexen Identifikationsprozess und lassen sich bei der Wahl ihres Vereins von verschiedenen Motiven leiten. Ein wichtiger Grund ist häufig die lokale Bindung, die für den Kreisligisten ebenso gilt wie für den Top-Verein aus der Millionenstadt. Kriterien sind aber auch die spezifischen Vereinskulturen, die Werte, die der Club und seine Mannschaft verkörpern, das soziale Milieu, für das er steht, oder die ethnische Zugehörigkeit seiner Mitglieder. Eine Rolle kann dabei auch die vorwiegende politische Ausrichtung der Fans eines Clubs spielen – oder eben nicht. Dies gilt etwa in Ländern wie der damaligen DDR oder dem Iran, wo Fußball eine Rückzugsmöglichkeit vor einem politisierten Alltag bot oder bietet. Besonders Fußballfans mit Migrationshintergrund können zudem multiple Fan-Identitäten entwickeln. So ist es z. B. für Münchner Türkischstämmige durchaus möglich, gleichzeitig die Lokalvereine Türkischer SV 1975 München und FC Bayern München sowie – in Bezug auf Familienherkunft und nationale Identifikation – Beşiktaş Istanbul und die türkische Nationalmannschaft zu unterstützen.

Vereinsidentitäten sind häufig eher imaginiert, als dass sie der Realität entsprechen, die Traditionen, die sich um sie ranken, oft bewusst eingeführt oder nicht weit zurückreichend. Und auch die Identitäten der Fans können kreiert sein. Ein weithin bekanntes Beispiel für dieses Phänomen sind in Europa die »jüdisch« imaginierten Vereine wie etwa Ajax Amsterdam oder Tottenham Hotspurs: Fans dieser Clubs schaffen sich als Reaktion auf antisemitische Schmähungen eine explizit »jüdische« Fan-Identität, die sich gleichsam verselbständigt hat.

Der Verein als eine »zweite Heimat« hat seine Wurzeln in der Gemeinschaft der Spieler, denn viele Clubs wurden als Spielvereinigungen gegründet. Vor allem auf dem Land leben auch heute noch unterklassige, in das Gemeindeleben integrierte Amateurvereine von

The power of football to emotionalise contributes to mobilising and demonstrating loyalties and can, therefore, also convey identity. From local neighbourhood games to international championships football provides a forum for the expression of collective identities. The formation of these identities goes hand in hand with clear demarcation from «the other side» in terms of football – a club from another part of the city, the rival team for the national championship or another country's national eleven. Identification and emotion are lived out in positive reinforcement but also in negative transference and are expressed in all sorts of different ways – the gamut ranges from exhortations and insults, paeans of praise and satirical ditties, banners and graffiti bearing vows of loyalty or insults to joyous fraternisation or naked violence.

Even though reporting of international football so often tends to focus on the supporters of the national teams, the fan scene in many countries tends rather to be shaped by supporters of football clubs. In their relationship to their club, they go through a complex process of identification and their choice of club is determined by all sorts of different motives. Local ties are often an important reason for a particular choice and this is just as true of local leaguers as it is of top-ranked teams from big cities. Other criteria, however, are the culture specific to a club, the values embodied by a club and its team, the social environment for which the club stands or the ethnicity of its members. The political bias of a majority of fans in a club can also play a role – or again it may not. It did and still does in countries such as the former GDR or Iran, where football provided or provides an opportunity of withdrawing from a politicised way of life. Football fans from an immigrant background tend to develop multiple fan identities. People of Turkish origin in Munich, for instance, can belong to both the local club, Türkischer SV 1975 München, and FC Bayern München while also supporting

Hooligans beziehen den »Kick« vor allem aus gewalttätigen Auseinandersetzungen mit gegnerischen Fans vor und nach dem Spiel wie hier bei der EM 2000. Hooligans really get a kick out of violent pitched battles with fans of the opposing team before and after a game, for example at the 2000 European Cup match. ©Photo: Reinhard Krause, Reuters/Corbis

Nach der Niederlage der russischen Mannschaft gegen Japan bei der WM 2002 kam es in Moskau zu schweren Unruhen. Severe rioting in Moscow followed the defeat of the Russian team by Japan in the 2002 World Cup. ©Photo: Sergei Kaprilkin, Corbis

dieser engen Verbindung von Spielern und Anhängern. Die globale Verbreitung des Fußballs war hingegen ein Migrationsphänomen. Die ersten außereuropäischen Vereine wurden meist von englischen oder anderen europäischen Migranten gegründet, die einheimische Bevölkerung schloss man häufig aus Rassismus und Klassendünkel aus. Die heute weit verbreiteten Fußballclubs als »Unterabteilungen« von Migrantenvereinen dienen anderen Zwecken. Abgesehen von der Freude am Spiel helfen sie – als Zusammenschluss von Angehörigen derselben Ethnie oder Schicksalsgemeinschaft –, die kollektive oder soziale Identität zu stärken.

Auch scheinen die Identifikation mit dem Verein und die Zusammensetzung der Mannschaft mittlerweile zu divergieren. Sind bei lokalen Vereinen die Spieler ein Teil der Gemeinschaft, muss bei den professionellen Clubs trotz Kommerzialisierung und globalem Spielertransfer darauf geachtet werden, dass der Verein die Funktion des *Local Players* übernimmt und versucht, heimatliche Bindung zur Stadt aufzubauen oder gar den Status einer gesellschaftlichen Institution zu erreichen. Deshalb spielt etwa das »traditionelle« Speisenangebot von der Bratwurst (Deutschland) bis zum heißen grünen Tee (Japan) in den Stadien eine wichtige Rolle. Auch ist die emotionale Bindung der Fans nicht gänzlich abgelöst von bestimmten Spielerpersönlichkeiten. Der Wechsel eines »Helden« zu einem anderen Verein kann ihm den Hass der gesamten Fangemeinde einbringen, der aus tief enttäuschter Liebe resultiert. War es in den 1960er Jahren für die Spieler der ethnisch definierten Fußballclubs in Kenia im wahrsten Sinne des Wortes lebensgefährlich, sich bei einem rivalisierenden Verein zu verpflichten, so ist es für Fans von A. E. K. Athen bis heute ein Ding der Unmöglichkeit, dass ein Spieler zum Erzrivalen Olympiakos wechselt. Und der heutige deutsche Bundestrainer Jürgen Klinsmann musste sich als aktiver Spieler bei seinem Wechsel vom VfB Stuttgart zum FC Bayern München mit Schmähungen überschütten lassen.

Im Kontext des weltweiten Fußballs bildeten sich zudem Kulturen und Traditionen aus, die z. T. nur gewisse Zeit bestehen, sich ausbreiten und wandern, einen Generationenwechsel anzeigen oder sich Moden, Zeitströmungen oder politischen Veränderungen anpassen. Sie greifen auf lokale gesellschaftliche und kulturelle Gegebenheiten und Entwicklungen zurück, verdeutlichen auf ihre Weise aber auch den Übergang zu einer zunehmend globalisierten Welt. Die in den Stadien sichtbaren Fankulturen sind ein Teil dieser Entwicklung,

»Danke Papa – dass du mich damals ins Westfalenstadion mitgenommen hast!« Fan-Schal von Borussia Dortmund.
«Thanks, Dad – for taking me with you that time to the Westfalenstadion!» A Borussia Dortmund fan scarf.

Auto-Nummernschild, vergeben von der »Republik Fenerbahçe«, für Fans von Fenerbahçe Istanbul.
Car number plate issued by the «Republic of Fenerbahçe» for Fenerbahçe Istanbul fans.

– and this relates to their familial origins and national identity – Beşiktaş Istanbul and the Turkish national team.

Club identities tend to be imaginary rather than matching reality. The traditions associated with them have often been deliberately introduced or may not go back all that far. And even fan identities can be artificial. Well-known examples of this phenomenon in Europe are the clubs perceived as «Jewish» such as Ajax Amsterdam or Tottenham Hotspurs. Fans of these clubs have created an overtly «Jewish» fan identity as a reaction to anti-Semitic insults and this identity has, as it were, continued to develop on its own.

The club as a «home away from home» is rooted in the community represented by the players since many clubs were founded as player associations. In rural areas especially, low-ranking amateur clubs that are integrated in community life are still fed by this close link between players and supporters. The global spread of football, on the other hand, was a migratory phenomenon. Most of the earliest non-European clubs were founded by English or other European emigrants seeking to exclude the indigenous population because of racism and class-based snobbery. The nowadays widespread football clubs representing subdivisions of immigrant clubs, however, serve other ends. Apart from the universal delight in the game, they help – as an association of people belonging to the same ethnic group or all those sharing a similar fate – to strengthen collective or social identity.

Identification with a club and the ethnic composition of its team now seem to be diverging. Even though the players supported by local clubs are part of the community, professional clubs must take into consideration that, despite commercialisation and global player trading, the club assumes the function of local player and tries to build up local ties to the city or even to attain the status of a social institution. That is why aspects such as the «traditional» regional bill of fare such as Bratwurst (Germany) and hot green tea (Japan) play an important role in the stadiums. And fans have not entirely broken off emotional ties to particular celebrated players. If a «local hero» transfers to a different club, the move can earn him the hatred of the entire local fan community, an emotion that grows out of a profound disappointment in love. In the 1960s players associated with the ethnically defined football clubs in Kenya risked their lives in the literal sense of the term if they committed themselves to a rival club. Similarly today, fans of A. E. K. Athens would not put up with a player of theirs transferring to their arch rival, Olympiakós. And Jurgen Klinsmann, now trainer of the German national team, was deluged with insults when he transferred from VfB Stuttgart to FC Bayern München in the days when he was still an active player.

In the context of global football, moreover, cultures and traditions, some of which are in any case of a transient nature, spread and migrate, pinpoint a change in generation or adjust to fashions, prevailing trends or political change. Such cultures and traditions go back to local societal and cultural conditions and developments but also mark in their way the transition to an increasingly globalised world. The fan cultures visible in the stadiums are

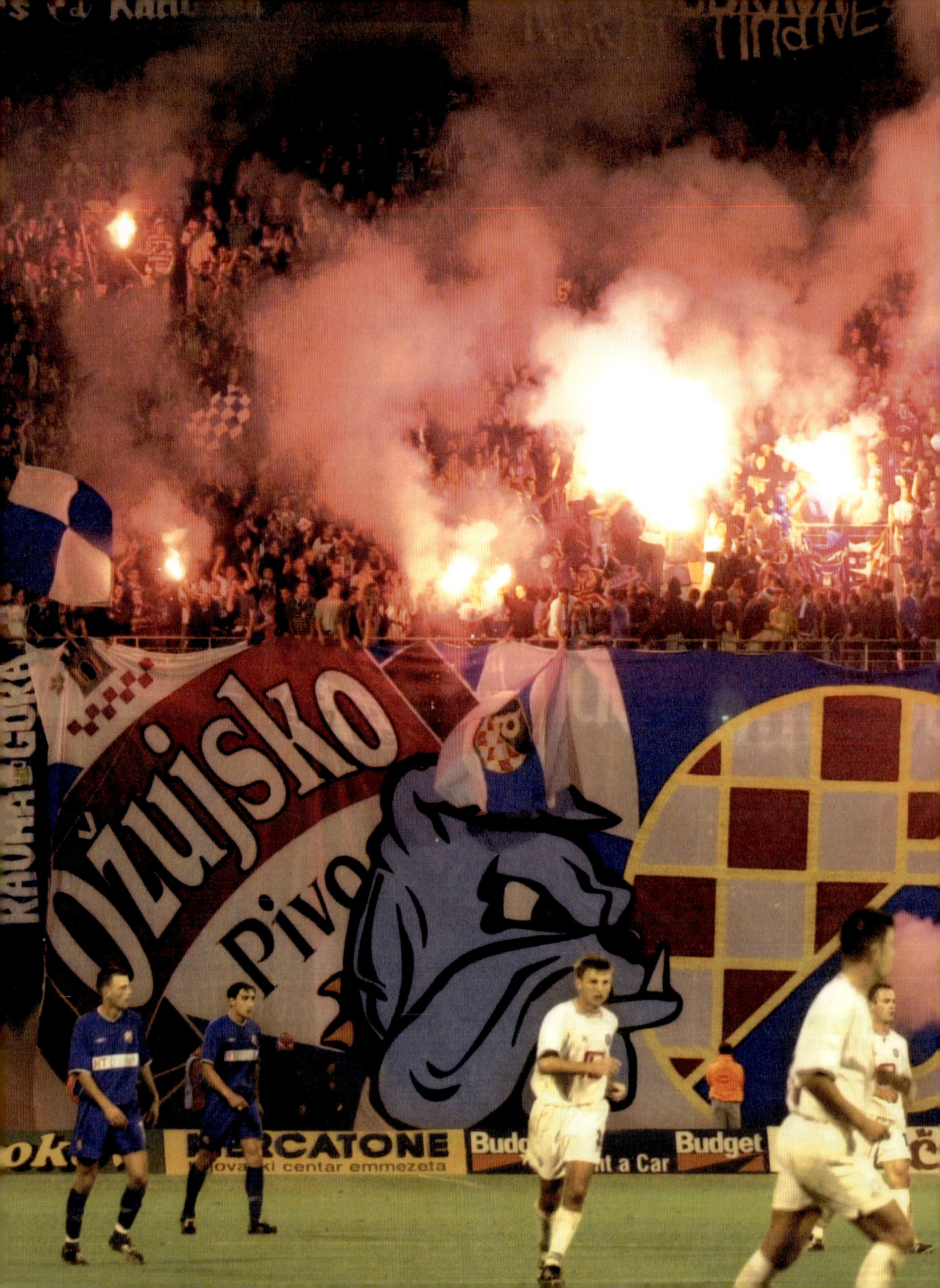
Ožujsko
Pivo
ERCATONE
Budget

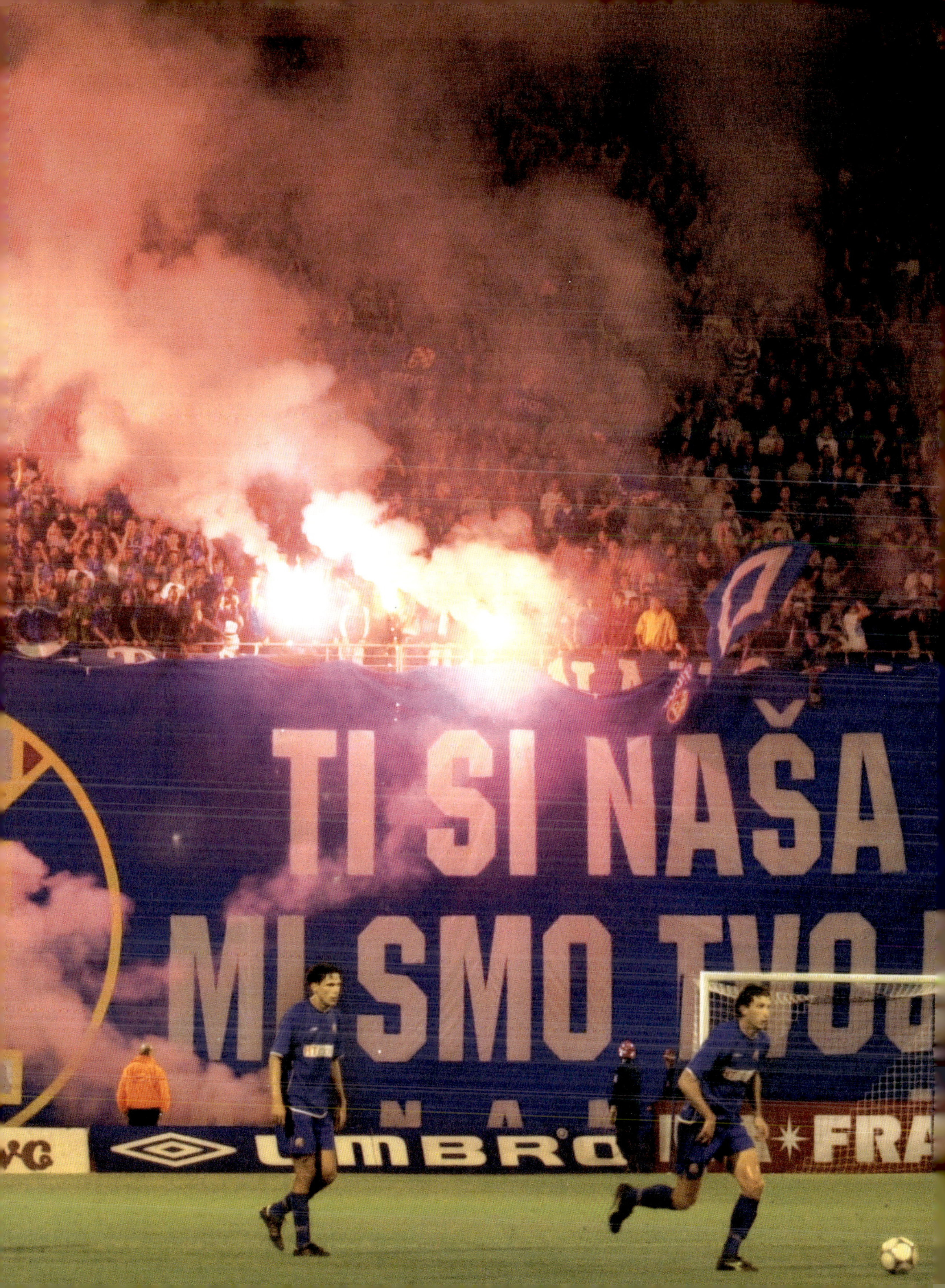
TI SI NAŠA
MI SMO TVO
UMBRO
FRA

Gelungene Choreographien der Ultras in den Stadien mit Schwenkfahnen, Papptafeln und Farbbändern bedürfen einer langen Vorbereitungszeit, eines beträchtlichen Budgets und einer ausgefeilten Logistik. Successful Ultra choreography with waving fans, cardboard placards and coloured banners requires lengthy preparation, a considerable budget and sophisticated logistics.

← Die 1950 gegründeten »Torcida« des kroatischen Clubs Hajduk Split gelten als die älteste Fanorganisation Europas. Vorbild für ihre enthusiastische Unterstützung waren die brasilianischen Fans, die Torcidas. Founded in 1950 the «Torcida» of the Croatian club Hajduk Split are believed to be Europe's oldest fan organisation, modelled on the Torcidas, the Brazilian fans.
© Photo: Mike Redmann

die in den letzten Jahren – besonders in den oberen Ligen und auf internationaler Ebene – vom zunehmend kommerzialisierten Showcharakter des Fußballs geprägt ist.

Fankulturen stehen auch für bestimmte Ideen und Einstellungen gegenüber dem Spiel und der Mannschaft und für politische Gesinnungen. Beispiele sind etwa in Europa die »Kuttenfans« (vgl. *Fankultur und Jugendkultur – die Kutten,* S. 168), die von der in den 1970er Jahren in Italien entstandenen »Ultra-Bewegung« mit ihren aufwändigen Choreografien abgelöst werden. Deren Anhänger agieren inzwischen weltweit in den Stadien, weisen aber starke lokale Unterschiede etwa hinsichtlich ihrer Gewaltbereitschaft oder dem Grad ihrer Politisierung auf. Ein ebenfalls weltweites Phänomen stellen die Hooligans dar. Ursprünglich im englischen Arbeitermilieu entstanden, berauschen sich mittlerweile Angehörige aus allen Schichten als »Hools« weniger am Spiel als am »Kick«, denen ihnen der gewalttätige Kampf mit gegnerischen Fans verleiht.

Phänotypische Merkmale für Fankulturen sind etwa Kleidung oder Equipment für den Stadionbesuch wie Fahnen, Lärminstrumente oder Vereinsdevotionalien. Die gerne zitierte Sambakultur der »Brasilianer« in den Stadien äußert sich auch in Musik und Gewändern. (Fußball-)politische Gesinnungen kommen dagegen in Sprechchören und Vereinsliedern, Fangesängen und Gebärden, auf Bannern und in »Fanzines« zum Ausdruck.

Letztlich ergibt sich die Vielfalt auf den Stadienrängen aus der kulturellen Heterogenität der Zuschauer – aber auch aus ihrer Bandbreite vom »Gelegenheitstäter« bis zum »echten Fan« – und ihren unterschiedlichen matchbezogenen Intentionen: dem Wunsch nach einem schönen Spiel, nach einem unbedingten Sieg der eigenen Mannschaft oder dem Ausleben intensiver Emotionen.

Fans von Genua 93 im Spiel gegen Sanpeloroa in der Saison 2001/02. In der gleichen Stadt sollen sich etwa 30 Jahre früher Fans von Sampdoria Genua als erste »Ultras« genannt haben.
Genoa 93 fans at the game against Sanpelorca during the 2001/02 season. In Genoa, fans of Sampdoria Genoa are said to have been the first to call themselves the «Ultras» thirty years ago.
© Photo: Mike Redmann, 2002

part of this development, which in recent years – particularly in the upper leagues and on the international level – has been shaped by the increasingly commercialised show character of football.

Fan cultures also stand for specific ideas and attitudes to the game and the team as well as political ideas. This is exemplified in Europe, for instance, by the *Kutten* (cf *Fan Culture and Youth Culture – «Kutten»*, p. 168), who were supplanted by the «Ultra movement» with its elaborate choreographies, which sprang up in 1970s Italy. Its adherents are now active in stadiums world-wide yet reveal pronounced local differences, especially with regard to their attitudes to violent behaviour or the degree to which they have been politicised. Hooligans are another world-wide phenomenon. Originally a product of an English working-class environment, «hools» are now recruited from all classes. They get less of a «kick» from the game than they do from violent battles with fans of an opposing team.

Phenotype markers of fan cultures are kit or gear for stadium use such as banners, noise-makers and club memorabilia. The frequently cited «Brazilian» samba culture in stadiums also expresses itself in music and clothing. (Football-related) political ideologies, on the other hand, are aired in chanting and club songs, fan songs and gestures, on banners and in fanzines.

Ultimately, however, the diversity displayed in the stadium tiers results from the cultural heterogeneity of the spectators – although also from their position on the scale ranging from the «occasional spectator» to «genuine fan» – and the differences in their intentions regarding a game: the desire for a fine game, for victory at any price by the home team or an opportunity for indulging in excessive emotion.

Die Welt der Fanartikel

Christiane Lembert / Barbara Rusch

Kultureller Hintergrund, persönliche Vorlieben und *last but not least* der Geldbeutel bestimmen die bunte Vielfalt an materiellen Zeichen, durch die viele Fußballfans im Stadion und im Alltag ihre Zugehörigkeit, Loyalitäten und Abneigungen eindeutig und sichtbar ausdrücken. Diese öffentlichen Bekenntnisse blicken auf eine lange Tradition zurück. Die Tendenz, sich speziell für das Spiel zu kleiden, gab es schon zu Beginn des organisierten Fußballs. Kopfbedeckungen und Schals, die heute weltweit zum klassischen Fanarsenal zählen, haben britische Wurzeln. Bereits im Jahr 1884 (!) bezeichnete die *Pall Mall Gazette* die Fans aus Blackburn in London anlässlich des F. A. Cup Final als »Nordische Horde in wunderlichen Trachten und mit liederlichen Flüchen.« (»A northern horde of uncouth garb and strange oaths.«). Die *supporters* trugen individuell gestaltete »Mützen, Schals und Schirme in den jeweiligen Vereinsfarben.« In England gründet die öffentliche Darstellung von Zugehörigkeiten durch Farben auf der Tradition der Public Schools und den Symbolfarben ihrer einzelnen Häuser sowie später ihrer Schülermannschaften. Lautstarke Unterstützung gaben die Fans um 1900 mit hölzernen Ratschen, die einen Höllenlärm verursachen konnten. In den 1960er Jahren »exportierte« die britische Fankultur als akustischen Beistand Gesänge, die der Beat- oder Popkultur entlehnt waren. Auf einem historischen Foto von 1926 sieht man zudem bereits ein Fan-Statement: Am Hut eines Mannes prangt die handgeschriebene Aufforderung »Up Fulham. Let'em all come. The bigger the better« (»Hoch Fulham. Sie sollen nur kommen. Je stärker, desto besser«). Vereinzelte Wimpeln und Fahnen wurden ab den 1920er Jahren in die deutschen Stadien mitgenommen.

Mittlerweile staffieren sich Fans in vielen Regionen der Welt für den Besuch im Stadion mit einem ganzen Arsenal an Utensilien aus. Neben Schals und Kopfbedeckungen sieht man auf den Tribünen Trikots, Fahnen mit den Vereinswappen oder den Nationalfarben, Spruchbanner, Zubehör für Choreographien und Musikinstrumente, zur Fankleidung umgestaltete Versatzstücke lokaler oder nationaler Trachten. Häufig wird dabei auf glorreiche oder »wildere« vergangene Zeiten zurückgegriffen. Mexikanische Fans favorisieren aztekische Kopfputze, bei Skandinaviern sind Wikingerhelme beliebt und französische Fans geben sich bisweilen »gallisch« mit Helm und nacktem Oberkörper. In Regionen, wo die in Industrieländern weit verbreiteten typischen Merchandising-Artikel für die allermeisten nicht erschwinglich sind, zeigen Fans beim Stadionbesuch ihre Vereinszugehörigkeiten etwa durch normale Kleidung in den Clubfarben.

Fanartikel fanden bereits in den Frühzeiten des Fußballs ihren Weg in das Alltagsleben. Ende des 19. Jahrhunderts etwa zierten Fußballmotive Pfeifen, Uhren und kunstgewerbliche Artikel. Mit Tischfußball und anderen Gesellschaftsspielen amüsiert der Fußball ebenfalls schon seit über 100 Jahren auch außerhalb des Stadions. Und in England gab es in jener Zeit auch schon die *Baines Cards,* die ersten Sammelkarten mit Vereinsemblemen und Spielerfotos.

Die »Kommerzmaschine« Fußball hat inzwischen eine wahre Flut von Gegenstände für alle möglichen und unmöglichen Alltagssituationen des Fanlebens geschaffen. Feuerzeuge, Bettwäsche, Gläser, Tassen, Schlüsselanhänger, Taschen, Geldbeutel, Hundekörbchen, Unterwäsche – die Industrie scheint vor nichts Halt zu machen. Die lokale Anbindung drückt sich im landestypischen Geschirr, in der Kleidung oder im Schmuck aus. Das Angebot von industriellen Fanartikeln folgt dabei streng marktwirtschaftlichen Kriterien. So werden etwa in Marokko zwar Wimpel, Fahnen, Poster oder Trikots von international gefeierten Stars oder Spitzenclubs wie FC Barcelona und FC Bayern München verkauft, hingegen aber kaum Fanartikel lokaler, marokkanischer Clubs. Es lohnt sich offensichtlich nicht!

The World of Fan Memorabilia

Christiane Lembert / Barbara Rusch

Cultural background, personal preferences and, last but not least, personal finances determine the amount and splendour of the material signs through which many football fans unequivocally flaunt their allegiance, their loyalties and their dislikes in the stadium and everywhere else on a daily basis. These publicly displayed professions of allegiance look back on a long tradition. The tendency to dress specially for the game has existed since the beginnings of organised football. Caps and scarves, which today are part of the classic fan arsenal world-wide, have British roots. Back in 1884 (!) the *Pall Mall Gazette* was spluttering over fans from Blackburn who were in London for the FA Cup Final as «a northern horde of uncouth garb and strange oaths.» These pioneering supporters were sporting individually designed caps, scarves and umbrellas in the club colours. In England the public display of allegiance by wearing the colours is based on the Public School tradition with its symbolic House Colours and later the Public School teams. By 1900 fans were making a hell of a lot of noise with wooden rattles to show their support. In the 1960s the British fan culture started «exporting» songs borrowed from rock or pop culture as an acoustic display of support. In a historic photo from 1926, a man is shown wearing a hat with what is already a hand-written fan statement: «Up Fulham. Let'em all come. The bigger the better.» Pennants and flags began to appear in German stadiums from the 1920s.

Nowadays fans in many parts of the world are kitted out for a visit to the stadium with an entire arsenal of gear and memorabilia. Not just scarves and headgear are seen in the blocks. Jerseys, flags and the club crest or the national colours, banners emblazoned with verbal encouragement, choreographic equipment and musical instruments, local or national dress transformed into fan garb for the occasion are the order of the day in the stadium. A glorious or more «savage» past is often evoked. Mexican fans favour Aztec headgear. Scandinavians, of course, turn out in Viking helmets, and French fans occasionally look like ancient Gauls wearing helmets and flaunting bare manly torsos. In regions where most people cannot afford the typical merchandise available everywhere in industrialised countries, fans show their club allegiance by appearing in the stadium dressed normally but in the club colours.

Even in the early days of football, club memorabilia were a factor to be reckoned with in everyday living. By the late 19th century, football motifs were mushrooming on pipes, watches and other merchandise. In the form of table football and pinball, football has been a source of amusement outside the stadium for over a century. And in England there were *Baines Cards* back then, the first cards for fans to collect with club emblems and photos of players.

The commercialisation of football has created a host of articles for all possible and impossible everyday situations in the life of a fan. Lighters, bed linen, glasses, cups, keyrings, bags, wallets, pet baskets, underwear – nothing is sacred to the memorabilia industry. Local allegiance is expressed in crockery, clothing or jewellery typical of the region. The range of mass-produced club memorabilia available strictly observes the laws of the marketplace. In Morocco, for example, the flags, banners, posters and jerseys associated with internationally famous stars or such premiership clubs as FC Barcelona and FC Bayern München are sold but hardly any memorabilia for fans of local Moroccan clubs. They are evidently not marketable!

Wimpel von drei marokkanischen Fußballvereinen: Oft ist es einfacher, in Nordafrika Fan-Utensilien großer internationaler Vereine zu erwerben als solche von einheimischen Mannschaften. Pennants of three Moroccan football clubs: it's often easier to buy the gear of large international clubs than that of local teams.

Fan-Schals zeigen die Farben und Embleme von Mannschaften, erinnern an bestimmte Spiele oder Meisterschaften und transportieren häufig Parolen über das Selbstverständnis von Verein oder Fanclub. Fan scarves display the colours and crests of teams, commemorate particular games or championship tournaments and are often vehicles for slogans expressing the self-image of a team or fan club.

Fanartikel fanden bereits in den Frühzeiten des Fußballs ihren Weg ins Alltagsleben. Diese Tonpfeife ziert ein Fußballstiefel. Fan articles entered everyday life in the early days of football. This clay pipe is decorated with a football boot.

Clubloyalität für Heimwerker: Zollstöcke für Fans der Teams Erzgebirge und Wismut Aue. Club loyalty for do-it-yourselfers: yardsticks for fans of the Erzgebirge and Wismut Aue teams.

Noch in den 1970er Jahren strickten in Westdeutschland viele Mütter ihren Söhnen Schals und Mützen in den Farben des Lieblingsvereins – hier des TSV 1860 München. In the 1970s, many West German mothers still knit scarves and caps for their sons in the colours of their favourite club – here TSV 1860 München.

Das Fußball-Marketing erobert traditionelles Brauchtum: Aus Trockenfrüchten gebastelte »Hutzelmännchen« sind in Süddeutschland und Tirol um die Weihnachtszeit beliebte Mitbringsel. Football marketing conquers traditional custom: «Hutzelmännchen» are popular items in southern Germany and the Tyrol at Christmas time.

Bereits Unterwäsche für Kleinkinder ist mit Bekenntnissen für den Verein bedruckt. Never too young to start: baby underwear printed with professions of club allegiance.

Für kleine Barça-Fans: Die bei spanischen Kindern heißbegehrten knallbunten Lutscher – verziert mit dem Vereinswappen. For little Barça fans: Spanish kids love these lollies – sporting the club crest.

Handtuch für Fans von Arsenal London. Towel made for fans of Arsenal London.

161

Edgar Davids als Corinthian-Figur. Edgar Davids as a Corinthian figurine.

Der Fußball erobert den Alltag – hier in Form von Espresso-Tassen, die in keinem italienischen Haushalt fehlen dürfen. Espresso Tassen AS-Roma. Football conquers everyday living – here in the form of Espresso cups, which are a must in all Italian households. AS Roma espresso cups.

In chinesischen Fußballzeitschriften findet man als Beilage häufig Sammelbildchen von Spielern aus europäischen Ligen. Collectable pictures of European-league players are often encountered in Chinese football magazines.

Auch in Westafrika durchdringen Fußball-Motive immer stärker die Alltagswelt: Streichholzschachtel aus dem Senegal. Football motifs pervade everyday living in West Africa, too: a matchbox from Senegal.

Passagen
Ein Lebensweg mit dem Verein

Christiane Lembert / Barbara Rusch

Im Zusammenspiel zweier Sinnstifter können Riten eine besondere Dynamik entwickeln. So berichtet die DFB-Schiedsrichterzeitung von 1933 über Fußballgottesdienste in der englischen Stadt Kingston, deren Besuch »außerordentlich groß« gewesen sei. Dazu wurden im Kirchenschiff Fußbälle aufgehängt und die Stühle mit Fußballtrikots verhängt. In den Gängen standen Linienrichter mit Fähnchen, im Mittelschiff ein Tor, und der Geistliche leitete seine Predigt mit einem Pfiff in die Schiedsrichterpfeife ein. Doch kommt nicht nur der Fußball zur Kirche, sondern auch die Kirche zum Fußball: Was in Lateinamerikas Arenen bekannt ist, findet auch in Europa von Barcelona bis Gelsenkirchen zum Wohl beider Institutionen Nutzen: Stadionkapellen.

Besondere Bedeutung besitzen diese Kirchen im Kontext der *rites de passage*. Diese lebenszyklischen Übergangsriten markieren den Wechsel von einem Lebensabschnitt in den anderen, Veränderungen im sozialen Status und die Eingliederung in soziale Gemeinschaften. Sie begleiten etwa Geburt, Heirat und Tod eines Menschen, aber auch seinen Eintritt in das Erwachsenenalter. Feierliche Riten wie Taufe oder Hochzeit betonen die Bedeutung dieser Übergänge, beinhalten durch ihren öffentlichen Charakter für die Akteure aber auch Bekenntnis und Verpflichtung.

Echte Fans haben oft das Bedürfnis, den eigenen Lebensweg mit ihrem Verein zu verknüpfen und ihre wichtigsten Lebensereignisse im emotional stark besetzten Stadion des geliebten Clubs zu markieren. Die in der Fußballliteratur gerne geschilderte »klassische« Initiation in einen Verein wird in der Regel mit dem ersten Besuch im Stadion gleichgesetzt. Doch die Zugehörigkeit und Liebe zu ihrem Club wollen Vereinsfans oft schon »von Anfang an« auf ihre Kinder übertragen. So werden bereits die Jüngsten als Clubmitglied angemeldet, während sie noch am Schnuller mit Vereinslogo nuckeln. Die Möglichkeit zu einer profanen und sakralen Initiation bieten etwa der brasilianische Fußballclub Vasco da Gama in seiner Stadionkirche, aber auch der deutsche Traditionsverein Schalke 04 in der ökumenischen Kapelle seiner Veltins Arena. Hier wie dort können Fans ihre Kinder taufen lassen. In Gelsenkirchen schließt zudem nicht nur der Geistliche Hochzeiten, man kann sich auch standesamtlich trauen lassen. Die Fans geben so ein mehrfaches Bekenntnis ab: zu ihrer Religion, ihrem Lebenspartner, ihrer Familie – und zu ihrem Verein.

In britischen Stadien – etwa von Manchester United oder der Bolton Wanderers – kann man solche Bekenntnisse an den *Walkways of Fame* abgeben. Dort künden Hunderte Inschriften von der Hingabe namentlich genannter Fans und von wichtigen Ereignissen in ihrem Leben wie die Geburt von Kindern, »runde« Geburtstage und Jubiläen. Auf Gedenksteinen sind Namen und Lebensdaten von Fans verewigt. Die »Ruhmeswege« finden die Aufmerksamkeit vieler Besucher, die dort verweilen, um nach Namen von Bekannten zu suchen.

Eine profane und sakrale Initiation in den Verein bietet Schalke 04 in der ökumenischen Kapelle seiner Veltins-Arena. Dort haben sich Bettina und Stefan »Örwin« Krohn trauen lassen – beide Gründungsmitglieder des Schalke-Fanclubs Höxter-Warburg. Schalke 04 provides both a profane and a sacred initiation into the club in the ecumenical chapel at their Veltins Arena. Bettina and Stefan «Örwin» Krohn – both founding members of the Höxter-Warburg Cohalke fan club – got married there.
© Photo: Klaus Wieschus

Als erste Schalker Fans ließen Monika Haack und Frank Ebbing ihre Tochter Marie Christin am 17.08.2001 in der Veltins-Arena auf Schalke taufen. Die Idee stammte von der Mutter. Monika Haack and Frank Ebbing were the first Schalker fans to have their daughter, Marie Christin, baptised in the Schalke Veltins Arena on 17 Aug. 2001. It was Mum's idea. © Photo: www.fcschalkenullvier.de, Joachim Haack

Passages
Lifelong with the Club

Christiane Lembert / Barbara Rusch

Rites can develop a special dynamic in the interplay of two significant institutions. The DFB referee newspaper reported in 1933 on football divine service held in Kingston, England, which were «exceptionally well attended». Footballs were suspended in the church nave for it and the pews were hung with football jerseys. Linesman with flags stood in the aisles, a goal was set up in the middle aisle and the clergyman started his sermon by blowing a referee's whistle. However, football not only goes to church; the Church goes to football. What is familiar from Latin American stadiums is also encountered in Europe from Barcelona to Gelsenkirchen: stadium chapels.

These churches possess particular significance in the context of *rites of passage*. These are rites marking the transition from one segment of the life cycle to the next, changes in social status and integration in social communities. They accompany birth, marriage and death as well as coming of age. Solemn rites such as baptism or the marriage ceremony emphasise the importance of such transitions but their public nature also exacts allegiance and commitment of those taking part in them.

Genuine fans often feel a need to link their own lives with their club and to celebrate the most important events in them in the emotionally charged stadium of their beloved club.

Bestattungsunternehmen bieten Fans fußballförmige Urnen in den Farben ihrer Vereine an. Urne für Anhänger von Borussia Dortmund. Undertakers offer fans football-shaped urns in their club colours. Urn made for supporters of Borussia Dortmund.

Auch die letzte Passage im Leben aller Menschen kann ein Bekenntnis ausdrücken. Für die Fans der Revierrivalen Borussia Dortmund und Schalke 04 bieten Bestattungsunternehmen fußballförmige Urnen in den Farben der Vereine oder Särge an, die mit den Vereinsinsignien geschmückt sind. Auf diese Weise können Fans noch auf ihrem letzten Weg ihre Liebe zum Fußball und zu ihrem Verein kundgeben.

In anderen Ländern bieten sich dank liberalerer Bestattungsgesetze ganz andere Möglichkeiten. In den Niederlanden finden Anhänger von Ajax Amsterdam ihre letzte Erfüllung auf dem Amsterdamer Friedhof Westgaarde, wo Rasenstücke aus dem Stadion zu einer Aschenstreuwiese zusammengelegt wurden. Selbst die Namensschilder haben die Form eines Fußballs. In Großbritannien muss man sich nicht nur symbolisch mit dem Stadion als Bestattungsort zufrieden geben. Dort bieten einige Clubs ihren *supporters* an, im Stadion ihre sterblichen Überreste in Form von Asche feierlich verstreuen zu lassen. Bekannt ist dies etwa vom FC Swansea oder vom Birmingham FC. Je nach Wunsch werden die Bestattungszeremonien von einem Priester ausgeführt, und auch der rituelle Grundstock des Übergangs bleibt erhalten: Die Feier in einer Trauergemeinschaft, die Prozession zum Bestattungsort, die Übergabe in ein anderes Element (Feuer und Erde) und das Gedenken.

Die Themenbestattungen, Gedenksteine und Stadionbegräbnisse sind Ausdruck neuer Strömungen in der westlichen Trauerkultur mit ihren christlich basierten Traditionen. War diese seit dem frühen 20. Jahrhundert zunehmend von funktionalisierter Routine, Verdrängung und Anonymisierung geprägt, so verstärkt sich in den letzten Jahrzehnten eine gegenläufige Bewegung: Trauer wird zunehmend individuell präsentiert und wieder öffentlich gezeigt. Im Rahmen dieser Entwicklung werden die Friedhöfe langsam als wichtigste Stätten der öffentlichen Trauer von anderen Orten abgelöst, etwa den Stadien. Die »Fußballbegräbnisse« zeugen aber vor allem von einem ganz besonderen Phänomen – der tiefen Liebe zum Fußball und der starken Identifikation mit dem auserwählten Club.

The «classic» initiation into a club so often described in publications dealing with football is usually equated with the first visit to the stadium. However, club fans often want to transfer to their offspring «right from the beginning» the feelings of belongingness and love they have for their club. Even the youngest are registered as members while they are still sucking on comforters adorned with the club crest. The Brazilian football club Vasco da Gama provides the possibility of a profane and a sacred initiation in its stadium church but so does the tradition-minded German club Schalke 04, in the ecumenical chapel at its Veltins-Arena. Fans can have their children baptised at both. In Gelsenkirchen, moreover, clergymen not only conduct the marriage service; you can even plight your troth at a civil marriage here. Thus fans profess several things: their religion, fidelity to their partner in life, their family – and their football club.

At British stadiums – such as that of Manchester United or the Bolton Wanderers – you can make such vows at the *Walkways of Fame*. There hundreds of inscriptions testify to the commitment of fans, who are mentioned by name, and to important events in their lives such as the birth of children, «even» birthdays and anniversaries. The memorial stones immortalise fans' names and significant dates in their lives. The *Walkways of Fame* attract the notice of many fans and visitors, who like to linger there, perhaps to look for a friend's name or just to read the inscriptions.

Even the last passage in all our lives can be expressed as a profession. Undertakers offer football-shaped urns in the club colours or coffins decorated with club crests to proclaim the love for football and their club professed by fans of Borussia Dortmund and Schalke 04, rival clubs in the coalmining district, on their last way.

In other countries, thanks to more liberal funerary laws, there are possibilities of an entirely different kind. In the Netherlands supporters of Ajax Amsterdam are in seventh heaven in the knowledge that their ashes can be scattered over a blanket of turf taken from the stadium and laid out in Westgaarde Cemetery in Amsterdam. Even the nameplates are in the form of footballs. In Britain you need not content yourself with the stadium as your last resting place in the purely symbolic sense. Some clubs even reward their supporters by having their cremated mortal remains ceremonially scattered in the stadium. Fans of FC Swansea and Birmingham FC are known to have taken advantage of this generous offer. Depending on a fan's last wish, the funeral service can be officiated by a priest or minister and even the ritual basis of the transition is retained: the ceremony in a congregation of mourners, the cortège to the place of burial, consignment to the elements (fire and earth) and the memorial.

Themed funerals, commemorative stones and funerals in stadiums express new trends in Western funerary culture which is based on Christian tradition. This Western funerary culture had been in decline since the early 20th century, when it became functionalised routine, repressed from the general conscious and anonymous. In recent years there has been a counter-movement: mourning is being individualised and once again shown publicly. In the context of this development, cemeteries are being replaced as the most important sites for public mourning by different places, such as stadiums. Most of all, however, «football funerals» attest to a very special phenomenon – fans' great love for football and strong identification with their chosen clubs.

Memento mori
Das Stadion als heiliger Ort

Christiane Lembert / Barbara Rusch

Der englische Traditionsverein Birmingham City FC bietet seinen Fans die Möglichkeit, sich im St Andrew Stadium des Clubs bestatten zu lassen. In einer feierlichen, nach Wunsch von einem Priester begleiteten Zeremonie wird die Asche der Verstorbenen von den Angehörigen in die leere Arena gebracht und am Rand des Spielfelds verstreut. Nicht nur die im Stadion bestatteten, sondern auch andere verstorbene Fans können zudem im clubeigenen *Book of Remembrance*, am *Walkway of Fame* des Stadions sowie auf einer Website verewigt werden. Da die Besonderheit des Begräbnisortes in der christlich geprägten, europäischen Trauerkultur eine wichtige Rolle spielt, zeigen die Bestattungen und das öffentliche Gedenken an die Toten, welch herausragende Stellung das Stadion für die engste Fangemeinde als emotionale »Heimat« einnimmt. Sie verleihen der Arena eine Bedeutung, die weit über diejenige einer reinen Stätte des Spiels hinausgeht. Das Stadion wird zur Stätte des Kults und der Totenwürde: zum heiligen Ort.

Memento mori
The Stadium as a Holy Place

Christiane Lembert / Barbara Rusch

The venerable English club Birmingham City FC offers its fans the possibility of being buried in the club's very own St Andrew Stadium. In a solemn ceremony, at which a clergyman can officiate if desired, the dead fan's ashes are brought by family members into the empty stadium and scattered at the edge of the pitch. In addition, deceased fans other than those thus buried in the stadium can be immortalised in the club's *Book of Remembrance*, at the stadium's *Walkway of Fame* and on a website. Since the special status enjoyed by the place of burial in the European culture of mourning, informed as it is by Christianity, plays an important role, the funerals and public commemoration of the dead show the status of the stadium for the close-knit community of fans as their emotional «home». It charges the stadium with a significance that goes far beyond its role as the place where the game is played. The stadium has become a place where a cult is observed and the dead are honoured: a holy place.

In Großbritannien bieten einige Clubs ihren leidenschaftlichsten Fans an, im Stadion ihre sterblichen Überreste als Asche feierlich verstreuen zu lassen. St Andrew Stadium, Birmingham City FC. Some British clubs offer their most ardent fans the chance of having their mortal remains ceremonially scattered as ashes in the stadium. St Andrew Stadium, Birmingham City FC. ©Photo: Sarah Gould

In britischen Stadien wie etwa dem Reebok Stadium der Bolton Wanderers künden an den »Walkways of Fame« Hunderte Inschriften namentlich genannter Fans von ihrer Hingabe zu ihrem Verein. In British stadiums such as Bolton Wanderers' Reebok Stadium, hundreds of inscribed names along «Walkways of Fame» record fans' devotion to their club. ©Photo: Roger Penn

Fankultur und Jugendkultur
Die »Kutten«

Christiane Lembert / Barbara Rusch

Vor allem in Mittel- und Westeuropa waren ab den 1970er Jahren in den Stadien jugendliche »Kuttenfans« die prägnantesten Protagonisten der Fanszene. Sie dominierten die aufkommenden Fanclubs und zogen mit den heute klassischen Fan-Attributen und -Verhaltensweisen in die Tribünenblocks ein. Ihre typischen Jeanswesten mit den abgetrennten Ärmeln (*cut off,* daher der deutsche Name »Kutte«) entstammen dem stark maskulin geprägten Rockertum. Die Wurzeln der Kuttenfans liegen in der »Halbstarken«-Revolte der 1950er Jahre und verweisen auf eine in den USA geborene und eher mit der Arbeiterschicht verbundene Jugendkultur, deren Insignien der Rebellion die Jeans und der Rock'n'Roll waren. Ihre Loyalitäten und Abneigungen dokumentieren Kuttenfans durch aussagekräftige Aufnäher – etwa Vereinsembleme, Fanclub-Abzeichen oder »Hass-Aussagen« gegen gegnerische Clubs und deren Anhänger – mit denen sie ihre Kutten in hingebungsvoller und geduldiger Arbeit zu textilen Kunstwerken gestalten. Heute gelten sie als Vertreter einer traditionsverhafteten Fankultur.

Fan Culture and Youth Culture
«Kutten»

Christiane Lembert / Barbara Rusch

Since the 1970s, youthful fans wearing *Kutten* (the German term for sleeveless denim jackets in the Hell's Angel's style) have been the stand-out protagonists of the fan scene in the stadiums of central and western Europe. They have come to dominate emerging groups of organized fans and have moved into the stands along with what are now classic fan attributes and behaviour patterns. Their typical jeans tops with cropped (cut-off) sleeves (from which the German name *Kutte* derives) originated in the Rockers, a very masculine culture. The roots of this fan culture go back to the Rockers revolt of the 1950s, a youth culture born in the US and associated primarily with the working class, whose insignia of rebellion were jeans and rock'n'roll. Fans wearing *Kutten* document their loyalties and pet hates with sewn-on badges that make powerful statements – eg team emblems, club badges and «hate statements» against rival teams and their adherents – labours of love with which they style their tops into textile art works. Nowadays *Kutten* are regarded as representative of a fan culture steeped in tradition.

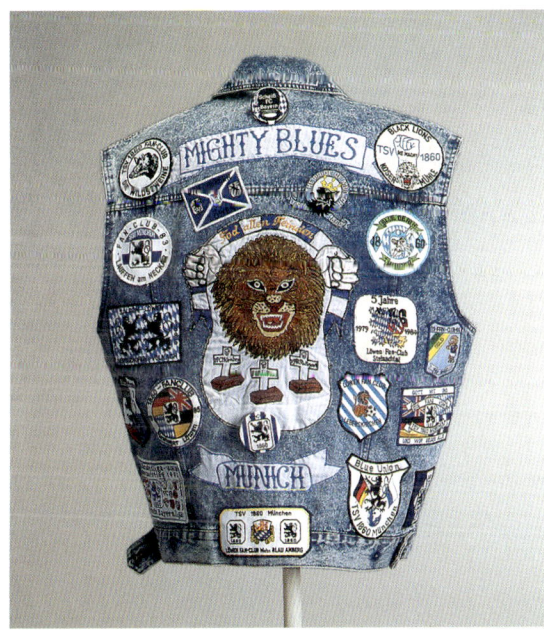

Die Kutte des leidenschaftlichen 1860er Fans Siegfried Lukas erzählt ein Stück Lebens- und Vereinsgeschichte. The «Kutte» worn by passionate 1860 fan Siegfried Lukas tells his lifestory and club history.

»Die Urheimat des Spieltriebs«? – In der Fußballwelt ist wohl kein anders Land derart von Stereotypen, Halbwahrheiten und Mythen geprägt wie Brasilien. «The original home of the urge to play»? – In the world of football no other country has been so mirrored in stereotypes, half-truths and myths as Brazil.

Karneval und Fußball in Brasilien

Alex Bellos

Einer der Gründe, warum der brasilianische Fußball sich weltweit so großer Beliebtheit erfreut, ist das Verhalten der Fans. Jeder, der schon einmal ein großes Spiel in Brasilien gesehen hat, weiß das. Die Fans sind nicht nur Zuschauer – sie sind auch Akteure in dem Spektakel. Sie bringen Blechinstrumente und Trommeln mit, um den Spielen ihren eigenen synkopischen Soundtrack zu geben. Anstatt still zu stehen, halten sie einander Arm in Arm, in langen Reihen, und springen auf und ab und zur Seite, als wären sie Tänzer, die einer Choreographie folgen. Sie kostümieren sich nicht nur in den Farben ihrer Mannschaft, sondern bringen auch Requisiten mit – wie etwa kleine Särge in den Farben des gegnerischen Teams. Anstelle von kleinen Fähnchen machen sie sich unerhört riesige Banner, die sie über sich selbst ausbreiten, wenn das Spiel beginnt, und danach bei jedem Tor, das für ihre Mannschaft fällt. Die Extravaganz, die Musikalität und das Gemeinschaftsgefühl des sportlichen Ereignisses werden perfekt von den Zuschauern widergespiegelt.

Während das Verhalten von Fans anderer Nationalitäten auch Elemente dieses Überschwangs aufweist – insbesondere im Zeitalter der Fernsehübertragung und der Homogenisierung des Weltfußballs – hat es doch den Anschein, dass keiner es so sehr übertreibt wie die Brasilianer. Ihre Ausgelassenheit, ihr Temperament und ihr Selbstdarstellungsdrang sind einzigartig.

Warum? Für dieses Problem gibt es eine semantische Lösung. Im Englischen etwa »unterstützt« man ein Fußballteam (*supporter* = »Unterstützer« im Sinne von »Fan«) – man ist zuverlässig, stark und loyal. In Brasilien verwendet man statt dessen das Verb *torce* – wörtlich übersetzt bedeutet das »biegen« oder »verdrehen«. Das Wort beinhaltet die Vorstellung von Bewegung, (Mit-)Leiden und Menschlichkeit.

Es scheint offensichtlich, dass es zwischen den Tatsachen, dass Brasilien das Land des Fußballs und gleichzeitig auch das Land des Karnevals ist, eine klare Verbindung gibt.

Carnival and Football in Brazil

Alex Bellos

One of the reasons Brazilian football is so universally appealing is because of the behaviour of the fans. Anyone who has ever been to a big game in Brazil knows this. The fans are not just spectators – they are also performers in the spectacle. They bring along brass instruments and drums to give the games their own syncopated soundtrack. Instead of standing still, they hold each other arm in arm, in long lines, and jump up, down and sideways like they are choreographed dancers. Not only do they dress up in team colours, but they also bring along props – such as small coffins painted in the colours of the opposing team. Rather than just small flags, they make outrageously large banners, which they roll out over themselves at the beginning of the game and then whenever the team scores. The flamboyance, musicality and togetherness of the sporting game is perfectly reflected in its audience.

While the behaviour of fans of other nationalities has elements of this exuberance – especially since the advent of televised games and the homogenisation of world football – there is a sense that no one exaggerates quite like the Brazilians. They have a unique playfulness, humour and exhibitionism.

Why? There is a semantic clue. In English you «support» a football team –you are solid and strong and loyal. In Brazil you *torce* – literally, you «bend» or «twist». The word contains the idea of movement, suffering and being human.

It would seem obvious that there are links between the fact that Brazil is the country of football and also the country of carnival. There are strong links – yet not always the expected ones. Football and carnival developed concurrently, strongly influencing each other, and in so doing establishing important pillars of popular culture.

Football arrived in late 19th century Brazil. The game was originally the preserve of the country's white, Europhile elite. At Fluminense's luxurious Laranjeiras' stadium in Rio, for example, spectators attended as a way of reaffirming the superiority of the European way of life in the tropics. Already there was a feeling that by attending you were on show. Fans would dress conspicuously in the latest fashions, with coloured ribbons coming from their boaters, and shout «hip hip hurrahs» at the goals.

Blacks at first were not allowed to play football with whites – they were forced to eavesdrop the games at Fluminense by sitting on neighbouring rooftops. They had no choice but to play the game among themselves in streets and parkland. It was only in the 1930s that this apartheid ended and football became properly «Brazilian».

Professionalism changed the game and also the business of the game. The press was also becoming more sophisticated. A crucial figure was Mário Filho, the young sports editor of Rio daily *O Globo,* who had a precocious understanding of hype. If he could create more interest in games, he would sell more papers. Perhaps his most fondly remembered marketing ruse was to coin the phrase »Fla-Flu«, meaning the derby between two of Rio's big teams, Flamengo and Fluminense.

Tatsächlich gibt es Verbindungen, doch sind dies nicht unbedingt diejenigen, die man erwartet. Fußball und Karneval entwickelten sich zeitgleich, beeinflussten sich dabei gegenseitig und wurden so zu wichtigen Säulen der populären Kultur.

Der Fußball ist im späten 19. Jahrhundert in Brasilien angekommen. Das Spiel war ursprünglich eine Domäne der weißen, europaphilen Elite des Landes. Den Besuch des luxuriösen Laranjeiras-Stadions von Fluminense in Rio zum Beispiel betrachteten die Zuschauer als Bestätigung der Überlegenheit der europäischen Lebensweise auch in den Tropen. Schon zu diesem Zeitpunkt stellte sich das Gefühl ein, beim Besuch des Stadions auf dem Präsentierteller zu sitzen. Die Fans kleideten sich auffallend nach der neusten Mode, mit farbigen Bändern an den Strohhüten, und schrieen »Hip Hip Hurra«, wenn ein Tor fiel.

Schwarzen war es zu Beginn nicht erlaubt, mit Weißen Fußball zu spielen – sie waren gezwungen, sich auf die benachbarten Dächer zu setzen, um die Spiele von Fluminense ansehen zu können. Sie hatten keine andere Wahl, als miteinander auf der Straße oder im Park Fußball zu spielen. Erst in den 1930er Jahren – als die ersten professionellen Ligen gegründet wurden – endete diese Apartheid und der Fußball wurde tatsächlich »brasilianisch«.

Das Berufssportlertum veränderte das Spiel und ebenso das Geschäft des Spiels. Auch die Presse entwickelte sich weiter. Eine entscheidende Rolle spielte Mário Filho, der junge Sportredakteur von Rios Tageszeitung *O Globo,* der bezüglich des Begriffs *hype* seiner Zeit deutlich voraus war. Sein Ziel war es, größeres Interesse an den Spielen zu wecken, um mehr Zeitungen zu verkaufen. Sein Marketing-Trick, der sich vielleicht am tiefsten eingeprägt hat, war die Wortschöpfung »Fla-Flu«, mit der er ein Derby zwischen den zwei großen Teams von Rio, Flamengo und Fluminense, bezeichnete. Um die Spiele zwischen Fla und Flu so stark wie möglich zu hypen, beschloss Mário Filho, einen Wettbewerb zwischen den Fans der beiden Mannschaften auszurichten. Sie wurden ermutigt, während des Spiels so laut und bunt wie möglich zu sein – er hielt sie dazu an, Trommeln, Instrumente, farbige Banner und Feuerwerke mitzubringen. Mit anderen Worten, sie sollten so karnevalesk wie möglich sein. *O Globo* wählte dann diejenigen Fans zum Gewinner, die das lebendigste Schauspiel geboten hatten. Ob Mário Filho nun die »brasilianische Art« der Fan-Unterstützung erfunden hat oder nicht, er hat sicherlich den Anstoß dazu gegeben.

Die Wettbewerbe zwischen den Fans der verschiedenen Mannschaften waren ein voller Erfolg. Bereits in den 1940er Jahren brauchten die brasilianischen Fans keine Anregung von außen mehr, um bei Fußballspielen ein großes Spektakel zu veranstalten. Sie übernahmen diese Aufgabe ganz von alleine. Der möglicherweise bekannteste Fan war Jayme de Carvalho, der immer dafür sorgte, dass eine Schar bunt zusammengewürfelter Freunde mit Blechinstrumenten bei den Spielen von Flamengo anwesend war. Die Band nannte sich Charanga und stellte Brasiliens Prototyp eines Fanclubs dar. Nach Charanga war ein brasilianisches Match ohne Trommeln oder Musik undenkbar.

Jayme war ein untergeordneter Staatsbeamter, ein namenloser Mann mit einem namenlosen Job. Während der Spiele jedoch war er der strahlende Mittelpunkt der Party, eine Berühmtheit der Ränge, immer aufgedreht und immer geschmückt mit den Farben seines Teams. Es war ein zeitaufwändiges Hobby, da in dieser Zeit kaum Merchandising-Produkte erhältlich waren, und Jaymes Frau Laura verbrachte ihre Tage damit, Stoff in den Farben von Flamengo zu färben und die einzelnen Materialien zusammenzunähen. Statt nur kleine

»Fla gegen Flu« ist das klassische Derby des brasilianischen Fußballs. Flamengo gilt als der beliebteste Club Brasiliens. Er findet seine Fans vor allem in den Armenvierteln – im Gegensatz zum vornehm-aristokratischen Fluminense. «Fla vs Flu» is the classic Derby of Brazilian football. Flamengo is Brazil's most popular club. Its fans come mainly from the favelas – just the opposite of elegant, aristocratic Fluminense.

Die Corinthians von São Paulo wurden 1910 von ihren Gründungsvätern nach der damals berühmten englischen Mannschaft gleichen Namens benannt. Heute gelten sie als »Freude der Armen«. The São Paulo Corinthians were named by their founding fathers after an English team celebrated at the time. Now they are regarded as «joy of the poor».

In order to hype the «Fla-Flus» as much as he could, Mário Filho decided to create a competition between both sets of fans. They were encouraged to be as noisy and colourful as possible during the game – he urged them to bring drums, instruments, coloured streamers and fireworks. In other words, to be as carnivalesque as possible. *O Globo* would judge the winner as the side that put on the most exhilarating display. Whether or not Mário Filho invented the «Brazilian way» of supporting, he certainly set it on its way.

The competitions between sets of fans were a success. By the 1940s, Brazilian fans didn't need any external stimulation to make a song and a dance at football matches. Fans took this role unto themselves. Perhaps the best known was Jayme de Carvalho, who always arranged for a motley collection of friends playing brass-instruments to attend Flamengo's matches. The band was called the Charanga, and was Brazil's prototype supporters' club. After the Charanga, the idea of a Brazilian match without drums or music became unthinkable.

Jayme was a low-level state functionary, an anonymous man in an anonymous job. During matches, however, he was the life and soul of the party, a terrace celebrity, always over the top and always bedecked in club colours. This was a time-consuming pastime, since in those days hardly any merchandising was available and his wife, Laura, would spend her weekdays dying cloth in Flamengo's colours and sewing the material together. Rather than just taking small firecrackers to matches, once Jayme lit a small bomb, which according to the (probably exaggerated) report by Mário Filho destroyed the grass where it landed and covered the stadium in smoke.

Jayme was known as a «torcedor-símbolo», a symbol-fan. The phrase itself says a lot about Brazilian attitudes to fandom. The «symbol fan» is not dismissed as an eccentric. Rather he is respected as a faithful representative of the passion that everyone else feels. He is a role

Die Brasilianisierung des internationalen Fußball-Fanwesens: Jubelnde Brasilianerinnen feiern 2002 auf dem Ku'damm den Einzug ihrer Nationalmannschaft ins WM-Finale. The Brazilianisation of international football fanism: cheering Brazilian women on the Berlin Ku'damm celebrate their national team qualifying for the 2000 World Cup finals. Photo: Theo Heymann, ddp

Feuerwerkskörper mit zu den Spielen zu nehmen, zündete Jayme einmal eine kleine Bombe, die dem (wahrscheinlich übertriebenen) Zeitungsbericht von Mário Filho zufolge das Gras, auf dem sie landete, zerstörte und das Stadion in Rauch hüllte.

Jayme war bekannt als ein *torcedor-símbolo,* ein »Vorzeigefan«. Allein dieser Ausdruck sagt einiges aus über die brasilianische Einstellung zum Fan-Sein. Der Vorzeigefan wird nicht als Exzentriker abgetan, sondern als getreulicher Repräsentant der Leidenschaft respektiert, die alle anderen empfinden. Er gilt als Vorbild, nicht als ein nach Aufmerksamkeit heischender Freak. Die Nationalmannschaft hatte sogar einen Vorzeigefan bei der Weltmeisterschaft 1958 in Schweden dabei. Cristiano Lacorte wurde letztendlich von der brasilianischen Regierung mit einer Medaille ausgezeichnet.

Karneval in Rio ist ein globaler Bezugspunkt für Hedonismus und Exzess. In Wirklichkeit handelt es sich bei der größten Parade – die im 60 000 Menschen Platz bietenden Sambadrom stattfindet – um eine hochgradig konkurrenzorientierte Veranstaltung, in der nichts dem Zufall oder der Improvisation überlassen wird. Zwei Nächte lang ziehen die besten 14 Sambaschulen zur Parade auf und erhalten Punkte für unterschiedliche Kriterien wie etwa das Trommeln, die Kostüme und den Tanz. Gewonnen hat die Schule mit der höchsten Punktzahl.

model, not an attention-seeking freak. The national team even had a «symbol-fan» at the 1958 World Cup in Sweden. Cristiano Lacorte was eventually awarded a medal by the Brazilian government.

Carnival in Rio de Janeiro is a global reference point for hedonism and excess. In fact, the main parade – which now takes place in the 700 m long, 60 000-capacity sambadrome – is a highly competitive event with nothing left to chance or improvisation. Over two nights, the 14 best samba schools in Rio parade for just over an hour each and are awarded points for several criteria such as drumming, costumes and dancing. The winner is the school with the highest points.

The carnival parade has several parallels with football – as well as the league format (the two schools with the lowest points are relegated to a lower division), each of the samba schools has its own colours, its own fans and its own community base. The competitive aspect of carnival has helped transform the parade into one of the most luxurious spectacles in the world. Hundreds of people work throughout the year, spending millions of pounds, preparing their schools for the big day. For many people, their samba school winning carnival is as important as their football team winning the league.

Again, a crucial figure in this development was Mário Filho. In 1931 he was editor of one of Brazil's earliest sports newspapers: *Mundo Esportivo*. The first issue coincided with the finals of the Rio state football championship. But when it was time for issue two there was no football left to write about. Mário Filho needed to look elsewhere to fill up his pages – it was the build up to carnival, so he decided to turn his thoughts to that.

At that time different carnival groupings used to come down from their communities and parade through the city's streets. *Mundo Esportivo* saw the rivalry and created a proper tournament between them. The paper invented a set of categories by which to compare the parades and appointed a set of judges. The competition has barely changed to this day. The Rio carnival parade may seem *sui generis* – yet it began as an ingenious way for football writers to sell newspapers in the off-season.

The culture of carnival parade and competing samba schools spread from Rio throughout Brazil during the 20th century. Almost all the main cities have some kind of parallel event during carnival. It has left its mark on urban architecture, too: as well as having a large football stadium large cities also count a monumental concrete sambadrome.

It was during the 1960s that Brazilian football consolidated itself as the best in the world. This decade was important also for social changes. It was when the urban population exceeded the rural population for the first time – and it coincided with the military coup. The industrialisation of Brazil shifted the country's centre of gravity to São Paulo, which – accentuated by Rio's loss of status as the capital to Brasilia – grew to become one of the largest cities in the world.

São Paulo was the engine of the Brazilian dictatorship's economic miracle, but also the cradle of the militancy that ultimately destroyed the military regime. In the authoritarian climate of repression and censorship one of the only spaces in which people were able to articulate themselves politically was football. The first and strongest example of this was the Corinthians supporters' club Gaviões da Fiel, founded in 1969, whose primary purpose was as a pressure group to change the Corinthians' presidency.

Die Karnevalsparade hat verschiedene Parallelen mit dem Fußball – sowohl das Prinzip der Ligen (die beiden Schulen mit der niedrigsten Punktzahl steigen in eine niedrigere Spielklasse ab), als auch die Tatsache, dass jede der Sambaschulen ihre eigenen Farben, ihre eigenen Fans und ihre eigene gemeinsame soziale Herkunft besitzt. Der konkurrenzbetonte Aspekt des Karnevals hat dazu beigetragen, dass die Parade zu einer der opulentesten Veranstaltungen der ganzen Welt geworden ist. Hunderte von Menschen arbeiten das ganze Jahr über und geben Millionen Euro dafür aus, ihre Schulen für den großen Tag vorzubereiten. Für viele Menschen ist der erste Platz ihrer Sambaschule beim Karneval ebenso wichtig wie der erste Platz ihrer Fußballmannschaft in ihrer Liga.

Wieder spielte Mário Filho eine entscheidende Rolle bei dieser Entwicklung. 1931 war er der Herausgeber einer der frühesten Sportzeitungen Brasiliens, der *Mundo Esportivo*. Die erste Ausgabe erschien zeitgleich mit den Endspielen der nationalen Meisterschaft in Rio. Als jedoch die zweite Ausgabe erscheinen sollte, gab es keine Fußballspiele mehr, über die man hätte schreiben können. Mário Filho musste sich nach etwas anderem umsehen, womit er seine Seiten füllen konnte – man befand sich gerade bei den Vorbereitungen zum Karneval, und so fasste er den Entschluss, sich damit zu beschäftigen.

Zu dieser Zeit pflegten verschiedene Karnevalsvereine aus ihren Gemeinden in die Stadt zu kommen und dort in den Straßen ihre Paraden durchzuführen. *Mundo Esportivo* erkannte die Rivalität zwischen ihnen und rief ein regelrechtes Turnier ins Leben. Die Zeitung stellte eine Reihe von Kategorien auf, anhand derer die Paraden bewertet wurden, und ernannte eine Jury. Bis heute hat sich dieser Wettbewerb kaum verändert. Der Karneval in Rio mag einzigartig erscheinen – dennoch begann er als eine erfinderische Methode von Fußballreportern, Zeitungen außerhalb der Saison zu verkaufen.

Die Tradition der Karnevalsparade und der konkurrierenden Sambaschulen verbreitete sich während des 20. Jahrhunderts von Rio aus in ganz Brasilien. Fast alle wichtigen Städte haben irgendeine vergleichbare Veranstaltung während des Karnevals. Auch in der urbanen Architektur hat das Ereignis seine Spuren hinterlassen: die großen Städte besitzen sowohl ein großes Fußballstadion als auch ein monumentales Sambadrom aus Beton.

Während der 1960er Jahre konsolidierte sich der brasilianische Fußball als der beste der Welt. Diese Dekade erlangte außerdem durch soziale Veränderungen Bedeutung. Zum ersten Mal übertraf der Anteil der städtischen Bevölkerung denjenigen der ländlichen – und gleichzeitig fand der Militärputsch statt. Durch die Industrialisierung Brasiliens verschob sich das Zentrum des Landes nach São Paulo, das – noch unterstützt durch Rios Verlust des Hauptstadt-Status zugunsten von Brasilia – zu einer der größten Städte der Welt wurde.

São Paulo war der Motor des Wirtschaftswunders der brasilianischen Diktatur, aber auch die Wiege der Militanz, die das Militärregime letztlich zerstörte. In dem autoritären Klima der Unterdrückung und Zensur war der Fußball einer der wenigen Bereiche, in denen die Bevölkerung sich politisch artikulieren konnte. Das erste und bedeutendste Beispiel dafür war der 1969 gegründete Fanclub der Corinthians, Gaviões da Fiel, dessen primärer Zweck die Bildung einer Interessensgruppe zum Wechsel der Präsidentschaft der Corinthians war.

Die Gaviões gelten als Brasiliens erster moderner Fanclub. Sie zogen nicht nur das Management zur Verantwortung, sondern arrangierten auch Reisen zu Spielen und organisierten Trommler, Flaggen und Banner. Die Gaviões wuchsen zu einer so starken Einheit zusam-

Der Karneval beeinflusst den Fußball – und umgekehrt. Weiblicher brasilianischer Fan auf den Rängen. Carnival influences football – and vice versa. Brazilian woman fan in the stadium.

The Gaviões are considered Brazil's first modern football supporters' club. As well as holding the club management to account, they arranged travel to games, organised drummers, flags and banners. The Gaviões became such a strong unit that it began to have life beyond football. During carnival or in the off-season, its members would get together – like Brazilians do all over the country – to drink beer, cook meat on a barbecue and sing samba. And the Gaviões had musicians at hand – the ones who played in the football stadiums.

These informal get-togethers became more formalised as the years passed. The Gaviões became a samba bloco – the name given to the small troupes that parade through the streets during carnival time. Then the bloco became a fully-fledged samba school, the largest and most prestigious carnival grouping, which parades every year in the São Paulo sambadrome.

Each year, each samba school chooses a different theme for its parade. A song is composed and costumes and floats designed that best illustrate that theme. The Gaviões

men, dass sie ein Gemeinschaftsleben auch neben dem Fußball zu entwickeln begannen. Während des Karnevals und außerhalb der Saison trafen sich die Mitglieder – wie es Brasilianer im ganzen Land tun – um Bier zu trinken, zu grillen und Samba zu singen. Und die Gaviões hatten Musiker zur Hand – diejenigen, die in den Fußballstadien spielten.

Diese ungezwungenen Zusammenkünfte wurden mit der Zeit mehr und mehr formalisiert, und die Gaviões entwickelten sich zu einer *samba bloco* (so nennt man die kleinen Truppen, die im Karneval durch die Straßen ziehen). Dann wurde der *bloco* zu einer vollwertigen Sambaschule, der größten und prestigeträchtigsten Gruppierung im Karneval, die jährlich im Sambadrom von São Paulo zur Parade aufzieht.

Jedes Jahr wählt jede Sambaschule ein neues Thema für ihre Parade. Ein Lied wird komponiert, Kostüme und Festwagen werden entworfen, die das Thema am besten veranschaulichen. Die Gaviões wählen von den Corinthians unabhängige Themen, auch wenn sie nie vergessen, dass das, was sie zusammenhält, die Tatsache ist, dass sie Fans dieser Mannschaft sind: Die Farben der Corinthians sind Schwarz und Weiß, ebenso wie die prominenten Farben der Sambaparade, und das Clubwappen ist deutlich sichtbar auf den Festwagen abgebildet. Die Gaviões sind das beste Beispiel für das karnevaleske Verhalten der brasilianischen Fans – da sie tatsächlich an der Karnevalsparade teilnehmen. Die Männer, die an den meisten Wochenenden in den Stadien Sprechchöre anstimmen, kleiden sich in Federn und Pailletten. Berühmte Models, gekleidet in nicht viel mehr als Bodypaintings, die über die enormen Festwagen wirbeln, ergänzen die Tausenden von Teilnehmern an der Parade – aber der innere Kern der Teilnehmer sind die treuen Gaviões. Auch die Hauptkonkurrenten der Corinthians, Palmeiras und São Paulo, haben einen Fanclub mit Sambaschule. Die Gaviões sind aber die am etabliertesten und erfolgreichsten. Mehrere Male schon haben sie den ersten Rang beim Karneval von São Paulo errungen.

In Rio hatten die originären Sambaschulen ihre Basis in den verschiedenen Gemeinden, und bei dem Wettbewerb ging es um nachbarschaftliche Rivalitäten. Die Tatsache, dass einige der Schulen in São Paulo aus Fußball-Fanclubs entstanden sind, spiegelt sowohl die Wichtigkeit des Fußballs und seine gemeinschaftsbildende Funktion wider, als auch die Zuwanderung und das beschleunigte Wachstum von São Paulo, wo sich die Menschen weniger an die lokalen Strukturen der Stadt gebunden fühlen.

Die mit Fußball-Fanclubs verknüpften Sambaschulen haben viel zur Leidenschaft des Karnevals in São Paulo beigetragen. Sie haben ihm seinen konkurrenzbetonten Charakter gegeben – da ihre eigene Existenz in der sportlichen Konkurrenz gründet. Es ist nicht nur so, dass die Wesensart der Fußballfans karnevalesker geworden ist – gleichzeitig ist der Karneval – im sportlichen Sinne – auch wettbewerbsorientierter geworden.

In anderer Hinsicht repräsentiert die Performance der Gaviões die auf den Kopf gestellte Kultur des Fußballs. Wenn die Gaviões zur Parade aufziehen, dann sind sie nicht länger Zuschauer: sie sind selbst zum Schauspiel geworden. Sie haben vom Zuschauerraum auf die Bühne gewechselt, sind zu Fußballfans geworden, die ihre eigenen Fans haben. So etwas geschieht in Brasilien leichter, da die Äußerungen der populären Kultur hier Aktivitäten sind, die jeden mit einschließen. Beim Karneval wie bei den Fußballspielen nimmt man also schon teil, indem man nur anwesend ist.

choose themes that are not connected to Corinthians, although they never forget that what links them together is that they are supporters of the club. Corinthians' colours are black and white, and the prominent colours of their parade are black and white, and the club crest is also displayed prominently on the floats.

The Gaviões are the best example of the carnivalesque behaviour of Brazilian fans – since they really do parade at carnival. The men who most weekends are usually chanting in football stadiums on this occasion are instead dressed in feathers and sequins. There are several other people that make up the thousands who take part in the Gaviões parade – famous models, dressed in not much more than bodypaint, gyrating on enormous floats – yet the core members are the Gaviões faithful.

It is not just Corinthians that has a supporters club that has also became a samba school that parades every carnival – their main rivals, Palmeiras and São Paulo, also do. The Gaviões, however, are the most established and the most successful. They have won the São Paulo carnival several times.

In Rio, the original samba schools were based in different communities and the competition between them was about neighbourhood rivalry. The fact that in São Paulo some of the schools originated from football supporters' clubs is both a reflection of the importance of football in providing a sense of community in Brazil, and also of the accelerated immigration and growth of São Paulo, where people feel less bound to the geography of the city.

The samba schools linked to football supporters' clubs have contributed greatly to the passion of the São Paulo carnival. They have given it a competitive edge – since their very existence came out of sporting competition. Not only has the nature of being a football supporter become more carnivalesque, but carnival has become more sportingly competitive.

In another way, the performance of the Gaviões represents the culture of football turned on its head. When the Gaviões are parading, they are no longer the spectators: they have become the spectacle. They have crossed from the audience to the stage. They have become the football fans who have their own fans. It is easier for this to happen in Brazil, where expressions of popular culture are inclusive activities. At carnival, as at football matches, just by turning up you are taking part.

Nippon Socca-Girlie
Zwischen Kimono, Barbie und Nakata

Patricia Müller

Fußball in Japan stellt geradezu ein betriebswirtschaftliches Musterbeispiel einer erfolgreichen Produkteinführung dar. Als am 15. Mai 1993 im Spiel zwischen Yokohama Marinos und Verdy Kawasaki vor 60 000 Zuschauern in Tokio der offizielle Anpfiff zur J-League erfolgte, waren zwei Ziele klar: Zum einen sollte sich der Fußball im Land der aufgehenden Sonne zu einer wirtschaftlich rentablen Sache entwickeln, zum zweiten eine Stärkung des Nationalteams erreicht werden. Profi-Fußball in Japan gleicht quasi einem Produkt, bei dessen Einführung nichts dem Zufall überlassen wurde. Eine der größten Marketingagenturen des Landes führte eine umfassende Analyse durch, die das Potenzial des professionellen Sportbetriebs ermittelte. Die daraus entwickelte Marketingstrategie zielte schließlich auf die Konsumkraft einer Klientel ab, die traditionell wenig mit Fußball zu tun hat: Junge Frauen in den Zwanzigern mit eigenem Einkommen, aber ohne eigenen Haushalt, die sich durch eine Kaufbereitschaft auszeichnen und eine gewisse Sogwirkung auf andere Konsumentenschichten ausüben. So wurden Club-Logos und bunte Maskottchen in »Girlie-Bonbon-Farben« kreiert, Fußball-»Beaus« wie Beckham und Nakata als goldene Mini-Plastikpüppchen verewigt, Barbies in Gestalt von Pop-Ikonen-tauglichen Nationalspielern aus aller Welt gestylt und Team-Songs zwischen Romantik und heißem *Dancefloor* komponiert, wobei der passende CD-Player in Fußballform gleich mitgeliefert wurde. Jungen Japanerinnen sollte auf diese Weise die Identifikation mit dem Sport oder den jeweiligen Teams leichter fallen – und ein Blick in die japanischen Fußball-Stadien seit der WM 2002 zeigt: Dieses »Ideal der Marketingstrategie« scheint tatsächlich aufzugehen.

Nippon Socca Girlie
Between Kimono, Barbie and Nakata

Patricia Müller

Football in Japan perfectly exemplifies the successful launch of a product on the market. When the whistle blew to start the J-League game between Yokohama Marinos and Verdy Kawasaki before a stadium of 60 000 spectators in Tokyo on 15 May 1993, two aims had been made clear. On the one hand, football was to develop comfortable profit margins in the Land of the Rising Sun and, on the other, the national team was to be strengthened. Professional football in Japan is like a product whose launch has been so carefully engineered that nothing has been left to chance. One of the country's marketing agencies carried out a comprehensive analysis to ascertain the business potential of professional sports. The marketing strategy developed from the study ultimately targeted the consumer potential of a clientele that has traditionally had little to do with football: young women in their twenties with disposable income but without household ties, a group that is distinguished by consumer eagerness and exerts a certain pull on other consumer groups. Consequently, club logos and colourful mascots were created in «Girlie candy colours», football «beaux» such as Beckham and Nakata were immortalised as golden plastic mini-dolls. Barbies were styled in the form of national players from all over the world as potential pop icons and team songs were composed in registers somewhere between mood music and hot dancefloor, with a suitable CD player shaped like a football thrown in for good measure. All this was supposed to make it easier for young Japanese women to identify with the game or a particular team – and a glance at Japanese football stadiums since the 2002 World Cup shows: this «ideal marketing strategy» really seems to be working.

↑ Der japanische Star-Fußballer Hidetoshi Nakata wird auf Postern gerade auch für die weiblichen Fans inszeniert. Posters feature Japanese football star Hidetoshi Nakata to appeal especially to his female fan following.

↗ Fußball und Kommerz in Japan: Die Marketing-Strategen entwickeln für die vorwiegend weibliche Klientel immer neue Produkte – vom CD-Player in Fußballform bis hin zu den plüschigen »Beanies« zur WM 2002. Commercialised football in Japan: marketing strategists keep developing new products for a mainly female clientele – from a CD player in the form of a football to plush «beanies» for the 2002 World Cup.

→ Ein Symbol für Freiheit und Ungebundenheit gerade auch in Japan: Jamaikanischer Fußball-Reggae-Boy. A symbol of carefree freedom in Japan especially: a Jamaican football reggae boy.

»You'll Never Walk Alone!« – Der FC Liverpool, einer der erfolgreichsten Vereine der Welt, wurde Ende des 19. Jahrhunderts in einem der damals größten Industriegebiete Englands gegründet. Wimpel von den »Reds« aus Liverpool.
«You'll Never Walk Alone!» – Liverpool FC, one of the world's most successful clubs, was founded in what was one of England's greatest industrial regions in the late 19th century. A Liverpool «Reds» pennant.

Kampf der Hütten gegen die Paläste?
Reale und imaginierte Identitäten im Fußball

Kathrin Steinbichler

Geht es nach den Statuten des Weltverbands FIFA, dann ist Fußball nur ein Spiel. Ein leicht verständliches Mannschaftsspiel, das durch klar definierte Regeln einen fairen Wettbewerb ermöglichen soll und so allein durch die fußballerischen Fähigkeiten der Spieler über Sieg oder Niederlage entscheidet. Geht es nach den Fans und denjenigen, die vom und für den Fußball leben, dann ist Fußball oft kein Spiel, sondern Metapher des Lebens. »Einige Leute halten Fußball für einen Kampf um Leben und Tod. Ich mag diese Einstellung nicht. Ich versichere Ihnen, dass es viel ernster ist«, sagte einmal Bill Shankly, legendärer Trainer des FC Liverpool in den 1960er Jahren. Shankly forderte von seinen Spielern absolute Identifikation mit dem Verein, mit der Mannschaft, mit dem Siegeswillen. Und niemand in der englischen Arbeiterstadt Liverpool lachte darüber. Denn es war das, was die Fans im Stadion an der Anfield Road selbst Spieltag für Spieltag lebten und inszenierten. Wenn durch das Stadion das berühmte Vereinslied *You'll Never Walk Alone* schallt, besingen die Fans nicht nur den Verein und die Spieler, sondern auch sich selbst. Es gab und gibt kaum einen anderen

A Contest of Huts vs Palaces?
Real and Imagined Identities in Football

Kathrin Steinbichler

According to the statutes of FIFA, the International Federation of Football Associations, football is just a game. A team sport easy to understand, which makes a fair contest possible through clearly defined rules so that players' skills alone decide about win or defeat. According to the fans and those who live on and for football, football often is a metaphor rather for life than for a game. Bill Shankly, legendary 1960s trainer of FC Liverpool, once said: «Some people believe football is a matter of life and death. I'm very disappointed with that attitude. I can assure you it is much, much more important than that.» Shankly demanded of his players to identify absolutely with their club, with their team, with the will to win. And no one in working-class Liverpool laughed about that. Because this was what football fans in the Anfield Road stadium were experiencing and staging again and again, match for match. When the famous club song, *You'll Never Walk Alone* rings out in the stadium, the fans are not just singing to the team and the players but about themselves as well. Hardly any other public place has ever existed in which people can regularly convene in such a large number, with such a volume and such expressive emotions as they can for football. The real world of the football fans blends with the identities of their teams and clubs as they imagine them. Football has become a place for cultural showcasing and social exchange. It outgrew the pitch long ago.

What actually counts in football is the principle of physical performance: The stronger one, the better one wins. Nevertheless, fans ascribe identities and qualities to football players and teams which are based on national or regional boundaries or related to the local history of the club. Thus hierarchy becomes a category determined by attributed social classification and not just by sporting qualities. Accordingly, the footballer who is supported is not necessarily the better one but rather the one fans are willing to support because of the identity they have given him. Apart from quantifiable results, events are important that happen outside the area of sport. If the team of FC Schalke 04 before the beginning of the season takes its annual trip to one of the coalmines around the region, it's not just a day trip. It also represents a ritually demanded confession to the history and lifestyle of the region in which both club and fans have their roots. Maintaining a clearly recognizable image is part of the way clubs keep the support of their spectators and part of their marketing strategy that in turn ensures revenue. This is especially important since the players themselves have long been uprooted, changing employers almost with the seasons like modern migratory labours. Teams and clubs make use of and work on their image, cultivating it through interviews, gestures, marketing articles, club crests, the colours of their jerseys and stagings of support in the stadium.

öffentlichen Ort, wo Menschen sich in derart großer Zahl, Lautstärke und Emotionalität regelmäßig treffen können wie beim Fußball. Die realen Welten der Fans vermischen sich dabei mit den imaginierten Identitäten ihrer Mannschaften und Vereine. Fußball ist zum Ort kultureller Inszenierung und sozialen Austauschs geworden und längst über den Rasen hinaus gewachsen.

Eigentlich gilt im Fußball allein das Prinzip der körperlichen Leistung: Der Stärkere, Bessere gewinnt. Dennoch schreiben die Fans Fußballern und Mannschaften Identitäten und Eigenschaften zu, die sich an nationalen oder regionalen Grenzen orientieren oder auf die lokale Geschichte des Vereins beziehen. Hierarchie wird so zu einer Kategorie, die sich nicht allein am Sportlichen, sondern auch an der sozialen Zuschreibung festmacht. Unterstützung erhält demnach nicht derjenige, der besser ist, sondern derjenige, dem der Fan sie aufgrund seiner Identifikation gewährt. Neben dem messbaren Ergebnis werden dabei Ereignisse wichtig, die außerhalb des Sportlichen liegen. Wenn also die Mannschaft des Revierclubs FC Schalke 04 vor Beginn jeder Saison in eines der umliegenden Kohlebergwerke einfährt, ist das nicht nur ein Ausflug, sondern auch ein rituell abverlangtes Bekenntnis zu Geschichte und Alltag der Region, in der der Verein und seine Fans verwurzelt sind. Ein klar erkennbares Image zu haben, ist für Clubs zum Bestandteil ihrer Zuschauerbindung, ihrer Vermarktung und damit ihrer finanziellen Einkünfte geworden. Umso mehr, da die Spieler selbst längst nicht mehr verwurzelt sind, sondern wie moderne Wanderarbeiter fast Saison für Saison den Arbeitgeber wechseln. Mannschaften und Vereine benutzen und erarbeiten ihre Images und kultivieren sie durch Interviews, Gesten, Fanartikel, Vereinswappen, Trikotfarben und Stadioninszenierungen.

Ob Groß gegen Klein, Reich gegen Arm, Links gegen Rechts, Stadt gegen Region oder Hütte gegen Palast – einmal entwickelte Selbstbilder und Rivalitäten bleiben erhalten, sind dem Selbstverständnis von Verein und Fans eingeschrieben und reproduzieren sich oft selbst. Nicht nur in München etwa verstehen sich die Anhänger der beiden großen Clubs der Stadt als strikt unterschiedliche Gruppen. Obwohl beide Vereine im ehemaligen Arbeiterviertel Giesing angesiedelt sind, galt und gilt der 1900 gegründete FC Bayern als der weltläufigere Club der Reichen und Erfolgreichen, der Emporkömmlinge und Stars – auf dem Spielfeld wie auf den Zuschauerrängen. Der TSV München von 1860 dagegen hat zahlenmäßig weder die Finanzen, die Mitglieder noch die Erfolge wie der FC Bayern und steht für den heimatverbundenen einfachen Mann, der zwar stets den Erfolg sucht, ihn aber doch nie so recht hat. Die Identität ist eng mit angeblicher oder gewünschter sozialer Herkunft und gesellschaftlichem Selbstvertrauen verbunden.

In Rom feinden sich die Anhänger der beiden *Seria A*-Clubs von Lazio und AS Rom nicht nur sportlich, sondern auch politisch heftig an. Während das 1900 gegründete Lazio als ein Verein gilt, dessen Klientel in den ersten Jahrzehnten oft rechtskonservativ und heute teils offen rechtradikal ausgerichtet ist, pflegt AS Rom sein Image des edelmütigen und zugleich liberal gesinnten Clubs. In der Darstellung seines Selbstverständnisses greift AS Rom auf sinnträchtige Symbole zurück. »Sangue e oro, aristocrata e popolare, asr core e simbolico della citta eterna« heißt der Vereinsspruch der Fans, der sich auf die prägenden Farben, die Geschichte und die Bevölkerung des antiken Roms bezieht: »Blut und Gold, edel und volksnah, ist AS Rom Herz und Symbol der ewigen Stadt«. 1927 als Zusammenschluss dreier

Erzrivalen in München: Die Anhängerschaft zu einem der beiden traditionsreichen Vereine FC Bayern und 1860 wird auch durch regionaltypische Biergläser und -krüge zum Ausdruck gebracht. Arch rivals in Munich: membership of one of the two venerable clubs FC Bayern and 1860 is also demonstrated by beer glasses typical of the region.

Whether big vs small, rich vs poor, left-wing vs right-wing, city vs region or hut vs palace – once developed, self-image and rivalry remain, are written into the way the club and fans see themselves and are often self-perpetuating. It is not just in Munich that supporters of the two big city clubs view themselves as strictly different groups. Although both clubs are located in Giesing, which once was a working-class area of the city, FC Bayern has always been regarded – on the pitch and at the stadium tiers – as the more cosmopolitan club, supported by the rich and successful, parvenus and stars. TSV München of 1860, on the other hand, has never had as much money, as many members nor as much success as FC Bayern and embodies the man in the street with strong local ties, who is always on the lookout for success which, however, always seems elusive. So far, identity is closely linked with alleged or desired social origins and social confidence.

In Rome the supporters of the two *Seria A* clubs Lazio and AS Rome are markedly hostile to one another both in sports and in politics. Whereas Lazio, founded in 1900, is regarded as a club serving a clientele that was in the early decades often right-wing conservative and today is in part obviously radical right-wing, AS Rome cultivates a club image of being noble-minded and liberal. To represent its self-image AS Rome reverts to heavily laden symbolism: «Sangue e oro, aristocrata e popolare, asr cuore e simbolico della citta eterna» («Blood and gold, aristocratic and popular, AS Rome is the heart and symbol of the Eternal City») is the fans' club motto, which refers to the emblematic colours, the history and the people of ancient Rome. In 1927, when it was founded as a merger of three small Roman clubs,

Der AS Rom pflegt seine liberale Ausrichtung. Er beansprucht auch durch die Wahl seines Wappens, das sich auf den Gründungsmythos der Stadt bezieht, »das wahre Rom« zu verkörpern. Fahne des AS Roma. AS Rome cultivates a liberal stance. Its choice of crest, referring to the founding myth of the city, also supports its claim that it stands for »the real Rome«. An AS Roma flag.

römischer Kleinvereine gegründet, wollte AS einen auf breite Unterstützung gestellten Gegenpart zum politisch wie wirtschaftlich dominierenden Norden Italiens bilden. Gemäß der prägenden Elemente des alten Roms wählte sich AS rotgelbe Trikots und ein Vereinswappen, das den Ursprungsmythos der Stadt abbildet: Die wilde Wölfin, die die späteren Stadtgründer, die königlichen Zwillinge Romulus und Remus säugt. Bis heute beansprucht AS, das »wahre Rom« zu verkörpern.

In Frankreich etwa stilisierte die Öffentlichkeit von Mitte der 1980er bis Mitte der 1990er lange Jahre Olympique Marseille zu einem Symbol für Integration, Mut und Kreativität, in dem sich die vielfältigen, in der südfranzösischen Hafenstadt ansässigen Ethnizitäten widerspiegelten. Was anderswo Grund gesellschaftlicher Abgrenzung und negativer Stereotype war, deuteten die Anhänger Olympiques durch den Fußball positiv um. Die Vielzahl von Spielern ausländischer Herkunft war nicht länger ein Problem, sondern die Voraussetzung für Spielwitz. Der leidenschaftliche Spielstil Olympiques stand plötzlich für das Selbstverständnis der Stadtjugend: »Droit au but!« skandierten die Fans im Stadion, »Direkt aufs Tor!«, und appellierten damit im Grunde nicht nur an die Spieler, sondern auch an sich selbst und ihre gesellschaftliche Situation. Ohne Umwege und Zögern das Ziel suchen, das war es, was sie in der für sie oft verschlossenen etablierten Gesellschaft erreichen wollten. Und die Mannschaft Olympiques bot ihnen bereitwillig die Identifikationsfläche dazu. Das Wettkampfergebnis der eigenen Mannschaft dient so letztlich als Bestätigung oder Herausforderung für den eigenen Alltag und das eigene Bemühen. Der Autor Ror Wolf schrieb dazu: »Die Welt ist zwar kein Fußball, aber im Fußball, das ist kein Geheimnis, ist eine ganze Menge Welt.«

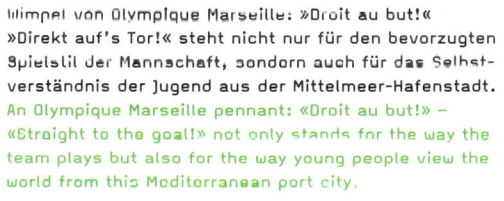

Wimpel von Olympique Marseille: »Droit au but!«
»Direkt auf's Tor!« steht nicht nur für den bevorzugten
Spielstil der Mannschaft, sondern auch für das Selbst-
verständnis der Jugend aus der Mittelmeer-Hafenstadt.
An Olympique Marseille pennant: «Droit au but!» —
«Straight to the goal!» not only stands for the way the
team plays but also for the way young people view the
world from this Mediterranean port city.

Pflege einer klar erkennbaren Club-Identität? — Coladosen mit den Emblemen
deutscher Fussballvereine. Cultivating a highly visible club identity? —
Coke cans with the crests of German football clubs. Installation: Münchner
Stadtmuseum.

AS wanted to form a broad-based counterweight to the politically and economically dominant north of Italy. Paving tribute to the determinant elements of ancient Rome, AS chose red and yellow jerseys and a club crest that represents the myth of the city's origin: the savage wolf feeding the royal twins Romulus and Remus, who later founded the city. Even today AS claims to embody the «real Rome».

In France between the mid-1980s and the mid-1990s the public stylised Olympique Marseilles into a symbol of integration, courage and creativity in which the diverse ethnic groups which formed the population of the seaport in the South of France were reflected. What elsewhere would have been a reason for social segregation and negative stereotyping was positively re-interpreted through football by Olympique supporters. The multitude of players of foreign origin was no longer a problem, but the premise for adroit play. The stormy style of play demonstrated by Olympique suddenly represented the self-image of the city's youth. «Droit au but!» («Straight to the goal!») chanted the fans in the stadium, thus addressing not just the players but themselves and their social situation. To head for the goal without making a detour and without hesitating was what they wanted to achieve at the society whose establishment was often closed to them. And the Olympique team was more than willing to provide them with a surface on to which they could project their identification. After all, the results achieved in matches by one's home team serves as a confirmation or as a challenge to one's own everyday life and efforts. As the writer Ror Wolf has put it: «The world may not be a football but in football, that's no secret, there is a lot of world.»

Mehr als ein Spiel, mehr als ein Club!
Fußball als Spielfeld regionaler Identitäten in Spanien

Christiane Hirsch

Zinédine Zidane, Ronaldo, Ronaldinho und David Beckham – die Liste der Namen, die spanische Clubs in den letzten Jahren vom internationalen Transfermarkt auf ihre Plätze holten, liest sich wie das *Who is who* der aktuellen Fußball-Superstars. Für diese beeindruckende Riege hat das Land auch die höchsten Ablösesummen weltweit gezahlt. 73 Millionen Euro flossen allein für Zidane an Juventus Turin. Damit erschöpfen sich aber auch schon fast die Gemeinsamkeiten spanischer Fußballclubs. In Spanien selbst interessieren ohnehin viel eher die Unterschiede der Vereine – je nach regionaler Herkunft: Katalanen singen für den FC Barcelona – liebevoll Barça genannt –, Madrilenen schwärmen für das »weiße Ballett« von Real Madrid und Basken fühlen mit Athlétic Bilbao oder Real Sociedad. Vor allem in den Begegnungen zwischen dem FC Barcelona und seinem großen Rivalen Real Madrid geht es um mehr als nur ein Spiel! Ausgespielt werden Siege und Niederlagen in der Arena regionaler und lokaler Identitäten, Katalanen gegen Madrilenen. Beide verbindet und trennt eine in Jahrzehnten gewachsene Feindschaft, die geprägt ist von unterschiedlichen Ansichten und Alltags-Einstellungen. Umgekehrt bestimmen die beiden Vereine das alltägliche Zusammenleben von Katalanen und Madrilenen ganz entscheidend. Wie sehr die Menschen davon betroffen sind, zeigt sich in den Folgen von »Grenzübertritten«: Im Jahr 2000 wechselte der 1995 für den FC Barcelona verpflichtete Luís Figo für eine Ablösesumme von rund 55 Millionen zu den »Königlichen«, zu Real Madrid. Bei seinem ersten Einsatz gegen den FC Barcelona im selben Jahr konnte sich Figo im Spiel nie der Eckfahne nähern: Anhänger des FC Barcelona bewarfen ihn mit Handys, einem Regen von Münzen und einem Schweinskopf und beschimpften ihn als Judas – eine der harmloseren Beleidigungen der aufgebrachten Fans. Figos Kopf wurde auf riesigen Pesetenscheinen abgebildet, versehen mit der Aufschrift: *Figo pesetero*. Als Grund für seinen Wechsel wurde ihm Geldgier unterstellt.

    Die Barça-Anhänger haben zu Spielerkauf und Finanzen eine ganz eigene Einstellung. Der FC Barcelona ist stolz auf seinen Ethos, den Club möglichst allein durch die Beiträge seiner Mitglieder, den *socios*, zu finanzieren. So waren die Clubtrikots in 100 Jahren Vereinsgeschichte immer frei von Sponsorennamen. Auch die Erweiterung des Heimatstadions Camp Nou 1994 wurde teilweise durch die Beiträge der *socios* finanziert. Für jeweils gut 50 Euro verkaufte man Wandfliesen, die mit dem Namenszug der Käufer versehen wurden – was die Verbundenheit der Mitglieder mit dem Club symbolisch zementieren sollte. Findige Fans von Real Madrid hatten das Ziel, das Projekt lokaler Identitätsstiftung zu unterlaufen: Sie sollen versucht haben, über den Ankauf von Wandfliesen Camp Nou ihre feindliche Handschrift aufzuprägen.

Bekenntnis zum FC Barcelona als Ausdruck katalanischer Identität – gerade zu Zeiten der Militärdiktatur Francos. Auch Joan Miró bezog Stellung und entwarf das Plakat zum 75-jährigen Clubjubiläum.
Allegiance to FC Barcelona as an expression of Catalan identity – particularly under Franco's military dictatorship. The artist Joan Miró showed his true colours in designing the poster commemorating the club's seventy-fifth birthday. ©VG-Bildkunst, Bonn 2006

Vereinsverbundenheit symbolisch zementiert: Die Erweiterung des Stadions von Barça wurde teilweise durch Clubmitglieder finanziert. Sie konnten Fliesen mit ihren Namenszügen erwerben, die heute im Camp Nou angebracht sind. Club allegiance symbolically cemented: the enlargement of the Barça stadium was partly financed by club members. They bought tiles with their names on them that are now on the walls in Camp Nou Stadium.

More than a Game, More than a Team! Football as the Pitch for Regional Identity in Spain

Christiane Hirsch

Zinédine Zidane, Ronaldo, Ronaldinho and David Beckham – the roll of illustrious names Spanish teams have acquired in recent years by trading reads like a *Who's Who* of current football superstars. For these impressive acquisitions the country has also paid the highest transfer fees world-wide. Seventy-three million euros were paid to Juventus Torino for Zidane alone. But that is about all Spanish football teams have in common. In Spain itself interest tends to centre on the differences between the teams – based on regional origin: Catalans sing out for FC Barcelona – affectionately nicknamed Barça – Madrilenos rave about the

Der Verein begleitet den Tag: Café-Tasse mit Barça-Emblem. *Living with your club all day: a coffee cup with the Barça crest.*

Fan-Bekenntnis im Alltag: »Porrón«, eine Karaffe, die mit Wein gefüllt auf dem Tisch steht, mit dem Vereinsemblem des FC Barcelona. *Fan allegiance all day, every day: a «porrón», a caraffe filled with wine standing on a table, boasts the FC Barcelona crest.*

Dies war nur ein weiterer Sabotage-Versuch in der langen Geschichte der Gegnerschaft zwischen den beiden Vereinen: Ihren Zenit erreichte sie während der Militärdiktatur von Francisco Franco von 1939 bis zu seinem Tod 1975. Die zentralistische Politik des Galiciers Franco zielte auf die Vereinheitlichung aller Regionen des Landes ab. Als Leitbild galt das Spanische, die Werte, Sprache und Lebensart der Zentralregion Kastilien, welche mit Slogans wie »Wenn du Spanier bist, sprich spanisch!« verbreitet wurden. Baskische und katalanische Kultur und Sprache waren verboten, politischer Widerstand konnte das Leben kosten. Die Anhänger des FC Barcelona sahen in Real Madrid zu dieser Zeit vor allem *el equipo del régime,* Francos Lieblingsclub. 1943 verlor der FC Barcelona bei einem Rückspiel gegen Real Madrid mit dem vernichtenden Ergebnis von 1:11 – die Militärpolizei soll den Spielern für den Fall eines Sieges mit Ausweisung und anderen Repressionen gedroht haben.

Etwa zwanzig Jahre später war der FC Barcelona bereits vollends mit den politischen Zielen der »katalanischen Sache« aufgeladen. Mit diesen hatte schon der Vereinsgründer, der Schweizer Hans Kamper sympathisiert, der seine katalanische Einstellung durch eine Namensänderung auf Joan Gamper demonstrierte. Bis heute wird er anerkennend als »Katalane im Herzen« bezeichnet. Dies war nur ein Zeichen für die ungeheure Wichtigkeit, die einer katalanischen Gesinnung von Spielern und Trainern im FC Barcelona über die Jahrzehnte hinweg zukam. Die Clubflagge der Blaubraunen, der *Azulgranas,* enthielt darüber hinaus nicht nur die Trikotfarben blau und braun, sondern auch die gelb-roten Streifen der katalanischen Flagge. In den 1960er Jahren ersetzte die Clubflagge bei Demonstrationen der politischen Opposition gegen Franco dann die verbotene gelb-rot gestreifte Flagge *Senyera* der katalanischen Autonomiebewegung. Das Fußballstadion wurde zu einem Ort, an dem die Zusammenkunft von Gleichgesinnten möglich war. Kurz: Der FC Barcelona wurde zum Medium katalanischer Identität und Politik zugleich und war damit für seine Anhänger weit mehr als ein Verein. Diese enorme politisch-kulturelle Bedeutung fand 1973 Ausdruck in dem katalanischen Clubslogan *més que un club*. Doch die Gleichsetzung von Real Madrid mit den Interessen des Francoregimes ist nur die halbe Wahrheit: Zwar wurde Real Madrid ab 1956 mit seinen Siegen und der geschickten Finanz- und Spielerpolitik seines regimetreuen Präsidenten Santiago Bernabéu im Ausland zum Erfolgssymbol des zentralistischen Spaniens. Exzel-

«white ballet» staged by Real Madrid and the Basques feel for Athlétic Bilbao or Real Sociedad. Especially when FC Barcelona meets its big rival Real Madrid, more is at stake than just a game! Victories and defeats are played out in the arena of regional and local identity: Catalans vs Madrilenos. They are united and divided in hostilities that have grown over the decades and are shaped by differing ways of viewing things and mundane attitudes. Conversely, the two teams crucially mould the way Catalans and Madrilenos get on with each other on a daily basis. How much people are affected by all this is shown in the consequences of «crossing borders»: in 2000 Luís Figo, who had signed up with FC Barcelona in 1995, moved to the «Royals», Real Madrid, for a transfer fee to the tune of roughly 55 million euros. In his first match against FC Barcelona that year, Figo never even got close to the corner post. FC Barcelona fans hurled mobile phones, coins and even a pig's head at him and he was subjected to violent verbal abuse – Judas was one of the printable terms used by the enraged fans. Figo's head was depicted on giant peseta notes bearing the inscription *Figo pesetero*. His motive for transferring was obviously put down to greed.

Barça fans have a distinctive attitude to buying players and finances. FC Barcelona is proud of the ethic which ensures the team is financed as far as possible by the contributions of club members, *los socios*. Club kit has been free of sponsor names for the hundred years of the team's history. Even when Camp Nou, the home stadium, was enlarged in 1994, the contributions made by the *socios* financed its refurbishment. Wall tiles bearing the purchaser's name were sold for what would now amount to at least 50 euros – which was supposed to symbolically consolidate the loyalty of members to their team. Inventive Real Madrid fans tried to subvert this project for enhancing local identity. They are said to have done their best to stamp their hostile signature on Camp Nou by buying wall tiles.

This was just one more act of attempted sabotage in the history of hostility between the two fan clubs, which was at its height during the military dictatorship of Francisco Franco between 1939 and his death in 1975. The centralist policies of Franco, a native of Galicia, aimed at unifying the country's regions. Spanish was to be the unifying factor: the Spanish values, language and lifestyle practised in Castile, the central region, which were disseminated by slogans such as «If you're a Spaniard, speak Spanish!» The Basque and Catalan languages and cultures were proscribed. Political resistance was on pain of death. The fans of FC Barcelona viewed Real Madrid at that time above all as *el equipo del régime*, Franco's pet team. In 1943 FC Barcelona lost a return game against Real Madrid by a devastating 1:11 – the military police were said to have threatened the players with deportation and other repressive measures if they won.

Twenty years later, FC Barcelona was completely taken up with the political aims of the «Catalan cause». The founder of the team, a Swiss named Hans Kamper, was fully in sympathy with them when he felt called upon to demonstrate his pro-Catalan stance by changing his name to Joan Gamper. Even today he is fondly remembered as a «Catalan at heart». This was just one indication of the enormous importance attached for decades by FC Barcelona players and trainers to allegiance to the Catalan cause. Moreover, the club colours of the Blues and Browns, the *Azulgranas*, sported the yellow and red stripes of the Catalan flag in addition to the kit colours blue and brown. In the 1960s demonstrations mounted by the political opposition against Franco, the club colours substituted for the *Senyera*, the for-

Real Madrid: Der Traditionsverein aus der Hauptstadt ist der Erzrivale des katalanischen FC Barcelona. Real Madrid: this venerable club from the capital is the arch rival of Catalan FC Barcelona.

Ronaldinho ist als Topstar des FC Barcelona auch dessen Hauptwerbeträger und Verkaufsschlager. Sein Konterfei zierte um die Weihnachtszeit 2005 sogar einen Weihnachtsstern. Ronaldinho is, as the top star of FC Barcelona, the main vehicle for advertising and a marketing dynamo. His likeness even adorned a Christmas star in 2005.

lente Spieler wie der Argentinier Alfredo di Stéfano und der Ungar Ferenc Puscás galten als das Aushängeschild für den Erfolg des Zentralismus des Regimes. Rückblickend war der Publicity-Erfolg im Fußball für Francos Politik wohl größer als der Profit, den der Club aus seinem Image ziehen konnte.

Heute haben der FC Barcelona genau wie Real Madrid als weltweit überaus erfolgreiche Vereine ein völlig neues Gesicht. Seit den 1990er Jahren sind beide gigantische Wirtschaftsunternehmen, die ihren Club mit eigenem Fernsehkanal und über den Verkauf von Werbeflächen und -artikeln vermarkten. Beide kämpfen seit der Jahrtausendwende gegen Schulden in Höhe von mehreren hundert Millionen Euro. Real Madrid gelang es, über den Verkauf seines Stadions an die Stadt Madrid für die Olympia-Bewerbung 2012 wieder schwarze Zahlen zu schreiben. Der FC Barcelona tastet nun das letzte Tabu des Clubs an und verhandelt mit möglichen Sponsoren für Trikotwerbung. Doch auch im Zeitalter des globalen Spieleraustauschs und der immer stärkeren ökonomischen Ausrichtung finden die verschiedenen Clubidentitäten noch lokalen Ausdruck. So zum Beispiel in Madrid: Der *Cibeles*-Brunnen ist der traditionelle Ort für Siegesfeiern von Real Madrid. Als Ronaldo im Sommer 2002 bei Real Madrid antrat, war ihm das noch nicht bewusst. Auf seiner Homepage präsentierte er sich also vor dem *Neptun*-Brunnen, nur 200 Meter entfernt, was ihm Hohn und Spott der realtreuen Sportzeitung *Marca* einbrachte: Der *Neptun*-Brunnen gilt als Wahrzeichen des Lokalrivalen Atlético Madrid ... So stehen regionale Identitäten immer wieder neu auf dem Spiel – nicht nur auf dem Fußballfeld!

bidden yellow and red striped flag of the movement for Catalan autonomy. The football stadium became a venue for all those who thought alike. In brief, FC Barcelona became the medium for Catalan identity and politics and meant, therefore, much more to its fans than a football team normally would. The enormous political and cultural significance attached to it was expressed in 1973 in the Catalan team slogan *més que un club*. The equation of Real Madrid with the interests of the Franco regime, on the other hand, is at best half apt: from 1956 Real Madrid was viewed as a symbol for centralist Spain thanks to the victories it won and the clever financial and player policies embraced by its president, Santiago Bernabéu, a regime loyalist. This meant that outstanding players such as Alfredo di Stéfano of Argentina and Ferenc Puscás, a Hungarian, were regarded as figureheads advertising the success of the centralist policies promoted by the regime. Viewed in retrospect, the success enjoyed by the publicity for Franco's politics provided by football probably outweighed any benefits accruing to the team from its own image.

FC Barcelona also depended on state support in 1962 because building the Camp Nou stadium, which was finished in 1957, had burdened it with enormous debts. In 1966 the team was only able to raise what in today's terms amounted to 25 million euros by selling properties around the old home stadium, *Les Corts,* because the government changed the status of what had been green-field zones to building sites.

Nowadays both FC Barcelona and Real Madrid are very successful world-wide and have developed into big corporations. Since the 1990s both have been giant businesses, which market their teams through their own TV channels and sales of advertising space and memorabilia. Since the millennium both have been battling debts amounting to several hundred million euros. Real Madrid managed to get back into the black by selling its stadium to the city of Madrid when it was competing for the 2012 Olympics. FC Barcelona is now infringing its last taboo by entering on negotiations with possible sponsors for kit-supported advertising. Nevertheless, even in an age of world-wide player trading and growing emphasis on financial considerations, club identities still find distinctive local expression. Take Madrid for instance: the *Cibeles* Fountain is the traditional venue for Real Madrid victory celebrations. When Ronaldo joined Real Madrid in summer 2002, he was still unaware of that fact. He duly presented himself on his homepage posing in front of the *Neptune* Fountain, only 200 metres away, a mistake that earned him a deluge of mockery and sarcasm from the sport paper *Marca,* which supports Real: the *Neptune* Fountain is the emblem of its local rival, Atlético Madrid... Regional identity still matters – and not just on the pitch!

Metropole versus Provinz im türkischen Fußball

Tanıl Bora

Man könnte meinen, Fußball und Oligarchie hätten nichts miteinander zu tun. Zumindest für die Fußballlandschaft in der Türkei stimmt das nicht. Seit 1959, als über den unterschiedlichen Regionalligen eine Nationalliga institutionalisiert wurde, haben es gerade mal vier anatolische Mannschaften geschafft, die Meisterschaft für sich zu entscheiden. Ankara mit seinen vier Millionen Einwohnern hat nie einen Meister hervorgebracht. Und damit nicht genug: Die drittgrößte Stadt des Landes, Izmir, oder die viertgrößte Stadt, Adana, haben seit Jahren keinen Vertreter mehr in der ersten Liga!

Seit Jahren dominieren drei Istanbuler Großclubs den gesamten türkischen Fußball. Ihre Vorherrschaft ist geradezu erdrückend. Die Anzahl ihrer Meistertitel spricht Bände: Fenerbahçe 16, Galatasaray 15, Beşiktaş 10. In den letzten Jahren ist sogar die Position des viertgrößten türkischen Vereins, Trabzonspor, gefährdet, der die Hegemonie der Istanbuler Clubs mehrfach gebrochen hatte.

Die Vormachtstellung der drei Istanbuler Topvereine spiegelt das gewaltige Gewicht der Stadt im wirtschaftlichen und sozialen Leben des Landes wider. Noch vor der Gründung der Nationalliga stand Istanbuls Fußball im Zentrum des Interesses und der Macht. Das hat auch damit zu tun, dass die Metropole schon lange auch Mediensitz ist und fleißig an Fußballmythen bastelt. Mit der Industrialisierung des Fußballs verfestigte sich diese Situation parallel zur Gründung der Nationalliga.

Einen Hoffungsschimmer konnten die Fußballfans in den Jahren zwischen 1968 und 1980 erblicken. Damals schien die Istanbuler Vormacht ernsthaft zu bröckeln. Auch das ist kein Zufall. Die Siebziger Jahre waren die Ära der selbstbewussten jungen Linken in der Türkei. Die außerparlamentarische Opposition erlebte damals so etwas wie eine »Nachspielzeit«, die das alte Establishment mit ihrem Selbstverständnis erschütterte und erst durch den »Schlusspfiff« des Militärputsches im Jahre 1980 beendet werden sollte. Das schlug sich auch im Fußball nieder. Zuerst drängten sich Göztepe aus Izmir, danach Eskişehirspor aus Eskişehir, Musterstadt der nachgeholten Industrialisierung der Provinz, an die Spitze und verfehlten im letzten Moment nur knapp die Meisterschaft. Dies gelang dann 1975 Trabzonspor. Trabzon, das sich auf dem hügeligen Stadtgelände der Schwarzmeerküste durch eine eigenständige Straßenfußball-Folklore hervortut, vereinte sein Potential mit unnachgiebigem Kampfgeist und zwang – stellvertretend für alle anatolischen Clubs – Istanbul in die Knie. Das war kein Glücksfall, Trabzonspor gelang das, was zuvor unmöglich schien und krönte seinen einzigartigen Aufstieg zwischen 1975 und 1984 gleich mit sechs Meisterschaften.

Seit Mitte der 1980er Jahre aber erfuhr die Kommerzialisierung des türkischen Profifußballs eine ungeahnte Dynamik und führte zu einem erneuten Ungleichgewicht zugunsten der Istanbuler Oligarchie. Istanbul, das ohnehin ein Industrie-, Finanz- und Medienzentrum war, gewann durch seine Standortvorteile eine Vormachtstellung, die den Rest des Landes

Wimpel der türkischen Fußball-Nationalmannschaft.
Pennant of the Turkish national football team.

Metropolis vs the Provinces in Turkish Football

Tanıl Bora

You might think football and oligarchy have nothing to do with each other but this certainly isn't true of football teams in Turkey. Since 1959, when a national league was established above the various regional leagues, merely four Anatolian teams have divided up the championship between them. Ankara, with its population of four million, has never managed to win the national cup. And that isn't all: the country's third biggest city, Izmir, and the fourth biggest, Adana, haven't sent anyone to the premier league for years and years!

Three big Istanbul clubs have dominated Turkish football for decades. Their virtually uncontested primacy is oppressive. The number of title matches they have won speaks volumes: Fenerbahçe sixteen, Galatasaray fifteen, Beşiktaş ten. In recent years even the position of the fourth biggest Turkish club, Trabzonspor, has been at risk. In the past it succeeded in breaking into the hegemony of the Istanbul clubs several times.

The supremacy of the three top Istanbul clubs reflects the enormous socio-economic weight of the city in the country as a whole. Even before the national league was founded, Istanbul football was the focus of attention and the hub of power. The predominance of Istanbul in football is also due to the fact that the metropolis has long been the seat of the media and has been busy building up the football legend. With the industrialisation of football, this situation was consolidated in parallel with the foundation of the national league.

Football fans had a glimmer of hope in the years between 1968 and 1980, when the primacy of Istanbul really seemed to be crumbling. That, too, is not a coincidence. The 1970s

geradezu an den Rand drückte. Die Zuschauerzahlen der drei Istanbuler Clubs, aber auch von Trabzonspor, sind seit Jahren fünfstellig, die der anderen Vereine bleiben vierstellig. Dies bedeutet für die Topclubs Vorteile – nicht nur bei Heimspielen (im Grunde sind ihnen Auswärtsspiele fremd): Als würde diese Unterstützung nicht reichen, können sich die türkischen Topklubs auch über Präsenz in den Medien nicht beklagen.

Die »Drei Großen« weisen tradierte Eigenschaften auf. Fenerbahçe – transferfreudig, spektakelverliebt *à la Brasil* und arrogant – wurde in den 1970er Jahren dem türkischen neureichen Bürgertum zugeordnet. Galatasaray, dessen Gründer und Führung dem gleichnamigen, westlich orientierten Elitegymnasium nahe stehen, gilt als Europa zugewandt. Kenner ordnen diesem Verein Innovationskraft, aber auch den Snobismus der urbanen Aristokratie zu. Beşiktaş, der als am stärksten lokal verwurzelte Club auf ein Milieu der Gemeinschaft zurückgreift, kultiviert im Schatten von Fenerbahçe und Galatasaray den »Stolz der Geächteten und Bedrängten« Zu ihm passt seine kollektivistische, kämpferische Spielweise, mit deren Geist sich die Anhängerschaft identifiziert. Hier trifft noch heute die Bezeichnung »Arbeitermannschaft« zu.

Seit Galatasaray in den 1990er Jahren regelmäßig an europäischen Wettbewerben wie der Champions League teilnahm und im Jahre 2000 sogar den UEFA-Cup und den Super-Cup gewann, messen sich die »Großen« an den Ergebnissen in der europäischen Arena. Erfolge in den letzten Jahren sind aber eher die Ausnahme. Was bleibt, ist die zynische Etikettierung der heimischen Clubs als infantile »Mama Liga« – wie die Galatasaray-Fans den innertürkischen Wettbewerb in der überaus erfolgreichen Ära der 1990er Jahre getauft hatten, um das trübe Lokaldasein ihrer Rivalen zu verspotten.

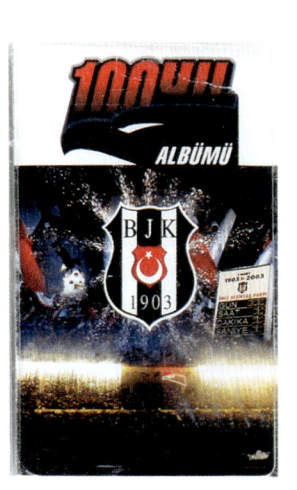

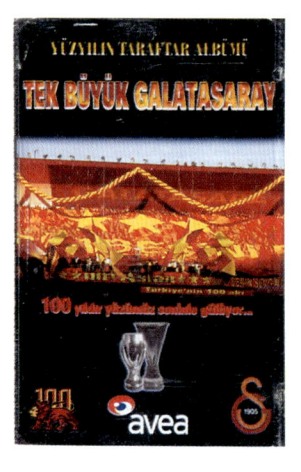

Musik-Kassetten für Fans der vier türkischen Spitzenmannschaften Fenerbahçe, Beşiktaş, Galatasaray und Trabzonspor.
Music cassettes for fans of the four top Turkish teams: Fenerbahçe, Beşiktaş, Galatasaray and Trabzonspor.

Einer der wenigen Top-Clubs außerhalb Istanbuls: Trabzonspor Kulübü – der »Trabzon-Sport-Club«. One of the few top clubs outside Istanbul: Trabzonspor Kulübü – «The Trabzon Sport Club».

Baby-Latz mit dem Slogan: »Ich wurde als Beşiktaş-Fan geboren.« A baby bib with the slogan: «I was born a Beşiktaş fan.»

were the era of the self-assured young leftists in Turkey. At that time the «extraparliamentary opposition» experienced something like «extra time», which shook the old establishment and its self-image and did not end until the military coup of 1980 blew the «final whistle» on this interlude. This upheaval also affected football. First Göztepe of Izmir, followed by Eskişehirspor of Eskişehir, a model of belated provincial industrialisation, surged to the top of the league, just missing Premiership at the last minute by a whisker. Trabzonspor did make it in 1975. Trabzon, which boasts a body of street football lore of its own, is a hilly city on the Black Sea coast. Its team united talent with a fiery fighting spirit and it brought – as the doughty champion of all Anatolian clubs – Istanbul to its knees. That was not just luck. Trabzonspor really did succeed in doing what had till then seemed impossible and went on to crown its meteoric rise with six national cup wins between 1875 and 1984.

Since the mid-1980s, however, the commercialisation of Turkish professional football has taken on a dynamic of its own and again led to the hegemony of the Istanbul oligarchy. Istanbul, which in any case has always been the hub of industry, finance and the media, provides the ideal location to support this supremacy and has proceeded to marginalise the rest of the country. Spectator figures for the three Istanbul clubs as well as Trabzonspor have remained in five digits whereas the other clubs have had to make do with four. This has brought advantages to the top clubs – not just at home games (in fact, they hardly know anything but home games) and, as if this were not enough, the top Turkish clubs cannot complain about the space devoted to them in the media.

The «three big ones» have all the traditional right qualities. Fenerbahçe – trading feverishly, spectacle-enraptured *à la Brasil* and as arrogant as they come – became the bailiwick of Turkish parvenus in the 1970s. Galatasaray, whose founders and directors are close to the elite, western-oriented secondary school of the same name, is regarded as European in outlook. Experts attribute powers of innovation to this club along with the snobbery of the urban aristocracy. Beşiktaş, the club with the strongest local community roots but

Die Ausrichtung der Istanbuler Großclubs an den europäischen Wettbewerben spiegelt sich in der Verpflichtung renommierter ausländischer Trainer wie etwa des Deutschen Christoph Daum. The orientation of the big Istanbul clubs at the European Cups is reflected in the recruitment of renowned foreign coaches such as the German Christoph Daum. © Photo: pixathlon

Das Ressentiment der Provinz gegenüber Istanbul wächst ständig. Die türkische Metropole steht für Globalisierung, Obrigkeit und uneingeschränkte Macht des Geldes. Sie ist aber auch Sinnbild für Kosmopolitanismus und »Entartung«. Es kommt daher nicht von ungefähr, dass manche »anatolischen« Fan-Initiativen sich als Mission gegen »Byzanz« verstehen. So verkörpern die »Anti-Byzantiner« die Reaktion der Verdrängten und Modernisierungsverlierer – manchmal aber auch nur provinzial-nationalistische Borniertheit.

overshadowed by Fenerbahçe and Galatasaray, cultivates the «defiance of the down-trodden and oppressed». It is known for a collectivist, combative style of play and its fans identify with it in spirit. This is a case in which the term «working men's team» actually applies.

Since Galatasaray regularly participated in European tournaments at Champions League level in the 1990s and in 2000 even won the UEFA Cup and the Super Cup, the «big ones» have been measured by the standards of the European arena. In the past few years, however, successes have been few and far between. What remains is the cynical labelling of the home club as an infantile «Mamma's League» – as Galatasaray fans took to calling the inner Turkish competition in the successful era of the 1990s to disparage the dreary local status of their rivals.

The resentment felt by provincial clubs towards Istanbul continues to grow apace. The Turkish metropolis stands for globalisation, authority and the untrammelled power of finance. But it also symbolises a cosmopolitan outlook and «decadence». It is no coincidence, therefore, that some «Anatolian» fan initiatives view themselves as a mission against «Byzantium». The «anti-Byzantines» represent the reaction of the oppressed losers in the struggle for modernisation – although this can at times amount to blinkered provincialism or nationalism.

Hauspantoffeln mit aufgesticktem Schriftzug: »Eines Tages wird jeder ein Fenerbahçe-Fan sein.«
Slippers with the following embroidered inscription: «One day everybody will be a Fenerbahçe fan.»

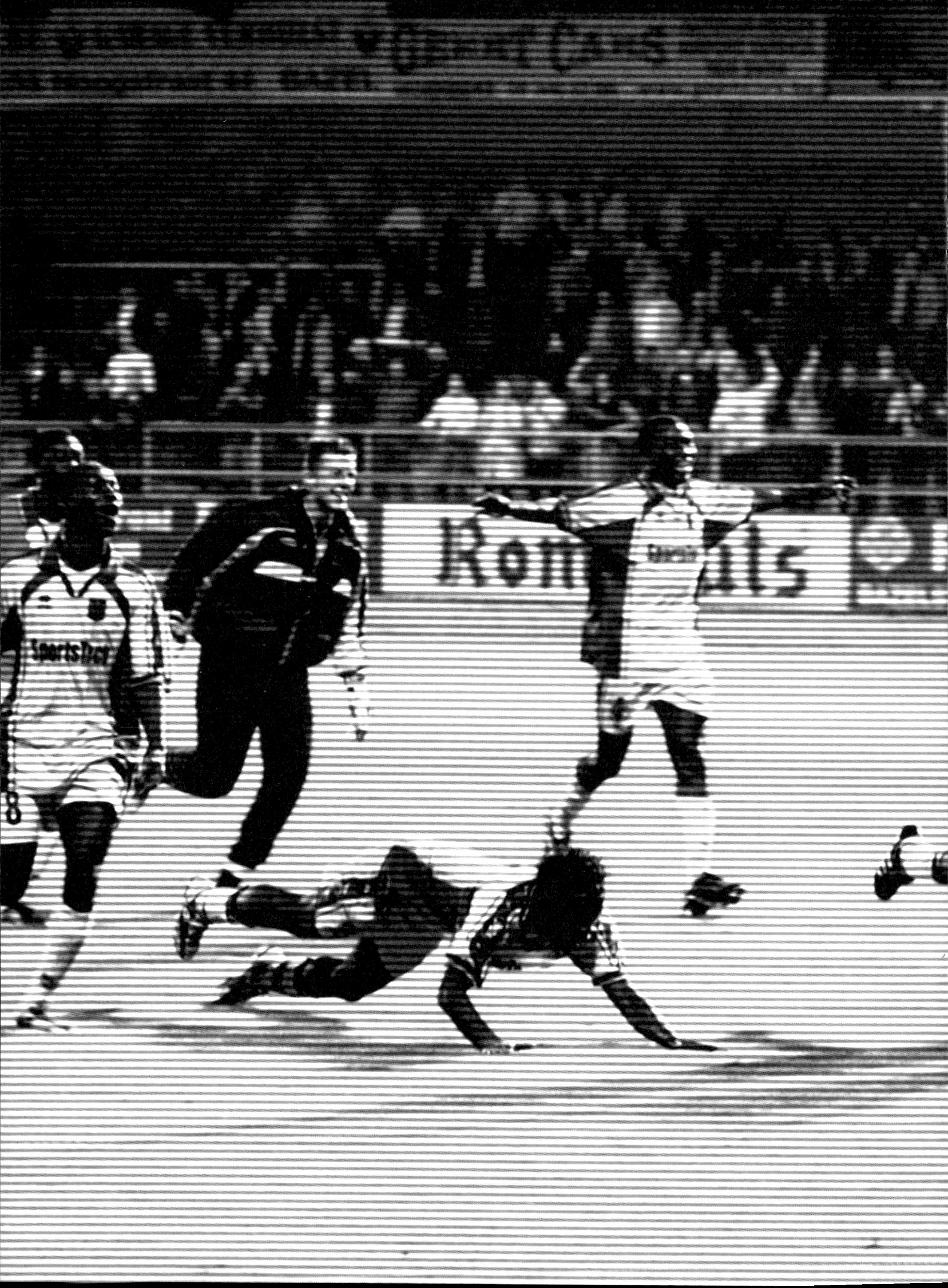

Brot und Spiele
Bread and Games

Fußball als Fortsetzung der Politik mit anderen Mitteln?

Stefan Eisenhofer

Schon 1880 verspottete der englische Schriftsteller Rudyard Kipling den Fußball und die »kleinen Seelen, deren Hunger durch die verdreckten Idioten gestillt werden kann, die ihn spielen«. Und knapp hundert Jahre später bemerkt Hubert Fichte in seinem Roman *Explosion* über Brasilien: »Inmitten größter Armut und Perspektivlosigkeit ein Stadion für 40 Millionen. Das ist nicht niedlich und bloß kurios. Das evoziert Fragen.«

Unterschiedliche Kreise standen und stehen dem Fußball immer wieder skeptisch gegenüber. Die einen fürchten, dass bei diesem Spiel durch animalische Instinkte und Ignoranz Kultur und menschliche Vernunft zerstört würden. Die anderen konstatieren, dass der Fußball die Masse verdummen, revolutionäre Ideen in falsche Bahnen lenken und die Arbeiter über ihre Ausbeutung und Unterdrückung hinwegtrösten soll. Alle zusammen schließlich beklagen die Rolle dieses Sports als willfähriges Vehikel eines immer hemmungsloser agierenden globalen Kapitalismus.

Freilich fehlt es während des gut hundertjährigen Siegeszugs des Fußballs durch die Welt auch keineswegs an Rehabilitierungsversuchen gegenüber diesem Sport, gerade auch von Intellektuellen. Seine völkerverbindenden Aspekte werden betont, seine Türöffner-Funktion, seine – im Gegensatz etwa zu Golf oder Boxen – klassenüberschreitenden Eigenschaften – und sein grunddemokratischer Charakter, bei dem die persönliche Leistung die Herkunft aus »gutem Hause« in den Hintergrund treten lasse. Schließlich wird auch immer wieder auf die zahllosen Sozialprojekte quer über die Welt hinweg verwiesen, bei der perspektivlose Jugendliche Selbstbewusstsein und Aufstiegsmöglichkeiten erlangen und ehemalige Kindersoldaten soziale Kompetenz einüben können.

Die Popularität des Fußballs und seine leichte emotionale Aufladbarkeit, seine »Kultfähigkeit« und seine Massenkompatibilität sowie seine identifikationsstiftenden Eigenschaften werden jedenfalls seit hundert Jahren für unterschiedlichste Zwecke genutzt. Als Symbolträger funktioniert Fußball auf den verschiedensten und vielfältigsten Ebenen: Vom Dorf und Stadtviertel über die Stadt und Heimatregion bis hin zur Nation und zum Erdteil, von der gesellschaftlichen Schicht über das politische System bis zur Religionszugehörigkeit. Dabei müssen die Anknüpfungspunkte keineswegs immer real sein; im Gegenteil, oft viel mächtiger sind erträumte und erwünschte Identifikationsmuster.

Trotz idealistischer und bisweilen auch recht naiver Bestrebungen, den Fußball als »Sport um des Sports willen« von äußeren Einflüssen »rein« halten zu wollen, ging die Verbreitung dieser Ballspielart von Anfang an mit Versuchen einher, sie für ehrenwerte und weniger ehrenwerte Zwecke einzuspannen. Schon vor hundert Jahren benutzte die europäische Großindustrie den Fußball als Bild für ein intaktes soziales Gefüge, das sich auf den eigenen Betrieb übertragen lässt: Jeder setzt für ein gemeinsames Ziel an seinem Platz seine Kräfte

Die italienischen Faschisten um Mussolini hielten Fußball lange für zu wenig »militärisch« und für »zu englisch« statt »italienisch«. Bald nutzten aber auch sie die Fußball-Massenbegeisterung für ihre Propaganda. Duce-Inschrift am Olympia-Stadion in Rom. For a long time the Italian Fascists around Mussolini considered football not «military» enough and «too English» rather than «Italian», but they soon exploited the mass enthusiasm for football for their propaganda. A Duce inscription on the Rome Olympic stadium. © Photo: Roger Penn

Football as Politics with Different Means?

Stefan Eisenhofer

Back in 1880 the English writer Rudyard Kipling made fun of football and the «little souls» whose hunger can be satisfied by the «dirty idiots» that play it. And just a century later, the German writer Hubert Fichte remarked on Brazil in his novel *Explosion:* «In the midst of great poverty and lack of perspectives a stadium for 40 million. That is not amusing and merely odd. That elicits questions.»

There have always been groups that are sceptical about football. Some are afraid that culture and rationality are destroyed in this game by bestial instinct and ignorance. Others insist that football dumbs down the masses, steers revolutionary ideas into wrong channels and is intended to console working-class men for being exploited and oppressed. All sceptical groups are unanimous in deploring the role of this sport as the arbitrary vehicle of a global capitalism that is acting ever more uninhibitedly.

Militärischer Drill im Training und Fußballer als »sportliche Soldaten«: Rigoros wurde der Fußball in die Ideologie der Nazi-Machthaber eingebunden. Beliebte Spieler wurden als faschistische Aushängeschilder instrumentalisiert, jüdische Fußballer schikaniert und ausgeschlossen. Military drill in training and footballers as «athletic soldiers»: football was closely linked with the ideology of the Nazi regime. Favourite players were instrumentalised as Fascist figureheads while Jewish players were badly treated and finally banned from football.

maximal für das Ganze ein. Durch die Gründung von Betriebsmannschaften versprach man sich sowohl bei den aktiven Spielern als auch bei den Zuschauern eine stärkere Identifikation mit dem eigenen Unternehmen. Zudem wurde der gesundheits- und arbeitskraftfördernde Aspekt des Fußballs – Bewegung an der frischen Luft statt Kneipen, Tabak, Alkohol und Drogen – betont. Hier trifft sich die Philosophie der damaligen Industriellen mit den Ideen von Sozialprojekten heutiger Tage, die den Fußball zur Förderung sozialer Kompetenzen, als Mittel zur gesellschaftlichen Wiedereingliederung und zur Traumabewältigung nutzen.

Der Fußball als Heilsbringer ist beileibe keine neue Erfindung. Schon in der frühen Kolonialzeit reisten europäische Mannschaften um die Welt, um den Fußball und seine Ideale zu verbreiten. Fußball wurde dabei auch zum »Instrument der Zivilisierung«, um europäische Zucht, Ordnung und Disziplin einzuüben. Mit dem Ball sollten denn auch gesunde Gesinnungen in gesunde Körper gedrillt werden – und zwar nicht nur bei »den Wilden daheim«, sondern auch bei denen in der Ferne. Entsprechend wurden Erfolge »schwarzer Spieler« als Triumph der Kolonialpolitik gefeiert. Als »schwarze Bürger im Fußballdress« galten diese als lebende Beweise dafür, dass »weiße Werte« verinnerlicht worden waren.

Während in den Kolonien der Fußball lange ausschließlich aus London, Paris und Brüssel ferngesteuert war – bis in die 1940er Jahre hinein durften nur »Weiße« als Schiedsrichter fungieren – wurde der Ballsport in der ausklingenden Kolonialperiode zur Bühne und zur Arena für antikoloniale Widerstandsbewegungen.

So nutzte etwa Benjamin Nnamdi Azikiwe den Fußball als Propagandamittel gegen die europäische Kolonialregierung. Stadien und Vereine wie sein Zik's Athletic Club fungierten dabei als Foren für unauffällige Versammlungen, bevor Azikiwe in der Folge zum ersten Staatspräsidenten von Nigeria wurde.

Wie eng Fußball, Unabhängigkeitsstreben und nationale Selbstbehauptung verknüpft sein können, zeigt auch das Beispiel Algerien, das mitten im Unabhängigkeitskrieg gegen

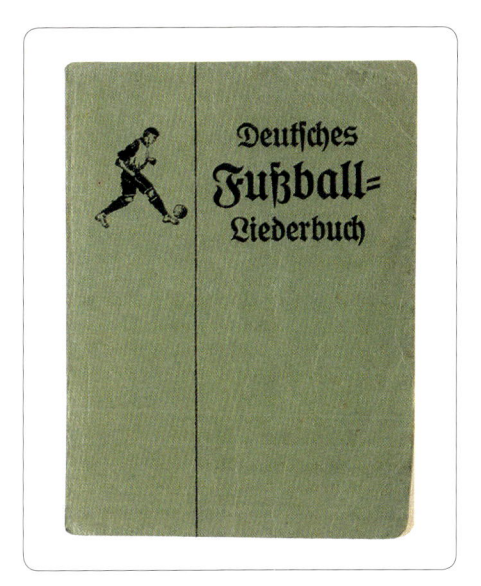

Fußball wurde in den europäischen Kolonien als Träger »weißer Werte« auch zum »Instrument der Zivilisierung«, um den dort lebenden Menschen »europäische Zucht, Ordnung und Disziplin einzuüben«. Koloniales Liederbuch mit Fußball-Liedern. In the European colonial era football was a vehicle for the values espoused by the colonialists, an «instrument of civilisation» to «teach the people living in the colonies law, order and discipline». A colonial song book with football songs.

Of course there has been no lack of attempts at re-establishing football's reputation during the hundred years or so during which the game has swept through the world in triumph and intellectuals have even been in the vanguard of this movement. Its way of bringing people together is a positive aspect of the game that has been emphasised, the way football opens doors, crosses class boundaries – unlike golf or boxing – and its fundamentally democratic character, which makes «coming from a good family» unimportant. Finally, the many social projects throughout the world are pointed out which help young people with no prospects to become self-confident and able to enter a different social sphere. Boys who may have once been child soldiers can practise core social competence skills with football.

The popularity of football and the fact that it is so easily charged with emotion, its «cultability» and its universal compatibility as well as its capacity for strengthening personal and national identity have also been drawn on for various purposes for a century. As a vehicle for symbolism, football operates on all sorts of levels: from the village and the quarter of a city through the city and region to nation and continent, from social class to political system and religious affiliation. The associations need not be real; on the contrary, imagined and desired identification patterns are often far more powerful.

For all the idealistic and occasionally rather naïve attempts to keep football «free» of external influences as a «sport for sport's sake», the spread of this type of ball game has always been accompanied by attempts to exploit it for honourable and not-so-honourable purposes. Even a century ago European heavy industry was using football as the emblem of an intact social fabric which might be translated to its own operations: everyone was to use his strengths at the workplace to the best of his ability for the good of the whole. In founding company teams, industrialists expected to foster stronger ties of identification with the company both in active players and spectators. What is more, the healthful aspect of football and the way it promoted a strong workforce – exercise in the fresh air instead of pubs, tobacco,

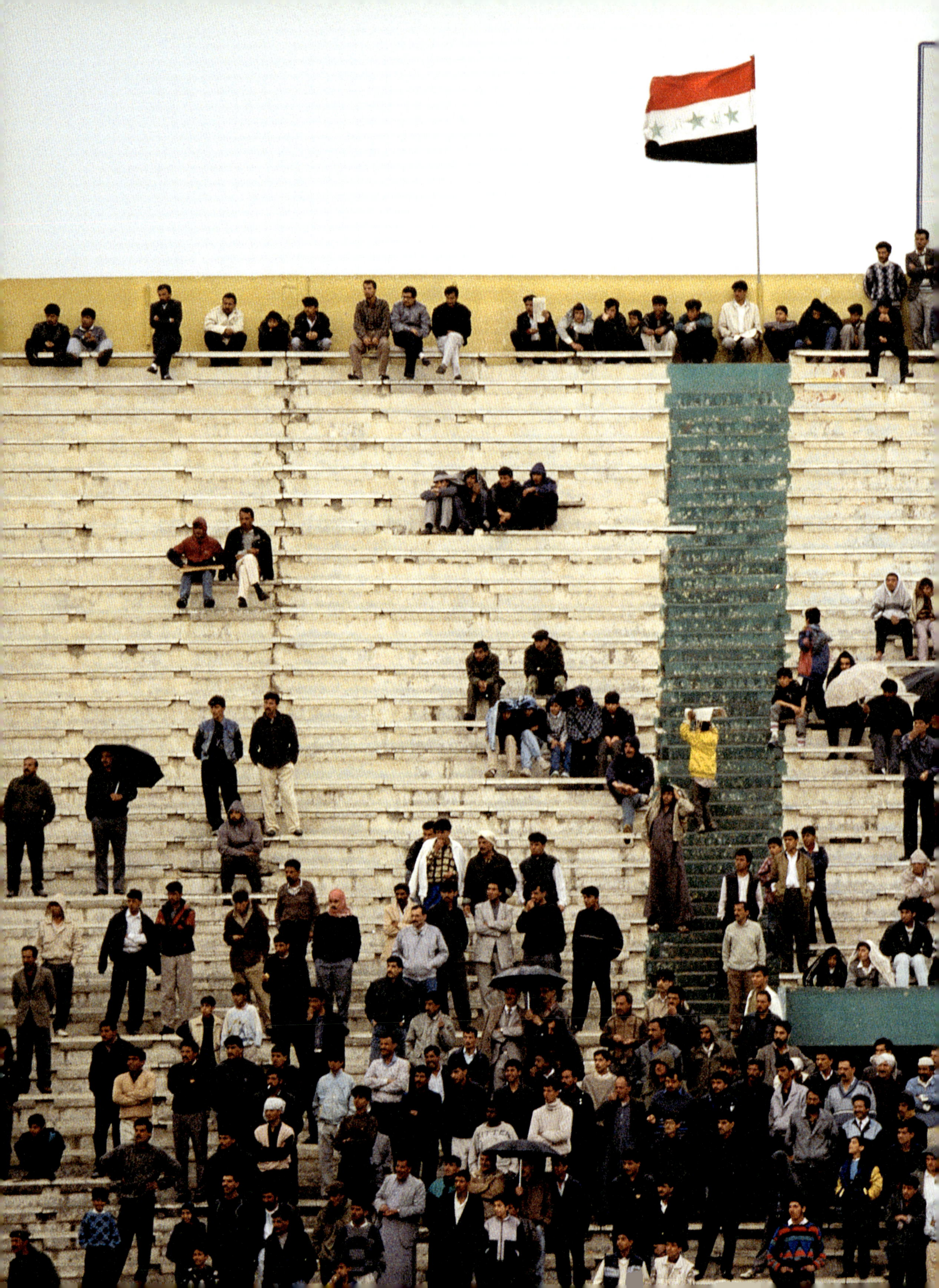

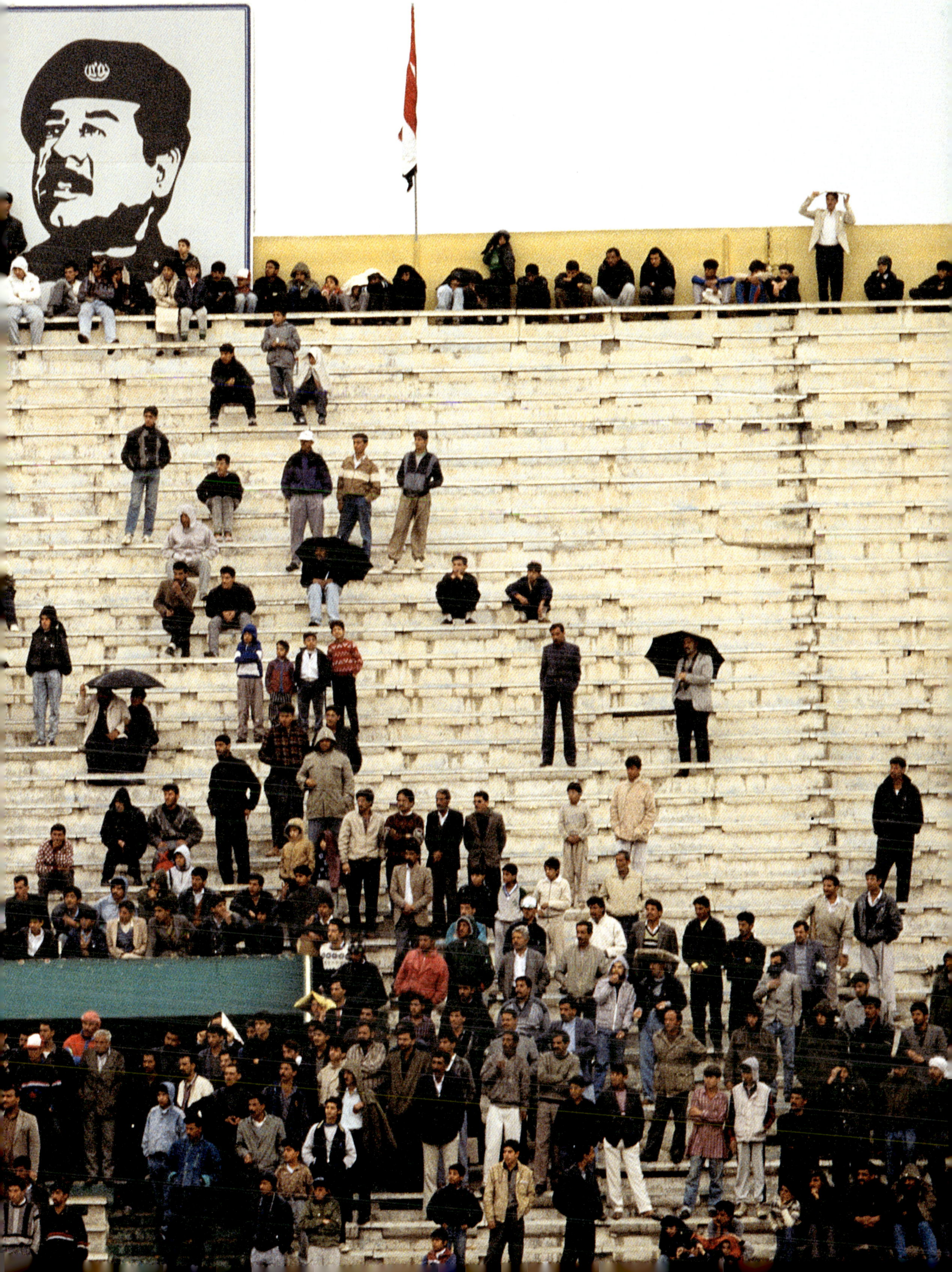

Der Fußball als Spiegel der politischen Verhältnisse eines Landes: Im Iran ist iranischen Frauen mittlerweile der Zutritt in Fußballstadien wieder verboten – Ausländerinnen hingegen nicht. Football mirrors political conditions in a country: Iranian women – but not foreign women – have again been banned from Iranian football stadiums. © Photo: Hasan Sarbkshian, AP Press, Teheran

← Gerade in totalitären Staaten können Fußballstadien zwei sehr gegensätzliche Gesichter annehmen: Einerseits als Triumphstätten der Machthaber, andererseits als Foren des Widerstandes. Stadion Bagdad, 1991. Football stadiums can have two faces in totalitarian countries: on the one hand, as place for regimes to celebrate triumphs and, on the other, as forums for resistance. A Baghdad stadium, 1991. © Photo: Les Stone, Sygma, Corbis

Frankreich im Jahr 1958 eine Nationalmannschaft aufstellte. Dabei wurden Fußballer wie Rachid Mekhloufi als Mitglieder des algerischen »Rebellenteams«, das als Politikum und als Affront gegen die Kolonialmächte verstanden wurde, zu Ikonen antikolonialen Widerstands. In vielen Clubnamen vor allem Afrikas kommt dieses damalige Unabhängigkeitsstreben noch heute zum Ausdruck, wenn führende Vereine den Namenszusatz »National« tragen – wie etwa beim wichtigsten ägyptischen Club *Al Ahly Cairo*. Eine besondere Art der Vergangenheitsbewältigung bietet der Fußball auch, wenn ein Sieg über die einstigen Kolonialherren erreicht wird – dies umso mehr in einem Sport, der von den Kolonisten einst selbst in die Kolonien gebracht worden war.

Nach der Unabhängigkeit erwies sich der Fußball auch mit neuen Herausforderungen als kompatibel. In den 1960er Jahren kam es in den neuen Staaten zu einer ganzen Reihe von Vereinsgründungen, die als Ausdruck von Souveränität und Selbstbewusstsein einzelner Bevölkerungsgruppen gedacht waren. So ist in vielen Ländern der Welt die Nationalmannschaft bis heute weniger ein Team der besten Fußballer des Landes, als vielmehr eine »Klammer« mit der Aufgabe, die unterschiedlichen im Land lebenden Gruppen zusammenzuhalten und nationale Anliegen gegenüber anderen Interessen in den Vordergrund zu stellen. Da gerade Fußballspiele auch gerne dazu genutzt worden waren, regionalistische und tribalis-

Ein Stück wiedererworbene Normalität in einem vom Bürgerkrieg gezeichneten Land: Fußballspielende Kinder in Angola. A glimpse of normality in a land ravaged by civil war: children playing football in Angola. © Photo: Eleanor Curtis, Panos Pictures

alcohol and drugs – were emphasised. Here the philosophy espoused by industrialists in those days concurs with the ideals informing social projects nowadays, which use football to promote social skills as a means for re-integration in society and overcoming trauma.

Football as a redemptive force is certainly not a new idea. Back in the early colonial era, European teams were travelling round the world to spread football and the ideals it embodied. Football thus became a «civilising instrument» for practising European law, order and discipline. The ball was supposed to inculcate *mens sana in corpore sana* – and not just in «the savages at home» but also in those far away in the colonies. Consequently, the success of «black players» was celebrated as a triumph of colonial policy. As «black citizens in football uniform» they were regarded as living examples of how «the white man's values» might be internalised by the black man.

While football in the colonies was entirely under remote control from London, Paris and Brussels – until well into the 1940s only «white men» were permitted to be referees – the ball game became a stage and arena for anti-colonial resistance movements in the declining colonial era.

Benjamin Nnamdi Azikiwe was one footballer who used the game as a vehicle for propaganda against the European colonial regime. Stadiums and clubs such as Zik's Athletic

Fußbälle werden oft unter Missachtung sozialer und ökologischer Mindeststandards hergestellt. Seit kurzem bemühen sich aber immer mehr westliche Importeure darum, den NäherInnen höhere Löhne zu garantieren, damit deren Kinder die Schule besuchen können anstatt für das Aufkommen des Familieneinkommens mitarbeiten zu müssen. »Fair Trade«-Ball und »kinderarbeitsfreier« Ball. Footballs are often made under conditions that flout minimum social and ecological standards. Recently, however, western importers have been trying to guarantee higher wages for the men and women who sew footballs so children can go to school instead of helping to support the family. A «Fair Trade» ball and a ball «child labour free».

tische Auseinandersetzungen zu schüren, folgte denn auch eine Reihe von Umbenennungen von Vereinsnamen, die antistaatliche Momente zugunsten neutralerer Bezeichnungen ausmerzten. Ähnliches kennt man aus den Staaten des ehemaligen Warschauer Pakts, wo Vereinsnamen wie »Dynamo«, »Vorwärts« oder »Empor« als Ausdruck politischer Zielsetzungen eine Blüte erlebt hatten, und wie verkürzte Parteiprogramme eingesetzt worden waren.

Überhaupt sind Mannschaften oft ein Spiegel unterschiedlicher Interessen außerhalb des rein Sportlichen. Viele Teams verkommen dabei zum Spielball der politisch und wirtschaftlich Mächtigen. Fußball ist sowieso meistens »Chefsache«. Kaum eine Diktatur und kaum ein totalitäres Regime der letzten hundert Jahre auf dieser Welt hat es unversucht gelassen, den Fußball als Medium zur Selbstdarstellung und zur Einflussnahme auf große Bevölkerungsteile zu nutzen. Die Instrumentalisierung des Fußballs ist jedoch ein zweischneidiges Schwert. Zu unsicher ist der Erfolg, zu schnell können Niederlagen in Unmut gegen die Mächtigen umschlagen. In der DDR beispielsweise genossen daher Sportarten, bei denen der Erfolg kalkulierbarer war, deutlich mehr Sympathien und Fördermittel von Seiten der maßgeblichen Politkreise. Tatsächlich wurde der Fußball durch seine starke emotionale Aufladbarkeit immer wieder zum Bumerang. Dies erfuhr unter anderem die argentinische Militärregierung, die sich durch die Weltmeisterschaft im eigenen Lande vor allem auch verstärkte Unterstützung durch die Bevölkerung versprach. Aber trotz des Erfolgs des Nationalteams skandierten die Fans kurz darauf lauthals, dass die Militärdiktatur zu Ende gehen solle.

Was für den Fußball im allgemeinen gilt, trifft auch für die Orte zu, an denen er gespielt wird: die Stadien. Ihre Rolle als Ort für Emotionsabfuhr und Missstands-Ablenkung ist ebenso wenig zu leugnen, wie die Tatsache, dass sie als Folterstätten, als Triumphstätten von Diktatoren und als Kathedralen geldwaschender Kapitalisten herhalten müssen. Schon allein ihr Standort ist oft von politischem Kalkül bestimmt, wenn etwa von der marokkanischen Regierung in der besetzten Westsahara ein Stadion mit 30 000 Plätzen gebaut wurde – als Manifestation des »Marokkanischen« und als Anreiz für Marokkaner, dorthin umzuziehen und die einheimische Bevölkerung zur Minderheit zu machen.

In zahlreichen Sozialprojekten wird Fußball als Mittel zur Steigerung von Teamfähigkeit und sozialer Kompetenz sowie zur Förderung von Selbstbewusstsein eingesetzt. Ball, SOS-Kinderdorf Äthiopien.
Many social projects rely on football as a means to building team spirit and social skills as well as promoting self-confidence.
A ball, SOS Children's Village, Ethiopia.

Club functioned as forums for discreetly subversive gatherings long before Azikiwe became the first president of Nigeria.

How closely football was linked with struggles for independence and nation-building is exemplified by Algeria, which set up a national team in 1958 in the midst of the war for independence against France. Footballers such as Rachid Mekhloufi became icons of national resistance as members of the Algerian «rebel team», which was regarded as a political factor and an affront to the colonial powers. Many club names, especially in Africa, still express this old struggle for independence when «National» is part of a leading club's name – this is the case with *Al Ahly Cairo,* Egypt's top club. Football also aids as a special way of coming to terms with the past when a team thrashes their former colonial overlords – and this in a sport that was introduced to the colonies by those same colonialists.

After a country gained its independence, football also proved to be compatible with the new challenges the fledgling nation now faced. In the 1960s quite a number of clubs were founded in new countries, intended to express the sovereignty and self-confidence of particular demographic groups. In many countries throughout the world, the national team is not so much a team made up of a country's best footballers as a «parenthesis» for holding the various groups in the country together and thrusting national rather than ethnic concerns to the fore. Since football matches in particular had also been used to foment regional and tribal strife, quite a few clubs were given neutral names to eliminate implicitly anti-national aspects. Similarly, club names such as «Dynamo», «Forwards» and «Upwards» had flourished in the countries of the former Warsaw Pact as the expression of official political aims and were used as party programmes in a nutshell.

Teams in fact often mirror interests above and beyond sporting ones. Many teams are degraded in the process to the status of pawns of the political and economically powerful. Football is anyway usually «a matter for the boss». Rarely has a dictator or totalitarian regime of the past century failed to take advantage of football as an ideal medium for showcasing themselves and keeping large sections of the population under their thumbs. However,

Auch der bauliche Zustand von Stadien wird bisweilen politisch instrumentalisiert. So ließ der langjährige Präsident von Ghana, Jerry Rawlings, die großen Stadien des Landes absichtlich eine Zeitlang verfallen – als Zeichen dafür, dass er statt Fußball die »Arbeiter und Bauern« zu fördern gedenke. Die Symbole des wirtschaftlichen Niedergangs von Ghana wurden so in Mahnmale für andere gesellschaftliche Gewichtungen umgedeutet.

Jedenfalls dienten Stadien keineswegs immer und überall nur zur ablenkenden Volksbelustigung. Gerade auch in totalitären Staaten kam ihnen immer wieder die Rolle als Stätten des Widerstandes und von Foren relativer Freiheit zu. Hier bot sich noch am ehesten die Möglichkeit zu Versammlungen in größerer Zahl und zur Artikulation oppositioneller Ansichten – etwa in Nordafrika, in Zimbabwe oder im Iran.

Ob nun erfreulich oder nicht – für viele Gesellschaften dieser Welt kann man sich bei der Einschätzung der Phänomene rund um den Fußball ziemlich sicher sein, dass es sich dabei nicht um Nebensächliches oder Randerscheinungen handelt. Sehr oft haben sie ihren Ursprung in der Mitte der jeweiligen Gesellschaften und können die Augen öffnen für deren zentrale Fragen, Probleme und Herausforderungen – gerade auch in gesellschaftlicher, politischer und ökonomischer Hinsicht.

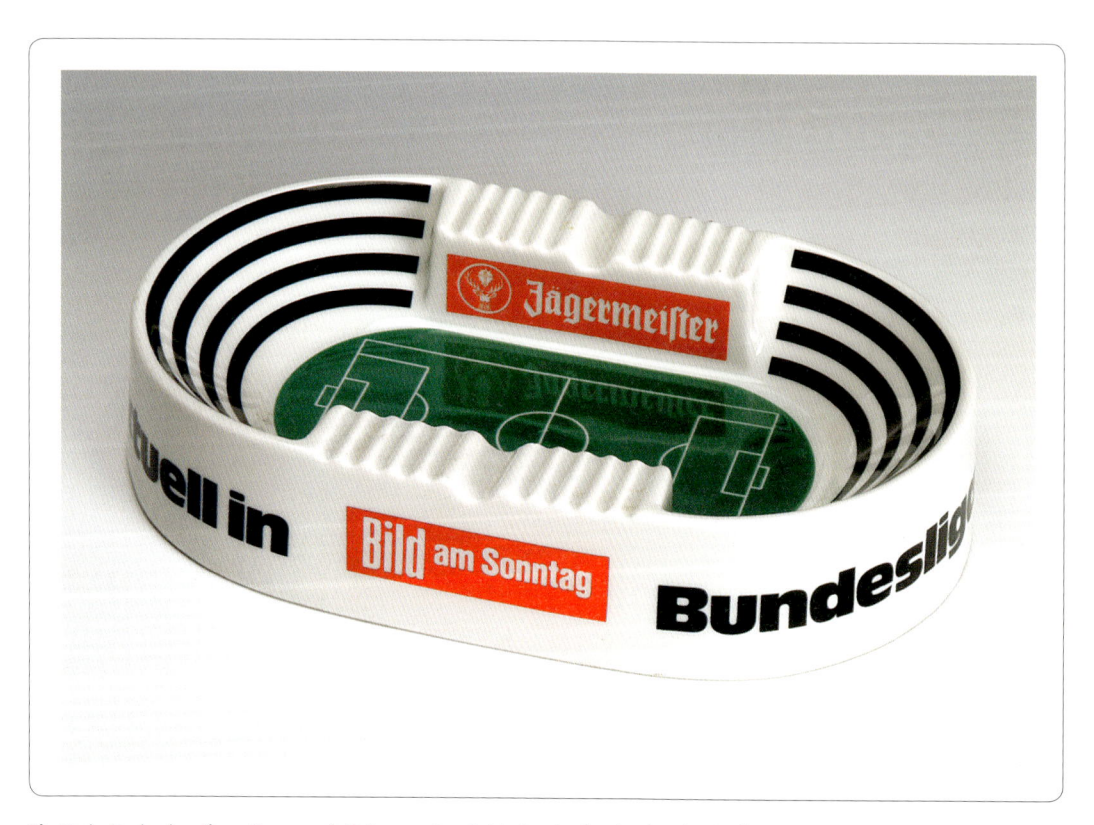

Ein Vorbote der heutigen Kommerzialisierung des Fußballs: Aschenbecher in Stadionform mit Reklameaufschrift aus den 1970er Jahren. A harbinger of today's commercialisation of football: ashtray in the form of a stadium with 1970s advertising.

the instrumentalisation of football is a two-edged sword. Success is too uncertain, defeats can turn into surliness addressed to those in power. That explains why sports in which success was calculable enjoyed considerably more sympathy and were much more heavily funded by the paramount political circles in the GDR, for example. In fact, just because football is so charged with emotions, it keeps turning into a boomerang. One regime that experienced this was the Argentine military government, which had pinned its hopes on consolidating its support at home when the World Cup was due to take place in Argentina. Despite the success of the national team, however, fans lost no time in chanting that the military dictatorship should step down.

What is generally true of football also holds for the places where it is played: the stadiums. Their role as places for emotional catharsis and distraction from harsh living conditions cannot be denied any more than the fact that they have been abused as places of torture, arenas in which dictators have celebrated their triumphs and as cathedrals consecrated to the machinations of money-laundering capitalists. Even their location is often a matter of political calculation, for instance, when the Moroccan government built a stadium seating 30 000 in the occupied Western Sahara – as a manifestation of «Moroccanism» as well as an incentive for Moroccans to move there and turn the indigenous population into a minority.

Even the state of stadium maintenance has occasionally been politically instrumentalised. Jerry Rawlings, for years president of Ghana, deliberately allowed the country's biggest stadiums to become dilapidated – as a sign that he intended to promote the «workers and farmers» instead of football. The symbols of economic decline in Ghana were thus loaded with new significance for other social priorities.

In any case stadiums have certainly not been used merely to keep the populace amused and their minds off political issues. In totalitarian countries especially they have always assumed the role of places of resistance and forums providing relative freedom. The stadium provides the best opportunity for dissidents to assemble in large numbers and voice views counter to the officially approved line – in North Africa, Zimbabwe and Iran.

Whether this is pleasant to contemplate or not – in evaluating football-related phenomena, one can be sure that in many societies throughout the world football is not something minor or a fringe activity. These phenomena often originate at the very heart of the society concerned and can open eyes to the pivotal issues, problems and challenges it faces – and especially from the social, political and economic angle.

Fußball und Demokratie in Südafrika
Vom Honeymoon nach der Wahl zur Weltmeisterschaft

Fiona Rankin-Smith

Am 25. Mai 2004 um 12 Uhr 21 machte FIFA-Präsident Sepp Blatter die historische Ankündigung, dass es für Afrika und Südafrika an der Zeit sei, das größte Sportereignis der Welt zu auszurichten. Südafrikas ehemaliger Präsident Nelson Mandela, der neben Blatter saß, konnte seine Tränen nicht zurückhalten. Danny Jordaan, der der südafrikanischen Bewerbung auf die Ausrichtung der Weltmeisterschaft vorstand, äußerte sich begeistert: »Der Traum einer Nation ist heute wahr geworden. Die Weltmeisterschaft wird helfen, unser Volk zu vereinen. Wenn es eine Sache auf diesem Planeten gibt, die die Macht hat, Menschen zu verbinden, dann ist es der Fußball.«

Die Aufregung über den Zuschlag für die Ausrichtung der Weltmeisterschaft erinnerte an den kurzen Zeitraum der Euphorie nach dem Wunder des Übergangs von Südafrika zur Demokratie. Einige der am lebhaftesten im Gedächtnis gebliebenen Momente des Feierns waren diejenigen, die mit den Erfolgen der nationalen Sportmannschaften in Zusammenhang standen. 1995 war Südafrika der Gastgeber der Rugby-WM, und am Anfang des Finales in Ellis Park zwischen Südafrika und Neuseeland brachte Präsident Nelson Mandela das Stadion zum Kochen, indem er dort in einem Springbok-Trikot mit der Nummer 6 des Kapitäns, Francois Pienaar, erschien. Die Macht dieser Geste initiierte das, was viele für die Magie hielten, die dazu führte, dass Südafrika die Meisterschaft gewann. 1996 gewann Südafrikas Fußball-Nationalteam *Bafana Bafana* den African Cup of Nations, wiederum nachdem Präsident Mandela das Trikot des Kapitäns, Neil Tovey, angelegt hatte.

Das Fußballspiel ist schon immer ein effektiver Nivellierer und ein Mittel zur Förderung des Stolzes unter den Massen gewesen. Fußballstars sind kraftvolle Beispiele für die Versöhnung innerhalb der südafrikanischen Gemeinschaft. Die Wirkung von Lucas Radebe und Mark Fish war groß. Mark wurde oft als »farbig« angesehen, da die Fans instinktiv seine Fähigkeit erkannten, die Grenzen zu verwischen und weder wirklich schwarz noch wirklich weiß zu sein. Das gleiche gilt für Lucas mit seinem immensen Erfolg in der überwiegend weißen Welt von Leeds und der Leichtigkeit, mit der er ohne Unterschied Schwarze wie Weiße anspricht. Diese beiden Stars zeigen mehr als Toleranz für »Rassenunterschiede« – sie zeigen den Wunsch und die Fähigkeit, sich über die Kluft hinwegzusetzen, indem sie in einer Gemeinschaft Erfolg haben, aus der ihre Hautfarbe sie früher wohl ausgeschlossen hätte.

Frühere Wurzeln der Fußballs: »Rassentrennung« und Apartheid
Die weiße Herrschaft in Südafrika drängte die schwarze Bevölkerung in verarmten Ghettos und ländlichen *homelands* zusammen. Die besten Freizeiteinrichtungen und Fußballplätze waren für Schwarze nicht zugänglich. Schwarze Spieler mussten schmerzlich erleben, dass

Soccer and Democracy in South Africa
From Post-election Honeymoon to World Cup

Fiona Rankin-Smith

At 12:21 on 15 May 2004, in Switzerland, FIFA President Sepp Blatter made the historic announcement that it was the time for Africa and South Africa to stage the world's greatest sporting festival. Sitting next to Blatter, South Africa's former president Nelson Mandela could not hold back his tears.

Danny Jordaan, head of South Africa's world cup bid enthused «The dream of a nation has come true today. The world cup will help unify our people. If there is one thing on this planet that has the power to bind people together, it is football».

The excitement over the world cup bid was reminiscent of the short period of euphoria after the miracle of South Africa's transition to democracy. Some of the most vividly remembered moments of celebration were those connected with the achievements of the national

Ein Symbol des »neuen Südafrika«: Das Fußball-Nationalteam mit Spielern aller Hautschattierungen beim African Cup of Nations 1996 mit Nelson Mandela (achter von rechts). A symbol of the «new South Africa»: the national football team, a rainbow coalition, at the 1996 African Cup of Nations with Nelson Mandela (eighth from the right). Johannes Mashego Segogela, »Nkosi Sikelele«, 1997.

Eine charakteristische Kopfbedeckung von Fußballfans in Südafrika: Helme aus Plastik, kreativ umgestaltet mit Emblemen und Slogans der bevorzugten Mannschaften, hier von »Bafana Bafana«, dem Nationalteam. Typical football-fan headgear in South Africa: plastic helmets, creatively restyled with crests and slogans of one's favourite team, here «Bafana, Bafana» for the national team.

Helm eines Fans der Johannesburger »Kaizer Chiefs«, eines der Top-Teams in Südafrika. A helmet made for a fan of the Johannesburg «Kaizer Chiefs», a top South African team.

ihre Fähigkeiten und Talente nie vollständig zum Einsatz kamen, dass man ihnen ihre Karrieren gestohlen hatte.

Die Lebensbedingungen für Schwarze in den 1950er Jahren waren erschreckend. Vor dem Hintergrund der Armut bedeutete Fußball die Aussicht auf aufregende Wochenendunterhaltung in Form endloser Debatten, was im Kontrast zu den düsteren Lebensbedingungen der Werktage stand. Sportarenen boten eine Plattform, um gegen die unterschiedlichen Formen der Unterdrückung zu kämpfen, und viele schwarze Südafrikaner konnten ihre Fähigkeiten und ihre Kreativität auf dem Spielfeld oder als Fans zum Ausdruck bringen.

Vom Widerstand zur Demokratie

In den 1950er Jahren verlangten schwarze Fußballorganisationen einen südafrkanischen Fußballverband ohne Rassentrennung und ein Nationalteam, das durch Auswahl der Besten zusammengestellt wird, ohne Rücksicht auf deren Hautfarbe. Diese Forderungen wurden ignoriert und die nur aus Weißen bestehende Organisation Football Association of South Africa (FASA) wurde von der internationalen Organisation FIFA anerkannt.

Wachsender Druck durch den African National Congress (ANC) und andere progressive politische Organisationen einschließlich der Liberalen hatte zum Ergebnis, dass die FASA 1960 von der Confédération Africaine de Football (CAF) und 1961 von der FIFA ausgeschlossen wurde. Fußballsanktionen gehörten zu den ersten internationalen Anklagen gegen das Apardheitsregime.

Ohrenbetäubende Kakophonien aus tausenden von Vuvuzela-Plastikhörnern sorgen in südafrikanischen Stadien für eine vor allem die gegnerische Mannschaft beeindruckende Klangkulisse. The ear-splitting cacophony emitted by thousands of plastic vuvuzela horns provides deterrent background noise primarily to impress the opposing team.

sporting teams. In 1995 South Africa hosted the Rugby World Cup and at the beginning of the final at Ellis Park between South Africa and New Zealand, President Nelson Mandela ignited the stadium by appearing in a Springbok rugby jersey bearing the number 6 of the captain, Francois Pienaar. The power of this gesture led to what many believed was the magic that won the cup for South Africa. In 1996, South Africa's *Bafana Bafana* went on to win the CAF Cup, the African Cup of Nations, again after President Mandela donned the jersey of the captain, Neil Tovey.

The game of soccer has always been a great leveller and means of building pride amongst the masses. Soccer stars are powerful metaphors for creating reconciliation in the South African community. The impact of Lucas Radebe and Mark Fish has been profound. Mark was often perceived as being «coloured», by fans instinctively recognising his ability to straddle boundaries and to be neither strictly black nor white. The same can be said for Lucas, with his immense success in the predominantly white world of Leeds, and the ease with which he reaches out to white and black children without differentiation. Both these stars show more than a tolerance of «racial» difference – they show a desire and an ability to embrace across the divide, thriving in communities where their skin colour once might have set them apart.

Earlier Roots of Soccer; Segregation and Apartheid.
White rule in South Africa compressed black people into impoverished urban ghettos and rural «homelands». The best recreation facilities and soccer grounds were off limits to black people.

Fans des Nationalteams von Südafrika während des Spiels gegen Tunesien beim Africa Nations Cup 2006. The 2006 Africa Nations Cup: South Africa fans wearing their team colours during the match against Tunisia. © Photo: Neil Marchand, Corbis

In der zweiten Hälfte der 1980er Jahre legten der ANC und das Nationalist Government die Grundlagen für ein Ende der Apartheid. Im Dezember 1991 begann man mit offiziellen Verhandlungen in Form der *Convention for a Democratic South Africa* (CODSA). In seinen frühen Aufrufen zur Aufhebung des internationalen Sportboykotts machte Nelson Mandela sich für eine Anschauung von Sport als heilende Instanz stark. Im Gegensatz zu Sportarten wie Rugby oder Kricket, wo es farbige Spieler praktisch nicht gab, hatte Fußball den Vorteil, dass man hier eine Anzahl schwarzer und weißer Spieler finden konnte, die alle talentiert genug waren, um aufgrund ihrer Fähigkeiten ausgewählt zu werden. Diskussionen über die Errichtung eines nicht nach Hautfarben getrennten Kontrollorgans führten schließlich, im Jahr 1991, zur Gründung der alle Bevölkerungsgruppen integrierenden South African Football Association, die 1992 durch die FIFA wieder in die Welt des Fußballs aufgenommen wurde.

Die Afrikanisierung des Fußballs

Im Durban des frühen 20. Jahrhunderts war ein Teil der Rituale zur Vorbereitung auf ein Spiel verbunden mit traditionellen Zulu-Reinigungspraktiken, wie sie früher von den *amabutho* des 19. Jahrhunderts, den »Altersklassenregimentern«, vor kriegerischen Auseinandersetzungen durchgeführt worden waren. Dazu gehörte, dass die Teams in der Nacht vor dem Match zusammen campierten und nackt an einem Feuer schliefen, wobei sie von einem *inyanga,*

Black players felt that their skills and talents never got to be fully utilised; that their careers were stolen.

Living conditions for blacks in the 1950s were appalling. Against a backdrop of impoverishment, soccer presented the prospect of weekend excitement in the form of endless debates in contrast to the gloomy conditions of working days. Sporting arenas provided a platform to fight against various forms of oppression and it was on the playing fields and in the role of supporters that many black South Africans could give expression to their abilities and creativity.

From Resistance to Democracy

In the 1950s, black soccer institutions demanded a non-racial inclusive national association and a national team based on selection of the best players despite their race. These calls were ignored and the whites' only organisation Football Association of South Africa (FASA) was recognised by the international organisation FIFA.

Mounting pressure from African National Congress (ANC) and other progressive political organisations including liberals resulted in FASA being suspended from the Confédération Africaine de Football (CAF) in 1960 and from FIFA in 1961. Football sanctions were among the first international indictments of the apartheid regime.

In the latter half of the 1980s the ANC and Nationalist Government laid the foundations for a negotiated end to apartheid. In December 1991, formal negotiations in the shape of the Convention for a Democratic South Africa (CODESA) were begun. Nelson Mandela, in his early calls for the lifting of the international sports boycott, was pushing an agenda of sports as healer. Unlike rugby or cricket where players of colour were virtually non-existent, soccer had the advantage of a spread of black and white players all good enough to be selected on merit. Discussions for the formation of a non-racial controlling body lead finally in 1991 to the creation of an integrated South African Football Association, which was welcomed back into world soccer by FIFA in 1992.

Africanisation of Soccer

In Durban in the earlier part of the 20th century, part of the pre-match rituals involved purificatory traditional Zulu practices previously performed by 19th century Zulu *amabutho*, the age regiments, before military encounters. This involved the teams camping together the night before a match, sleeping naked around a fire while being given *umuthi*, a traditional medicine, by the *inyanga*, the traditional healer. The morning before the match, players would drink a strong mixture followed by a vomiting (and therefor cleansing) ritual similar to those practised by Zulu soldiers before going into battle. Once inside the stadium, the teams drew on *ukugiya* (war dancing) traditions entering the field with a choreographed stylised trotting step.

More recently, *isangoma* the diviners and *inyanga* are approached for their traditional medicine and ritual practices to ensure a winning performance of their favoured team and for protection from the magic of rival traditional practitioners. *Inyanga* prepare *muti* that is rubbed on the players legs to strengthen them. Match rituals involve throwing of bones to foresee the outcome of the game.

Fan-Helme des Fußballclubs der Witwatersrand-University (»Wits«) sowie des südafrikanischen Top-Teams »Kaizer Chiefs« aus Johannesburg. Helmets made for fans from the Witwatersrand University («Wits») fan club and fans from the South African top team «Kaizer Chiefs» of Johannesburg.

einem traditionellen Heiler, *umuthi*, eine traditionelle Medizin, bekamen. Am Morgen vor dem Match tranken die Spieler eine starke Mixtur, die anschließend bei einem reinigenden Ritual – ähnlich denen der Zulu, bevor sie in die Schlacht zogen – wieder erbrochen wurde. Beim Einzug in das Stadion beriefen sich die Mannschaften auf die Traditionen des *ukugiya* (Kriegstanzes), indem sie das Spielfeld in einem choreographierten stilisierten Trab betraten.

In jüngerer Zeit werden *inyanga* und *isangoma* (Wahrsager) mit ihrer traditionellen Medizin und ihren rituellen Praktiken hinzugezogen, um sich selbst oder dem favorisierten Team den Sieg zu sichern und um sich vor den schädlichen Kräften der *inyanga* und *isangoma* der Gegenseite zu schützen. *Inyanga* bereiten *muti* zu, das auf die Beine der Spieler gerieben wird, um sie zu stärken. Zu den Ritualen gehört auch das Werfen von Knochen, um den Ausgang des Spiels vorherzusehen.

Sich selbst mit den Farben und Insignien des unterstützten Teams auszustatten, ist ein sehr wichtiger Bestandteil des Zuschauer-Spektakels bei Fußballspielen. Gesichtsbemalungen in den Farben der favorisierten Mannschaften werden kombiniert mit Kriegshelmen, bei denen es sich um Umbildungen von Bauarbeiterhelmen handelt. Diese werden aufgeschnitten und durch Erhitzung des Plastiks so verformt, dass die Konturen wie handgeschnitzt wirken. Diese Helme werden mit den Bildern und Zeichen des jeweiligen Teams versehen, ähneln aber den Kopfbedeckungen, die von den einheimischen afrikanischen Bevölkerungsgruppen getragen werden. Eine relativ neue Erscheinung bei afrikanischen Fußballspielen ist die sogenannte *vuvuzela*, ein Horn aus Plastik. Es hat möglicherweise in dem Rinderhorn seinen Ursprung, das bei vielen traditionellen afrikanischen Ritualen verwendet wird. Die ohrenbetäubenden Kakophonien von Tausenden von *vuvuzelas*, die auf einmal geblasen werden, sind ein unvergessliches Erlebnis. Visuell-verbale Wortspiele bei den Matches sind ebenfalls ein wichtiger Bestandteil der Fußballkultur. Wenn Mark Fish auf dem Feld ist, kommt es nicht selten vor, dass Zuschauer riesige tote Fische in die Luft halten, während die Menge »Fiiiiiisshh« brüllt, kaum dass er den Ball berührt.

Branding oneself in the colours and insignia of one's team is a huge part of the spectator spectacle at soccer matches. Face painting with colours of favoured teams is associated with donning warrior helmets that are transformations of plastic construction site safety headgear. The hats are cut open and remodelled by heating the plastic into carved shapes that include images and branding associated with their preferred clubs but resemble indigenous head-dresses worn by African communities. A recent addition to contemporary African soccer matches is the *vuvuzela*, a plastic horn possibly based on the cattle horn used in many traditional African rituals. The deafening cacophonies of thousands of *vuvuzela* being blown at once are unforgettable. The visual/verbal punning that is part of soccer culture is also evident at matches. When Mark Fish plays it is not uncommon to find spectators wielding huge dead fish aloft while the crowds roar to the sound of «Feeeeeessshh» each time he connects with the ball.

Fans des südafrikanischen Fußballstars Mark Fish nehmen neben Dosenfisch bisweilen auch echte Fische als Fan-Utensilien mit ins Stadion. Fans of the South African football star Mark Fish don't stop at tinned fish; they take real fish into the stadium to show their support. © Photo: pixathlon

Bern 1954
Ein Finale und seine Folgen

Anikó Szalay

Am 4. Juli 1954, einem verregneten Sommertag, trat der hohe Favorit Ungarn gegen den Außenseiter Deutschland im Berner Wankdorfstadion zum Finale der Fußball-Weltmeisterschaft an. Die ungarische Mannschaft war seit 34 Spielen unbesiegt, war amtierender Olympiasieger und hatte die Engländer erstmalig auf deren Insel geschlagen – mit einem klaren 6:3. Doch den Deutschen gelang, was damalige Spitzenmannschaften nicht vermocht hatten: Sie besiegten die Ungarn mit 3:2.

Für die Deutschen wurde der Sieg in der Folge zum »Wunder von Bern«. Die deutsche Mannschaft wurde gefeiert – sie hatte ihrem Land, das noch an seinen Wunden des Zweiten Weltkriegs litt, auf der internationalen Bühne wieder Anerkennung verschafft.

Doch auch für die Ungarn bedeutete das Spielergebnis mehr als nur das Resultat eines sportlichen Ereignisses. Das Land hatte nach dem Ersten Weltkrieg zwei Drittel seines Staatsgebiets eingebüßt und wurde nach Ende des Zweiten Weltkriegs der sowjetischen Einflusszone zugeteilt. Die Siege der »Goldenen Mannschaft« bedeuteten einen Lichtstrahl und boten die nahezu einzige Möglichkeit für patriotische Gefühle. Der Weltmeistertitel schien 1954 zum Greifen nahe. Umso größer war die Enttäuschung nach dem Endspiel. Die Niederlage diente als Ventil, und in Budapest kam es zu Ausschreitungen, deren eigentlicher Adressat jedoch nicht die Mannschaft, sondern das ungeliebte Regime war. Dieses reagierte schnell, und so wurde das heimkehrende Team nicht nach Hause, sondern in ein Trainingslager gefahren. Dort gratulierte der kommunistische Parteiführer Rákosi zwar zur sportlichen Leistung, wies aber gleichzeitig darauf hin, dass er beim nächsten Mal einen Sieg erwarten würde. Bis dahin bräuchte niemand Angst vor Konsequenzen zu haben.

Die unmittelbar darauf dann doch folgenden Repressalien trafen den Torwart Gyula Grosics am härtesten. Wegen seiner offenen systemkritischen Haltung hatten die zu Auslandsspielen mitreisenden Geheimpolizisten der Staatssicherheit bereits vor der Weltmeisterschaft Belastungsmaterial gesammelt. Kurz nach der Niederlage wurde er angeklagt wegen »Verdachts auf Spionage, welche den Begriff des Landesverrats ausschöpft.« Und wäre er nicht der beliebte Nationaltorwart, wäre er schon längst gehängt – fügte man der Anklage hinzu. Ein Jahr lang wurde Grosics jeden Montag abgeholt und zum Verhör in die Zentrale der gefürchteten Staatssicherheit ÁVH gebracht, eingeschüchtert und bedroht. Jahrelang durfte er nicht in der Nationalmannschaft spielen. Von seinem Budapester Verein Honvéd wurde er zum frischgebackenen Erstligisten Tatabánya in die Bergbauprovinz zwangsversetzt. Und noch bis 1990 wurde Grosics beobachtet, wie Akten des Geheimdienstes belegen. Auf die Frage, ob es zu diesen Repressalien gekommen wäre, wenn die Ungarn an jenem 4. Juli 1954 in Bern gewonnen hätten, antwortet er noch heute mit einem bestimmten »Nein, niemals«.

Ein wegweisender Moment für zwei Nationen – auch außerhalb des Fußballplatzes: Helmut Rahn zieht zum 3:2 ab und macht Deutschland zum Weltmeister. A ground-breaking moment for two countries – even off the pitch: Helmut Rahn about to make Germany world champions with a 3:2 win. Volker Hildebrandt: »3:2«, 2001, Acryl auf Leinwand / acrylic on canvas, 150 × 200 cm. Courtesy Galerie Jörg Heitsch, München

Bern 1954
A Finals Game and its Repercussions

Anikó Szalay

On a rainy summer's day, 4 July 1954, Hungary was favoured to win against Germany, then a rank outsider, in the Wankdorf Stadium in Bern, Switzerland. It was the World Cup finals. The Hungarian team had had a winning streak of thirty-four consecutive victories and were the current Olympic champions. They had even thrashed the English 6:3 on their own home territory – a first. The Germans, however, succeeded in doing what the then top-ranked teams had not been capable of: they defeated Hungary 3:2.

To Germans the victory afterwards came to be known as the «Miracle of Bern». The German team was fêted – they had made their country, which was still licking its wounds from the second world war, respectable players once again on the world stage.

Die legendäre »Goldene Mannschaft« zerfiel nach der Revolution gegen das kommunistische Regime im Jahre 1956. Viele Spieler emigrierten: Puskás setzte seine Karriere bei Real Madrid fort, Kocsis und Czibor bei Barcelona. Auch viele Nachwuchsspieler verließen das Land. Die Daheimgebliebenen erzielten trotz dieses Aderlasses bis in die 1960er Jahre beachtliche Erfolge, konnten aber an die große Zeit der »Goldenen Mannschaft« nicht mehr anknüpfen. Die Namen der emigrierten Spieler wurden zum Tabu erklärt – und somit der ungarische Fußball und die heranwachsende Spielergeneration auch ihrer Vorbilder beraubt.

Überdies griff der Staat in die Strukturen der Vereine ein. Alte traditionsreiche Clubs wurden zerschlagen und umbenannt, Finanzen nach politischem Belieben verteilt und die Vereinsführungen neu aufgestellt. Zudem konnte Ungarn – wie andere sozialistische Staaten – mit der zunehmenden Professionalisierung des Fußballs im Westen nicht mithalten und suchte nach Nischensportarten, in denen Sieg und Ruhm bei internationalen Wettkämpfen sicherer waren.

Wimpel von Honvéd Budapest: Der 1909 gegründete Kispest AC (Athletic Club) wurde 1949 nach der Verstaatlichung der Sportvereine in »Budapest Honvéd« umbenannt. Als Armeeclub wurde er zum Vorzeigeverein des sozialistischen Ungarn. Pennant of Honvéd Budapest: Kispest AC (Athletic Club), founded in 1909, was renamed «Budapest Honvéd» in 1949 after sport clubs were nationalised. An army club, it became the figure-head club of socialist Hungary.

Der ungarische Torwart Gyula Grosics war nach der WM-Niederlage 1954 massiven politischen Repressalien ausgesetzt. The Hungarian goalkeeper Gyula Grosics was subjected to massive political repression after the Hungarian 1954 World Cup defeat. Volker Hildebrandt: »Gyula Grosics«, 2006, Acryl auf Leinwand/acrylic on canvas, 120 x 150 cm. Courtesy Galerie Jörg Heitsch, München

However, the outcome of the game meant more to Hungary, too, than simply winning or losing in a sporting event. After the first world war the country was left deprived of two thirds of its territory and the second world war ended with Hungary consigned to the Soviet sphere of influence. The victories achieved by the «Golden Team» were a ray of light that provided the country with its only chance of expressing patriotic feelings. Winning the 1954 World Cup seemed within the team's grasp and that made the final all the more disappointing. The defeat was used by Hungarians to ventilate their frustration and in Budapest there were riots, which were aimed at the hated regime, not the team. The regime reacted so quickly that the team members were even not allowed to go home but were instead sent straight to a training camp. There Rákosi, head of the Communist Party, congratulated them on their achievement on the pitch but made it plain that he expected victory next time. No one would have any reason to fear any consequences until then.

But retribution followed in spite of his words. Goalkeeper Gyula Grosics suffered most. Because he had been openly critical of the regime, the secret police, who were sent

Trotz jeder Bemühung, die Fußballhelden von 1954 totzuschweigen, blieb die Verehrung vieler Ungarn für sie ungebrochen. Ihre mitreißend schönen und kämpferischen Spiele sowie die Tatsache, dass sie den Ungarn in schwierigen Zeiten vielfach zu Momenten großer Freude verholfen hatten, bleiben unvergessen.

Fragt man Jenö Buzánszky, einen der noch lebenden Spieler von 1954, nach den Ursachen der Niederlage – ob es denn am Regen lag, an der schlaflosen Nacht aufgrund der lauten Stadtfeierlichkeiten in Solothurn direkt vor den Fenstern der ungarischen Mannschaft oder am Schiedsrichter, der einen regulären Treffer von Puskás nicht anerkannt hatte –, antwortet er: »Es gibt zahlreiche Gründe, aber letztendlich haben wir verloren… Das bleibt, und das tut immer noch weh… Der Sieg war uns nicht vergönnt, aber das ist das Spiel, das ist Fußball…!« Und die Wehmut weicht einem fast jungenhaften Lächeln auf seinem achtzigjährigen Gesicht.

Besonderer Dank für die Interviews gilt:
Gyula Grosics (Torwart im WM-Finale 1954)
Jenö Buzánszky (rechter Verteidiger im WM-Finale 1954)
Zoltán Magyar (von 2000 bis Mai 2004 Manager der ungarischen Nationalmannschaft und der olympischen Mannschaft von Atlanta 1996)
Lajos Szabó (Direktor des Ungarischen Sportmuseums, Budapest)

Einer der maßgeblichen Gründe für den Sieg der deutschen Mannschaft? – Die neuen Schraubstollen-Fußballschuhe, die den unterschiedlichen Bodenverhältnissen angepasst werden konnten. Did they underpin the German victory? – State-of-the-art football boots that could be adjusted to ground conditions.

abroad with the team to keep tabs on them, had collected evidence to be used against him even before the World Cup finals. Just before the defeat Grosics was accused of «suspected espionage, which meets the definition of treason». And if he had not been the popular national goalkeeper, he would have been hanged – this was appended to the accusation. For a whole year Grosics was picked up every Monday and taken to the forbidding security police headquarters ÁVH for examination, where he was intimidated and threatened. For years afterwards he was not permitted to be in the national team. He was banished from his Budapest club, Honvéd, to Tatabánya, a fledgling Premiership club in a provincial mining region. Moreover, Grosics was under observation until 1990 as secret police records show. Asked whether he would have been subjected to such repressive treatment if Hungary had won that 4 July 1954 in Bern, he still answers firmly «no, never».

The legendary «Golden Team» fell apart after the 1956 revolt against the Communist regime. Many players emigrated: Puskás continued his career with Real Madrid, Kocsis and Czibor went to Barcelona. Many young hopefuls left the country. Those who stayed at home still managed to chalk up some considerable successes on into the 1960s despite the loss of so many crucial players but they were minor compared to what the «Golden Team» achieved in its heyday. The names of the emigrated players were officially taboo – and thus Hungarian football and the new generation of players were deprived of role models.

If that were not enough, the state intervened to restructure the clubs. Venerable clubs that looked back on a long tradition were disbanded and renamed. Funding depended on toeing the official Party line. Club management was restructured. Further, Hungary – like other Socialist countries – was unable to keep up with the increasing professionalisation of football in the West and was forced to engage in sports in which victory and fame were ensured at international contests.

Even though so much was done to banish the names of the football heroes of 1954 from the public consciousness, many Hungarians continued to revere them. Their enthralling technique and dynamic game as well as the fact that they had given Hungary so many moments of sheer joy in hard times were unforgotten.

If you ask Jenö Buzánszky, one of the 1954 players still alive, why Hungary lost then – whether it was due to the rain, the sleepless night beforehand because the celebration in Solothurn made so much noise right under the windows of the Hungarian team or whether the referee was the cause because he had not accepted a goal by Puskás – he answers. «There are lots of reasons but after all, we did lose ... Nothing can change that and it still hurts ... We were not meant to win but that's just the game, that's football ...!» And the melancholy gives way to a boyish smile on this eighty-year-old footballer's face.

We are indebted for interviews to:
Gyula Grosics (goalkeeper at the 1954 World Cup final)
Jenö Buzánszky (outside defender on the right in the 1954 World Cup final)
Zoltán Magyar (manager of the Hungarian national team from 2000 to May 2004 and at the 1996 Olympic Games in Atlanta)
Lajos Szabó (director of the Hungarian Sport Museum, Budapest)

Türkischstämmige MigrantInnen feierten freudig und enthusiastisch in vielen Städten Deutschlands – wie hier in Berlin – den Einzug der türkischen Nationalmannschaft ins WM-Viertelfinale 2002. In many German cities – here in Berlin – men and women from Turkey living in Germany enthusiastically celebrated the Turkish national team qualifying for the 2002 World Cup quarter finals. © Photo: Janine Albrecht

Zuhause und in der Fremde
Der Migrantensport Fußball

Christiane Lembert / Barbara Rusch

Im November 2005 beantragte eine Delegation der indigenen Gemeinschaften Argentiniens eine Audienz bei Präsident Néstor Kirchner. Als sie nicht empfangen wurden, beschlossen die Indigenas, vor dem Präsidentenpalast in Buenos Aires so lange auszuharren, bis ein Treffen zustande käme. Als Ausdruck ihrer Zugehörigkeit zum argentinischen Staat zogen sie sich die Trikots der Fußballnationalmannschaft an, obwohl sie Fußball nicht als Teil ihrer Kultur sehen.

Dass die Indigenas ihre nationale Identifikation durch das Trikot der Nationalelf zeigen, ergibt Sinn, ist doch in Argentinien der Fußball Nationalsport und kollektive Leidenschaft. Interessanterweise entwickelte sich dieses Phänomen zusammen mit der Ausbildung einer typisch argentinischen, »kreolischen« Spielweise. Erstmals verwendet wurde der Begriff nach dem Sieg der Landesmeisterschaft durch die Elf des Racing Club Buenos Aires 1913. Deren Spieler waren zwar Nachfahren spanischer und italienischer Immigranten, empfanden sich aber im Gegensatz zu den britischen Einwanderern als explizit argentinisch. Der aus verschiedenen Spielweisen kreierte neue, »kreolische« Stil galt als unabhängig vom Migrationshintergrund, wurde als eine argentinische Tradition überhöht und als unverzichtbarer Beitrag der Immigranten zur Herausbildung einer nationalen Identität gesehen.

At Home and Abroad
Football as an Immigrant Sport

Christiane Lembert / Barbara Rusch

In November 2005 a delegation from the Argentinean indigenous communities petitioned for an audience with President Néstor Kirchner. When he did not receive them, the Indigenas resolved to stage a sit-in at the presidential palace in Buenos Aires until a meeting might be arranged. To demonstrate their allegiance to the state of Argentina, they wore the jerseys of the national team even though they do not regard football as part of their culture.

It does make sense for Indigenas to show their identification with their country by donning the jerseys of the national eleven since football is the national sport in Argentina and a collective passion. Interestingly, this phenomenon has developed along with the formation of a typically Argentinean «Creole» style of play. The term was first used after the national championship victory won in 1913 by the Buenos Aires Racing Club eleven. The players were descendants of Spanish and Italian immigrants but, unlike the British immigrants, they regarded themselves as staunchly Argentinean. The new «Creole» style created from various other styles was viewed as independent of the players' ethnic backgrounds and was emphasised as an Argentinean tradition and as an indispensable contribution made by immigrants to the formation of a national identity.

The world-wide spread of football through the agency of the British and its adoption by British emigrants overseas and in Africa has often been described. In some countries it took longer than in others to inaugurate the first club *for* «natives» of the countries concerned and members of the working class or the founding of clubs *by* «natives» of a country or non-British immigrants. All those groups have made an impact on local and regional styles of play.

In the Ruhr in Germany, for instance, BVB Borussia Dortmund was established in 1909 in an environment dominated by the Church of the Holy Trinity which had been built primarily for Catholic workmen from Poland near the Hoesch-Westphalia foundry. Early in the 1920s Polish immigrant clubs in Germany even founded their own league. Those football players who had emigrated to Germany from eastern Europe contributed substantially to raising football in Germany to an international standard.

Greeks driven out of Asia Minor by the war between Greece and Turkey (1921–23) founded A.E.K. Athens (Athlitikí Énosi Konstantinoupóleos) in 1924. Before the Níkos Goumás Stadium was to be demolished in 2004, fans in Athens demonstrated with banners neatly uniting past and present: «Expelled by the Turks in 1922. Driven out by Greeks in 2004.»

Nowadays national teams bear witness to the many complex causes of migrations. This becomes abundantly evident in the former European colonial powers becoming the destination of choice for people emigrating from countries that had once been their colonies. Zinédine Zidane is the son of Algerian immigrants to France, Lilian Thuram comes from Guadaloupe, Claude Makelele from the D.R. Congo and David Trezeguet from Argentina.

Die weltweite Verbreitung des Fußballs durch Briten und seine Aufnahme durch englische Immigranten vor allem in Übersee und Afrika wurde oft beschrieben. Die Öffnung der ersten Clubs *für* »Einheimische« und Angehörige der Arbeiterschicht bzw. die Gründung von Clubs *durch* Einheimische oder nicht-britische Migranten erfolgte in den verschiedenen Ländern nach unterschiedlich langen Zeitspannen. Alle diese Gruppen beeinflussten dabei die lokalen bzw. regionalen Spielweisen. Im Ruhrgebiet formierte sich z. B. der BVB Borussia Dortmund 1909 im Umfeld der vor allem für katholische Arbeiter aus Polen errichteten Dreifaltigkeitskirche nahe der Hoesch-Westfalenhütte. Anfang der 1920er Jahre bildeten in Deutschland die polnischen Migrantenvereine sogar eine eigene Liga. Es waren *auch* diese Fußballspieler mit osteuropäischem Migrationshintergrund, die dem Fußball in Deutschland zu internationalem Niveau verhalfen.

Die in Folge des Griechisch-Türkischen Kriegs (1921–23) aus Kleinasien vertriebenen Griechen gründeten 1924 den Fußballclub A.E.K. Athen (Athlitiki Énosi Konstantinoupoleos). Vor dem Abriss des Stadions »Nikos Goumas« 2004 demonstrierten die Fans in Athen mit Spruchbannern, auf denen Vergangenheit und Gegenwart eine Verknüpfung erfuhren: »1922 Vertreibung durch die Türken. 2004 Vertreibung durch die Griechen.«

Heute spiegeln die Nationalteams Migrationsbewegungen, deren Ursachen vielfältig und vielschichtig sind. Deutlich wird dies etwa an den ehemaligen europäischen Kolonialmächten, die zum Einwanderungsziel von Menschen aus den früheren Kolonien geworden sind. So ist etwa Zinédine Zidane der Sohn algerischer Einwanderer, Lilian Thuram stammt aus Guadeloupe, Claude Makelele aus der D. R. Kongo und David Trezeguet aus Argentinien.

Fußballteams spiegeln heute auch in Deutschland die moderne Gesellschaft wider. Das U-21-Team ist ähnlich multiethnisch wie die französischen oder englischen Nationalteams. In fast allen Clubs spielen Angehörige bzw. Nachfahren jener jüngeren Migrationsströme mit, die durch den Arbeitskräftemangel in Westeuropa nach dem Zweiten Weltkrieg ausgelöst wurden. Zu Integrationsfiguren für die türkischen Migrantenjugendlichen in Deutschland wurden etwa Erdal Keser und Ilyas Tüfekci.

In den 1970er und 1980er Jahren bildeten sich europaweit innerhalb der Migrantencommunities Fußballmannschaften, die zu ethnischen Vereinen gehörten. Bekannt ist der Club des 1971 von syrisch-orthodoxen Einwanderern aus der Türkei gegründeten Kulturvereins Assyriska in der Industriestadt Södertälje bei Stockholm. Er spielte sich im Lauf von drei Jahrzehnten (kurzfristig) bis in die erste schwedische Liga.

Durch die Kommerzialisierung des Fußballs und den Transfer von Spielern aus aller Welt entstand das Phänomen des *Global Player*. Die Spieler unterschiedlicher ethnischer Herkunft gehören zwar zu den Aushängeschildern der europäischen Topvereine, doch müssen auch sie mit Diskriminierung und Rassismus rechnen und leben.

Der Fußball ist also eindeutig auch ein Migrantensport. Er war es immer schon und ist es bis heute geblieben – wenngleich auch unter anderen Vorzeichen und Bedingungen. Ebenso geblieben sind die Probleme, mit denen sich Migranten und *Global Players* in den jeweiligen Gesellschaften konfrontiert sehen. Projekte wie etwa »Football Against Racism in Europe« (FARE) können zwar immer wieder Erfolge verzeichnen, doch so lange Fremdenfeindlichkeit, rassistische Klischees und Vorurteile in der Alltagswirklichkeit unserer Gesellschaften nicht verschwinden, werden sie auch im Fußball vorhanden bleiben.

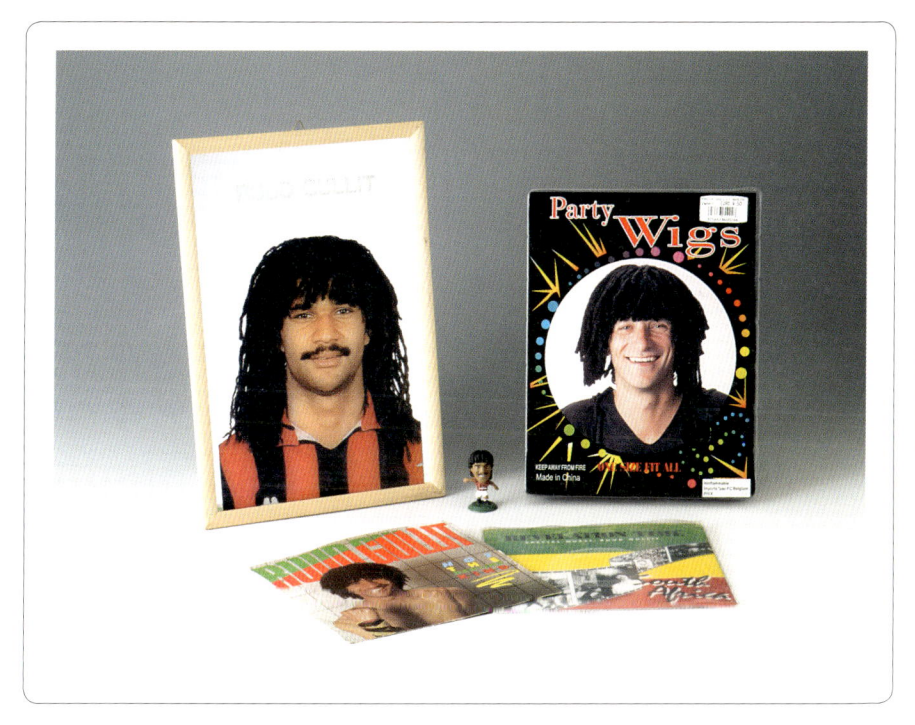

Ruud Gullit, dessen Vorfahren aus Surinam stammen, wurde zum internationalen Vorzeigeathleten der Niederlande. Er engagierte sich vehement gegen Rassismus und widmete die ihm als Europas Fußballer des Jahres 1988 verliehene Trophäe Nelson Mandela. Ruud Gullit, whose ancestors came from Surinam, is a model Dutch sportsman. A vocal opponent of racism, he dedicated the trophy he won as European Footballer of the Year in 1988 to Nelson Mandela.

Griechisches Männerkettchen (Komboloi) von Fans des Clubs A.E.K. Athen, der 1924 in Athen von aus Kleinasien vertriebenen Griechen gegründet wurde. Greek komboloi (worry beads) for fans of A.E.K. Athens, founded in Athens in 1924 by Greeks expelled from Asia Minor.

In Germany, too, football teams mirror the ethnic make-up of modern society. The U-21 team is just as multiethnic as the French and English national teams. Members or immediate descendants of those involved in recent migrations triggered off by the urgent need to replenish the workforce in Western Europe depleted by the second world war play in most teams. Erdal Keser and Ilyas Tüfekci, for instance, became role models for Turkish immigrant youths in Germany.

In the 1970s and 1980s football teams associated with ethnic clubs were founded throughout Western Europe within immigrant communities. A well-known example is Assyriska, founded by Syrian Orthodox immigrants from Turkey in the industrial city of Södertälje near Stockholm in 1971. Within a timespan of three decades it reached (for a short while at least) the Swedish premier league.

The phenomenon of the *global player* was created by the commercialisation of football and – concomitantly – players being traded throughout the world. Players of widely diverse ethnic origins are among the token figures so proudly displayed by European premiership clubs, but even they – like the immigrant population at large – must contend with discrimination and racism and learn to live with them.

Football is, therefore, unequivocally also an immigrant sport. It has always been – even though different attitudes and conditions prevail nowadays. What has also remained are the problems confronting immigrants and *global players* in the societies concerned. Projects such as «Football against Racism in Europe» (FARE) continue to chalk up successes, but until xenophobia, racist clichés and prejudices have vanished in the everyday reality of modern society, they will linger in football as well.

Zinédine Zidane
Kind von Migranten, Heros der Nation

Wolfgang Wohlwend

Nach dem Finalspiel der WM 1998 scheint ganz Paris auf die Champs Elysées zu strömen. Auf den Arc de Triomphe wird ein Foto projiziert: Es ist das Portrait von Zinédine Zidane, überlebensgroß lächelt es bescheiden auf das freudentrunkene Frankreich. Zidane – Retter der Nation. Zizou – Kind der Nation. Ist Zidane Frankreichs neuer Nationalheros? Zinédine Zidane wächst als Sohn einer algerischen Einwandererfamilie im sozial benachteiligten Marseillaiser Viertel La Castellane auf. Ständig feilt er dort an seinem spielerischen Talent und wird in jungen Jahren von einem Spieler-Scout entdeckt. Seine steile Karriere in der Fußballwelt beginnt mit dem AS Cannes und kulminiert im Weltmeisterschaftstitel und in Verpflichtungen bei Juventus Turin und Real Madrid. Trotz Ruhm und Erfolg bleibt er bescheiden, statt Ausschweifungen und Frauengeschichten liebt er seine Familie, und zu seinen engsten Freunden zählen immer noch diejenigen aus der Castellaner Zeit. Die Mythenfigur Zidane ist vielschichtig: Für eine ganze Generation nordafrikanischer Migranten ist er ein Vorbild in ehrlicher Haltung, Strebsamkeit und Selbstbehauptung. Für die *grande nation* hingegen ist Zidane der Retter französischer Fußballehre. Und – an der Spitze einer Mannschaft mit Spielern unterschiedlicher sozialer und ethnischer Herkunft – wurde er zur Symbolfigur für eine gelungene Integration von Kindern aus Migrationsfamilien, zur Ikone des idealisierten Bildes eines »multikulturellen Frankreichs«.

Zinédine Zidane
Child of Immigrants, National Hero

Wolfgang Wohlwend

After the final game of the 1998 World Cup, le tout Paris thronged the Champs Elysées. A photo was projected on to the Arc de Triomphe: a portrait of Zinédine Zidane. Monumentally enlarged, it smiled modestly down on France caught up in the delirium of victory. Zidane – Saviour of the Nation. Zizou – Child of the Nation. Is Zidane the new French national hero?
Zinédine Zidane grew up as the scion of an Algerian immigrant family in the socially disadvantaged La Castellane quarter of Marseilles. Constantly attracting notice there for his talent as a player, he was discovered at an early age by a talent scout. His meteoric rise in the world of football began with AS Cannes and culminated in the World Cup and playing for Juventus Turin and Real Madrid. For all his success and fame, he has remained modest. Not given to debauchery, he loves his family and his closest friends are still those he knew when he was a poor boy in La Castellane. As a mythic figure, Zidane is multi-faceted: he sets a good example for a whole generation of North African immigrants by being clean-living, hard-working and assertive. In the eyes of the *grande nation,* on the other hand, Zidane is the saviour of French honour in football. And – at the head of a team of players of various social and ethnic origins – he has become a figure symbolic of the successful integration of children from immigrant families, an icon as the idealised image of a «multicultural France».

Banner mit Bild von »Zizou« Zinédine Zidane, Frankreich.
A banner with the portrait of «Zizou», Zinédine Zidane, France.

KSK Beveren
Belgiens »neue Diamanten«
Ben Kerste

Was auf den ersten Blick wie ein afrikanisches Vereinsteam wirkt, entpuppt sich bei näherem Hinsehen als der flämische Erstligist KSK Beveren in Belgien. Dieser wurde über Jahre hinweg bis zum Januar 2006 von dem Franzosen Jean-Marc Guillou geleitet, der in der ivorischen Hauptstadt Abidjan eine »Fußball-Talentschmiede« unterhält. Als Beveren 2001 kurz vor dem finanziellen Bankrott und Abstieg stand, nutzte Guillou den Moment. Er hatte ein Schaufenster gefunden, um seine noch unbekannten Talente in europäische Topclubs zu hieven. Zeitweise stammten allein 18 der 26 Spieler aus der westafrikanischen Republik Elfenbeinküste.

In Beveren kulminierten seitdem viele Fragen einer globalisierten kapitalistisch bestimmten Fußballwelt. So warf man Guillou vor, er verkaufe die Identität des Vereins, ja ganz Flanderns. Auch Vergleiche zur Rohstoffveredelung im Rahmen des Diamantenhandels der belgischen Kolonialzeit wurden gezogen, ein Ausbluten afrikanischer Ligen durch das Abwandern zahlloser Talente beklagt.

Die Situation erweist sich jedoch als weit komplexer. So profitieren die Spieler und ihre Familien in dem krisengeschüttelten Staat Elfenbeinküste durch die relativ hohen Gehälter. In Belgien werden Fremdenfeindlichkeit und Stereotypen aufgebrochen und neue Identitäten sowie Fremdenbilder geschaffen. Und auch wenn durch den schnellen Wechsel vieler Spieler die Fan-Identifikation erschwert wird, lassen sich immer mehr Belgier begeistern vom eleganten und technikorientierten Spiel »ihrer« Afrikaner.

KSK Beveren
Belgium's «New Diamonds»
Ben Kerste

What at first sight looks like an African team, turns out at second glance to be the first league Flemish KSK Beveren, based in Belgium. It was managed for years up to January 2006 by a Frenchman, Jean-Marc Guillou, who maintains a «football talent farm» in Abidjan, the capital of Côte d'Ivoire. When Beveren was faced with imminent bankruptcy and decline in 2001, Guillou seized an advantage. He had found a window for showcasing his as yet unknown talents for sale to top European teams. Temporarily eighteen of Beveren's twenty-six players came from the west African republic of Côte d'Ivoire.

Since then many issues related to the globalisation and capitalist orientation of modern football have converged on Beveren. Guillou has been accused of selling the identity of the team, indeed of Flanders itself. Invidious comparisons have been drawn with the processing of raw materials, specifically diamond cutting and polishing, during the Belgian colonial era. The weakening of the African leagues by the loss of so much talent has been deplored.

However, the situation turns out to be far more complex than that. Players and their families in crisis-ridden Côte d'Ivoire benefit from the relatively high salaries. In Belgium prejudice against foreigners and racist stereotyping are being broken down so that new identities and ideas of foreigners are being created. And even though players are being traded off so fast that fans have trouble identifying with the players in their team, more and more Belgians are enthusiastic about the elegant, technique-centred game played by «their very own» Africans.

»Rohstoffveredelung« auf dem Fußballplatz? – Die Mannschaft des KSK Beveren. «Upgrading raw materials» on the pitch? – the KSK Beveren team.

Bibliografie (Auswahl)
Selected Bibliography

Alegi, Peter
  2004. Laduma! Soccer, politics and society in South Africa. Durban
Appadurai, Arjun
  1986. The social life of things – commodities in cultural perspective. Cambridge
Apraku, Eva / Hesselmann, Markus
  1998. Schwarze Sterne und Pharaonen – Der Aufstieg des afrikanischen Fußballs. Göttingen
Archetti, Eduardo P.
  1997. Argentinien.
  In: Eisenberg, Christiane (ed.): 149–170
  1999. Masculinities – Football, Polo and the Tango in Argentina. Oxford
Armstrong, Gary
  1998. Blade Runners – Lives in Football. Sheffield
  2000. Football Hooligans – Knowing the Score. Oxford / New York (1st edition 1998)
Armstrong, Gary / Giulianotti, Richard (eds.)
  1997. Entering the Field – New Perspectives on World Football. Oxford / New York
  1999. Football Cultures and Identities. Houndmills / London
  2004. Football in Africa – Conflict, Conciliation and Community. Houndmills / Hampshire
Ball, Phil
  2003. Morbo – The Story of Spanish Football. London
Barth, Reinhard / Buschan, Peter u.a. (eds.)
  1986. Die größten Fussball Stars aller Zeiten. Weinheim
Bausenwein, Christoph
  1995. Geheimnis Fußball. Auf den Spuren eines Phänomens. Göttingen
Beiersdorfer, Dietmar u.a.
  1993. Fußball und Rassismus. Göttingen
Belliger, Andréa / Krieger, David J. (eds.)
  2003. Ritualtheorien – Ein einführendes Handbuch. Wiesbaden (2nd edition; 1st edition 1998)
Bellos, Alex
  2004. Futebol – Fußball. Die brasilianische Kunst des Lebens. Berlin (original edition London 2002)
Biermann, Christoph
  2004. Wenn du am Spieltag beerdigt wirst, kann ich leider nicht kommen – Die Welt der Fußballfans. Köln (4th edition; 1st edition 1995)
  2005. Fast alles über Fußball. Köln
Blume, Georg
  2002. Im freien Raum. In: DIE ZEIT 23/2002
Brändle, Fabian / Koller, Christian
  2002. Goooal!!! Kultur- und Sozialgeschichte des modernen Fußballs. Zürich
Bromberger, Christian
  2001. Le Match de Football – Ethnologie d'une passion partisane à Marseille, Naples et Turin. Paris (3rd edition; 1st edition Paris 1995)
  2003. Fußball als Weltsicht und Ritual. In: Belliger, Andréa / Krieger, David J. (eds.): 285–301
Brüggemeier, Franz-Josef / Borsdorf, Ulrich / Steiner, Jürg (eds.)
  2000. Der Ball ist rund. Essen
Buford, Bill
  1992. Geil auf Gewalt – Unter Hooligans. München / Wien (original edition London 1991)
Burns, Jimmy
  1998. Barça. A People's Passion. London
Dal Lago, Alessandro / Moscati, Roberto
  1992. Regalateci un sogno. Miti e realtà del tifo calcistico in Italia. Mailand
Diketmüller, Rosa
  2002. Frauenfußball in Zeiten der Globalisierung – Chancen und Risiken. In: Fanizadeh, Michael / Hödl, Gerald / Manzenreiter, Wolfram (eds.): 203–226
Dimeo, Paul / Mills, James (eds.)
  2001. Soccer in South Asia – Empire, Nation, Diaspora. London

Dirmoser, Dietmar (ed.)
  1995. Lateinamerika – Analysen und Berichte 19: Sport und Spiele. Bad Honnef
Downing, David
  2003. England V Argentina. World Cups and other small wars. London
Dunning, Eric
  1999. Sport Matters – Sociological Studies of Sport, Violence and Civilization. London / New York
Eisenberg, Christiane (ed.)
  1997. Fußball, soccer, calcio – Ein englischer Sport auf seinem Weg um die Welt. München
Elias, Norbert / Dunning, Eric
  1986. Quest for Excitement – Sport and Leisure in the Civilizing Process. Oxford / New York
Fanizadeh, Michael / Hödl, Gerald / Manzenreiter, Wolfram (eds.)
  2002. Global Players – Kultur, Ökonomie und Politik des Fussballs. Frankfurt am Main
Fechtig, Beate
  1995. Frauen und Fußball. Interviews – Porträts – Reportagen. Dortmund
Fischer, Gerd / Roth, Jürgen
  2005. Ballhunger – Vom Mythos des brasilianischen Fußballs. Göttingen
Fischer, Gerhard / Lindner, Ulrich
  1999. Stürmer für Hitler – Vom Zusammenspiel zwischen Fußball und Nationalsozialismus. Göttingen
Fischer, Norbert
  2002. Zur Geschichte weltlicher Bestattungskultur – Vortrag auf dem Kolloquium Weltliche Bestattungskultur in Berlin am 25. Mai 2002 im Krematorium Berlin-Baumschulenweg
Fishwick, Nicholas
  1989. Association Football and English Social Life, 1910–1950. Manchester
Foer, Franklin
  2006. Wie man mit Fussball die Welt erklärt. München (original edition New York 2004)
Friedman, Graeme
  2001. Madiba's Boys. The stories of Lucas Radebe and Mark Fish. Cape Town
Friedrich-Ebert-Stiftung (Hg.)
  2001. Art in Politics – Sanaa katika Siasa: The first East African competition on political caricatures and cartoons. Dar es Salaam
Galeano, Eduardo
  1997. Der Ball ist rund. Zürich (original edition Montevideo 1995)
Gehrmann, Siegfried (ed.)
  Bedeutung einer populären Sportart. Münster / Hamburg / London
Gisler, Omar
  2003. Die größten Vereine der Welt – Top Clubs Fußball. München
Goethals, Gregor T.
  2003. Ritual und die Repräsentation von Macht in Kunst und Massenkultur. In: Belliger, Andréa / Krieger, David J. (eds.): 303–322
Guttman, A.
  1994. Games and Empires – Modern Sports and Cultural Imperialism. New York
Happel, Berthold
  1996. Der Ball als All – Mythos und Entzauberung des Fußballspiels. Münster/Westfalen
Hauser-Schäublin, Brigitta / Braukämper, Ulrich (eds.)
  2002. Ethnologie der Globalisierung – Perspektiven kultureller Verflechtungen. Berlin
Herzog, Markwart (ed.)
  2002. Fußball als Kulturphänomen: Kunst – Kult – Kommerz. Stuttgart
Hesse-Lichtenberger, Ulrich
  2003. Tor! The Story of German Football (revised edition). London

Hoffmann, Eduard / Nendza, Jürgen
  2005. Verlacht, verboten und gefeiert. Zur Geschichte des Frauenfußballs in Deutschland. Weilerwist
Husmann, Rolf / Krüger, Gundolf (eds.)
  2002. Ethnologie und Sport. Frankfurt am Main / London
Kasza, Peter
  2004. Fußball spielt Geschichte. Das Wunder von Bern 1954. Berlin
King, John
  1997. The Football Factory. London (1st edition 1996)
Kuper, Simon
  2003. Football against the enemy. London (1st edition 1994)
Kuper, Simon (ed.)
  2002. Magnum Fussball. Berlin
Lanfranchi, Pierre
  1997. Frankreich und Italien.
  In: Eisenberg, Christiane (ed.): 41–64
Lanfranchi, Pierre / Taylor, Matthew
  2001. Moving with the ball – The migration of professional footballers. Oxford / New York
Lindner, Rolf (ed.)
  1980. Der Fußballfan – Ansichten vom Zuschauer. Frankfurt am Main
  1983. Der Satz »Der Ball ist rund« hat eine gewisse philosophische Tiefe. Berlin
Lindner, Rolf / Breuer, Heinrich Th.
  1978. »Sind doch nicht alles Beckenbauers« – Zur Sozialgeschichte des Fußballs im Ruhrgebiet. Frankfurt am Main
Manzenreiter, Wolfram / Horne, John
  2001. Moderne Körper, moderne Orte.
  In: Minikomi 2, Wien
  2004. Football goes East. New York
Maradona, Diego Armando
  2001. El Diego. München (original edition: Yo soy el Diego. Buenos Aires 2000)
Marino, Nicola
  2000. Totem und Ragú. Neapolitanische Spaziergänge. München
Martin, Simon
  2004. Football and Facism – The national game under Mussolini. Oxford / New York
Mason, Tony
  1980. Association Football and English Society 1863–1915. Brighton
  1989. Football. In: Mason (ed.) 1989. Sport in Britain – A Social History. Cambridge 146–186
  1997. Großbritannien.
  In: Eisenberg, Christiane (ed.): 22–40
Meier, Marianne.
  2004. »Zarte Füsschen am harten Leder ...«. Frauenfussball in der Schweiz 1970–1999. Frauenfeld
Morris, Desmond
  1981. Das Spiel – Faszination und Ritual des Fußballs. München / Zürich (original edition London 1981)
Niola, Marino
  2000. Totem und Ragú – Neapolitanische Spaziergänge. München
Osses, Dietmar
  2000: Das kleine Spiel – Gesellschaftsspiele rund um den Fußball. In: Brüggemeier, Franz-Josef / Borsdorf, Ulrich / Steiner, Jürg (eds.): 203–211
Parusel, Bernd
  2005. »Nicht hinlegen, nicht sterben« – Abstieg eines Hoffnungsträgers: Der schwedische Multikulti-Fußballklub Assyriska Föreningen aus Södertälje wird wieder zweitklassig.
  In: Junge Welt, 6.10.2005

Penn, Roger
2005. Cathedrals of Sport: Football Stadia in Contemporary England. Online-Veröffentlichung der Lancaster University. www.cas.lancs.ac.uk/papers/roger/

Pfister, Gertrud (ed.)
1980. Frau und Sport. Frankfurt am Main
1996. Fit und Gesund mit Sport. Berlin

Pieper, Werner
1992. Der Ball gehört allen. Fakten. Fans. Faszination. Löhrbach

Plüer, Sebastian
2000: Englischer Sport. In: Brüggemeier, Franz-Josef / Borsdorf, Ulrich / Steiner, Jürg (eds.): 78–85

Pöppl, Michael
2002. Fußball ist unser Leben – Eine deutsche Leidenschaft. Berlin

Prosser, Michael
2002: »Fußballverzückung« beim Stadionbesuch. In: Herzog, Markwart (ed.): 269–292

Quinn, John
1998. Jungle Tales – Celtic Memoirs of an Epic Stand. Edinburgh (1st edition 1994)

Santander, Carlos Fernandez
1990. El Fútbol Durante La Guerra Civil Y El Franquismo. Madrid

Schmidt-Lauber, Brigitta (ed.)
2004. FC St. Pauli – Zur Ethnographie eines Vereins. Münster (revised edition; 1st edition 2003)

Schönau, Birgit
2005. Calcio – Die Italiener und ihr Fußball. Köln

Schulze-Marmeling, Dietrich
2000. Fußball – Zur Geschichte eines globalen Sports. Göttingen

Schulze-Marmeling, Dietrich (ed.)
1992. Der gezähmte Fußball – Zur Geschichte eines subversiven Sports. Göttingen
1995. »Holt Euch das Spiel zurück!« – Fans und Fußball. Göttingen

Schümer, Dirk
1998. Gott ist rund – Die Kultur des Fußballs. Frankfurt am Main (1st edition 1996)

Schurian, Christian
2000. Fußballfans: vom Zuschauer zum Aktionär. In: Brüggemeier, Franz-Josef / Borsdorf, Ulrich / Steiner, Jürg (eds.): 336–345

Secretan, Thierry
1994. Going into Darkness – Fantastic Coffins from Afrika. London

Selmer, Nicole
2004. Watching the Boys Play – Frauen als Fußballfans. Kassel

Spittler, Gerd
2002. Globale Waren – Lokale Aneignungen. Berlin. In: Brigitta Hauser-Schäublin / Ulrich Braukämper (eds.): 15–30

Stadtarchiv München (ed.)
1997. München und der Fußball – Von den Anfängen 1896 bis zur Gegenwart. München

Sugden, J. / Tomlinson, A. (eds.)
1994. Hosts and Champions – Soccer Culture, National Identities and the USA World Cup. Aldershot

Tamaki, Masayuki
1999. Supotsu to wa Nani ka. Tokio

Taylor, Chris
1998. Samba, Coca und das runde Leder. Stuttgart

Theweleit, Klaus
2004. Tor zur Welt – Fußball als Realitätsmodell. Köln

Uden, Ronald
2005. Totenwürde zwischen Discountbegräbnis und Erinnerungskultur. In: Deutsches Pfarrerblatt 10, 2005. Online-Ausgabe: www.deutsches-pfarrerblatt.de

Ulloa, Rodrigo Dosal
2006. El fútbol: un juego de identidad. Online-Veröffentlichung von efdeportes.com 10/92, Buenos Aires, Januar 2006. www.efdeportes.com/efd92/ident.htm

Wagg, Stephen (ed.)
1984. The Football World – A Contemporary Social History. Brighton
2004. British Football and Social Exclusion. Abingdon

Walvin, J.
1994. The People's Game – The History of Football Revisited. Edinburgh

Williams, John
2001. Into the Red – Liverpool FC and the Changing Face of English Football. Edinburgh / London

Wolf, Ror
1978. Punkt ist Punkt – Alte und neue Fußballspiele. Frankfurt am Main (1st edition 1971)

Yapp, Nick
2000: Football. Soccer. Fußball. Köln

Websites
www.maradona10.com
www.iglesiamaradoniana.com
www.vivadiego.com
www.fifa.com

Bullige Stürmer und massive Abwehr: Fußballspielende Elefanten in Thailand.
Thick-skinned forwards and massive defence: elephants playing football in Thailand.

Danksagung / Acknowledgements

Die Realisierung von Ausstellung und Publikation wäre ohne die Unterstützung zahlreicher Institutionen und Privatpersonen nicht möglich gewesen. Es fehlt an Platz, um an dieser Stelle alle diejenigen aufzuführen, die uns in den letzten Monaten mit Rat und Tat zur Seite gestanden sind.
The exhibition and the publication could not have been realised without the support of so many institutions and private individuals that there is not enough space here to thank all those who have helped us over the past months with advice and hard work.

Besonderer Dank gebührt der DFB-Kulturstiftung, die dieses Projekt so großzügig und mit viel Engagement unterstützt hat, insbesondere Herrn Dr. Volker Bartsch (Geschäftsführer der DFB-Kulturstiftung) und Frau Agnes Wegner (Projekt-Betreuerin) sowie Judith Hehne, Monique Jajo, Dr. Reinhard Alings und Claudia Assmann.
Particular thanks, however, to the DFB-Kulturstiftung, who have supported this project with such generosity and commitment, first and foremost to Dr. Volker Bartsch (chairman of the DFB Kulturstiftung) and Agnes Wegner (project consultant) and also to Judith Hehne, Monique Jajo, Dr. Reinhard Alings and Claudia Assmann.

Ein ebenso großer Dank geht an OB Christian Ude, den Stadtrat der Landeshauptstadt München, an das Referat für Arbeit und Wirtschaft sowie an das Kulturreferat der Landeshauptstadt München, allen voran Frau Professor Dr. Dr. Lydia Hartl sowie Stefanie Reichelt M.A., Franz Krisch und Patricia Müller M.A. We are equally grateful to Mayor Christian Ude, the Munich City Council, the Referat für Arbeit und Wirtschaft and the Kulturreferat der Landeshauptstadt München, first and foremost to Dr. Dr. Lydia Hartl, Stefanie Reichelt M.A., Franz Krisch and Patricia Müller M.A..

Einen herzlichen Dank an das Münchner Stadtmuseum und sein Team für die große Unterstützung in allen Phasen der Realisierung der Ausstellung, vor allem an Herrn Direktor Dr. Wolfgang Till für sein unermüdliches Engagement für das Projekt und seinen Zuspruch in schwierigen Phasen. Our heartfelt thanks to the Munich City Museum and team for their unwavering support in all phases of preparing and realising the exhibition, first and foremost to Director Dr. Wolfgang Till for his untiring commitment to the project and his encouragement when the going got tough.

Ein besonderer Dank für die Unterstützung auch an die Recherche-Mitarbeiter sowie an die ProjektassistentInnen für die außergewöhnlich engagierte Mitarbeit. Our particular thanks also to the researchers as well as the project assistants for their support and for the unswerving commitment they have shown to the project.

Und *last but not least* herzlichen Dank an die Arnoldsche Verlagsanstalt, Stuttgart, und insbesondere an Winfried Stürzl für das unermüdliche Engagement sowie an Silke Nalbach und Karina Moschke für die schöne Gestaltung der Publikation. And, last but not least, many thanks to Arnoldsche Art Publishers in Stuttgart and especially to Winfried Stürzl for his unswerving commitment to the project. We are also indebted to Silke Nalbach and Karina Moschke for their superlative book design.

Darüber hinaus danken wir für Rat, Unterstützung und Exponatbeschaffung:
In addition, we thank the following for their advice, support and commitment to ensuring that exhibits were forthcoming:
Peter Amann
Elisabeth Angermair (Stadtarchiv München)
Bayern Magazin
Bilderdienst des Süddeutschen Verlags
Uwe Birras (1. FC Köln GmbH & Co. KGaA)
Madeleine Boll
Angelika Brunner
Dr. Inés de Castro
Tom Cole
Wilfried Eckstein (Goethe-Institut Bangkok)
Walter und Eva Eisenhofer
Leonie Emeka
Doris Fitschen (DFB, Frankfurt am Main)
Lotte und Helmut Guggeis
Prof. Dr. Frank Heidemann (Institut für Ethnologie und Afrikanistik der Universität München)
Paul Hempel, M.A. (Institut für Ethnologie und Afrikanistik der Universität München)
J-Village, Shizuoka (Japan)
Noemie Jaeger
Dr. Gunther Joppig
Christoph Karbacher (Beauftragter Kunst und Kultur des OK FIFA WM 2006)
Mechthild Katzorke und Volker Schöwerling (catlinafilm Berlin)
Sadahiko Kishi, Kyoto (Japan)
Dr. Alexander Knorr (Institut für Ethnologie und Afrikanistik der Universität München)
Prof. Dr. Manfred Lämmer (Leiter des Instituts für Sportgeschichte der Deutschen Sporthochschule Köln)
Jeannette Leitner
Fußballverband und Landesvereine Liechtenstein
Friso Maecker (Goethe-Institut München)
Marianne Meier (SAP, Biel, Schweiz)
Susanne Meierhenrich (Leitung Koordination und Redaktion von literaturhaeuser.net)
Uwe Möller, München
Angeline Mukum
Holger Obermann
Klaus Paysan
Angelika Piller
Barbara Plankensteiner (Museum für Völkerkunde Wien, Österreich)
Dr. Margrit Prussat (Institut für Ethnologie und Afrikanistik der Universität München)
Ramon Pujol (Barça Museum, Barcelona)
Hella Rabbethge-Schiller
Fiona Rankin-Smith (University Art Galleries, University of the Witwatersrand, Johannesburg)
Lourdes Ros-el-Hosni und Mustafa el-Hosni
Prof. Dr. Klaus Schneider (Direktor des Rautenstrauch-Joest-Museums, Köln)
Kofi Setordji (Art Haus Accra, Ghana)
Karin Sommer
Kathrin Steinbichler
Lajos Szabó (Direktor des Ungarischen Sportmuseums, Budapest)
Dr. Bertram Turner (Max-Planck-Institut für Ethnologische Forschung, Halle/Saale)
Andreas Veithoefer (Club Nr. 12, FC Bayern Fan-Museum München)
Dr. Christian Wacker (Direktor, Deutsches Sport & Olympia-Museum Köln)
Jörg Weck (Sammlungsleiter, Deutsches Sport & Olympia-Museum Köln)
Südafrikanisches Konsulat München
Sugimoto Yoshinori, Shizuoka (Japan)

Folgenden Leihgebern sind wir zu großem Dank verpflichtet:
We are greatly indebted to the following for donating exhibits:
Khodr und Karin Abdallah
Alexander Altendörfer
Ingo Barlovic
Rasso Bernhard
Deutsches Sport & Olympia-Museum Köln
Zisis Dimoudis
Dr. Stefan Eisenhofer
Bela Erasmus
Girma Fisseha/Slg. SOS-Kinderdorf, Addis Ababa, Äthiopien
Doris Fitschen
Ulrike Folie
Nadim Frembgen
Themis Giparis
Belinda Greinert
Bernd Guggeis
Helmut Guggeis
Karin Guggeis
Christiane Lembert
Hagen Liebing
Liechtensteiner Fußballverband und Landesvereine
Münchner Stadtmuseum
Siegfried Lukas
Marianne Meier
Elisabeth Nagelstutz
Peter Niedersteiner
Lourdes Ros-el-Hosni
Barbara Rusch
Volodymyr Slyvko
Dr. Wolfgang Stäbler
Standard Bank African Collection (Wits Art Galleries), Johannesburg (Südafrika)
Kathrin Steinbichler
Joachim von Stieglitz
Dr. Wolfgang Till
Dr. Bertram und Jutta Turner
Andreas Veithöfer, FC-Bayern Fan-Museum
Yabirag Sinahí Venegas Garibay
Bernhard Walch
Dr. Uta Weigelt
Wilma Wohlwend

Ein großer Dank auch an die Künstler, deren Werke unsere Ausstellung bereichern:
Our heartfelt thanks also to the artists whose work has graced our exhibition:
Luis Basto, Maputo
Joe Big-Big, Paris
Lucia Dellefant, München
Silke Eberspächer, München
Rodriguez Emerson, Recife, Brasilien
fischerartwork
Nikolaus Heidelbach, Köln
Oliver Heisch, Köln
Volker Hildebrandt, Köln
Pieter van der Houwen, Amsterdam
Jumnong Jantaphant, Bangkok
Dr. Paa Joe, Labadi, Ghana
Loomit, München
Américo Mariano, Paris
Gottfried Müller, München
Otobong Edet Nkanga, Lagos, Nigeria
Boris Tomschiczek, München

Die Herausgeberin und das Konzept-Team
The Editor and the Concept Team

Autoren / Authors

Dr. Jigal Beez
Ethnologe, Geograph und Entwicklungshelfer mit Forschungsschwerpunkt Ostafrika. Langjähriger Mitarbeiter des DED und der Universität Bayreuth. Cultural Anthropologist, geographer and foreign aid worker, focuses in his research on East Africa. Has worked for the DED and Bayreuth University for many years.

Alex Bellos
Journalist und Autor des Buches *Futebol – Die brasilianische Kunst des Lebens*. Langjähriger Südamerika-Korrespondent für den *Guardian* und den *Observer*. Journalist and author of *Futebol – The Brazilian Way of Life*. South America correspondent for *The Guardian* and *The Observer* for many years.

Tanıl Bora
Politologe und Soziologe. Dozent an der Politikwissenschaftlichen Fakultät der Universität Ankara. Chefredakteur der Zeitschrift *Toplum ve Bilim* (»Gesellschaft und Wissenschaft«). Autor mehrerer Publikationen über türkische Fußballkultur und wöchentlicher Liga-Kolumnist der Tageszeitung *Radikal*. Political scientist and sociologist. Teaches at the Political Science Faculty of Ankara University. Editor of *Toplum ve Bilim* («Society and Science») magazine. The author of books and articles on Turkish football culture, he also writes a weekly column on football for the daily *Radikal*.

Dr. Stefan Eisenhofer
Ethnologe und Historiker. Leiter der Abteilung Afrika am Staatlichen Museum für Völkerkunde München und Dozent am Institut für Ethnologie und Afrikanistik der Ludwig-Maximilians-Universität München. Zahlreiche Ausstellungen und Publikationen zur Kunst und Geschichte Afrikas. Cultural Anthropologist and historian. Chief curator of the Africa Department at the Staatliches Museum für Völkerkunde München and lecturer at the Institut für Ethnologie und Afrikanistik at Ludwig-Maximilians University, Munich. Has curated numerous exhibitions and written prolifically on African art and history.

PD Dr. Juergen Wasim Frembgen
Leiter der Abteilung Islamischer Orient am Staatlichen Museum für Völkerkunde München und Privatdozent für Islamstudien an der Universität Erlangen-Nürnberg. Forschungen und zahlreiche Publikationen zur ost-islamischen Welt. Chief Curator of the Islamic Studies Department at the Staatliches Museum für Völkerkunde München and private lecturer in Islamic Studies at Erlangen-Nürnberg University. A prolific researcher, he has published numerous books and articles on the Islamic world.

Dr. Natalie Göltenboth
Ethnologin, Dozentin am Institut für Völkerkunde und Afrikanistik der Ludwig-Maximilians-Universität München. Publikationen und Forschungen zu Kunst, Religion und Alltagskultur in Süditalien, Kuba und München. Cultural Anthropologist, lecturer at the Institut für Ethnologie und Afrikanistik at Ludwig-Maximilians University, Munich. Her publications and research deal with the art, religion and way of life in southern Italy, Cuba and Munich.

Karin Guggeis, M.A.
Ethnologin. Mitarbeiterin am Museum für Völkerkunde München. Forschungen und Publikationen zur Repräsentation von Afrika und zur außereuropäischen Kunst. Kuratorin der Ausstellung *Fußball: Ein Spiel – Viele Welten*. Cultural Anthropologist, working at the Museum für Völkerkunde München. Research and publications on representations of Africa and on arts of the non-western world. Curator of the exhibition *Football: One Game – Many Worlds*.

Christiane Hirsch, M.A.
Landschaftsplanerin und Ethnologin. Forschungen zu Kultur- und Identitätstheorien, Praxis- und Performanzkonzepten sowie museologischen Fragestellungen. Landscape planner and Cultural Anthropologist. Researches on cultural and identity theory, praxis and performance concepts as well as museological issues.

Dr. Wolfgang Kapfhammer
Ethnologe, Dozent am Institut für Ethnologie und Afrikanistik der Ludwig-Maximilians-Universität München. Forschungen und zahlreiche Publikationen zur Ethnologie Brasiliens, insbesondere Amazoniens. Cultural Anthropologist, lecturer at the Institut für Ethnologie und Afrikanistik at Ludwig-Maximilians University, Munich. His research and numerous publications on the anthropology of Brazil focus on the Amazon Basin.

Ben Kerste
Studium der Ethnologie, Geschichte und Religionswissenschaften an der Ludwig-Maximilians-Universität München. Projektassistent beim Projekt *Fußball: Ein Spiel – Viele Welten*. Studies Cultural Anthropology, history and the history of religions at Ludwig-Maximilians University Munich. Project assistant with the *Football: One Game – Many Worlds* project.

Christiane Lembert, M.A.
Ethnologin. Wissenschaftliche Mitarbeiterin an der Universität Augsburg im Fach Europäische Ethnologie/Volkskunde. Untersuchungen und Publikationen zur Migrationsforschung, Koordinatorin des EU-Projekts *MigraNet*. Cultural Anthropologist, lecturer at Augsburg University in Europäische Ethnologie/Volkskunde. Her research and publications deal with migrants and migration, co-ordinator of the EU *MigraNet* project.

Patricia Müller, M.A.
Ethnologin und Japanologin. Zuständig für *Eine Welt Kultur* sowie urbane Kultur beim Kulturreferat der Landeshauptstadt München. Zahlreiche Projekte zum kulturellen und politischen Wandel in Afrika, Asien und Lateinamerika. Cultural Anthropologist, Specialist in Japan Studies. Responsible for *Eine Welt Kultur (One-World Culture)* at the Kulturreferat of the City of Munich. Has worked on numerous projects dealing with cultural and political change in Africa, Asia and Latin America.

Fiona Rankin-Smith
Kuratorin an der University of the Witwatersrand Art Galleries in Johannesburg. Zahlreiche Ausstellungen und Publikationen zur Kunst, Kultur und Geschichte Südafrikas. Diplom in Fine Arts am Technikon Natal und HDE an der Universität Natal. Curator at the University of the Witwatersrand Art Galleries in Johannesburg; she has curated numerous exhibitions and has participated in publishing a number of catalogues. She qualified with a diploma in Fine Arts at the Technikon Natal and HDE from the University of Natal.

Barbara Rusch, M.A.
Ethnologin und Kommunikationswissenschaftlerin. Autorin, Übersetzerin und Lektorin. Buchkonzepte und Publikationen zu kulturwissenschaftlichen und ethnologischen Themen. Cultural Anthropologist and Specialist in communication studies. Author, translator and reader for publishing houses. Book concepts and publications on cultural history and cultural anthropology.

Kathrin Steinbichler
Freie Journalistin. Redakteursausbildung an der Deutschen Journalistenschule (DJS) in München und Studium der Ethnologie, Soziologie und Politik. Mitarbeiterin der Sportredaktion der *Süddeutschen Zeitung*. A freelance journalist, she trained as an editor at the Deutsche Journalistenschule (DJS) in Munich. Studies anthropology, sociology and political science. Currently a sports editor on the *Süddeutsche Zeitung*.

Anikó Szalay, M.A.
Politikwissenschaftlerin und Psychologin. Mitarbeit bei verschiedenen Kulturprojekten, u. a. bei der Ausstellung *Fußball: Ein Spiel – Viele Welten*. Political scientist and psychologist. Has worked on numerous cultural projects, including *Football: One Game – Many Worlds*.

Dr. Wolfgang Till
Volkskundler, Kunsthistoriker und Ausstellungsmacher. Nach längeren Wanderjahren seit 1987 Direktor des Münchner Stadtmuseums. Forschungen zu Bildern und Zeichen religiösen Volksglaubens, zur Kulturgeschichte Bayerns und zum gegenwärtigen Zustand Münchens. Cultural Anthropologist, Art Historian and exhibition curator. After years of travel and freelance activity, has been director of the Munich City Museum since 1987. His research deals with devotional images and signs, Bavarian cultural history and the present state of the city of Munich.

Yabirag Sinahí Venegas Garibay
Studentin der Ethnologie an der Ludwig-Maximilians-Universität München. Projektassistentin beim Projekt *Fußball: Ein Spiel – Viele Welten*. Studies Cultural Anthropology at Ludwig-Maximilians University, Munich. Project assistant with the *Football: One Game – Many Worlds* project.

Wolfgang Wohlwend
Studium der Ethnologie, Turkologie und Slawistik an der Ludwig-Maximilians-Universität München. Projektassistent beim Projekt *Fußball: Ein Spiel – Viele Welten*. Studies Cultural Anthropology, Turkish Studies and Slavic languages and literature at Ludwig-Maximilians University, Munich. Project assistant with the *Football: One Game – Many Worlds* project.

Zé do Rock
Zé do Rock is vor verdammt langer zeit in Brasilien geboren, hat 14630 tage gelebt, 1357 liter alkohol gesoffen, 940 stunden flöte und 648 stunden fussball gspilt, 200000 km in 1457 autos, flugzeugen, shiffen, zügen, oxenkarren und traktoren geträmpt, 104 lända und 16 gefengnisse besucht, sich 8 mal ferlibt, ain film gedreet, aine kunstsprache erfunden, ain ferainfachte doitsh kreirt, 3 buches gshriben, hat nix studirt und lebt noch hoite, maist in Mynchen. Zé do Rock was born a damd long time ago in Brazil, livd 6570 days, drank 1357 liters of alcohol, playd 940 ours of flute and 648 ours of soccer, hichhiked 200000 km in 1457 cars, planes, ships, tranes, ox carts and tracters, visited 116 cuntrys and 16 prisons, fell in love 8 times, made a film, invented an artificial languej, created simplified spellings for sevral languejes, rote 3 books, didnt studdy enything and he's stil alive, spending moast of his time in Munic, Germany.

© 2006 ARNOLDSCHE Art Publishers, Stuttgart, Münchner Stadtmuseum und Autoren / and the authors

Alle Rechte vorbehalten. Vervielfältigung und Wiedergabe auf jegliche Weise (grafisch, elektronisch und fotomechanisch sowie der Gebrauch von Systemen zur Datenrückgewinnung) – auch in Auszügen – nur mit schriftlicher Genehmigung von ARNOLDSCHE Art Publishers, Liststr. 9, D-70180 Stuttgart, art@arnoldsche.com.
All rights reserved. No part of this work may be reproduced or used in any forms or by any means (graphic, electronic or mechanical, including photocopying or information storage and retrieval systems) without written permission from ARNOLDSCHE Art Publishers, Liststr. 9, D-70180 Stuttgart, art@arnoldsche.com.

Herausgeberin / Editor
Karin Guggeis M.A.
im Auftrag des Münchner Stadtmuseums und des Kulturreferats der Landeshauptstadt München
Commissioned by the Munich City Museum and the Department of Culture, City of Munich

Unter konzeptioneller Mitarbeit von / Concept Team
Dr. Stefan Eisenhofer, Dr. Wolfgang Habermeyer, Christiane Lembert M.A., Patricia Müller M.A., Barbara Rusch M.A.

Redaktion / Editorial work
Winfried Stürzl, Stuttgart

Übersetzungen ins Englische / Translations into English
Joan Clough, München
Dr. Ruth Schubert, München (Einleitung, Umschlag-Rückseite / Introduction, back cover)

Grafik / Layout
Silke Nalbach, Karina Moschke, nalbachtypografik, Stuttgart

Offset-Reproduktionen / Offset-Reproductions
Repromayer, Reutlingen

Druck / Printing
Leibfarth & Schwarz, Dettingen/Erms

Dieses Buch wurde gedruckt auf chlorfrei gebleichtem Papier. This book has been printed on paper that is free of chlorine bleach.

Gedruckt auf EuroBulk 150 g/m² von M-real.
Printed on EuroBulk 150 g/m² by M-real.

EuroBulk
m-real

Bibliografische Information
Der Deutschen Bibliothek
Die Deutsche Bibliothek verzeichnet diese Publikation in der Deutschen Nationalbibliografie; detaillierte bibliografische Daten sind im Internet über **http://dnb.ddb.de** abrufbar.

Bibliographic information published by Die Deutsche Bibliothek
Die Deutsche Bibliothek lists this publication in the Deutsche Nationalbibliografie; detailed bibliographic data is available on the internet at **http://dnb.ddb.de.**

ISBN 3-89790-242-7

Made in Germany, 2006

Bildnachweis / Photo Credits
Alle Angaben beziehen sich auf die Seitenzahlen.
All data refer to pages.
Stefan Eisenhofer/Karin Guggeis: 10
Jürgen Wasim Frembgen: 33 o.
Christiane Hirsch: 189 r., 192 r.
Münchner Stadtmuseum: 70
Münchner Stadtmuseum, Patricia Fliegauf / Dorothee Jordens-Meintker: 11, 12, 17 l.+m., 18, 20, 21 l.+m., 23; 30, 31; 33, 35–37, 47, 50, 59, 60, 63, 64, 66–68, 70 l., 81, 84, 85, 106, 107, 109, 112, 115, 119, 121, 124, 127–130, 133, 134, 137, 149, 152, 153, 156, 160, 161, 164, 169, 170, 173, 181, 182, 185, 186, 187, 189 l., 190, 192 l., 195–199, 205, 210, 212, 216, 217, 224, 226, 231, 233
Wayne Oosthuizen: 22, 215
Stadtarchiv München: 17 m., 84, 124, 204
Daniel Urban: 237
Uta Weigelt: 21 r.

Für alle anderen Abbildungen befindet sich der Nachweis direkt beim Bild. Photo credits otherwise under the pictures.

Für die Abdruckgenehmigung wurden die jeweiligen Rechteinhaber kontaktiert; einige konnten bisher nicht ermittelt werden. Das Münchner Stadtmuseum bittet in solchen Fällen um Kontaktaufnahme. As far as possible each copyright holder has been notified. However, since we have not been able to contact all copyright holders, we therefore request any and all concerned to contact the Munich City Museum in this matter.

Diese Publikation erscheint anlässlich der gleichnamigen Ausstellung des Münchner Stadtmuseums vom 19. Mai 2006 bis zum 3. September 2006. This book is published to accompany the exhibition under the same title at the Munich City Museum from 19 May 2006 to 3 September 2006.

Leihgeber von Objekten im Katalog / Donators of objects in the catalogue
Alle Angaben beziehen sich auf die Seitenzahlen.
All data refer to pages.
12 l.: Barbara Rusch; 12 r.: Yabirag Sinahí Venegas Garibay; 18 l.: Karin Guggeis; 20 m., 21 l.+m.: Joachim von Stieglitz; 22: Standard Bank African Collection (Wits Art Galleries), Inv. Nr. 1998.16.0; 23 l.: Kathrin Steinbichler; 23 r.: Wolfgang Stäbler; 31, Abb. 6: Marianne Meier; 31, Nr. 10: Yabirag Sinahí Venegas Garibay; 33 u.: Nadim Frembgen; 47, 50 r.: Stefan Eisenhofer; 64: Karin Guggeis; 85: Doris Fitschen; 106: Stefan Eisenhofer; 107 r.: Volodymyr Slyvko; 115: Figur der Virgen de Guadalupe: Yabirag Sinahí Venegas Garibay; 130: Stefan Eisenhofer; 156: FC-Bayern Fan-Museum, Andreas Veithöfer; 160, 1. Reihe l., 2. v. l.: Volodymyr Slyvko; mittlere Reihe l.: Barbara Rusch; Reihe unten, 2. v. l.: Bernd Guggeis; Reihe unten, r.: Christiane Lembert; r. o.: Stefan Eisenhofer; 161 l. u.: Uta Weigelt; 161 r. u.: Wolfgang Till; 169: Siegfried Lukas; 205: Wolfgang Till; 210 r.: Bela Erasmus; 211: Girma Fisseha / Slg. SOS-Kinderdorf, Addis Ababa, Äthiopien; 212: Wolfgang Till; 215: Standard Bank African Collection (Wits Art Galleries), Inv. Nr.1997.10.01–17; 216/217: Karin Guggeis; 226: Deutsches Sport & Olympia Museum Köln

Die Ausstellung ist ein offizieller Beitrag des Kunst- und Kulturprogramms der Bundesregierung zur FIFA WM 2006™ in Zusammenarbeit mit dem OK FIFA WM 2006. This exhibition is an official Element of the Artistic and Cultural Programme of the Federal Government for the 2006 FIFA World Cup™ in cooperation with the 2006 FIFA World Cup Organising Committee.

Gefördert durch die / Sponsored by the Nationale DFB Kulturstiftung WM 2006 gGmbH

FUSSBALL FOOTBALL
Ein Spiel – Viele Welten   One Game – Many Worlds

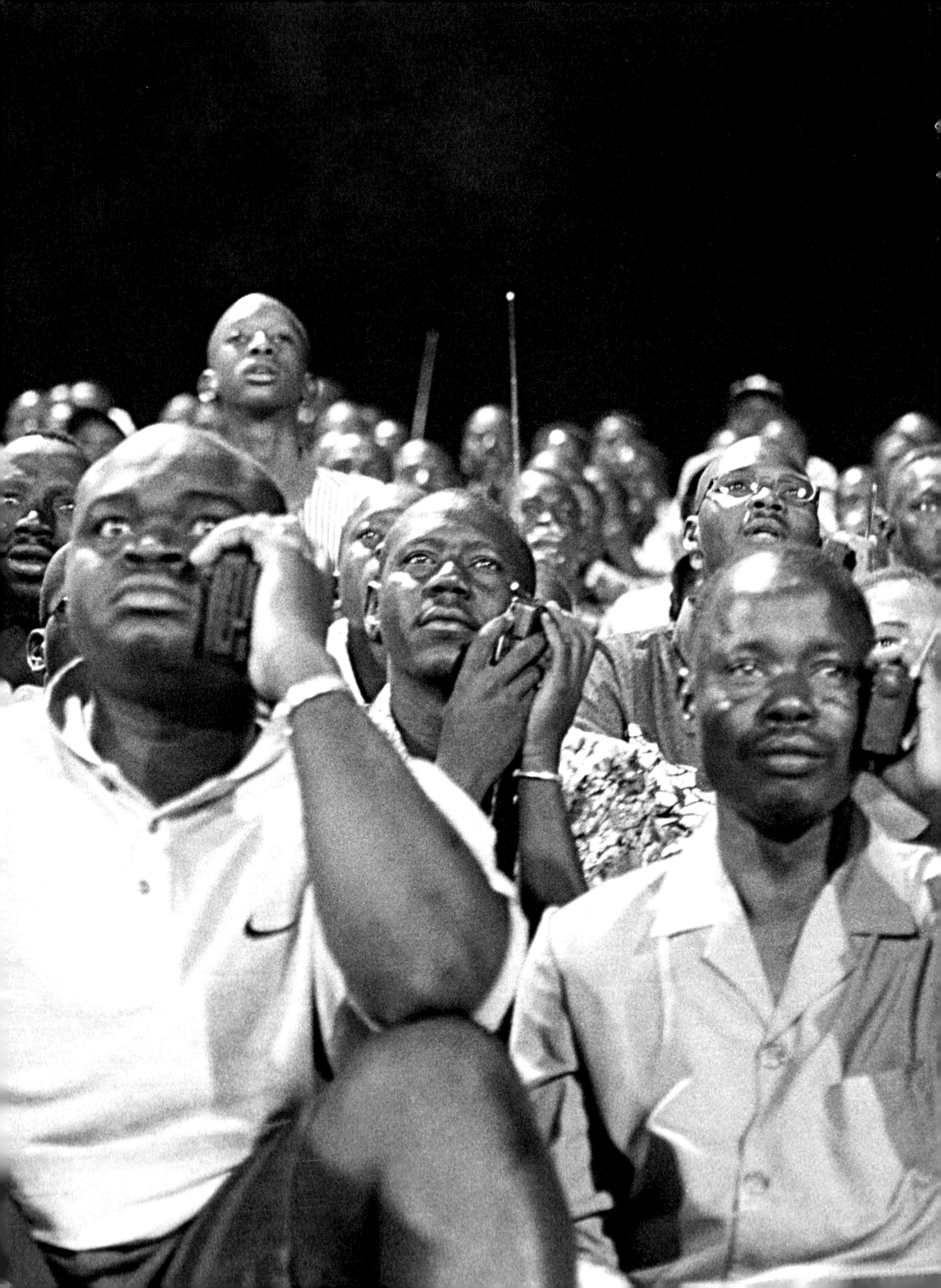